Monetary Orders

A volume in the series
CORNELL STUDIES IN POLITICAL ECONOMY
edited by Peter J. Katzenstein
A full list of titles in the series appears at the end of the book.

Monetary Orders

Ambiguous Economics,
Ubiquitous Politics

Edited by
JONATHAN KIRSHNER

CORNELL UNIVERSITY PRESS

ITHACA AND LONDON

First published 2003 by Cornell University Press
First printing, Cornell Paperbacks, 2003

Printed in the United States of America

Library of Congress Cataloging-in-Publication Data

Monetary orders : ambiguous economics, ubiquitous politics / edited by Jonathan Kirshner.
       p. cm. — (Cornell studies in political economy)
Includes bibliographical references and index.
   ISBN 0–8014–4060–2 (cloth : alk. paper) — ISBN 0–8014–8840–0 (pbk. : alk. paper)
   1. Monetary policy. 2. Monetary policy—Developing countries. 3. Monetary policy—United States. 4. Developing countries—Economic policy. 5. United States—Economic policy. 6. Globalization—Economic aspects. 7. International Monetary Fund. I. Kirshner, Jonathan. II. Series.
   HG230.3 .M6357 2003
   332.4'6—dc21

                              2002013242

Cornell University Press strives to use environmentally responsible suppliers and materials to the fullest extent possible in the publishing of its books. Such materials include vegetable-based, low-VOC inks and acid-free papers that are recycled, totally chlorine-free, or partly composed of nonwood fibers. For further information, visit our website at www.cornellpress.cornell.edu.

Cloth printing 10 9 8 7 6 5 4 3 2 1
Paperback printing 10 9 8 7 6 5 4 3 2 1

Contents

Contributors

RAWI ABDELAL is Assistant Professor at Harvard Business School.

MARK BLYTH is Assistant Professor of Political Science at Johns Hopkins University.

MICHELE CHANG is Assistant Professor of Political Science at Colgate University.

FRANCIS GAVIN is Assistant Professor at the LBJ School of Public Affairs at the University of Texas at Austin.

ILENE GRABEL is Associate Professor of International Finance at the Graduate School of International Studies at the University of Denver.

WILLIAM W. GRIMES is Assistant Professor of International Relations at Boston University.

ERIC HELLEINER is Associate Professor in the Department of Political Studies, Trent University.

JONATHAN KIRSHNER is Associate Professor of Government at Cornell University.

HECTOR E. SCHAMIS is Assistant Professor in the Department of Government, Cornell University.

DAVID STASAVAGE is Lecturer in the Department of International Relations at the London School of Economics.

HONGYING WANG is Assistant Professor of Political Science at the Maxwell School of Citizenship and Public Affairs, Syracuse University.

Acknowledgments

The chapters in this volume were developed over the course of two workshops held at Cornell University, in April and October 2000. Primary support was provided by the International Political Economy Program of the Einaudi Center for International Studies, Cornell University. Additional support was provided by the Peace Studies Program and Institute for European Studies at Cornell, and the Ben and Rhoda Belnick Fund in the Government Department. The meetings benefited enormously from the active and thoughtful participation of the discussants, and I thank Alan Carlson, Benjamin Cohen, Matthew Evangelista, Rachel Epstein, Shinju Fujihira, Peter Johnson, Peter Katzenstein, Phil McMichael, Kathleen O'Neill, Beth Simmons, and Christopher Way for making this a better and more coherent volume. Brian Bow, Rachel Epstein, and Matt Ferchen helped organize the workshops and prepare the manuscript. I also thank Roger Haydon and two anonymous referees at Cornell University Press for their help in sharpening the final product.

Chapter 3 also appears in modified form in Eric Helleiner, *The Making of National Money: Territorial Currencies in Historical Perspective* (Cornell University Press, 2003).

J. K.

Ithaca, New York

CHAPTER ONE

The Inescapable Politics of Money

Jonathan Kirshner

The rise to preeminence of monetary phenomena is one of the principal defining characteristics of the contemporary global economy.[1] For most of the second half of the twentieth century, the real side of the economy dominated the agenda. International concerns centered largely on questions of trade, especially strategy, liberalization, and integration, while within societies lively conflicts over taxes, transfers, and subsidies defined the political scene. These issues have lost much of their salience over the course of the last decade and have been eclipsed by financial liberalization, monetary unification, inflation fighting, and central bank independence (CBI).

Although monetary phenomena define the contemporary economic scene, insufficient attention has been given to their political content and consequence. While the practice of strategic trade and debates over taxation are easily recognizable as political matters, issues such as financial liberalization and CBI are not. In fact, such measures are often expressly represented as *apolitical*, as steps that remove a contentious issue from the political sphere. However, monetary phenomena are *always* and *everywhere political*. In each of the four issue areas just mentioned (financial liberalization, monetary unification, inflation fighting, and CBI), the aggregate economic consequences are ambiguous and modest, and certainly less than the political and distributional effects. It is illogical to assume that policy choices derive from the modest effects of the former rather than the intense motivations produced by the latter. A renewed focus on the importance, and indeed the primacy, of political forces in shaping monetary decisions and outcomes is necessary.

The widespread acceptance that monetary and macroeconomic policies can be depoliticized has served to mask underappreciated distributional and other political conflicts. Fundamentally political struggles about money are routinely cloaked in economic terms, often throwing

1. I thank Rawi Abdelal, Ilene Grabel, Eric Helleiner, and two referees. This chapter draws on the second half of Kirshner 2000 and also parts of Kirshner 1999a, 2001.

students of politics off the scent. The purpose of this volume is to contribute to and encourage an emphasis on the study of the *politics* of money.

The principal argument in this volume is that economic theory is indeterminate in its ability to account for most of the monetary policy choices and reforms that are observable in the world today. While market forces are strong—perhaps stronger than ever in the monetary sphere—the difference between many plausible policies is of ambiguous or, at most, modest economic effect. Economic logic limits the range of policy choices to a plausible set, but the outcomes observed are largely attributable to politics—ideas, interest group conflict, and international relations. In this chapter I illustrate this claim with reference to some fundamental decisions about the management of money at the national and international level.

AMBIGUOUS ECONOMICS

Capital Mobility and the Geography of Money

Macroeconomic policies are often veiled by a cloak of economic legitimacy. But on closer examination, it is clear that behind the assertion of efficiency, the aggregate economic benefits of various policy decisions are ambiguous, modest, and dwarfed by their political and differential effects. In the international context, uninhibited financial liberalization is the most obvious example of this. This matters, because, as I discuss later, the perception of legitimacy can be self-fulfilling, nullifying the prospects of otherwise plausible alternative policy options.

The idea that capital flows should not be regulated is more than just self-fulfilling (though that is remarkably consequential). It is also the express policy of powerful states like the United States and of the international institutions that are supposed to oversee the smooth functioning of the global economy. The support for, and salience of, the idea of freeing capital gathered increasing momentum in the 1990s. In the wake of this trend, the International Monetary Fund (IMF) embarked on a fundamental revision of its charter, announcing in May 1997 plans to amend its constitution—the Articles of Agreement—"to make the promotion of capital account liberalization a specific purpose of the IMF and give it jurisdiction over capital movements" (*IMF Survey* 5/12/97). This proposed revision represented a dramatic change—in fact the very *opposite* of what the founders of the IMF intended. They thought that capital controls were necessary to ensure the smooth functioning of an open international economy. Thus, the Bretton Woods era, currently considered the "golden age of capitalism," was a period characterized by the widespread practice of capital control.[2] Now, however, the IMF has asserted that capital liberalization is the only legitimate path to economic efficiency, and has explicitly proclaimed that "forces of globalization must be embraced" (*IMF Survey* 5/26/97). Its new policy has been characterized repeatedly as a proposition "to make unrestricted capital flows a condition of membership in the global economy" (*Wall Street Journal* 9/2/98; *Asian Wall Street Journal* 9/2/98).

It should be noted that there are good deductive reasons to believe in the elimination of capital controls. Openness to capital inflows expands the resources available to the local economy, and the elimination of restrictions on capital outflows gives foreigners the confidence to invest their funds. Not only are investors confident that they will be able to repatriate their profits, but also states that allow unrestricted capital flows enjoy greater credibility: market actors assume that they are more likely to follow "sound" policies, because if they failed to do so, they would be subject to hemorrhaging of both foreign and domestic capital. More generally, free capital seems to follow the logic of free trade—few deny that an open market to goods results in a more efficient allocation of resources, expanded consumption choices, and a host of other benefits such as the discipline imposed by international competition.

But at the same time, there are competing deductive arguments suggesting that some positive level of capital control is optimal from the perspective of economic efficiency.[3] The free flow of capital differs in important ways from the free flow of goods. Two attributes in particular make capital quite distinct from most real goods. First, contemporary technology allows investors to move huge amounts of money almost instantaneously, at very little cost. Second, to an important extent, financial assets are worth what people think that they are worth. Given these elements, fears regarding what other people are thinking can cause herding behavior, unleashing financial stampedes with economic consequences that veer far from the path suggested by any reading of the economic "fundamentals."

Additionally, in a world of perfectly mobile capital, investors can scan the globe for the best rates of return, and this creates pressure for conformity across countries' macroeconomic policies. But it is simply implausible to assume that it is economically optimal for all states to pursue the same macroeconomic policies. On the contrary, states face diverse economic conditions and need to tailor their economic policies accordingly. But in the absence of any restrictions on capital flows, governments that de-

2. As Keynes, one of the principal architects of the Bretton Woods system, wrote, "Nothing is more certain than that the movement of capital funds must be regulated" ([1942] 1980, 149).

3. It is important to note the qualified nature of this argument. The competing argument is not that capital flows are bad but rather that completely deregulated capital would lead to a suboptimally high level of flows.

viate from the international policy norms, even when those policies are entirely appropriate for local needs, are "punished" by capital flight, often with such force that the policies have to be abandoned or even reversed. Further, and more subtly, if states feel pressure to attract foreign capital or to enhance the reputation of their currencies, they may engage (even unwittingly) in competitive interest rate increases. Thus, fully unregulated capital creates pressure toward not only macroeconomic convergence but also convergence with a contractionary bias (Kirshner 1998).[4]

What is particularly striking, especially given the existence of competing deductive arguments, is that the widespread faith in the logic of unregulated capital does not rest on a foundation of empirical support. Jagdish Bhagwati, noted champion of free trade, recently took many of his fellow economists to task for simply inferring the case for unregulated capital from the case for free trade. Proponents of free trade, he observed, have provided mountains of evidence to support their claims; the supporters of free capital have not. In fact, he concluded, "the weight of evidence and the force of logic point in the opposite direction, toward restraints on capital flows" (Bhagwati 1998, 12; see also Cooper 1999). The challenge to capital flow liberalization is only reinforced by the recent study of Dani Rodrik (1998, 61), whose analysis from a sample of one hundred countries showed "no evidence that countries without capital controls have grown faster, invested more, or experienced lower inflation."[5] Ultimately, explaining the consensus on capital deregulation must be found somewhere other than from the decisive demands of economic efficiency.

Similarly, if less spectacularly, it is clear that economic efficiency does not explain the geography of money—which money is used where and why. For one thing, as Benjamin Cohen (1998a, 82–84) observed, while there are economic theories of "optimum currency areas," it is clear that the use of money is defined by political concerns (Goodhart 1995, Helleiner 1998). Most agree, to take a prominent example, that the European Monetary Union (EMU) is *not* an optimum currency area.[6] Indeed, as Michele Chang points out in this volume, policy discussions have transformed from whether the EMU is an optimum currency area to what measures should be taken to make it an optimum currency area. Thus, a predictive theory has become a policy prescription. Little regard is paid to the fact that the process of monetary integration cannot be divorced from international politics, and more pointedly, that the aggregate efficiency gains from monetary

4. For an illustration of the potentially disastrous consequences of interest rate competition, derived in part from a concern with market reputation, see Eichengreen 1992a.

5. Another important skeptic of the case for capital deregulation is Susan Strange. The folly of capital deregulation is one of the main themes of her book *Mad Money* (1998b). See also Strange 1998a, 6, 17–18.

6. See, for example, Eichengreen and Frieden 1993. More generally on this issue, Cohen showed how political factors such as power and ideology explain which monetary unions succeed and which fail. See Cohen 1998a, 82, 85, 87, 91; 1993; also Rockoff 2000.

union (such as the reduction in transactions costs) are surely dwarfed by the differential effect the union will have on various groups.

It is also difficult to rely on economic logic to understand which currencies will be used internationally. Here economists have produced an interesting set of diverse theories to address the question. Yet again it is hard to escape the conclusion that even from an economistic perspective, politics will play a central role.[7] The decisive role that politics will play here is underscored even further by the economic evidence on a related issue—the costs and benefits of issuing a currency that is used internationally. A debate that derives from the U.S. balance-of-payments concerns of the 1960s produced a number of studies, the results of which suggest that the economic costs and benefits of international currency fall into the "modest and ambiguous" camp (Cohen 1971; Aliber 1964; Salant 1964; Karlik 1968).

Thus, with regard to the regulation of international capital, international use of currency, and basic questions about the contours of monetary geography, economic theory rarely tells us anything definitive about when and where and almost never tells us why.[8] Once again, it should be emphasized that economic forces certainly (and powerfully) affect basic policy decisions regarding the management of capital, the use of international money, choice of exchange rate mechanism and monetary association, and the mechanisms of adjustment. Further, in any given setting economic logic will effectively rule out certain options. But there will also almost always remain a range of policies that are plausible—that is, economically coherent. And here economic theory will have little to tell us about the path chosen from this plausible set. Even in the cases where the difference between the aggregate economic consequences of one choice over another is discernable, those consequences typically will be dwarfed by the considerable differential and political effects that the choice of one policy over another will have.

The indeterminacy of economic theory as a guide to policy goes much deeper than issues relating to the international use of money—it reaches down to the very core of macroeconomics, to the management and control of money. Over basic issues such as inflation and CBI, the study of money suffers from the same problems—modest and ambiguous economic findings that cannot account for the policy choice—even as the result is routinely attributed to the inevitable logic of economic theory.

---

7. Cohen (1998a, 161, 164) noted, for example, that the extent to which the yen is used as an international currency is essentially a policy choice, and that both the Europeans and the Japanese manage the use of their currencies with an eye toward avoiding confrontation with the United States. For theories on the international use of currency, see also Kindleberger 1967; Cohen 1971; Krugman 1984.

8. Similarly, it can be noted that the choice of the adjustment mechanism is made from a range of options with minor differences in their relative efficiency but dramatic variation in their political consequence. See Simmons 1994.

Inflation and Macroeconomic Policy

The extent to which economic legitimacy reifies one policy choice while cloaking profound political consequence is even more pronounced in the domestic sphere. With regard to domestic economic management, contemporary macroeconomic theory and policy has at its core the widely held assumption that inflation carries real economic costs and that the principal goal of macroeconomic policy should be the maintenance of low inflation. Vigilance against the threat of inflation must be the primary, if not the sole, goal of macroeconomic policy. This view derives from the recognition, supported by evidence, that governments cannot call forth greater employment and production in the long run via monetary expansion. But the only conclusion that can be drawn from this is that governments should not purposefully promote inflation to expand output. It does not address the question of whether inflation itself is costly or "bad" or whether the suppression of inflationary embers need be the principal goal of policy. In fact, the costs of moderate inflation are extraordinarily difficult to establish.

Once again, there are lots of deductive reasons why inflation might impose real economic costs (Fischer and Modigliani 1986). Inflation, for example, can weaken the informational role of prices (Ackley 1978; Laidler 1979). This can also reduce efficiency by increasing uncertainty. There is empirical support for some of these propositions, as inflation has been shown to be associated with greater variability in prices and the variability of real output (Parks 1978; Louge and Sweeney 1981). Models can also be constructed to simulate why inflation should be costly in practice. In particular, Martin Feldstein (1997, 1999b, 1999c) argued that even low rates of inflation impose significant and sustained real economic costs—as high as 1 percent of gross domestic product (GDP) per year. He argued that inflation interacts with and exacerbates inefficiencies in the tax system, resulting in large deadweight losses. This approach has been applied to a number of different national settings, all supporting the proposition that a permanent reduction in inflation will yield substantial real gains.[9]

On the other hand, competing arguments provide reasons why some inflation might actually be a good thing (i.e., the inflation rate associated with the maximum possible rate of economic growth is positive). Such arguments often center around the view that in an economy where nominal prices are slow to adjust downward, some inflation would allow for essential changes in relative prices to occur more quickly and efficiently. Very low inflation also might undermine monetary policy, given a nominal interest rate floor of zero percent. In fact, "inflation may be a necessary part of the process" (Duesenberry 1977, 265), and deductive models can be constructed and simulations run to show that in fact moderate inflation "per-

---

9. See many of the applications of the model presented in Feldstein's volume (1999b). See also Dotsey and Richmond 1996; Feldstein 1979.

mits maximum employment and output" (Akerlof, Dickens, and Perry 1996, 2).

Additionally, deductive arguments concluding that inflation is costly have been criticized both on their internal logic and on their practical significance (Foster 1972, 7). And the logic of models that show significant negative effects of inflation has been questioned. Feldstein-type models in particular have been sharply challenged (Fischer 1999a, 42; Dornbusch 1999; Tobin 1983; Ball 1997). In addition, such models may contain an important bias: Feldstein asserted that the costs of disinflation (which would be quite significant: 6 percent of GDP [1999c, 37]) would only be incurred once, because the reduction would be "permanent" (1997, 24; 1999b, 4). But in practice, inflation would tick up from time to time and would have to be suppressed, and these new efforts at disinflation would carry real costs as well. These costs would cut into the potential gains identified by Feldstein, especially since, even as currently constructed, the model does not expect the gains to outweigh costs for decades.

Here, faced with competing and indeterminate deductive arguments, scholars have taken great advantage of the relative abundance of data available on inflation rates and growth rates and produced numerous studies. And, as already noted, it turns out that the costs of moderate inflation are extraordinarily difficult to establish. Inflation hawk Robert Barro—who with David Gordon (1983, 104) had written that while economists assume that inflation is costly, they "have not presented very convincing arguments to explain these costs"—attempted to illustrate those costs. He concluded that the data reveal costs that, while apparently small, have a cumulative effect that is "more than enough to justify a strong interest in price stability." He noted, however, that the "clear evidence" of the costs of inflation comes from countries that have had inflationary episodes exceeding 10–20 percent per year (Barro 1995, 1, 9). In a follow-up article, the qualifications are even stronger: "For inflation rates below twenty percent per year . . . the relation between growth and inflation is not statistically significant" (Barro 1996, 159).

Almost all of the negative relationships found between inflation and growth are dependent on the consequences of very high levels of inflation.[10] Ultimately, any real economic costs of inflation, especially inflation below 20 percent, and certainly below 10 percent, are almost impossible to find. And even if a more consistent finding did actually emerge,

10. Two prominent examples of this are provided by Stanley Fischer and Michael Bruno, leading macroeconomists who have had great practical influence on public policy. Fischer (1993, 1996) compared the effects of inflation on growth for one country with an inflation rate of 110 percent with those for another with a rate of 10 percent. Yet his conclusion supports an inflation target of 1 to 3 percent. Although Bruno found "no evidence of any relationship between inflation and growth at annual rates less than 40 percent" (Bruno and Easterly 1996, 145), he argued for policies aimed at "keeping the inflation genie tightly in the bottle" (Bruno 1995, 35).

the question would remain as to whether the coexistence of inflation and low growth necessarily supports the pursuit of a disinflationary policy. Since disinflationary policies are unambiguously associated with output losses, the result of such policies might be lower inflation and even lower growth.

For those who study the politics of money, the final resolution of this debate is not of great concern. The evidence overwhelmingly supports the view that the inflation rate—at low or moderate levels—will have very little effect on the performance of the aggregate economy. Thus, there is no good reason to believe that even moderate inflation has a significant effect on economic performance, or that moderate inflation should be met with aggressive anti-inflationary policies. The enormous empirical literature has failed to come to a clear conclusion regarding the economic consequences of moderate inflation. The evidence suggests that most likely the net economic effect of such inflation is modest, ambiguous, and contingent on other factors (Temple 2000; Romer and Romer 1997a; Card and Hyslop 1997; Groshen and Schweitzer 1999).

But the idea that inflation is costly remains an article of faith held by mainstream economic theorists and, to an even greater extent, by related policy communities. Central bankers in particular are virtually missionary in their statements regarding the need to fight inflation at all costs.[11] This matters because the consensus on the costs of inflation is the basis for the proposition that central banks should be "independent," that is, insulated from the political process. Support for an independent central bank derives from the need to guard against inflation.

In fact, increased CBI is associated with lower rates of inflation. But there is no evidence that greater CBI is associated with enhanced economic performance.[12] This lack of association is surprising, as it was assumed, for example, that the greater credibility of independent central banks would cause disinflationary episodes to be both shorter and less costly. In fact, the opposite is true. "In direct contradiction" to the credibility hypothesis, "disinflation appears to be consistently *more* costly and no more rapid in countries with independent central banks" (Posen 1995a, 3, 13). Rather than receiving a bonus, independent central banks "have to prove their toughness repeatedly, by being tough" (Debelle and Fischer 1995, 205; see also Eijffinger and De Haan 1996, 36, 38, 64).

Yet the lack of real benefits has not affected the ingrained anti-inflationary perspective that stubbornly persists. The Federal Reserve Bank of Cleveland, for example, has twice published a scatter plot reporting a negative

---

11. See, for example, Hoskins 1991 (Hoskins was then president of the Federal Reserve Bank of Cleveland); McDonough 1994 (as president of the Federal Reserve Bank of New York); Crow 1989 (as governor of the Bank of Canada).

12. See Alesina and Summers 1993; also Cukierman 1994, 1440. For a good survey of this large literature, see Eijffinger and De Haan 1996; also Berger, De Haan, and Eijffinger 2001.

correlation of 0.28 between output and inflation in forty-five countries. This correlation, however, is almost wholly dependent on one dramatic outlier, and it is not statistically significant. The conclusion drawn by the bank, on the other hand, is quite significant: "Ultimately, a central bank can best contribute to a nation's economic health by eliminating the price uncertainties associated with inflation" (*Economic Trends* 2/97, 19; *Economic Commentary* 12/96, 3).

How dramatic is this bias? The breadth and dogmatism of the costly inflation faith are remarkable. In 1994, Alan Blinder asserted that the natural rate of unemployment in the United States was about 6 percent (*Washington Post* 9/8/94), and in 1997 he argued that the maximum sustainable rate of growth for the U.S. economy was about 2.5 percent (Blinder 1997b). In each case, exceeding these targets should be met with cautious monetary policy; otherwise there would be the danger of inflation.[13] Given that in the following two years growth in the United States exceeded 4.2 percent and unemployment fell to 4 percent, while inflation continued to recede to record lows, it is hard to characterize Blinder's assessments as anything but erring on the side of extreme caution.

Yet Blinder has been widely perceived as a reckless dove with regard to inflation. He only enhanced this reputation as vice chairman of the Federal Reserve Board, when he set off "an avalanche of press reaction" (*Washington Post* 9/8/94) to comments he offered after a conference on reducing unemployment. Blinder suggested that overly tight monetary policies had contributed to Europe's high unemployment rate. Blinder's commentary, especially about U.S. policy, was quite cautious. Indeed, Thomas Sargent (1999, 11), a leading figure among scholars who hold that even low inflation bears real economic costs, stated, "I do not believe that Blinder's comments would have excited controversy or exception at any leading macroeconomics seminar." But for policymakers, there was widespread discomfort even "with the implication of less than single-minded devotion to the battle against inflation that has become a creed among central bankers" (*Financial Times* 8/29/94).[14]

There is much at stake here, because monetary policy can be too tight, and disinflationary policies are unambiguously associated with output losses. Thus, in emphasizing inflation fighting, and especially when delegating responsibility for monetary policy to independent central bankers who share a creed of single-minded devotion to crushing inflation, there is a danger of disregarding this potential threat to the real side of the economy. If monetary policy is too tight, then output and employment will suffer. If it is too loose, inflation will rise. The puzzle is that the costs from

13. See also Blinder 1998.
14. At the time of Blinder's appointment to the Federal Reserve Board, Chairman Alan Greenspan was told that some of his publications were "soft on inflation." Greenspan reportedly quipped, "I would have preferred he were a communist" (Woodward 2000, 127).

macroeconomic policies that are a little too tight are unambiguous, while the costs of policies that are a little too loose are unclear. Yet the policy conclusion derived from contemporary macroeconomics is to sanctify institutional structures—independent central banks—that are designed to err on the side of being a little too tight. This puzzle cannot be resolved by looking solely at the aggregate effects of macroeconomic policy choices. It can only be resolved by shifting the focus of the analysis from economic efficiency to political forces and objectives.

UBIQUITOUS POLITICS

A political approach places renewed emphasis on the fact that there are in practice a range of plausible policy choices that differ only marginally with regard to their economic efficiency. Given that monetary policy has distributive consequences and additionally that states have concerns for power and autonomy, the choice of one policy over another is likely to be driven by political rather than economic calculation. Those politics are likely to derive from group conflict, ideas, and state power.

Ideas about Money: Cloak and Dagger

While ideas can of course be used instrumentally to advance particular interests, in the macroeconomic sphere they can have an additional and dramatic effect. There is a growing literature on the importance of ideas in international relations, as well as in international political economy (IPE), including some work that has addressed how ideas have shaped decisions made about money (see, e.g., Goldstein 1993; Goldstein and Keohane 1993; Haas 1992b; Helleiner 1999; McNamara 1998; Odell 1982). But there is something special about the role of ideas in monetary affairs that has not been sufficiently addressed to this point: With regard to money, the power of ideas does more than just shape the possible. It defines the feasible.

Money is different. It has no inherent value—its value derives solely from the fact that it can be exchanged for things of value. Thus, money is worth more than the paper it is printed on solely because people believe that it can be exchanged for other desirable things. Or, as Cohen stated, "Nothing enhances a currency's acceptability more than the prospect of acceptability by others."

But where does that acceptability come from? It comes from confidence in the currency, the assurance of which is provided by the pursuit of "credible strategies," which "make considerable concessions to market sentiment" (Cohen 1998a, 97, 122). It can be costly to establish a currency's reputation, and if its guardians are not vigilant, that reputation can vanish quite quickly.[15] Unlike a reputation for military power and resolve, the strength of a country's currency is put to the test every day—in fact, around the clock: in currency markets around the globe, traders monitor every policy choice and study each new descriptive statistic to form an assessment of just how strong others will perceive that currency to be.

Thus, what distinguishes money politics from other spheres of political economy is not simply the tendency for economic ideology to be used "to veil the conflict between special and national interests" (Strange 1998a, 15).[16] Rather it is this tendency, coupled with the unique link between ideas and "market sentiment" in money matters, and the overwhelming influence of that sentiment on the ability to practice macroeconomic policy. The Credible Policy is that policy which "the market" thinks is right. Policies that are not credible cannot be sustained because of the responses of market actors to such policies.

The role of beliefs and ideas in macroeconomics is unique, therefore, in that all macroeconomic policies require public confidence in order to work. The astonishing result of this is that in a hypothetical menu of five economic policies, each of which was plausible from the standpoint of economic theory, if three were *perceived* to be illegitimate, they would not in fact be sustainable, *solely for that reason*. Support for this constructivist proposition can be found in the halls of the University of Chicago economics department. In their classic text *A Monetary History of the United States, 1857–1969*, Milton Friedman and Anna Schwartz argued that abandoning the gold standard "might well have been highly preferable" for the United States in the 1890s. However, in a "fascinating example of how important what people think about money can sometimes be," that choice was not feasible. Instead, "the fear that silver would produce an inflation sufficient to force the United States off the gold standard made it necessary to have a severe deflation in order to stay on the gold standard." To some extent, then, the art of the feasible is both contestable and consequential (Friedman and Schwartz 1963, 111, 133; see also Grabel 1997, 2000).

This phenomenon is not an artifact of history but has an enormous contemporary influence on both economic theory and the practice of public policy. One of the reasons why states abandoned the Bretton Woods fixed exchange rate system was the expectation that flexible exchange rate sys-

---

15. As Cohen noted repeatedly, "The issue, ultimately, is a government's own credibility," which is a function of "how official policies interact with market preferences" (1998a, 67, 135; see also 121, 123, 130, 133 156, 160; on the cost necessary to maintain reputation, 141; on the ephemeral nature of reputation, 10–13). Regarding what makes a currency acceptable, one cannot help but be reminded of Sidney Greenstreet's line in *The Maltese Falcon*: "I'll tell you right out, I'm a man who likes talking to a man who likes to talk."

16. See also Strange 1998b, 190. Strange takes these points further than Cohen, emphasizing that the specific aspects of some macroeconomic policies are less important than the market's perception of them (1988b, 107, also 99, 108, 111, 121 on ideas, mood, and sentiment).

tems would afford macroeconomic policy autonomy. This was an implication of the influential Mundell-Fleming model, which remains an essential analytical device for students of the international economy and of IPE.

One of the understood "laws" of economic theory derived from the Mundell-Fleming model is that states could only select two items from the following menu: free capital flows, fixed exchange rates, and autonomous monetary policy (Kenen 1985; Fleming 1962; Mundell 1960). Thus, it was assumed that by abandoning fixed rates, states could pursue the monetary policies of their choice. But this did not turn out to be the case. In theory, given flexible rates, policy disparities should be mediated at the border. If a state's policies resulted in an inflation rate that was 5 percent above the international average, its currency would depreciate by 5 percent and that would be that. But if capital mobility is accompanied by a consensus with regard to what is a "correct" monetary policy, then the depreciation will not stop at 5 percent. Capital flight in this case will punish the state for pursuing a deviant policy. Failure to reverse that policy in the wake of a sustained depreciation will stimulate even further capital flight and depreciation, and so on. Thus, a state that preferred to pursue a more expansionist monetary policy than average, even one that was willing to tolerate the depreciation necessary to restore equilibrium in international prices, might be unable to chart such a course in the face of punishing (as opposed to equilibrating) capital flows. Hence, the "holy trinity" is a myth, because if there is an ideological consensus regarding macroeconomic policy, it is not possible to have capital mobility and policy autonomy at the same time.

Why does this matter? It matters because macroeconomic policies are often veiled in a cloak of economic legitimacy. Legitimate policies thrive, it is argued, because they are the most efficient and because those that deviate lose out in a Darwinian struggle—they fail because they are unable to deliver the goods. But two observations raise fundamental questions for this version of events. First, as Friedman and Schwartz argued with regard to the choice of a monetary standard, some policies, perhaps even the best policies, may be unsustainable solely because people (erroneously) think they are inefficient. Thus, "legitimacy" is not the inevitable revelation of optimality but a path-dependent self-fulfilling prophecy.[17]

Thus, ideas in and of themselves can affect policy choice. There are three principal mechanisms through which ideas about money can profoundly shape policy in ways divorced from the economic logic or merits of those ideas. First, beliefs, especially when they harden into an ideology (defined here as beliefs that are held as articles of faith and thus resistant to change even in the light of evidence), can skew the ways in which policymakers understand and react to problems. As Eric Helleiner shows in this

---

17. This does not mean, it should be added immediately and emphatically, that any policy is just as good as another. Rather, the argument is solely that there is a plausible set of macroeconomic policies that would provide roughly similar aggregate economic performance and that should be sustainable based on their internal logic.

volume, the markedly different rules and institutional structures of central banks established in the South after the Second World War are attributable to the prevailing economic beliefs of the great power whose influence held sway in each particular state.

Second, ideas, especially when they contribute to normative understandings about "appropriate" behavior, can create artificial yet powerful constraints on policy. (*Artificial* here means not derived from any economic "truth.") One prominent example of this is attitudes toward devaluation. From an economic perspective, devaluation or revaluation of a currency is a step taken to restore external equilibrium—it cannot be said that one direction for currency adjustments is "better" than the other. But in practice, devaluation (and depreciation) is associated with weakness, while a "strong" currency affords prestige to its issuer. As Charles Kindleberger (1970, 198) wrote, "A country's exchange rate is more than a number. It is an emblem of its importance to the world, a sort of international status symbol." Similarly, Robert Mundell stated that "great powers have great currencies" (quoted in Cohen 1998a, 121).[18] These sentiments, however true they may be, have no basis in economic logic, but they can guide policy. As Hongying Wang illustrates in chapter 7, devaluation was probably the appropriate course of action for China in 1997. However, the decision to stand pat was made not on the basis of economic logic but to demonstrate that by refusing to devalue its currency, China was behaving as a "responsible great power."

Finally, as discussed above, ideas about money can matter because they can be self-confirming, bestowing a legitimacy that convinces the winners they are right while masking sharp distributional conflicts. But many of these policies, justified and sustained principally on claims of their theoretical soundness (and superiority to other options), are of predominantly political origin and effect. Nothing more than the way people think about money can rule out some otherwise plausible options in favor of another. The aggregate economic consequences of this choice are not likely to be large. But political consequences—which groups, sectors, regions, and so on, are better off with one policy as opposed to another—may be extraordinary. In order to come to grips with this, students of the *politics* of money need to reconsider their conceptualization of macroeconomics. In particular, students of politics need to place greater emphasis on the differential as opposed to the aggregate effects of macroeconomic phenomena.

The Conflict of Interests

The use of aggregate data such as the gross national product statistic and other basic measurements common in macroeconomic analysis is problem-

---

18. Cohen (1998a, 121) then added, "What nation would not take pride in the esteem accorded one of its most tangible symbols?"

atic for most political analyses. Looking at the aggregate data obscures the most basic political disputes that can arise over economic policy. Although a national economy will have an aggregate growth rate, most of the time different income groups, regions, and sectors will have distinct and often markedly diverse economic experiences—some regions or sectors, for example, might be dramatically outperforming others. Outside of exceptional economic circumstances, it is the composition of growth, not the overall aggregate rate, that is of greater political significance.

Two important political issues become visible only when attention is shifted from the rate to the composition of economic growth. First, the perception of the "correct" macroeconomic policy might be quite different across individuals, sectors, and regions within a country, given their distinct economic circumstances. Those experiencing rapid growth of their own incomes might favor a cautious macroeconomic policy, while others, doing less well, could urge expansion. What is "optimal" from a national perspective is unclear. In practice, the balance of political influence across groups, combined with the specific experiences of those groups, will shape the ultimate policy choice.

Second, and much more significantly, it is not just that the distribution of growth affects macroeconomic policy choice. The converse is also true: *macroeconomic policies shape the distribution of growth*. Thus, because macroeconomic policies do not work their way uniformly through the economy, it is possible for some interests to eat their cake and have it too. Given high growth in their sector, they may favor cautious monetary policies and vigilance against inflation. In turn, tight money and low inflation might enhance the prospects for greater growth of their own sector. "Risking" policies that might slow the aggregate economy is not risky for such actors.

This dynamic is likely to be overlooked by analyses that take contemporary macroeconomic theory as their point of departure. Macroeconomic theorists today almost always impose strict homogeneity assumptions on their models, which effectively eliminates the issue of distribution from the study of monetary phenomena. Regardless of their theoretical starting points, most such models consider the economy as a unitary entity, composed of identical building blocs such as labor (possibly skilled and unskilled), capital, and consumers (typically with independent, identically distributed tastes) (see, e.g., Blanchard and Fischer 1989). Together these elements assume away the distributional consequences of macroeconomic phenomena in particular and almost all of the politics in general.

It should be noted that this approach is not necessarily inappropriate for macroeconomists (though even there the assumption has not been immune from sharp criticism [Kirman 1992; see also McCallum and Goodfriend 1989]). When one is studying the science of how the economy works in theory, it may make sense to hold outside the model the political factors that shape the functioning of the economy in practice. Further, for a subdiscipline focusing on aggregate outcomes, differential effects may be of limited significance. But this stringent assumption, however appropriate for many inquiries into macroeconomic theory, is a fundamentally unsound starting point for questions involving politics and political economy.

Of greatest significance here is a closely related assumption. Modern macroeconomic theory assumes aggregate monetary neutrality: that monetary phenomena do not affect the overall performance of the real economy in the long run. While embraced by the discipline as a working assumption, the issue of monetary neutrality is still debated by macroeconomic theorists (Patinkin 1989; Gale 1982; Hahn 1983; Ostrup 2000). Once again the resolution of this debate within the economics profession is of little concern here—and also, as with homogeneity assumptions, the neutrality assumption does not seem obviously unreasonable for a discipline concerned with long-run aggregate economic growth. But it too provides an inappropriate point of departure for most inquiries into politics. Because even if it is true that in the long run, monetary phenomena do not affect aggregate economic performance, they do have real distributional economic effects: shaping relative prices, income distribution, and the relative performance of different sectors and industries across the economy.

The effect of monetary phenomena on relative prices has been recognized even by economists who were passionate defenders of aggregate monetary neutrality. Irving Fisher, the patriarch of American monetarism, described his opus *The Purchasing Power of Money* as "at bottom simply a restatement of the old 'quantity theory of money.'" Yet he also argued that "prices do not, and in fact cannot, move in perfect unison." Aggregate monetary neutrality holds, in fact, because there exists "a compensation in price movements in the sense that the failure of one set of prices to respond to any influence on the price level will necessitate a correspondingly greater change in other prices" (Fisher 1920, vii, 196, 197; see also Hayek 1990, 82). Fisher and other macroeconomists, then, did not deny the existence of distributional effects; rather, those effects were simply not the object of their study.

This was not always the case. Classical economists, including "virtually all" of the quantity theorists of the late nineteenth century, believed that monetary phenomena have significant real consequences (Laider 1991, 17).[19] The main student of these phenomena was Richard Cantillon, whose eighteenth-century writings produced a research agenda that was sustained until the 1930s. Cantillon argued that changes in the money supply did not descend uniformly from heaven but had to flow from some source. The nature of the source and the recipients of the money would determine the dis-

---

19. Malthus ([1811] 1963, 96), for example, argued that it "must always be recollected" that real effects of monetary expansion are the result not of "the *quantity* of the circulating medium . . . but the *different distribution* of it."

tinct effect of a change in the money supply. Following a monetary expansion, the price level will rise, but not uniformly, owing to the different tastes and elasticities of those who receive the new money first (Bordo 1983).

According to Cantillon, "Everybody agrees that the abundance of money or its increase in exchange, raises the price of everything." But crucially, "Market prices will rise more for certain things than for others however abundant the money may be." There are real distributional effects as monetary phenomena work their way through the economy, just as "a river which runs and winds about in its bed will not flow with double the speed when the amount of water is doubled" (Cantillon [1931] 1964, 161, 179, 177).[20]

Cantillon was followed in the nineteenth century by John E. Cairnes ([1873] 1965; Bordo 1975) and in the twentieth by John Maynard Keynes. Keynes, in his *Treatise on Money*, followed Cantillon and Cairnes with his argument that changes in purchasing power that result from monetary contractions or expansions are "not spread evenly or proportionately over the various buyers." The "new distribution of purchasing power" will have "social and economic consequences" that "may have a fairly large lasting effect on relative price levels." Once again, the argument here is not that monetary disturbances affect aggregate output but that monetary phenomena have consequences even in the absence of such effects. "The fact that monetary changes do not affect all prices in the same way, to the same degree, or at the same time, is what makes them significant" (Keynes [1930] 1971, 81, 83–84).

Ironically, it was subsequent work by Keynes that led to the atrophy of this line of inquiry. In *The General Theory of Employment, Interest, and Money* (1936), which dominated the profession for a generation and ushered in the era of modern macroeconomics, Keynes shifted his emphasis away from monetary influences. The vigorous monetarist response that followed kept the debate at the aggregate level. But students of the politics of money need to revisit this literature, which was not superseded but rather was left to atrophy as the focus of the economics profession followed an alternate trajectory. It is the differential, political effects of macroeconomic phenomena that provide the missing link in the relationship between ideas and interests and clarify the extent to which the choice of a "legitimate" economic policy may be of greater political than economic consequence.

A more political approach can provide an answer for the puzzle introduced earlier—why do states seem to be erring in favor of a deflationary

20. W. Stanley Jevons (1881, 72) characterized Cantillon's tracing of monetary disturbances as "marvelous." It is important to note that Cantillon was no monetary crank; in fact, he was quite orthodox. He did not believe that a monetary expansion would increase economic activity in the long run. Rather, he was an opponent of inflation who believed that the inflationary process would have self-reversing effects with attendant real economic costs. And he was sensitive to the danger that macroeconomic policy might be manipulated by politicians for their own benefit. See Cantillon [1931] 1964, 323; Bordo 1983, 237, 251; Murphy 1986, 263, 277.

bias in their monetary policies, accepting the unambiguous pain of aggressive disinflation rather than risk the uncertain (but apparently, at the most, modest) costs of a bit more inflation?[21] A commitment to the primacy of inflation fighting and, relatedly, the assurance of CBI is the sole macroeconomic policy posture that has legitimacy in the contemporary world. What matters here is not this policy choice per se, but rather the way in which the winning policy is anointed and sustained. If vigilance against inflation were the unambiguously optimal economic policy for all, then these distributional quibbles would be of only marginal interest—all groups seem to support bad policies if they will help their narrow interests.

But as the economics become more modest and ambiguous, the demand for a political explanation must increase. If the hypervigilant policy is but one plausible policy available from a larger menu, then it is likely that the distinct distributional effects of each policy choice, not its economic efficiency, explain the outcome. This casts new light, for example, on the long-held understanding that inflation has distributional consequences,[22] and on the less appreciated but just as important observation by Charles Rist ([1940] 1966, 375) that "price stability, just as much as price instability, gives rise to inequalities as between the citizens of one and the same country." There is a deafening silence on this issue—the distributional effects of low inflation, and the distributional effects of policies designed to keep inflation low. Indeed, Feldstein (1997, 153; 1999c, 38) stated explicitly that his model did not address "the distributional consequences of the disinflation *or of the reduced inflation*" (emphasis added). But low inflation and, perhaps more important, the policies required to sustain it, will benefit some groups in society at the expense of others.

A focus on the real, differential effects of monetary phenomena clarifies the sharp politics, as opposed to the ambiguous economics, that is driving macroeconomic policy. As Adam Posen argued, low inflation is only sustainable if it has adequate political support. That support, he suggested, comes from numerous sources, but especially from "one historically prominent interest group: the financial sector." The financial sector supports CBI "as a long run means to price stability," and it could not be sustained "with-

21. It bears repeating that the ultimate resolution of the economic debate over optimal inflation policy is of small concern to students of politics, given the modest stakes. The purpose of this discussion is not to champion one policy over another but rather to illustrate that more than one policy is theoretically plausible, that the perception of legitimacy can be a crucial factor in determining which policy is chosen, and that the differential effects of each easily outweigh the difference in their aggregate economic consequences.

22. Few would dispute the notion, for example, that unanticipated inflation benefits debtors at the expense of creditors, or that this is one reason why financiers have always been strong proponents of price stability. Indeed, many of the opponents of inflation make their case on distributional grounds—that governments often use inflation as a means of increasing their resources relative to society. In fact, inflation affects distribution through a multitude of channels, with differential effects on various individuals, classes, sectors, and regions. See Kirshner 1998 and the literature cited therein.

out that group's ongoing protection of its counterinflationary activities" (Posen 1995b, 254, 256, 264).[23]

Posen's findings were challenged by other scholars who primarily suggested that he had overstated his case—in particular, they showed that CBI, along with a host of other factors, still has an independent effect on the rate of inflation (Franzese 1999; Temple 1998). But Posen's work remains an important contribution and a step forward in understanding the political foundations of macroeconomic policy choices.

In theory, CBI alone should not be sufficient to produce a low inflation outcome; it depends on what central bankers decide or are ordered to do.[24] In the United States, for example, the Federal Reserve System was originally designed to *balance* societal interests. Given the distributional issues at stake, the system was structured in a manner that "reflected a fear of both banker and populist control" (Faust 1996, 279). But in practice, the system is now run by the bankers, who see the world instinctively through the anti-inflationist eyes of their profession (or, in the words of one scholar, who will "listen with a more careful ear to the interests of the banking community" [Piga 2000, 28]). And the idea that any threat of inflation must be suppressed is the only one that is legitimate in contemporary mainstream economic theory—and policy. That consensus helps sustain low inflation policies and, more important, serves to undermine policies that might deviate from the norm, regardless of the soundness of such policies on the basis of their internal economic logic.

But the policies chosen affect the composition of growth to a much greater extent than they do the aggregate rate of growth, and tight macroeconomic policies privilege some sectors in society at the expense of others. Inflation hurts financial institutions. One study, for example, showed that the share prices of commercial banks are inversely related to inflation, and that bank shareholders benefited from the disinflation of the 1980s (Santoni 1986, 23). Ultimately, the "special relationship" that central bankers are likely to have with the financial sector offers a more compelling explanation for the primacy of the low-inflation school than do the economic merits of the case for such a policy (Epstein and Schor 1990, 58).[25]

Still a World of States

Even though states have lost considerable power and autonomy to market forces in the past few years, the world is still a world of states, actors with

23. Posen (1995b) also showed a correlation between the strength of the financial sector and the degree of central bank independence. See also Posen 1993.

24. This is captured in the well-known distinction between "goal" and "instrument" independence. See Debelle and Fischer 1995, 197.

25. Santoni (1986, 23) argued that the housing sector in the United States "was a major beneficiary of the inflationary process" from 1965 to 1980; see also Cargill and Hutchison 1990, 172–173. Other studies have also explored the differential effects of low inflation and tight monetary policies (see Epstein and Schor 1990; Frieden 1997).

strong preferences and the power to advance their interests. This has a formative influence on the pattern of international macroeconomics and is crucial to understanding the observed outcomes (again, from a range of plausible options available to states) with regard to their monetary arrangements. As already noted, for example, political factors explain the basic contours of what money is used where. The force of the economic logic of the "optimum currency area," however deductively coherent, has almost no predictive power.

The role of politics in shaping the choice of money extends beyond the issue of preferred legal tender to include a broad range of monetary arrangements, orientations, and alliances. Ultimately, it is impossible to divorce the pattern of monetary relations from international politics, as well as from the needs and preferences of governments themselves as they strive for autonomy and attempt to finesse their domestic political positions. As Rawi Abdelal illustrates in this volume, one cannot begin to understand the pattern of post-Soviet monetary relations without emphasizing international politics and the domestic political contest from which those international preferences derive. Similarly, but relying on different variables and approach, David Stasavage illuminates the political foundations of (and sustained political influence on) the CFA Franc Zone in Africa.

State power and politics define the basic contours of international money relations in numerous ways. Three issues in particular illustrate the formative role politics plays in determining the international use of money: the traditional role of power in shaping international relations, the tendency for states to be self-conscious about their exposure to the international economy, and the difficulties states find in coming to mutually beneficial agreements in the monetary arena.

Most basically, it should not be forgotten that even in the relatively specialized realm of money, international relations still reflect, to some extent, the interests of powerful states. Such states may shape the international system to enhance their relative autonomy, pursue unrelated political goals, or advance the interests of the financial sector within their own economy (see, e.g., Helleiner 1994, esp. 112–114; Kirshner 1995). Even with the relative shift in the balance of power from states to international financial markets, states pursuing their interests remain a key and probably the most important purposeful force in shaping monetary phenomena.

Given the realities of world politics, states are also often self-conscious about the way in which they interact with the international economy—that is, they have broader concerns than the pursuit of wealth or economic efficiency. In chapter 8, for example, William Grimes shows that internationalization (or lack thereof) of the Japanese yen has been the result of state policy—and one shaped almost entirely by international and domestic political considerations—not the result of consideration of its aggregate economic implications. Further, when states do choose to encourage the international use of their currencies, that too is for political reasons. For more than a century large states have often attempted to extend their influence through the formation and management of exclusionary monetary areas. These efforts, which are made to advance political goals, typically involve numerous perks to attract participants and are almost always money-losing propositions for the states that place themselves at the center of a currency area (Kirshner 1995).

Finally, the efficient functioning of an international monetary system often requires that states cooperate, that is, follow rules and make short-term sacrifices in the expectation of continued and long-term economic gains. The inevitable problem that must be addressed by any effort at international monetary cooperation is how to share the burden of adjustment. Disequilibria will arise in the international macroeconomic sphere. And while there are states that may not wish to allow their economies to expand or let their currencies appreciate, the greatest political pressures will emanate from the states that must retrench—and slow their economies—in order to sustain the smooth functioning of the international monetary order. Thus, some states will be asked to bear real and relatively narrow economic burdens for the sake of an abstract and fairly general international ideal.

International cooperation to share or at least coordinate and ease the burdens of adjustment is thus crucial. As Barry Eichengreen (1992a) argued, one of the principal reasons why the interwar monetary payments system utterly collapsed, in contrast to the smooth functioning of the prewar system, was international cooperation—present before the war and absent in its aftermath.[26] There is still no consensus on the conditions under which international monetary cooperation is likely to occur and, more important, to be sustained.[27] It is clear that such cooperation has rested squarely on the shoulders of international politics. However, as I elaborate in the conclusion to this volume, security concerns alone cannot explain the pattern of monetary cooperation—both the conflicts of interests and ideational factors must also be considered.

MONEY POLITICS: DISPARATE SETTINGS, COMMON THEMES

The unifying theme of this volume is the ubiquitous and inescapable political foundations of monetary phenomena. Each chapter explores a spe-

26. Eichengreen (1992a, 7) stated that "the credibility of the prewar gold standard rested on international cooperation."

27. It has been difficult, for example, to come to conclusions about how the international balance of power affects the prospects for monetary cooperation. While British and especially U.S. leadership contributed to monetary stability, unilateralism from the center has also been an important source of monetary instability, contributing, for example, to the collapse of the Bretton Woods system. See Eichengreen 1987, 1989; Rowland 1976; Walter 1991.

cific issue or puzzle relating to money. The chapters focus on a wide variety of countries, regions, and periods but share the same basic structure. They begin with the observation that economic theories by themselves offer little by way of explanation—economic pressures are ambiguous and/or modest. That is, economic theory offers either (1) no unambiguous choice (as to which policy or outcome is "better") or (2) a clear choice but one of little absolute significance. In either case the outcome or policy choice is more likely attributable to some other (political) factor. It should be clear that the shared foundational argument is not that the economic theories are wrong or incoherent, but rather that they are indeterminate—on the basis of economic logic alone, there are in theory a range of choices and outcomes that are plausible. To understand which choices and outcomes will emerge from that plausible range, one must turn to politics. Each chapter thus compares the ambiguous, relatively broad, and modest economic pressures with other political factors—ones that tend to produce powerful, more narrow, and divergent interests and preferences and that provide the missing link between the plausible set and the outcome observed.

Those political factors can be grouped into three categories—ideas, conflict, and power. As reviewed earlier, ideas can shape policy by shaping beliefs, hardening into ideologies, and constituting norms that circumscribe behavior. Ideas are of great interest with regard to money matters because of the unique role credibility plays in the macroeconomic sphere. Owing to this factor, one policy can develop a sole, consequential, and self-reinforcing claim to economic legitimacy. Thus, it is impossible to understand the choice of policy from the plausible set without understanding the role of ideas. More pointedly, policy legitimization, which appears to make one policy inevitable, can mask the profound differential and political consequence of that choice, or at the very least obscure and muffle the sharp political contestation that normally occurs under such circumstances. Once drained of rhetoric and self-reinforcing legitimacy, the conflictual elements present in macroeconomic policy choices become visible.

The second category of political forces that shape macroeconomic outcomes is conflict. Political conflict focuses on the differential economic influence that various policies have across actors within societies. The third category, power, considers the distinct problems raised by and the influence of relations between states as a source for understanding basic choices about the use of money.

In this chapter I have emphasized ambiguous economics and the conflict of interests—two foundations for the argument that monetary politics are inescapable. There is no "neutral" policy; rather, every macroeconomic phenomenon and monetary policy has significant and inevitable differential and political implications. In the next chapter, Ilene Grabel explores much more closely the role of ideology in shaping economic policy and the consequences of those choices. These two chapters are followed by two sets of empirically oriented studies that explore the ambiguous economics and sharp politics that characterize monetary phenomena in both the small and the great powers.

Part 2 focuses on smaller states. Along with the chapters by Abdelal, Helleiner, and Stasavage mentioned earlier, Hector Schamis's chapter evaluates money politics in Argentina. He shows that even given obvious and compelling economic pressures—such as hyperinflation, for which surely "something must be done"—the particular "something" is chosen on the basis of perceived credibility more than any other factor.[28] Part 3, on the great powers, includes chapters by Grimes on Japan, Wang on China, and Chang on the EMU. Also in this section Francis Gavin looks at U.S. policy making in the 1960s. Gavin's chapter illustrates the remarkable power that beliefs (even some mistaken ones) can have over policy, gives a practical example of just how intense conflicts over international adjustment can be, and shows the extraordinarily intimate interconnections between state power and national security present in international monetary relations.

Two chapters comprise the fourth and concluding part of the volume. First, Mark Blyth considers the political power of ideas in international financial markets, and why a system prone to crisis and characterized by increasing inefficiencies can be sustained. Finally, in the last chapter I revisit the political forces of power, ideas, and conflict and then illustrate how these forces are crucial to explain the continued drive for capital deregulation after the Asian financial crisis. I argue that deriving the bases of monetary conflict—whose interests will be affected by what policies—is necessary but not sufficient for understanding the choice of monetary policies. Rather, the material conflicts are filtered through and mediated by the interplay between power and ideas about money.

Individually, the chapters in this volume offer fresh insights into important debates in contemporary international relations and political economy. Taken together, they also underscore the point that wherever there is money, there is money politics—a subject that demands even greater attention in a global economy where monetary phenomena lead and the real economy follows.

---

28. The emphasis on policy credibility of course resonates with Sargent (1982). A crucial difference, obviously, is that Sargent, following rational expectations, holds that there is only one true credible path rather than a plausible set.

CHAPTER TWO

Ideology, Power, and the Rise of Independent Monetary Institutions in Emerging Economies

ILENE GRABEL

[handwritten annotation: neoliberalism = free trade, open markets, deregulation]

T he last quarter of the twentieth century will undoubtedly be regarded as an era of fundamental economic revolution—a revolution in which diverse economies in the South and East underwent
a radical transformation toward a neoliberal form of capitalism.[1] Like similar revolutions in the past (Polanyi 1944), this "great transformation" was
the product of political contest and ideological struggle rather than the un-
folding of some natural historical process. The theoretical justification for
this transformation in emerging economies is provided by new-classical
economic theory (Grabel 2000).[2] In particular, the new-classical theory of
"policy credibility" cements the case for the desirability and indeed inevitability of economic reconstruction along neoliberal lines. The concept
of policy credibility is central to the broader task of elevating the market as
the principal means of directing economic affairs and the effort to place severe constraints on state manipulation of economic policy toward particularist aims.

The movement to insulate the market and the policy-making process
from politics is particularly pronounced in the realm of monetary reform in
emerging economies. This effort to "depoliticize" policy is reflected in the
creation of central banks and currency boards that are beyond the reach of
state representatives. However, I believe that these institutional reforms fail

1. George DeMartino, and participants at the Cornell conference, especially Mark Blyth,
Benjamin Cohen, Shinju Fujihira, Peter Katzenstein, Jonathan Kirshner, Kathleen O'Neil,
Beth Simmons, and Hongying Wang, provided helpful comments. Peter Zawadzki, Robert
Fortier and Ritu Sharma provided excellent research assistance.

2. Two terms deserve clarification. The term *new-classical economic theory* refers to the extension of neoclassical theory that emerged in the 1970s and 1980s. It combines the "rational
expectations hypothesis" with a presumption of instantaneous market adjustment. The term
neoliberal economic policies refers to the free-market economic policies that derive from new-
classical theory.

on their own terms. Stated plainly, the effort to depoliticize financial policy via the creation of independent central banks and currency boards is ineluctably political.

The creation of independent institutions that set monetary and exchange rate policy stems from the widespread acceptance of the theory of policy credibility within the academic and policy community. I argue that the theory of policy credibility has powerful ideological aspects. First, the theory is elevated to the status of singular truth; as a consequence, its institutional corequisites are taken to be uniquely viable and efficacious. But despite these scientific pretensions, the theory and the policies inspired by it are fundamentally untestable and empirically irrefutable. They demand to be taken on faith, and at present, they are getting their way.

Second, the theory of credibility obscures the particular interests served by the institutions and policies it recommends. It regards these simply as serving the public good. It therefore suppresses an examination of contestation among opposing interests in society and the role of power in securing the design of monetary institutions and policy. In this connection, new-classical theorists treat a policy's viability as the consequence of the epistemological status of the theory that generates it rather than as the outcome of endogenous social and political factors.

At the broadest level, the rhetoric of economic theory critically understates and indeed obscures the underlying politics of monetary reform. Along with other contributors to this volume, I argue that choices about institutional innovations are informed as much—and indeed more—by politics than by the uncontestable logic of economic science (Cohen 1998a; Kirshner 2000). Monetary systems in emerging economies have been profoundly transformed by acceptance of the ideological aspects of the new-classical theory of policy credibility and by the exercise of political and economic power by influential actors.

INDEPENDENT CENTRAL BANKS AND CURRENCY BOARDS IN EMERGING ECONOMIES

The 1990s witnessed a global rise in statutory central bank independence (CBI). Governments in emerging economies took steps to create independent central banks where they did not exist, and enhanced the statutory independence of existing institutions.[3] Whether legal or statutory independence translates into operational independence is a critically im-

---

3. Helleiner (this volume) shows that the current trend toward CBI in emerging economies stands in sharp contrast to the creation of politically controlled, "developmentalist" central banks during much of the Bretton Woods era.

portant consideration in emerging economies.[4] In view of the problems with inferring operational from legal independence, Cukierman, Webb, and Neyapti (1992) developed several measures of CBI in a study of seventy-two countries (see Maxfield 1994, 1997).

In Latin America over the last decade, the governments of Argentina, Chile, Colombia, Ecuador, Mexico, and Venezuela took steps to increase CBI. Among emerging economies in Asia and the Indian subcontinent, the governments of South Korea, Pakistan, and Vietnam moved modestly toward creating independent central banks, as did the governments of Algeria and Egypt among the North African countries. In Eastern and Central European countries, efforts to enhance the statutory independence of central banks proceeded apace throughout the 1990s, though with questionable success in many cases (see fn. 4). Measures toward central bank statutory independence were implemented in Albania, Armenia, Belarus, Bulgaria, the Czech Republic, Estonia, Hungary, Kazakhstan, Latvia, Lithuania, Poland, Romania, Russia, the Slovak Republic, and Ukraine (Loungani and Sheets 1995; Maxfield 1997).[5]

While the responsibilities of independent central banks are well understood, the same cannot be said of currency boards. A currency board is a monetary institution that issues local currency fully backed by stocks of a hard foreign "reserve currency." By law, the local currency is fully convertible on demand and without limit into the foreign reserve currency at a fixed rate of exchange. The rate of exchange between the local and the foreign reserve currency is inviolable: the International Monetary Fund (IMF) recommends that the exchange rate be written into the currency board's constitution (*IMF Survey* 5/20/96; Hanke, Jonung, and Schuler 1993). The reserves held by the currency board consist of low-risk, interest-earning securities and other assets payable in the reserve currency. The amount of foreign reserves held by the currency board must typically be equal to 100 to 110 percent (as set by law) of the value of the local money stock.

Historically, some seventy countries have operated currency boards. Today, currency boards operate in Argentina, Bermuda, Bulgaria, Bosnia and Herzegovina, Cayman Islands, Djibouti, Estonia, Falkland Islands,

[handwritten margin note: currency board]

---

4. For example, a 1995 study of the former socialist countries by Loungani and Sheets found that the Armenian, Hungarian, Polish, and Romanian central banks had less operational independence than did the Albanian, Bulgarian, Czech Republic, and Estonian central banks. To place even this finding into its proper context, observers of the region note that the operational independence of the Estonian central bank is particularly weak (though the IMF continues to praise the country's progress in maintaining the operational independence of its central bank and currency board; see, e.g., *IMF Survey* 2/7/00, 42).

5. Though the Czech central bank has statutory independence, the lower chamber of the country's Parliament passed an amendment in July 2000 that contradicts this intent. The law enables the government to appoint the central bank's board members and requires the bank to consult the government before important policy decisions (*New York Times* 7/15/00).

Faroe Islands, Gibraltar, Hong Kong, and Lithuania (see Ghosh, Gulde, and Wolf 1998; Hanke, Jonung, and Schuler 1993, appendix C). Recent reports by IMF economists and consultants cited the success of existing boards in Argentina,[6] Estonia, and Hong Kong as a basis on which to argue for their adoption elsewhere (see *IMF Survey* 2/2/97, 5/20/96, 6/8/98, 3/9/98, 5/10/99, 7/19/99; Enoch and Gulde 1997; Ghosh, Gulde, and Wolf 1998; Hanke, Jonung, and Schuler 1993). At the cost of severe recessions, the Estonian board is credited with having stabilized the economy; the Argentine board, with having ended inflation and maintained stability during the Mexican financial crisis of 1994–95 and the subsequent Asian financial crisis; and the Hong Kong board, with having maintained stability during the Asian financial crisis and during the transition from British to Chinese rule (see Schamis's and Wang's chapters in this volume). In the period prior to the Brazilian election in October 1998 and the IMF's "preventative bailout" of the country, Dornbusch proposed the adoption of a currency board modeled on that of Argentina (*IMF Survey* 1/25/99, 24).[7] More recently, he advocated currency boards as the best way to avoid currency crises by "outsourcing monetary policy" (*IMF Survey* 6/21/99, 195) and divesting countries from control over their national currencies (*IMF Survey* 3/6/00, 74).

Currency boards complement the operations of independent central banks by providing an additional means by which the private sector can be assured that monetary management will proceed undisturbed by political pressures. Indeed, the credibility of currency boards is seen to exceed that of independent central banks because currency boards have the single responsibility of maintaining exchange rate fixity, while central banks (independent or not) have a broad range of responsibilities. Currency boards help fill the "credibility deficit" that confronts even independent central banks in countries where these institutions are new or where they have a poor track record. Like central banks, they are to be autonomous—with their members drawn from the ranks of technocrats, economists, and bankers and appointed for multiyear terms—to ensure that exchange rate policy is in the hands of an independent authority that does not have strategic incentives to veer toward an expansionary course.

---

6. As of this writing (final edit May 2002), the Argentine currency board exists in name only, having been overtaken and rendered impotent by that country's current financial and political crisis. Today Argentina's exchange rate policies are in flux, and it seems unlikely that the currency board will be restored in anything like its previous form. It is too early to say how currency board advocates will make sense of this apparent failure. No consensus has yet emerged among these advocates about the causes and implications of the Argentine experience.

7. Needless to say, currency board advocates no longer hold up Argentina's currency board as a model for replication elsewhere.

NEW-CLASSICAL ECONOMIC ARGUMENTS FOR
INDEPENDENT CENTRAL BANKS AND CURRENCY BOARDS

The preoccupation of development economists with the idea of policy credibility emerged on the heels of two developments—one empirical and one theoretical. On the empirical level, the failure of the ambitious neoliberal economic reconstruction of South America in the late 1970s and early 1980s prompted an anxious search for explanations. By the mid-1980s, a consensus had emerged among new-classical development economists that despite the inherent correctness of the neoliberal prescription for South America, the reform agenda nevertheless had failed to achieve its intended results because its architects had not taken into account the overall "policy environment" in which these programs were implemented (Grabel 1996).

On the theoretical level, the current preoccupation with policy credibility stems directly from the precepts of new-classical economic theory. The seminal work of Kydland and Prescott (1977) was particularly important to the development of the theory of policy credibility (Blackburn and Christensen 1989; Cottarelli and Giannini 1997). In this approach, rational agents use the *uniquely correct* economic model and take into account all available information when forming expectations about the future and making judgments about what actions to take. Among other factors, agents must assess the credibility of an announced policy. Unfortunately, however, assessing policy credibility is no simple matter. At issue are perceptions concerning the viability and effectiveness of announced policies, policymakers' *complications of policy* commitment to sustain them, and hence, the likelihood of policy reversal or collapse.

In light of the recognition of the importance of policy credibility, economists now faced a challenging question: How could economic policy be developed in this complex environment in which the success of policy depends critically on perceptions of its viability? Two choices presented themselves: one could shade policy toward existing popular sentiments, or one could implement "correct" policy, policy that respects the fundamentals of new-classical economic theory. The former option is ruled out on the simple grounds that "incorrect" policy (no matter how popular) could not possibly retain credibility in the wake of the disruptions that would inevitably attend it. In the context of open capital markets, for instance, incorrect policy would precipitate capital flight. In contrast, correct policy (no matter how unpopular) would induce credibility over time as it proved itself uniquely capable of promoting development and economic growth. A correctly specified policy would therefore impel rational agents to act "properly," at once attracting international private capital inflows, achieving growth and stability, and inducing the credibility necessary to sustain the policy regime.

Credibility Theory Applied to the Design of Monetary Institutions and Policy

The theory of policy credibility has proved to be influential in the design and operation of the institutions that govern monetary and exchange rate policy in emerging economies.[8] From the perspective of new-classical economic theory, the logic of extending the theory of policy credibility to the design of financial policy-making institutions is rather straightforward: to be credible, financial policy must be insulated from the vagaries of the political process, where shortsighted political goals often predominate. In the absence of this insulation, financial policy can be manipulated instrumentally by governments seeking to garner political support. Aware of this possibility, the (rational) public will know that announced financial policies "may lack credibility because they are economically inconsistent or politically unsustainable" (Schmieding 1992, 45–46).[9]

Problems of financial policy credibility may also arise if policymakers have a history of reneging strategically on established policies in order to achieve a short-term political or economic objective. This is the problem of "time inconsistency" (Kydland and Prescott 1977). In this context, rational economic actors are likely to expect policy reversals and will act accordingly (such as by hedging against reversal). At best, the policy will fail to induce the intended results; at worst, it will be sabotaged. Financial policy credibility (and hence, success) may also be threatened if financial and fiscal policies are at cross-purposes, introducing the problem of "Stackelberg warfare" (Blackburn and Christensen 1989).

From the perspective of new-classical economic theory, the task of gaining the public's confidence in the technical abilities and the anti-inflationary resolve of financial authorities in emerging economies is somewhat daunting. In such countries, it is reasonable to expect that the public will have limited confidence both in the personnel of financial policy-making institutions and in the likelihood that the institution will be able to stay the course of politically unpopular policies. It is even reasonable for the public to question the longevity of new or reformed financial policy-making institutions. These uncertainties may stem from the immaturity of the institutions themselves, from the legacy of high inflation, or from the rapid turnover of personnel in the government and financial institutions (Schmieding 1992, 45–46). In this context, new-classical economic theory maintains that it is necessary to staff apolitic financial institutions with nonpartisan technocrats in order to establish policy credibility.

public opinion

----

8. Institutions and policy are treated herein as analytically distinct, but in practice they are thoroughly interdependent. For example, new-classical economists' support for an independent central bank is tied to the view that such an institution is uniquely qualified to pursue credible (read: anti-inflationary) monetary policy.

9. Johnson (1973) anticipated many of these insights in an essay on the Panamanian monetary system.

Central Banks

The case for independent central banks in new-classical economic theory follows directly from this view on the prerequisites for credible policy. CBI imparts a degree of credibility to monetary policy that cannot be achieved when policy is developed by elected politicians. This credibility stems from the political insulation of the institution. Armed with respect for the precepts of new-classical economic theory and protected by institutional barriers from political contamination, the nonpartisan technocrats who staff independent central banks are able to pursue credible (and time-consistent) monetary policy in pursuit of an anti-inflationary course for the national economy (Blackburn and Christensen 1989).[10]

A vast empirical literature seeks to substantiate the theoretical claims for the anti-inflationary performance of independent central banks. Initial studies focused on central banks in wealthy countries; these tended to confirm the hypothesis (e.g., Alesina and Summers 1993; Blackburn and Christensen 1989). More recently, efforts have been undertaken to substantiate these claims in the context of emerging economies. One study of twelve former communist countries found that countries with independent central banks experienced lower levels of inflation and greater macroeconomic stability than did countries with dependent central banks (Loungani and Sheets 1995). However, substantial research on emerging economies presents mixed results (at best) on the relative performance of independent central banks (Bowles and White 1994; Cardim de Carvahlo 1995–96; Cukierman, Webb, and Neyapti 1992; Mas 1995; Maxfield 1994, 1997, chaps. 1 and 2). Indeed, Maxfield's (1997) thorough survey of the empirical literature makes clear that the data supporting the case for CBI in emerging economies is far from unambiguous, particularly in light of the sensitivity of the empirical results to measures of independence.

Despite the ambiguous empirical basis for CBI in emerging economies, independence is nevertheless taken as a necessary (though not sufficient) step for achieving monetary policy credibility. Where central banks are new institutions (as in the former communist countries) or where the public has little confidence in these institutions, it may also be necessary to import central bank credibility by adopting the actual operating guidelines of credible Western central banks or by employing central bank staff directly. Indeed, the German Bundesbank Law was adopted by the new Polish, Hungarian, Czechoslovak, and Bulgarian central banks. Credibility can also be created via externally imposed constraints on central bank operations. Such constraints are often embodied in IMF structural adjustment pro-

---

10. Some new-classical development economists argue that fiscal policy should also be designed by an independent authority in order to preclude the possibility of Stackelberg warfare (e.g., Mas 1995).

grams (SAPs) that tie financial and technical assistance to the central bank's adherence to certain operating practices, such as the refusal to finance government debt (Schmieding 1992).

The replacement of discretionary with rule-based monetary policy may also enhance central bank credibility.[11] As before, this can involve importing credible rules from abroad. Increasingly, these rules are taking the form of inflation or monetary growth targets, about which there exists a gathering international consensus among new-classical economists. But central bank credibility will only be enhanced by these constraints as long as the rules themselves do not introduce time inconsistency or Stackelberg warfare, and as long as the public is confident that the rules will not be breached. This introduces a game-theoretic dilemma in which central banks must search for increasingly credible means by which rules can be enforced. If the public does not find the central bank's commitment to policy rules sufficiently credible, then the central bank may seek to have these rules incorporated into the legal system of the country. If mere laws are not sufficiently credible, then a constitutional amendment (a "meta-rule") might be pursued (Schmieding 1992, 50).

There is a tension between the strictures of monetary rules and considerations of policy credibility. Unforeseen exigencies may necessitate bending rules, which will make them lose credibility. Anticipation of such potential problems should undermine the attractiveness of rule-based policy in the uncertain environment of many emerging economies. Perhaps because of these dilemmas, efforts to reform central banks tend to focus on creating statutory and institutional independence prior to establishing monetary or inflation targets.[12]

Currency Boards

Currency boards enhance the credibility of the local currency (and the exchange rate) via the establishment of a direct link between it and the board's hard foreign currency holdings. Provided that the currency board maintains sufficient holdings of the foreign reserve currency, investors and the general public can be confident of the board's ability (not just its willingness) to maintain a fixed exchange rate (Bhattacharya 1997; Enoch and Gulde 1997). Moreover, the public is also assured of protection against de-

---

11. The August 2000 announcement that Chile's President Ricardo Lagos had prepared a new reform package that would severely limit his discretion over fiscal policy underscores the continued resonance of the theory of credibility in discussions of economic policy. President Lagos announced plans to introduce reforms that mandate an average 1 percent surplus in the structural balance. His minister of finance explained the measure's rationale: "We want to arrive at a position where macroeconomic policy is not just sound. . . . It is based on rules" (*New York Times* 8/6/00).

12. However, currency board operations are rule-based (see below).

basement of the local currency.[13] This confidence in the fixed exchange rate may prevent the public from engaging in currency substitution, destabilizing speculation against the currency, and other actions that will undermine the stability of the domestic monetary system. Hence, even though currency boards do not render speculation against the currency impossible, they reduce the chances that speculators will lose confidence in the currency.

Currency boards epitomize the credibility advantages of rule-based financial policy; where currency boards have existed, they have operated in accordance with a strict set of simple, transparent rules.[14] As a consequence, they possess even less scope for discretion than do independent central banks—an important virtue for new-classical economists who are concerned about abuses of monetary discretion in emerging economies.[15] The legally and constitutionally binding rules that govern currency boards, coupled with institutional independence, preclude them from ceding to political pressures for monetary expansion.

Several prominent new-classical economists have endorsed currency boards on several grounds.[16] This support may seem surprising. After all, new-classical economics preaches the virtues of unfettered markets in which prices adjust instantly and without government interference in response to supply- or demand-side shocks. Currency boards prevent this adjustment by fixing the rate of exchange between the domestic and a foreign currency. But new-classical economists reconcile themselves to currency boards as an important "second-best" alternative for emerging economies, given the proclivity of governments to intervene in exchange markets and to print money to finance government expenditures. Insofar as these governments cannot be trusted to let foreign exchange markets operate freely or to exercise monetary discipline, currency boards provide a means for reducing government freedom while securing currency credibility. Moreover, the legal and institutional commitments under which currency boards op-

13. Indeed, a recent empirical study found that inflation in countries with currency boards (all else equal) was 4 percent lower than in countries with other types of pegged exchange rate regimes (Ghosh, Gulde, and Wolf 1998).

14. As Eichengreen (1999, 105) noted, "Closing off all avenues for discretionary monetary policy not just for a time but for the foreseeable future is something that few societies are prepared to do." This may account for the relatively small number of countries that today maintain currency boards as opposed to independent central banks. Eichengreen argued that public support for the Argentine board stems from the profound distrust of discretionary policy engendered by the country's experiences with hyperinflation (cf. Schamis, this volume).

15. Johnson (1973) argued that currency boards are more credible and cost-effective than independent central banks (see also *IMF Survey* 9/25/99, 11/8/99).

16. The "arguments [of new classical economics] lend support to the case for currency boards, since currency boards are rule-bound and have no discretion in monetary policy" (Hanke, Jonung, and Schuler 1993, 39).

erate render the resulting currency values far more credible than those that arise under fixed exchange regimes that lack currency boards (Ghosh, Gulde, and Wolf, 1998).[17]

As with independent central banks, the credibility of currency board rules can be enhanced through external mechanisms that ensure compliance with the rules. This may involve "importing" credibility by placing representatives of foreign central banks or multilateral institutions on currency boards or conditioning external financial or technical support on compliance with predetermined rules. A model currency board constitution prepared for Russia by U.S. consultants contains just such provisions for importing credibility from abroad. The proposed constitution requires a majority of the members of the board of directors to be foreigners, to "help prevent the government from bending the rules of the currency board" (Hanke, Jonung, and Schuler 1993, 110).

Some analysts have insisted that even external enforcement of currency board credibility will be an inadequate guarantor of its independence. For example, Dornbusch (1997) suggested that the Mexican government cannot be trusted to leave a currency board unmolested. For this reason, he proposed that Mexico adopt the extreme measure of importing currency credibility by simply adopting the U.S. dollar as its currency. The Ecuadorian government took precisely this step in September 2000.

Independent Institutions and the Neoliberal Agenda

Independent central banks and currency boards are institutions that allow emerging economies to fill the credibility deficit that confronts economic policy. They are staffed or directly monitored by external actors or are indirectly monitored by foreign investors, in order to "import" or "borrow credibility" from abroad.[18] These institutions act as monitors and enforcers of monetary and exchange rate policies that constrain inflation and currency risks, respectively. They are agencies of restraint that minimize "investors' risk of policy reversal and therefore help to establish the credibility of the chosen policy options vis-à-vis market participants" (Dhonte 1997, 6–7). Independent central banks and currency boards assure investors that governments will not bend to popular pressures to abandon the "right" policies. The penalties for policy reversal include the loss of investor confidence and the withdrawal of private capital flows.

Independent central banks and currency boards are posited as the insti-

---

17. This is not to say that all currency board arrangements are intrinsically credible. For example, the IMF rejected an Indonesian plan to implement a currency board in February 1998 because the government's commitment to a fixed exchange rate lacked credibility owing to low reserve holdings and political instability (*IMF Survey* 2/23/98, 50).

18. Cottarelli and Giannini (1997) made this argument in the context of SAPs, while the former prime minister of Estonia (quoted in Maxfield 1997, 35) made this point regarding the signaling effect of IMF standby agreements.

tutional foundation for a more aggressive neoliberal policy agenda (see Kirshner 1998). Bowles and White (1994, 237) described the synergy between these institutions and neoliberalism, arguing that "although the case for CBI is primarily based on providing lower inflationary outcomes, it also resonates with a wider agenda aimed at restoring 'discipline' and 'credibility' to economic decision-making in general." Maintaining CBI is one way that the public and investors (both domestic and foreign) can be assured that the central bank will pursue anti-inflationary monetary policy and hence foster a favorable investment climate.

The operation of currency boards also complements broader programs of neoliberal economic reform. Currency boards enhance neoliberal reform credibility by assuaging investor fears of policy reversal. They also promote reductions in government spending by precluding the printing of fiat money. This restriction, in addition, promotes privatization since central banks cannot be used to provide aid to ailing state-owned enterprises (Hanke 1997).

Currency board operations also complement neoliberal reforms that promote external economic openness. Currency board rules stipulate that the local money supply can be increased only following an increase in foreign exchange holdings. An increase in foreign exchange holdings may result from improved net export performance or from private capital inflows. Expansion of the local money supply is predicated on the success of capital and current account liberalization, themselves important components of neoliberal economic reform.

A POLITICAL EXPLANATION FOR INDEPENDENT
CENTRAL BANKS AND CURRENCY BOARDS

Against the new-classical economic explanation for the rise of independent central banks and currency boards, I argue that political factors chiefly explain the emergence of these institutions. Specifically, the creation of monetary and exchange rate institutions that are independent of elected governments stems from the widespread acceptance of the ideological aspects of the theory of policy credibility and from the exercise of political and economic power by influential actors.

Ideological Foundations

The theory of policy credibility—on which the case for independent central banks and currency boards rests—has two ideological dimensions. First, the theory of new-classical economics (in which credibility is nested) is elevated to the status of "science," and its conclusions are presented as unambiguously "true." However, contrary to Popperian methodological prescriptions, the concept of credibility serves to insulate this theory from meaningful empirical test or refutation. Therefore, it must be taken on faith. Second, credibility eliminates politics and power from view in new-classical accounts of the rise and fate of distinct policy regimes. A policy's success, in this account, depends solely on its analytical (and epistemological) merits, not on the power of the interests it serves.

A few points deserve clarification before I discuss the ideological aspects of the new-classical theory of policy credibility. The argument that there are ideological aspects to the theory is not equivalent to the argument that the theory is nothing but ideology. It is not the individual propositions of new-classical theory (e.g., that agents are "rational" in a particular way) but the epistemological claims that are made on behalf of these propositions that constitute its ideological content. It is in the elevation of this one theory to the status of singular truth, and in the consequent suppression of all alternative economic theories on grounds of their inherent falsity, that new-classical economics becomes something other than science.

Truth Status

Proponents of the theory of policy credibility make very strong epistemological claims on its behalf. Recall that a key premise of credibility theory is that all agents in an economy uniformly derive their expectations about the consequences of an economic reform program from the same correct (new-classical) economic model (this is the well-known "rational expectations hypothesis"). The purchase of the concept of credibility then requires the truthfulness of assumptions about the epistemic condition in which economic actors live and the economic models that these actors use to interpret the consequences of economic policies. The *assumption* that this is the uniquely true theory is projected onto the economic actors about whom the theory theorizes, and then their embrace of this theory is taken to secure the unique correctness of the policies that the theory generates. They are *rational*, after all, so they would not possibly choose the wrong theory. How elegant, wonderfully convenient, and irreducibly ideological!

If instead we assume (more realistically) that even reasonably knowledgeable agents in the economy rely on different economic (let alone political and social) models when they are forming expectations, then we will expect them to pursue diverse behaviors in any particular policy context. This diversity may then generate unpredictable macroeconomic outcomes, including outcomes that jeopardize the viability of any policy program (Frydman and Phelps 1983). Thus, a rejection of the assumption of rational expectations complicates any ex ante judgments regarding the credibility of any economic policy—new-classical or otherwise.

For the sake of argument, however, let us assume that agents form their expectations rationally. Let us assume further that this implies that *under normal circumstances* these agents assign the identical, correct probability distribution to the likelihood of a policy's effects and to the likelihood of its failure or reversal. In short, let us presume the validity of the rational expectations hypothesis. Nevertheless, the rational expectations presumption is implausible in the case of new or reformed institutions of monetary and exchange rate policy, particularly in contexts where agents may have reason to be skeptical or may be ill-informed about the direction or consequence of monetary and exchange rate policy. The problem here is that a lack of experience with independent institutions of monetary and exchange rate policy means that agents have no basis for applying past learning (Lucas 1973; Conley and Maloney 1995). In such circumstances, agents might be expected to form diverse and inconsistent subjective probability distributions regarding a policy's effects and longevity, and take actions that undermine the policies implemented by new or reformed central banks and currency boards.

Complicating matters further, the adjustment of expectations and behavior in the wake of radical shifts in the policy-making process occurs in real time. In the process of adjustment, we must recognize the influence of any number of informational asymmetries and imperfections that will necessarily affect agents' decision making (Agnenor and Taylor 1992). The behavior of agents in the short run, then, may very well generate economic outcomes that are inconsistent with the long-term policy objectives of independent central banks and currency boards.

All of these complications are seemingly ignored by today's proponents of independent central banks and currency boards. Their implication, after all, is that policy design is a much trickier business than is generally acknowledged by advocates of these institutions.

I say "seemingly" ignored because they are in fact dealt with implicitly and, unfortunately, with implications that are antipluralist in theory and practice. This is indeed the most problematic aspect of the way in which the criterion of policy credibility has been incorporated into the case for independent central banks and currency boards. This criterion has functioned to discredit the design of institutions of monetary and exchange rate policy that incorporate popular participation. Let us explore what is involved here.

On their face, the propositions that credible monetary and exchange rate policies are more likely to succeed and that policy credibility depends on empowering independent technocrats seem entirely innocuous. However, the ideological import of credibility theory is made quite clear when one explores its underlying epistemological assumptions. The truth status of the theory of credibility (and its application to discussions of optimal institutional form) can be best understood by reducing the theory to a straightforward set of five propositions: (1) monetary and exchange rate policies will garner credibility only to the degree that they are likely to survive; (2) monetary and exchange rate policies are likely to survive only to the degree that they attain their stated objectives; (3) monetary and exchange rate policies are likely to achieve their stated objectives only to the degree that they induce behaviors (in the aggregate) that are consistent with these objectives; (4) monetary and exchange rate policies are likely to induce consistent behaviors only to the degree that they reflect and operationalize the true theory of market economies; and (5) monetary and exchange rate policies reflect the true theory of market economies only to the degree that they are consistent with new-classical economic theory.

The antipluralist attribute of the theory of policy credibility is captured in propositions 4 and 5. Monetary and exchange rate institutions that are subject to state influence are summarily rejected on the grounds that they could not possibly meet the unforgiving credibility test, because such institutions could not implement or maintain credible policies. Hence, monetary and exchange rate policies implemented by such institutions are destined for failure, in part because of the inconsistent behaviors they necessarily induce. Writing on the intellectual maturation of new-classical economics, Frydman and Phelps (1983, 27–28) identified this aspect of the tradition as a barrier to intellectual pluralism. In their words, the "thoroughgoing implementation of the rational expectations [new-classical] method in policy-making would entail the official promotion, or 'establishment,' of one model over others."

Notice the epistemological foundation of the new-classical perspective. Advocates of independent central banks and currency boards impute credibility to policies based on the purported verisimilitude of the abstract theory from which these policies derive. Economic science then points us in the direction of the singular true model of policy making, and hence to a single institutional setting in which monetary and exchange rate policies can be designed. The best that could be said of monetary and exchange rate policies designed outside of a politically insulated setting is that agents will lack confidence in them. Therefore, these policies will induce inconsistent expectations and will fail.[19] In this manner, the credibility criterion discredits pluralistic discussions regarding the appropriate governance structure of the institutions that govern monetary and exchange rate policy. In short, the truth claims of the theory of policy credibility bar consideration of theoretical and practical alternatives to politically insulated policy making.

19. Part of the reason why these policies will fail is because conventional wisdom, or what Blyth (2000) referred to as "governing conventions," induces behaviors such as capital flight that precisely result in policy failure. See also Kirshner's (2000, this volume) discussions of the role of confidence in monetary policy success and the role of ideology in defining the feasible set of policy options. On this latter point, he suggests that the truth claims supporting the case for institutional independence preclude the success of policies that are inconsistent with these claims by inducing self-fulfilling perceptions of policy failure. Hence, policy failure is not an inevitable result of technical policy misspecification. The strength with which a theory's truth claims are held can be an independent cause of policy success or failure.

Many critics have argued that autonomous monetary authorities are incompatible with the principles of democratic governance (e.g., Arestis and Bain 1995; Berman and McNamara 1999; Epstein 1992). After all, these critics claim, monetary and exchange rate policies can and do have substantial distributive effects. Hence, these institutions must be accountable to elected government officials and, thereby, to the electorate.

New-classical economists dispense with these criticisms in part by claiming that monetary and exchange rate institutions must be insulated from political pressures to ensure policy credibility. To create an environment where good economic outcomes can obtain, the state must take steps to ensure that the processes of policy design and implementation are protected from democratic contestation by the populace and from capture by self-seeking politicians. Political contest over economic affairs might undermine confidence even in correct policy and thereby subvert its effectiveness. It is far better to take the domain of economic policy out of the orbit of politics, these economists argue. But this view makes sense only if we are prepared to accept the epistemological claims of the theory of policy credibility, along with the unified, harmonious view of society and the cynical view of the state assumed by new-classical economic theory (cf. Toye 1991). Only in this case is it legitimate to view the autonomous monetary authorities as champions of the national interest (cf. Blyth, this volume). If there is only one true economic theory, then the insulation of monetary and exchange rate institutions from political influence hardly amounts to a democratic deficit. The same is true if all citizens share the same values, interests, and goals, and if they are all affected by a particular policy in substantially similar ways. This is precisely the stand taken by new-classical economic theorists. In their view, only politically insulated technocrats can guarantee the kind of economic outcomes that will ultimately benefit all of society's members.

The Irrefutable Nature of the Case for Independent Central Banks and Currency Boards

Credibility fulfills a vitally important ideological function in new-classical economics by allowing for perpetual ad hoc theoretical adjustment. Insofar as it can always be asserted after the fact that the environment in which failed new-classical monetary and exchange rate policies were implemented was not credible, it is possible to insulate the policies or the institutions themselves from critique. The failure of an independent central bank to curb inflation or of a currency board to create confidence in the domestic currency is not attributed to the inappropriateness of the institutional structure or the underlying theoretical framework that gives rise to that structure. Rather, policy failure is explained by the presence of all manner of distortions that characterize the economy, by political uncertainty, by the public's lack of confidence in the longevity of technocrats, by the failure to guarantee the operational (rather than de jure) independence of policy-making institutions, and so on.[20] Credibility theory therefore precludes any substantive empirical refutation of the case for institutional independence.[21] It is the impossibility of testing (and therefore rejecting) its central propositions combined with its self-understanding as the uniquely adequate and objective economic science that imparts to the new-classical theory of policy credibility its ideological content.

Recall that empirical studies of the benefits of CBI in emerging economies have not provided unambiguous empirical support. But by allowing for perpetual ad hoc adjustment, credibility theory preserves the theoretical case for independence despite the empirical record. For instance, advocates of CBI can always invoke the gap between legal and operational independence. It should not be surprising, then, that the theoretical framework supporting this institutional innovation has never been revised in light of empirical experience. Ad hocery notwithstanding, this unwavering commitment to CBI in emerging economies—in the absence of unambiguous empirical evidence—exemplifies the ideological character of this monetary reform.

The Role of Power

In deriving policy credibility from the epistemological status of the theory that generates it, new-classical economic theorists deny the significance of factors that are endogenous to all societies and that significantly influence the likelihood of a policy's success and, hence, its credibility (cf. Burkett and Lotspeich 1993). Notably absent from discussions of policy credibility within new-classical economic theory, for instance, are considerations of class conflict and the distribution of income, wealth, and political power. The credibility of the policies implemented by independent central banks and currency boards is secured not by their inherent rightness but by enforcement strategies and capabilities of domestic and foreign capital and the state (see Kirshner 1995, 1998, 2000, this volume; other chapters herein). Together, these actors often have been able to suppress popular dissent against the social dislocation and recessionary consequences of the high-interest-rate policies associated with independent central banks and

20. Polanyi (1944) emphasized the propensity of advocates of free markets to explain their failure as stemming from insufficient liberalization rather than from the failure of markets themselves. He wrote, "Its apologists [defenders of market liberalization] are repeating in endless variations that but for the policies advocated by its critics, liberalism would have delivered the goods; that not the competitive system and the self-regulating market, but interference with that system and interventions with that market are responsible for our ills" (143).

21. In view of this predilection for ad hoc recuperation, the new-classical extension of neoclassical thought acquires the features of what Lakatos (1970) identified as a "degenerative research programme."

currency boards, and they have relied on the ideological and financial support of the international policy and investment community. The credibility of the policies implemented by independent central banks and currency boards is secured, then, through the mobilization of political and economic power. It does not arise as the natural result of autonomous decision making of economic actors forming rational judgments about the future and pursuing voluntary courses of action that intrinsically validate these policy options.

The way in which the credibility criterion is presently understood by new-classical economic theorists and policymakers reflects a particularly naive vision of society. That vision is of a society marked by largely homogeneous (or at least harmonious) goals and expectations, in which policymaking institutions, to the extent that they can free themselves from interest groups, are able to implement policies designed to secure these goals. In short, it is a vision of society free of class and other fundamental social and economic conflicts (cf. DeMartino 2000). To the extent that conflicts do exist (particularly among interest groups that seek to capture policy to serve their particularist aims), new-classical theorists propose the construction of institutions that *transcend* these conflicts.

What is absent from this view is an understanding that in societies stratified by wealth, class, and power, all economic policies (monetary, exchange rate, or otherwise) are inherently biased in terms of their effects. Policies always serve some interests against others.[22] Hence, a policy's credibility always requires securing the willful consent of some groups and the coercive acquiescence of others. This political-economy view is no less true of policies implemented by politically insulated institutions purporting to promote the national interest than of those designed under other institutional configurations. *Credibility, in short, is founded on politics, not metaphysics.*[23]

From this perspective, the support of foreign capital in the form of inflows of direct foreign and portfolio investments or loans (or the threat of withdrawal) and the financial and technical support of multilateral institutions are critical because they *create* policy credibility rather than simply *reveal* it. The importation of outside "experts" plays the same role: the act of "signaling credibility" should be understood to produce the effect of credibility rather than merely to reveal something that was already there, latent in the policy-making institution itself. In addition to the policy credibility created by foreign experts, domestic experts (including economists and members of the business community) likewise play a role in validating the case for independent central banks and currency boards.

The argument advanced here is different from (though not inconsistent

22. On economic policy and interest groups, see Cohen 1998a, 63–64; citations in Eichengreen 1998 and Frieden 1991.
23. Indeed, this is a theme that runs through many of the chapters in this volume (e.g., those by Blyth and Wang).

with) Maxfield's (1997) argument. From her perspective, emerging-economy governments use CBI strategically to signal to international investors and lenders their commitment to the "right" policies as a means of attracting external private capital flows. I argue that it is the success of this signaling effect (i.e., the response of external actors) that actually creates the credibility of the institutions and their policies. These institutions, and the policies they implement, are not inherently credible—their credibility results from the response of investors and multilateral agents whose actions provide important ideological and material capital to those who advocate the neoliberal agenda.

The exercise of political and economic power (in addition to ideology) also explains the creation of independent institutions. U.S. university faculties in economics have long sought to export ideas about monetary governance to emerging economies via education in the United States and educational programs sited in emerging-economy countries. The early-twentieth-century work of Princeton economics professor Edwin Kemmerer represents perhaps the most well-known effort to export the case for independent central banks to emerging economies (see Helleiner, this volume). This project was taken up in the 1970s by the University of Chicago in its work with Chilean economists (Becker 1997), by a consortium of U.S. universities to retrain Russian economists (Wu 1997), and by the IMF through its extensive technical training programs. The latter include the IMF Institute, which offers seminars for government and central bank officials, and various regional training institutes. The IMF's Monetary and Exchange Affairs Department also works with finance officials on central banking, exchange rate, and monetary policy issues.

When these educational initiatives have proved to be insufficient, the IMF has not hesitated to expend its political and economic capital to pressure emerging-economy governments to establish (or enhance the operational autonomy of) independent central banks and currency boards, such as through SAPs. For instance, during its 1996 negotiations with Bulgaria and Bosnia, the IMF explicitly tied the continued receipt of financial support—and hence the viability of the economy—to the creation of currency boards (Ghosh, Gulde, and Wolf, 1998; Bhattacharya 1997). In negotiations with Brazil in February–March 1999 over receipt of an installment of its (post-Asian crisis) bailout, the IMF pressed for and received assurances from the government that it would take steps to strengthen the operational autonomy of the central bank (see *IMF Survey* 2/8/99, 33; 3/22/99, 82). Increasing CBI was also among the preconditions for the IMF's April 2001 bailout of Turkey (*New York Times* 4/27/01).

Recent events in emerging economies illustrate the endogeneity of central bank and currency board credibility. The Estonian currency board experiment has largely been kept afloat by Finland and Sweden for geopolitical reasons. During the turmoil of the Asian financial crisis, the credibility of the Hong Kong currency board was secured by China's financial support of the fixed exchange rate (see Wang, this volume) and by the ability of the Hong Kong monetary authority to intervene aggressively in markets to support the economy. More generally, IMF–World Bank financial and technical support and SAPs play a pivotal role in maintaining investor confidence in the credibility of central banks and currency boards.

Conversely, central banks and currency boards can be rendered "noncredible" if the governments that attempt to put them into place are not able to secure the consent and support of development banks or the IMF. Governments that do not protect the independence of these institutions sometimes face capital strike. New-classical economists take this flight as evidence of the inherent noncredibility of such institutions. But investors deciding if and when to flee are not taking a referendum on the purported rightness of such institutions in the abstract; they are assessing their credibility in the context of the anticipated reaction of external *political and economic* actors to such state initiatives. Investors flee when they anticipate the withdrawal of external loans and loan guarantees, aid, trade credits, and technical assistance programs on which emerging economies often depend. In short, we have here a game-strategic situation in which the IMF can activate capital flight as a means of gaining leverage over recalcitrant national governments to ensure that they pursue policies that the IMF deems appropriate. It therefore rings hollow when IMF economists assert that the reactions of investors are an "independent" gauge of the rightness of economic policy. Signaling, then, is a far more complex phenomenon than is commonly recognized in the new-classical economics literature. It must be seen as a means to leverage and exercise power, not merely as a means to convey information.

IMF signaling can be vitally consequential. For example, the IMF's high-profile rejection of former President Suharto's plan to create a currency board in Indonesia during the Asian financial crisis essentially condemned his initiative. In the public wrangling over this issue, warnings from the IMF ensured that investors would act in ways that would undermine rather than support this institution. Confronting this likelihood, Suharto was forced to abandon his plan.[24]

If we adopt a political-economy approach to policy making, an approach in which conflict in economic interests, values, and goals is endemic to all societies, then it becomes quite clear that independent central banks and

---

24. The IMF rejected the currency board proposal because it did not trust the government to protect the institution's independence and because it did not want its bailout resources being used to protect the value of the currency. The former concern was no doubt warranted. However, the IMF appeared to have no difficulty with the latter strategy during its preventative bailout of Brazil in 1999. The Indonesian and Brazilian examples illustrate the endogeneity of credibility insofar as the success of the government's policy initiative depended on the actions of the IMF.

currency boards are hardly apolitical. They "do not exist 'above' or 'outside' politics" (Bowles and White 1994, 240) but instead represent a strategic means by which some groups seek to secure their own economic interests at the expense of the interests and goals of others (cf. Kirshner 2000, this volume). Policy-making institutions that are structurally precluded from capture by elected officials do not operate in some presumed "general" or "national" interest but rather in accordance with the particularist interests of some and against the particularist interests of others. In the case of independent central banks and currency boards that pursue neoliberal policy, the financial community represents the interest group whose concerns about monetary and exchange rate policy are paramount (see Posen 1995b).

One of the enduring challenges of policy making (and more broadly of democratic society) is to find ways to mediate the opposing claims of contending social groups. New-classical economic theory attempts to do what is simply impossible: to sidestep this challenge by pretending that it does not exist. In so doing, proponents have unwittingly produced a set of institutional reforms that allow those already best off in society to further their own economic interests—all under the ideological cover of apparently scientific economic theory.

Ideology-Power Interactions in Monetary Reform

In this section I examine the process by which ideology and power have codetermined the creation of independent institutions of monetary and exchange rate policy. For purposes of analytical clarity, the discussion is organized around a series of questions that follow the standard journalistic investigative formula: *Who* are the actors that are influenced by the ideological aspects of new-classical theory and by the expression of material and political power, and *by whom* are they influenced? Of *what* exactly are these actors convinced? *Why* do they institute the particular reforms *when* they do? Most important, *how* do these political factors codetermine the reform outcome?

Who?

Assessing *who* is being convinced of what *by whom* is a rather straightforward matter. The principal actors involved in negotiating the process of institutional reform in emerging economies are national-level politicians, technocrats employed in the government service, and members of the financial community (who may directly or indirectly influence decision making by government officials). Whether or not the populace (taken broadly) is supportive of the reforms undertaken is not directly relevant. In countries where the democratic process functions well, the preferences of the populace should map onto politicians' behavior. Where the democratic process is compromised, the question of whether the populace is influenced by the political factors under consideration is moot. The views of these internal actors are shaped and reinforced by powerful external actors who are, using Wade's (1998b) (extension of Bhagwati's [1998]) terminology, members of the "Wall Street–U.S. Treasury–U.S. Congress–City of London–U.K. Treasury–IMF complex."

The relative weight of internal and external actors in the reform process varies from country to country. In some countries, external and internal actors work in tandem to institute reforms consistent with the worldview of the neoliberal epistemic community. In others, external actors serve as a "push factor" in the reform process by either subtly "teaching" internal actors about the necessity of creating independent institutions or by playing a more determinative coercive role in pressing for institutional innovation; and in still others, internal actors strategically use external actors to legitimate or make palatable to the populace their own reform goals.[25] The efficacy of these "carriers" or "policy entrepreneurs" depends in part on their status and power within the system and the extent to which their ideas are institutionalized and embedded in organizational structures.[26] The internal and external actors carrying the mantle of independent central banks and currency boards to emerging economies fit this profile—together they command significant material, political, and intellectual capital.

What?

Regardless of national differences in the weight of internal and external actors in propelling financial reform, the issue as to *what* these actors are convinced of is unambiguous. Reformers behave as if they are convinced of the necessity of creating independent institutions of monetary and (in some cases) exchange rate policy.[27] This institutional structure is understood to ensure that financial authorities pursue policies that maintain a sound currency and hence preserve investor confidence in the economy. The assumed fit between institutional structure and desired macroeconomic outcomes stems directly from acceptance of the new-classical theory of policy credibility, a view that is validated by the expression of political and material capital by powerful actors.

For more than a decade, the necessity of institutional independence has

25. The terms "epistemic community" and "teaching" are borrowed from Haas 1992a and Finnemore 1993, respectively.

26. Berman (1998) did not introduce power in her discussion of carrier efficacy, but its inclusion here seems entirely appropriate.

27. I do not venture here into the question of whether reformers' decisions actually map on to their beliefs; for our purposes, it matters only that they undertake particular reforms. In some cases, reformers may actually believe in what they are doing; in other cases, powerful actors may coerce them into making these reforms; and in still others, they may implement these reforms as a strategic means to obtain resources from multilateral institutions or private investors.

taken on the status of a universal truth that holds for all countries regardless of the peculiarities of their economic, political, or historical development (cf. Helleiner, this volume). Given the standing of the theory of policy credibility, it is difficult to imagine a policymaker or an economic advisor making a (credible) case for the desirability of an alternative governance structure.[28] This belief in universality is maintained despite the fact that the link between macroeconomic outcomes and policy independence remains largely unsubstantiated empirically in the emerging-economy context. Moreover, the developmental contribution of government control over monetary and exchange rate policy in many Asian states (let alone in Western Europe during much of the post–World War II era) is simply ignored by advocates of independent central banks.[29]

Why?

As I argued earlier, there are numerous reasons *why* reformers create financial policy-making institutions that are independent of state direction. On the macrolevel, it is quite clear that the ideological aspects of the new-classical theory of policy credibility resonate with contemporary reformers precisely because they are embedded in a broader neoliberal worldview. In this context, embrace of the type of institutions that are the theory's coreq-uisites is hardly surprising. On the microlevel, receptivity to new-classical theory (and hence to its institutional counterparts) in the early to mid-1980s was enhanced by policymakers' shared understanding of the causes of past policy failures and the presentation of a comprehensive theoretical and practical alternative to past strategies. At that time (and continuing today), new-classical theory was presented by economists, foreign advisors, and policymakers as the only sound alternative to the failure of Keynesian-inspired statist policies during the Bretton Woods era and South American neoliberalism in the late 1970s and early 1980s. Needless to say, this policy was not (and is not) articulated in a political vacuum: it was pressed ideologically and validated materially by powerful actors sharing a common worldview. Absent the exercise of political power and material support, these reforms might never have been implemented, at least not to the extent they have been.

The causal explanation of institutional innovation that is advanced here is consistent with explanations of a range of policy innovations proffered by

---

28. With operational independence elevated to the status of universal truth, policy failure under alternative governance structures is guaranteed precisely because the perception of likely policy failure is self-fulfilling. See Berman's (1998) discussion of the power of ideas in shaping actors' perceptions of constraints.

29. In this connection, see Finnemore's (1993, 1996) discussion of norms in the absence of supporting evidence. See Wade 1992 on the developmental contribution of government control over monetary and exchange rate policy in Asian development (cf. the "revisionist view" [World Bank 1993b]) and Helleiner 1994 on the contribution to Western European and Japanese development.

a number of analysts in this volume (particularly, Abdelal, Blyth, Gavin, Helleiner, Kirshner, and Wang) and others. Berman (1998) demonstrated that ideology (though she used the term "programmatic beliefs") principally shaped the policy choices made by the Swedish and the German Social Democratic parties during the interwar period. In her study of European monetary integration, McNamara (1998) found that ideology played a critically important role in explaining why this historic economic policy convergence occurred across the majority of European governments beginning in the mid-1970s and solidifying in the 1980s.[30] In the work of Finnemore (1993, 1996) and Meyer et al. (1997), the existence of shared ideological constructs held by powerful actors (which the former terms "norms," and the latter terms "global culture") explains the presence of common institutional and policy innovations around the globe.

Why, we might ask, is educating policymakers on the need for a sound currency considered an insufficient means to ensure this result? Why is there the additional need for the institutional reforms advanced by newclassical economics? The answer is found in a related branch of neoclassical economics—the new political economy—that new-classical theorists fully embrace. Since new-classical theory begins with the proposition that government agents are rational, egoistic, utility maximizers, they should be expected to use the policy tools at their disposal to secure their own interests rather than those of the broader society they have been appointed to serve. They will manipulate economic outcomes (such as currency values) to further their own careers, unless the institutional framework in which they operate prevents these strategies (and ideally, rewards appropriate behavior).

It follows then that where credibility problems are most severe (e.g., in new countries, in countries with particularly dramatic histories of hyperinflation, and in countries where the turnover of government officials is high), even an independent central bank may be an insufficient guarantor of operational independence. In such cases, or where policymakers have a strong desire to attain exchange rate stability (and investor confidence) quickly, currency boards may be pursued. Currency boards represent a stronger and more rapid institutional fix for credibility problems because they operate under tighter restrictions than do independent central banks. In addition, currency substitution or "dollarization" (discussion of which is outside the scope of this chapter) might be pursued where problems of credibility are most severe, where the government cannot be trusted to respect currency board independence, or where policymakers seek the most rapid route to exchange rate stability. Hence, independent central banks,

---

30. McNamara (1998) also argued that the neoliberal consensus in Europe was driven by policy emulation. Neither Berman (1998) nor McNamara investigated whether power reinforces the ideology they identified. Moreover, one can interpret McNamara's findings as suggesting that the economic analysis underlying the new consensus in Europe is indeed "correct."

currency boards, and dollarization all represent means by which reformers might solve the credibility problem by eliminating discretion over monetary policy making.

Certainly factors other than the severity of the credibility problem and the speed with which policymakers seek to attain a sound currency can influence the choice among the institutional fixes considered here. In some cases, policymakers might be driven by strategic concerns.[31] Currency boards and dollarization might be used to signal a strategic commitment to countries to which the national currency is tied. The very success of this signaling process itself creates the credibility of the strategy, thereby reinforcing the ideological claims of its proponents. Alternatively, in countries where concerns about the protection of national identity are strongest, currency boards and especially dollarization are infeasible strategies. In such cases, policymakers will likely attempt to resolve the credibility deficit via the construction of an independent central bank. Thus, the historical, economic, and political context matters deeply in understanding why countries adopt one institutional fix to their credibility problem over another (as numerous contributors to this volume make clear [e.g., Abdelal, Blyth, Gavin, Helleiner, Schamis, Stasavage, and Wang]).

The concept of policymaker choice must not be overemphasized in the emerging-economy context, however. Power plays at least as important a role as policymaker choice in explaining the form of institutional innovation. To be sure, the degree of freedom granted emerging-economy governments by powerful external actors varies across countries and across time. (See Helleiner this volume, for a discussion of this variance.)

When?

Ideology and power codetermine *when* reformers in emerging economies create independent institutions of monetary and exchange rate policy. For "early adopters" of these reforms, it is clear that the ideological aspects of new-classical theory played a precipitating role in stimulating the institutional innovation. Reformers were receptive to new-classical ideas about the preconditions for policy credibility at precisely the time when older (Keynesian) models of state-led development were being discredited. The persuasiveness of economists as an epistemic community in pushing these ideas and in promulgating an interpretation of past policy failures cannot be understated.

In addition to the power of ideas in shaping these reforms, more traditional expressions of power (e.g., over external assistance and private capital flows) play a central role in explaining these reforms. Since the debt crisis of the 1980s, the power and autonomy of the IMF and the private

---

31. Stasavage (this volume) argues that for many African countries, continued participation in the CFA Franc Zone has been inextricably linked to strategic considerations.

financial community have increased vis-à-vis the policy decisions of emerging-economy governments (see Blyth, this volume). Thus, in the 1980s a search for alternative development strategies coincided with the ability of powerful actors to present a persuasive case that the right path was found in the new new-classical paradigm. As Ikenberry (1993, 82) noted, "Not all increments of time are equal," a point that underscores the particular temporality of the implementation of independent central banks and currency boards. Goldstein and Keohane (1993) wrote in a similar vein about the openness to new ideas during uncertain times when the old conventional wisdom is seen to break down. Moreover, Halpern (1993) described how following important upheavals, there is a tendency toward mimesis of imported strategies in policy design (or of policy emulation in McNamara's view [1998]).

Moving from earlier to later adopters, the initial momentum behind the creation of independent institutions creates a reform dynamic. For later adopters, ideology takes on an ex post facto role in validating and legitimating decisions to create these institutions. The more that countries are rewarded and validated for this institutional innovation (via the receipt of external assistance and private capital flows), the greater are the incentives and pressures for other countries to follow this path and no other.[32] In this manner, an international consensus around the inevitability of these reforms is cemented.

How?

Much of the above discussion anticipates the issue of *how* ideology and power drive the creation of independent central banks and currency boards. There are, in fact, several (mutually reinforcing) channels by which ideology and power promote this institutional innovation.

First, by supplying an abstract understanding of the causal link between institutional independence and desired macroeconomic outcomes, the ideological aspects of new-classical theory provide an intellectual justification for one type of governance structure over all others. Once an independent governance structure is established, inertia sets in largely because policy choices are path-dependent (unless and until a crisis of confidence emerges, forcing a rethinking of strategies). Goldstein and Keohane (1993) (and many of the essays therein) traced the manner in which ideas serve as important "causal pathways" or discourage policy innovation via ideational inertia.

Second, in the emerging-economy context, considerations of material power, as well as the power to persuade, must inform analyses of how new-classical ideas about institutional independence have been institutionalized

---

32. The political interpretation of monetary reform advanced in this chapter implies that mimesis is not simply a matter of adopting the institutional innovation that works best.

over competing views. For example, Berman's (1998) discussion of the mechanisms of policy entrepreneurship is relevant to understanding how an international epistemic community successfully leveraged its intellectual and political capital to establish new-classical theory as the conventional wisdom. By overlaying power on McNamara's (1998) model, one can better understand how new-classical policy entrepreneurs were able to articulate a particular explanation of policy failure in the 1980s and advance their approach as the only viable alternative to past strategies. Finnemore's (1993, 1996) approach implies that the institutional innovations considered here are a product of intellectual "marketing" and ideational and material coercion by influential actors (see also Finnemore and Sikkink 1998).

Third, once the case for institutional independence assumed the status of conventional wisdom, this innovation necessarily took on a life of its own as a necessity for all emerging economies. Processes of mimesis (Halpern 1993), policy emulation (McNamara 1998), and contagion (Jackson 1993) —reinforced by the expression of power and the continued sway of new-classical ideology in a neoliberal world—combine to diffuse further the adoption of institutional independence.

THE ROLE OF IDEOLOGY AND POWER IN SHAPING MONETARY REFORM IN THE TWENTY-FIRST CENTURY

I have argued that considerations of ideology and power are central to the task of understanding why independent central banks and currency boards are becoming increasingly common institutional forms in emerging economies (despite an ambiguous empirical record). From the perspective of new-classical economic theory, independent central banks and currency boards embody the singularly correct, inevitable resolution to the problems of monetary and exchange rate credibility in emerging economies. On examination, however, the theoretical edifice that provides intellectual justification for these institutions is found to have important ideological attributes, attributes that are the foundation for the belief that the theory and its institutional corequisites are uniquely efficacious and irrefutable. Moreover, the ideological attributes of the theory mask the critical role of power in establishing and defending independent central banks and currency boards.

By foregrounding these political variables, I have not completely rejected the new-classical economic arguments in favor of institutional independence. Rather I have argued that they critically understate and, in some cases, obscure the central role of politics (over economic science) in driving these reforms. Ideology and power figure not only into the positive decision to create independent central banks and currency boards but also into decisions not to consider alternative institutional forms.

This argument raises the question as to whether it is reasonable to assume that the ideology of new-classical economics and the power of the vested interests it serves will continue to secure and advance the neoliberal agenda in the early decades of the twenty-first century. The answer is yes. There are several reasons for reaching this conclusion.

1. The theory of policy credibility (and the new-classicism on which it depends) has served to revitalize neoclassical development economics. Credibility provides insulation from empirical refutation and so sustains the theory, despite recurring development disappointments and even disasters. This insulation may ultimately prove to be credibility's most enduring contribution to neoclassical theory.

2. More broadly, and partly as a consequence, new-classical economic theory, along with its embodiment in the fundamental aspects of the "Washington consensus," shows no sign of losing its hegemonic status within the economics profession.[33] The recent effort by the American Economics Association to purge the participation of heterodox economists from its annual conference does not prove this point, but it does underscore the power (and, I would add, the hubris) of new-classical economic theory within the profession today. Certainly, heterodox economists and others critical of the Washington consensus in policy were heartened by the brief moment of self-doubt that plagued new-classical economists following the Asian financial crisis (and following the earlier crisis in Mexico in 1995–96). However, with only a few notable exceptions, the destabilizing effects of the crisis for new-classical economic theory and its most important policy corequisites have largely disappeared (see Grabel 1999, 2000). The new-classical economic consensus has been restored. Polanyi would have predicted as much.

3. There is today an increasing emphasis worldwide on the need to place policy-making authority in the hands of technocrats, or what Williamson (1994), following Feinberg (1992), called "technopols."[34] This effort is not just confined to emerging economies, as the creation of an independent European central bank and independent national central banks in the region demonstrates. The delegation of authority to unelected technocrats around the world—whether in the realm of monetary, exchange rate, fiscal, or any manner of administrative, regulatory, or juridical functions—suggests that the trend toward the creation of independent central banks and currency boards is part of a larger movement to depoliticize economic policy making.[35]

As the chapters in this volume collectively make clear, politics does play

[handwritten marginal note: no such thing as technocrats]

33. "Washington consensus" refers to a broad set of economic policies embraced by the IMF, the U.S. Treasury, international investors, and market-oriented reformers in emerging economies (Williamson 1994, 26–28).

34. "Technopols" refers to economists in key policy-making positions.

35. For example, see Blinder's (1997a) proposal for an independent fiscal authority.

a significant and often determinative role in shaping monetary affairs. This is as it should be, insofar as monetary policy and institutions always have differential effects on the groups constituting society. As a result, the effects of these reforms should be identified, assessed, and contested—in a word, politicized. But politicization makes new-classical economists uncomfortable. For them, the economics they advance is an entirely objective science whose policy findings should be secured through thoroughly apolitical institutions. In short, new-classical theorists respond to political challenges by attempting to depoliticize economic policy making. However, the effort to depoliticize policy is a deeply ideological and radically political project itself.

[handwritten marginalia: Politics & economy cannot be separated]

PART 2

Small States in World Markets

CHAPTER THREE

The Southern Side of Embedded Liberalism
The Politics of Postwar Monetary Policy in the Third World

Eric Helleiner

In an important 1982 article, John Ruggie highlighted the central role of the ideology of "embedded liberalism" in influencing the construction of the global monetary order after World War II.[1] Proponents of embedded liberalism sought to build a global monetary order different from the gold standard that "classical liberals" had endorsed. Instead of celebrating the discipline of the gold standard, they sought to strengthen the capacity of national governments to pursue domestically oriented, activist monetary policies. National policy autonomy was bolstered through adjustable exchange rates, the international provision of balance-of-payments financing, and the endorsement of capital controls. The international monetary system was now to be more of a servant of the domestic Keynesian and welfarist goals that had emerged so prominently across many industrial countries in the wake of the Great Depression of the 1930s.

The position of Southern countries within the new embedded liberal global monetary order has received less attention than that of Northern countries. This neglect is unfortunate because in the early postwar years some Southern countries adopted dramatic monetary reforms that were in keeping with the new embedded liberal commitment to domestic monetary autonomy. In the first few decades of the twentieth century, many independent Southern countries created central banks whose mandate was one endorsed by classical liberals: maintaining an internationally convertible currency on the gold standard. In other parts of the South—particularly regions that were colonized—currency boards were introduced for the

1. I am very grateful to the Social Sciences and Humanities Research Council of Canada for helping to fund the research for this chapter as well as to Rawi Adbelal, Rachel Epstein, Gerry Helleiner, Jonathan Kirshner, and David Stasavage for their helpful comments.

same purpose. During the early post-1945 years, however, policymakers in many Southern countries followed their counterparts in the North in rejecting this "orthodox" approach to monetary policy.[2] In place of currency boards and the gold standard, they introduced capital controls, more flexible exchange rates, and politically controlled national central banks designed to serve the "nationalist" domestic goals of rapid industrial development and nation building.

The choice to reject monetary orthodoxy was not a uniform one across the South in the early postwar period. In many ex-British colonies, for example, the embedded liberal and nationalist monetary ideas seem to have had less influence. To be sure, most of these newly independent countries replaced colonial currency boards with new national central banks and national currencies. But these central banks and currencies were initially managed in quite orthodox ways. The experience of many ex-French colonies in Africa was even more striking. Many of these countries at independence rejected the idea of creating national currencies and central banks and instead maintained regional colonial currency boards that precluded national discretionary monetary management altogether.

What explains this diversity of experience? If we assume policymakers were driven only by concerns of economic efficiency, the divergent policy paths are difficult to explain. After all, many of the Southern countries that pursued radically different monetary policies in this period shared very similar economic circumstances and constraints. To account for the divergent policy decisions, we must instead turn to the theme of this volume: the importance of politics in shaping monetary policies. Given space constraints, I do not provide a comprehensive political explanation of monetary policy decisions across all Southern countries during the early postwar years. Instead, I focus attention on the specific role that dominant Northern states played in influencing these decisions. My goal is to show that the divergent monetary choices of Southern governments were strongly influenced by the political objectives of U.S., British, and French policymakers in their respective spheres of influence. As in the other chapters in this volume, my thesis is that political considerations—rather than any calculations of economic efficiency—played the central role in determining monetary outcomes (Kirshner 2000).

To develop this argument, I first examine how the United States provided important—and in some ways surprising—political support to countries within its sphere of influence that sought to reject orthodox monetary policies. This support stemmed partly from the commitment of American financial advisors to embedded liberal ideas but also from their recognition of the geopolitical value of not challenging the growing power of Southern

---

2. I use the term *orthodox* to refer to the objectives of classical liberals in the pre-1945 period.

economic nationalism in the postwar period. Next I clarify the significance of U.S. support for embedded liberal monetary reforms by examining two contexts where it was not present: regions coming under British and French influence. I highlight how Britain and France strongly opposed these kinds of monetary reforms in their ex-colonies for their own ideological, geopolitical, and interest-based reasons. Their attitudes, in combination with the ideological orientation of some specific Southern governments, help to explain why reforms took a more limited and cautious form in some parts of the South in the postwar period.

AMERICA'S NEW MONEY DOCTORS: THE SOUTHERN EXTENSION OF EMBEDDED LIBERALISM

To those familiar with U.S. foreign economic policy during the early twentieth century, U.S. policy toward monetary reforms in Southern countries after World War II may seem surprising. Before 1931, U.S. policymakers and private financiers played a lead role in encouraging many Southern countries to adopt the gold standard and set up national monetary authorities that could guarantee its maintenance (e.g., Rosenberg 1985; Drake 1989). Indeed, the American Edwin Kemmerer became the most famous of the foreign "money doctors" promoting monetary reforms along these classical liberal lines across Latin America and other parts of the South. In the early post-1945 years, however, U.S. policymakers did an about-face. Explicitly rejecting Kemmerer's approach, they came to be leading critics of orthodox monetary policy in the Southern countries and strong supporters of monetary reforms along the new unorthodox lines. Because of the dominant position of the United States in the postwar global monetary order, this policy reversal gave important strength to this trend of monetary reform.

Why did U.S. policymakers come to reject Kemmerer's ideas in the early postwar period? One might have expected the new unorthodox thinking to come from the U.S. Treasury, which during the early 1940s had become sympathetic to unorthodox international monetary ideas under the influence of Henry Morgenthau and Harry Dexter White. In fact, however, the first criticisms of orthodox "money doctoring" in the South came in the early 1940s from the U.S. Federal Reserve. The Federal Reserve's interest in this issue was triggered by a 1941 request for advice on monetary reform from the Paraguayan government. In response to this request, the chief of the Latin American section of the staff of the Federal Reserve's Board of Governors—Robert Triffin—launched an extensive process of consultation over several years with financial officials from the United States, Paraguay, and other Latin American countries (Triffin [1947b] 1966, 16, 112–114).

Out of this consultation process emerged the view among key Federal

Reserve officials that a different approach to money doctoring would be necessary in the postwar period. This new approach was first put into place in Paraguay in a set of monetary reforms in 1943–45 that the U.S. Federal Reserve (USFR 1945, 528) described as "a fundamental departure from the central banking structures previously established in Latin America." Triffin (1946, 25) himself described the Paraguayan reforms as "revolutionary." The Paraguayan model of reform was then promoted actively by Triffin and other U.S. officials in a series of money doctoring missions over the following decade in countries such as Ethiopia (1942–44), Guatemala (1945), the Dominican Republic (1947), Honduras (1950), the Philippines (1949), South Korea (1950), and Ceylon (1950).[3] In Kim's words (1965, 6), the new Bank of Paraguay's legislation "heralded much post-war central banking legislation that followed."

Various publications written by Federal Reserve officials in this period outline clearly their rationale for the new approach to money doctoring (USFR 1945; Triffin 1944, 1946, [1947a] 1966, [1947b] 1966). They argued that the interwar experience had highlighted the drawbacks of a passive monetary policy geared externally to respond automatically to changes in the balance of payments. In countries whose balance of payments were vulnerable to crop failures, dramatic changes in export markets, or volatile international capital movements, this "monetary automatism" was simply too costly in an economic and social sense. It magnified—rather than minimized—the impact of international instability on the domestic economy in this context.[4]

In the 1920s, for example, orthodox central banks in Latin America reinforced the inflationary impact of sudden capital inflows by expanding the money supply in response to the large balance-of-payment surpluses these inflows produced. Then when the balance of payments turned suddenly into deficit in the 1929–31 period (as capital flows suddenly collapsed and export markets dried up), orthodox central banks reinforced deflationary tendencies by contracting the money supply. In this way, orthodox monetary management subjected these economies to what Triffin (1946, 74) called "unbearable and often unnecessary disruptions." Triffin (1946,

---

3. Triffin (who was originally from Belgium), in his role as chief of the Latin American section of the Federal Reserve staff in the 1943–46 period, led many of these initial Federal Reserve money doctoring missions to Southern countries. Other U.S. officials involved in these missions included Bray Hammond, John Exter, Henry Wallich, David Grove, John De-Beers, Arthur Bloomfield, and John Jensen (Urquidi 1991; Kim 1965). I should make clear that the new central banks set up under U.S. assistance did not always pursue the nationalist policies that U.S. money doctors advised.

4. The money supply might have been less dependent on changing balance-of-payment conditions if trends in private bank lending had counteracted the direction of monetary policy pursued by currency boards or central banks in Southern countries. In reality, however, lending trends by private banks usually reinforced the policies of central banks or currency boards because the banking sector was dominated by foreign banks that responded primarily to the needs of the foreign trade sector.

79–80) also noted that these adjustments might not even be equilibrating in the way that orthodox theory predicted for countries whose exports were concentrated in a few products with inelastic demand or whose internal price levels were mostly determined by international prices of their exports and imports.

In the new American view, what was needed was a form of monetary management that *insulated* the national economy from international disruptions rather than *reinforced* the latter's impact on the former. Whereas Kemmerer's banks (and colonial currency boards) had prioritized the external stability of the currency and international equilibrium, the new priority was domestic economic development. In the Guatemalan reform of 1945, for example, the Federal Reserve highlighted that the goal was to create "guidance of monetary policy primarily by analysis of domestic developments, rather than in automatic response to changes in international reserves" (quoted in Laso 1957–58, 448). Similarly, one U.S. official involved in the 1950 Honduran reforms lamented that the monetary system had "not been used as an instrument to promote economic development" in the past, but that now it would be able "to assist the growth of the national economy" (Vinelli 1950, 420).

Indeed, this new domestic priority was clearly written into the constitutions of the central banks set up by the new U.S. money doctors. The Paraguayan central bank, which became the prototype of the new approach, described one of its key purposes as "the development of productive activities" (Triffin 1946, 115). A key goal of the new Philippine central bank established in 1948 was also "to promote a rising level of productive, employment and real income in the Philippines." Similarly, Ceylon's new central bank set up in 1949 was designed to serve, among other things, "the promotion and maintenance of a high level of production, employment, and real income in Ceylon, and the encouragement and promotion of the full development of the productive resources of Ceylon" (quoted from Kim 1965, 15 fn. 2).

To achieve these new domestic objectives, central banks had to have charters quite different from those written by Kemmerer. To begin with, their note issue and deposit liabilities were no longer regulated by rigid provisions linking them to gold or foreign exchange reserves. With this external constraint loosened, the national currency could be managed without such a strict connection to the condition of the balance of payments. To ensure that the international economy did not disrupt domestic goals, central banks were also allowed to adjust the exchange rate within limits in certain circumstances and to control capital inflows and outflows. Triffin [1947b] 1966, 141) acknowledged that many economic liberals would regard the endorsement of the latter in particular as "highly unorthodox," but he reminded them that the new Articles of Agreement for the International Monetary Fund (IMF) now permitted and even encouraged capital controls (by saying that IMF funds could not finance large capital outflows). Indeed, the principal negotiators of the Bretton Woods agreements, John Maynard Keynes and Harry Dexter White, had seen capital controls as a central element of the new embedded liberal monetary order (Helleiner 1994, chap. 2).

Federal Reserve officials also insisted that central banks be equipped with strong powers to promote the development of their national economies.[5] Central banks set up with Kemmerer's advice usually had been expected to influence the money supply through mechanisms such as discount rate changes and open market operations. In most Southern countries (as well as the British Dominions), U.S. officials noted that these tools were quite ineffective because domestic financial markets were underdeveloped and the banking system was often dominated by foreign banks that responded primarily to monetary developments only in their home country. To become more effective, central banks needed to be able to impose reserve requirements on private banks and to control private lending, and perhaps even to lend directly to the public.

Central bank involvement in lending to the public was advocated not just to strengthen central banks' abilities in national monetary management. It was also proposed as a means to promote developmental goals more directly. In contexts where foreign banks dominated the domestic banking system, there was often very little "developmental lending" for the domestic economy. A central bank could fill this void by taking on the role directly. Alternatively, it could play a key role in encouraging the establishment of domestically owned private financial institutions to do this kind of lending. Interestingly, U.S. officials also did not oppose provisions that allowed central banks to lend to their own governments. The reasoning was that it was simply unrealistic to expect a central bank to behave otherwise in the context of many developing countries (e.g., Triffin 1946, 23).

One final recommendation of U.S. money doctors in this period is worth noting in the context of contemporary interest for "dollarization." They encouraged Southern governments to eliminate the use of foreign currencies within their territory wherever that practice was widespread (e.g., in Honduras, the Dominican Republic, Paraguay, and Ethiopia). It was impossible, U.S. officials argued, for a central bank to develop a strong and independent monetary policy devoted to national development unless the currency it issued held a monopoly position inside the country. In the Dominican Republic, for example, Wallich and Triffin (1953, 24) noted how difficult it was to control inflationary pressures deriving from a balance-of-payments surplus in a context where the U.S. dollar was the main currency in use (as it had been since 1905). In Paraguay, where an (outdated) Argentine cur-

5. Indeed, in the case of Paraguay, Triffin (1946, 72) noted the powers of the central bank were "almost without precedent."

rency standard was widely used, U.S. officials also argued that the use of a foreign standard "throws doubt upon the stability" of the national currency (Triffin 1946, 60).

The decision of U.S. Federal Reserve officials to turn their backs on Kemmerer and endorse unorthodox monetary policy and institutional reforms in Southern countries requires political explanation, especially since it was often quite controversial at the time among orthodox thinkers and some parts of the business community.[6] A key part of the explanation is the new ideological commitment of U.S. policymakers in this area to embedded liberal ideas. Triffin and other economists in the U.S. Federal Reserve were clearly influenced by the Keynesian revolution that was underway. Policymakers who were sympathetic to embedded liberal ideas had been strengthened politically inside the United States by the shift away from financial and monetary orthodoxy that took place within the country in the wake of the Great Depression in the early 1930s. I have described elsewhere how the opposition of New Dealers to the liberal financial world of the 1920s had considerable influence in turning U.S. Treasury officials away from orthodox international monetary policy during the Bretton Woods negotiations (Helleiner 1994, chap. 2). The U.S. Federal Reserve had also been affected by the thinking of the New Deal, particularly after it became headed by Marriner Eccles, a non–New York banker with quite unorthodox views.

Even if U.S. officials were not themselves convinced by the new monetary ideas unleashed by the 1930s experience and the Keynesian revolution, they were forced to recognize the political power of these ideas abroad. Across the world, monetary policy had moved during the 1930s and wartime decisively away from the orthodox notion that monetary policy should be geared externally to respond automatically to changes in the balance of payments. In place of this "monetary automatism" was a new commitment to "autonomous monetary management" geared to *domestic* goals of monetary stability, full employment, and rapid growth (Triffin 1946, 22). Triffin ([1947b] 1966, 144) concluded from these changes that it was simply not politically feasible to try to return to orthodox policies: "Tomorrow's currencies will be managed currencies. . . . Any attempt to enforce rigid solutions patterned upon orthodox gold standard doctrines would be even more futile in the postwar than it already proved to be in the interwar period."

This shift away from orthodox monetary policies was particularly striking in Latin America, the region that strongly influenced the early views of Trif-

---

6. In the Philippines, for example, Cullather (1994, 81) noted the strong opposition of U.S. business to the introduction of capital controls in 1950 because it interfered with their ability to repatriate profits freely. The inflation that accompanied the monetary policy pursued by the new central bank of the Philippines was also strongly criticized by the U.S. business community (Hartendorp 1958, 255, 608).

fin and other Federal Reserve officials. When declining export markets and the collapse of U.S. lending produced dramatic balance-of-payment crises in the early 1930s, most Latin American countries abandoned the gold standard and introduced exchange controls rather than undergo dramatic deflations. Many of them also began to experiment with more activist monetary policies aimed at financing government spending and producing domestic economic growth. Exchange controls, which initially had been introduced as temporary measures, were often made permanent in order to allow this kind of monetary policy to be pursued independent of external constraints. Governments also became involved more directly—often via the central bank—in allocating credit to the private sector as a means of promoting economic growth and industrialization. In addition to reflecting Keynesian ideas, these various policies drew particular strength from economic nationalist thinking that placed a high priority on the goal of state-led industrialization as a tool of nation building.

In the early 1940s, U.S. Federal Reserve officials displayed a detailed understanding of the various policy innovations that had occurred in Latin America during the 1930s. Triffin (1944), in particular, was very knowledgeable about them and was explicit in acknowledging that they had strongly influenced his thinking. He made a special point frequently to cite his debt to Raul Prebisch's "pioneering work" in this area (Triffin [1947b] 1966, 141 fn. 2). Prebisch, who was head of the Argentine central bank between 1935 and 1943 and then became head of the UN Economic Commission for Latin America, was the leading theorist of the "structuralist" school that advocated economic nationalist policies of import-substitution industrialization. Triffin recognized his importance by consulting him in detail on the initial Paraguayan reforms.[7] Other Latin American governments, such as that in the Dominican Republic, also invited Prebisch for consultations with the Americans as part of the preparations for U.S.-led monetary reform programs (Wallich and Triffin 1953, 25).

U.S. officials, thus, were very familiar with the policy changes that had taken place across Latin America during the 1930s and understood the extent to which the new approach to monetary policy making had become politically entrenched in the region. To challenge this approach might be not only futile but also detrimental to broader U.S. geopolitical goals. In the important Paraguayan case, for example, U.S. monetary consultations took place at a time when U.S. policymakers were actively seeking to prevent, through aid packages and diplomatic efforts, the Paraguayan government from allying itself too closely with the Axis powers. Accommodating the nationalist leanings of the country's government, rather than challeng-

7. The head of the Bank of Colombia (Enrique Davila) was also very involved in consultations with Triffin concerning Paraguay, and both he and Prebisch spent three months in Paraguay in 1943 and 1945.

ing them, was the U.S. priority. And to many nationalist Paraguay officials, monetary reform served not just the goal of industrialization but also the objective of consolidating an exclusive national currency for the first time. Indeed, U.S. advisors played to nationalist sentiments when they advocated the elimination of the use of the old Argentine monetary standard on the grounds that it would help the country "reaffirm its monetary independence and sovereignty." They argued that the use of a foreign currency standard "has injured the prestige of the national currency both at home and abroad," and they encouraged the new currency to be called the *guarani*, a name which "derives from the racial origins of the Paraguayan nation" (USFR 1944, 46–47).[8]

By the late 1940s, geopolitical concerns in the new Cold War also encouraged an accommodating approach toward economic nationalism in the South.[9] In the Philippines, for example, local politicians after the war sought to replace the colonial currency board with a powerful central bank that would introduce capital controls and pursue expansionary monetary policies (Cullather 1994, 63–66). These local demands stemmed not just from the goal of rapid industrialization (and the pressing fiscal needs of the government) but also from broader nationalist sentiments that a currency board arrangement was "an unsuitable system for an independent Philippines."[10] Many U.S. officials were wary of the local demands for monetary reform and would have preferred to see more orthodox deflationary measures introduced by the late 1940s. However, as Cullather (1994, 64–71, 76, 81, 191) showed, Cold War fears of the growing power of left-wing rebels in the Philippines encouraged the United States to go along with local expansionary objectives and not to press for deflationary measures that might have given political strength to the rebels.

One further geopolitical motivation deserves mention. In newly independent countries emerging from European colonial rule, a more sympathetic approach to nationalist monetary reforms helped U.S. officials to gain influence. Some ex-British colonies, for example, explicitly sought out U.S. money doctors instead of British ones because the latter favored the maintenance of colonial boards (for reasons explained in the next section). In Ceylon, for example, the currency board "was looked upon as a financial appendage of colonial government and was recognized as part and parcel of the system of colonial administration" (Karunatilake 1973, 3).

8. In the Dominican Republic, Wallich and Triffin (1953, 24) also appealed to nationalist sentiment in making the case for the creation of an exclusive national currency: "In international affairs, it will strengthen the position of the Republic and put it on an equal footing with all other nations."

9. I have shown elsewhere the influence of the Cold War in also encouraging U.S. officials to accept European and Japanese preferences for monetary and financial interventionism in the early postwar years (Helleiner 1994, chap. 3).

10. Quotation from the U.S.-Philippine Finance Commission set up in 1946 to study the future of monetary arrangements (quoted in Golay 1961, 217).

The construction of a central bank came to be seen by its supporters as necessary to achieve "economic freedom"; indeed, one supporter argued that it was even more important than the Independence Bill (Karunatilake 1973, 8). Even the ability to adjust the national exchange rate—not possible under the currency board arrangements—was seen in political terms by the minister of finance in 1949 as creating a "free currency, the content of which, the value of which, we and we alone can determine according to the best interests of the people of Ceylon" (quoted in Karunatilake 1973, 13). Since U.S. officials were known to be more sympathetic to these nationalist goals, they—instead of Bank of England officials—were invited to help construct the country's first central bank. Indeed, local policymakers wanted a central bank like that recently constructed under U.S. advice in Korea and the Philippines (Karunatilake 1973, 5).

In British-occupied Ethiopia during the early 1940s, a similar situation took place. At this time, the money in circulation within the country was a motley collection of currency issued by the Ethiopian state, Maria Theresa thalers, traditional commodity-based, small-denomination money, and Italian and British currencies. Ethiopian policymakers sought to create an exclusive national currency for the first time in order to assert the state's authority over the whole country, and to create a monetary system that could be mobilized to promote rapid economic growth. The British were supportive of the objective of consolidating the national currency, but they pushed for it to be managed by a currency board. To the Ethiopians, however, a currency board was unacceptable since it prevented them from pursuing their nationalist monetary goals. They also saw the British proposal in highly political terms, as an attempt to turn the country into a protectorate or colony of the United Kingdom. To offset British influence, Ethiopian policymakers turned to U.S. officials for advice, recognizing correctly that the latter would support their goal of creating a powerful central bank guided by more nationalist thinking. Indeed, U.S. officials not only provided advice but also secretly printed Ethiopia's first notes and provided the central bank with its governors until 1959 (Degefe 1995).

Thus, U.S. support for the new approach to monetary policy had both ideological and geopolitical roots. Regardless of its sources, this support was important in encouraging the trend of nationalist monetary reforms in the South. Its importance stemmed not so much from the specific content of the advice provided by U.S. money doctors. After all, most of the countries that received U.S. advice were already committed to the course that U.S. money doctors recommended.[11] The 1930s experience, the rise of economic nationalism, and broader anticolonial sentiments had all played a role in encouraging Southern countries to reject the orthodox monetary economics. What was more important than the specifics of U.S. advice was

11. The same had been true of Kemmerer's missions (Drake 1989).

the simple fact that the political weight of the world's dominant financial power would not stand in the way of nationalist reforms.

DISCOURAGING "THE WRONG TENDENCIES": BRITISH RESISTANCE TO NATIONALIST MONETARY REFORMS

The importance of U.S. support is highlighted if we turn to examine some cases where it was not present. As mentioned already, British policymakers were quite opposed to nationalist monetary reforms, and they went out of their way to advise newly independent ex-British colonies not to implement them. Some countries—such as Ceylon and Ethiopia, as we have seen—simply ignored this advice, but others were forced to listen because of continuing close economic and political ties to Britain. In these latter countries, the introduction of nationalist monetary reforms took place more cautiously and slowly.

Why were British policymakers so opposed to the new approach to monetary policy in Southern countries? The opposition was partly ideological. The institution that took charge of British foreign economic policy in this area in the early postwar period was the Bank of England. Alongside Kemmerer, Bank of England officials had been leaders of orthodox money doctoring during the interwar period (e.g., Plumptre 1940). Despite the experience of the 1930s and the nationalization of the bank in 1944, its outlook remained largely orthodox throughout this period. The Bank of England's leading money doctors in the postwar period, such as J. B. Loynes, largely picked up where their predecessors had left off.

Equally if not more important in explaining British policy was the geopolitical goal of preserving the sterling area and Britain's privileged position within it (Bangura 1983). The continued existence of the sterling area after the war provided Britain with not just international prestige but also important balance-of-payments support. This support came partly from the fact that sterling area countries and colonial currency boards held their often considerable foreign exchange reserves in sterling and in London; indeed, in the case of currency boards, Balogh (1966, 30) noted that this arrangement ensured that any increase in the money supply within the Southern country resulted in a "de facto loan" to Britain (and often at below "market" rates since sterling balances earned very low rates of interest). The absence of capital controls and exchange rate risk within the sterling area—when combined with limited local money markets—also encouraged private banks, companies, and individuals in many sterling area countries to export savings and liquid funds to London markets. When this export of local savings was offset by long-term loans back to the colony from London, there might be no net balance-of-payments benefit to Britain. But the arrangement still provided one further interest-based benefit of the sterling area to Britain: that of bolstering the City of London's role as an international financial center.

If countries turned to unorthodox policies, these benefits of the sterling area to Britain would diminish. Activist domestic monetary management, for example, might produce balance-of-payment deficits that would force countries to draw down their sterling reserves and sterling assets in London. Demand for sterling and sterling assets in London, and for sterling more generally, would also be reduced if national currencies were backed with less than 100 percent reserves or if reserves were held in local government securities. Similarly, capital controls and the creation of domestic money and capital markets might reduce capital outflows to London and reduce the dependence of Southern borrowers on London financiers.

British hostility toward the new nationalist approaches to monetary policy initially took an interesting form: opposition to the creation of central banks in newly independent countries altogether. Throughout the 1940s and 1950s, at the same time that the United States was advocating the creation of powerful central banks, the Bank of England usually opposed their creation and still promoted the creation of currency boards in countries such as Jordan and Libya. In their various colonies, British officials went to great lengths to try to convince local policymakers not to create central banks and to maintain the colonial currency board arrangements after they attained independence.[12]

In some cases, British officials even sought initially to keep together the large currency zones that had been administered by one currency board in colonial times, such as that in East Africa (Tanzania, Uganda, Kenya, Aden) and in Malaya (Singapore, Malaysia, Brunei, Borneo, Sarawak).[13] In other regions, such as West Africa, however, the British were willing to accept what Loynes called "prestige and appearance" reasons for why countries would want to break up these zones and create national currencies immediately upon independence (as Ghana did in 1957, Nigeria in 1958, Sierra Leone in 1963, and Gambia in 1964).[14] Most newly independent countries, indeed, did place considerable symbolic value on the creation of a national currency. As Ghana's finance minister put it, "No nation could be regarded as fully independent which shared a common currency with its former colonial neighbours."[15] But the British hoped that the creation of these national

12. There were some exceptions. In the Gold Coast, Cecil Trevor (who had had experience with the Reserve Bank in India) unexpectedly recommended the creation of a central bank in a 1951 report, a conclusion that greatly annoyed Bank of England officials and led them to insist that he not be allowed to provide advice to Nigeria (Uche 1997).

13. These arrangements rarely lasted long, with the East African countries creating national currencies in 1965–67 and the Malayan common currency board breaking up completely by 1967.

14. Loynes quotation from his 1961 report to Sierra Leone (PRO [Public Record Office, London] CO [Colonial Files] 1025/127 E/57, March 1961, 8).

15. PRO CO 1025/42 59/13/04, "Speech for the Minister of Finance on the Occasion of the Signing of the Currency Notes Contract Between the Gold Coast Govt and Messrs Thomas de la Rue and Co. Ltd, London, Sept. 15, 1955."

currencies would not lead to what Loynes called privately "the wrong tendencies." He hoped they would simply provide a "national façade for the currency" (quoted in Uche 1996, 151). As the acting British governor of Sierra Leone put it in 1960, "Any reforms should be of a very conservative nature."[16]

In a further effort to prevent the creation of central banks, the British even began to reform currency boards to try to accommodate criticisms of their operations (e.g., EACB 1967, 1972; Lee 1986, 20). Some currency boards, such as those in East Africa in 1955 and Malaya in 1960, were allowed to begin issuing some unbacked money in an effort to increase the flexibility of their operations. These currency boards were also permitted to invest their reserves in nonsterling assets such as local government securities and dollars around this time. The East African currency board also began to cultivate a local money market in 1960 by discounting activities in the local treasury bill market and by allowing banks to hold balances with it and offering clearance and settlement services. In addition, the headquarters of these operations were moved from London to the regions themselves, and more local staff were recruited. Finally, colonial images on the notes and coins issued by currency boards were replaced with iconography more appropriate to newly independent countries: in 1959 in Malaya, the picture of the queen was replaced by a fishing craft, and in 1964 in East Africa, an image of Lake Victoria appeared on the notes.

The British opposition to central banks contrasted sharply not just with U.S. policy but also with the Bank of England's own policy during the interwar period. In that earlier era, the head of the Bank of England, Montagu Norman, played a lead role in encouraging countries around the world to set up independent central banks where none yet existed (including in some colonized regions such as India). These banks, he hoped, would help to insulate the management of money from political pressures and to preserve the international gold standard. Now that central banks had become associated with more activist monetary management, however, the Bank of England wanted nothing to do with them.

Central banks, it now argued, would only lead to inflationary pressures as politicians controlled them to finance government deficits. Moreover, efforts to promote economic development with expansionist monetary policies could also lead to inflation and balance-of-payment crises. Capital controls, British officials argued, were often ineffective and would discourage new inflows of capital (EACB 1966, 13). British officials also argued that modern central banking could not work in contexts where no local money and capital markets existed. Efforts to overcome this problem by involving the central bank directly in lending, as U.S. officials recommended, would only risk undermining confidence in the bank if losses were sustained. As a

16. PRO CO 1025/127 S.F.P. 9482, acting governor of Sierra Leone to Galsworthy, Oct. 7, 1960.

final point, the British often stressed that in comparison to currency boards, central banks were more expensive to run and required a kind of expertise that was often not available in newly independent countries (e.g., EACB 1965, 7–11; Uche 1997).

It quickly became clear to British officials, however, that most Southern governments disregarded these arguments and planned to establish central banks anyway. In part, the desire of Southern policymakers for a modern central bank reflected their belief that the creation of this institution would be a symbol of their political independence (Bangura 1983, 49; Basu 1967, 52; Schenck 1993, 427). Currency boards were also rejected because they precluded the kind of activist monetary policy that was seen as necessary to serve domestic goals of economic development. As Ghana's first finance minister put it, "A Currency Board is the financial hallmark of colonialism. . . . [It] is a dead thing . . . an automatic machine which has no volition of its own and could do nothing to assist in developing our own financial institutions" (Gold Coast 1956–57, 852).[17] President Julius Nyerere in Tanzania explained the decision to create a national central bank on similar grounds: "We found that it is impossible to control our economy and achieve the maximum development while our currency and credit was outside our control" (quoted in Rothchild 1968, 234).

In defying British preferences, these policymakers were sometimes supported by the United States, as we have seen in the cases of Ceylon and Ethiopia. Also important was the role played by U.S.-controlled international financial institutions, which made similar arguments as Triffin had. In Nigeria, for example, the Bank of England was frustrated by a 1954 report by the International Bank for Reconstruction and Development (IBRD) that called for the creation of a central bank much more quickly than the Bank of England was advising (Uche 1997). Similarly, the British were annoyed with an IBRD mission in Malaya during the next year that advocated the creation of a central bank with strong powers to pursue an autonomous domestic monetary policy and develop a local money market (Schenk 1993, 412–413). In addition to reserve requirements, the IBRD even recommended that the central bank be able to control the overseas assets of banks that were counterpart funds of Malay bank deposits. In Uganda in 1962, too, an IBRD report recommended the creation of a central bank on similar grounds (World Bank 1962, 71–72). One final example comes from Sierra Leone where Loynes was disappointed by the fact that after he recommended against the creation of a central bank, the government decided to get a second opinion from the IMF since it was known to favor the creation of central banks at that time (Uche 1996, 157 fn. 61).

The IBRD and IMF were not the only external forces interfering with British efforts to preserve orthodox monetary arrangements. Also impor-

17. See also Nkrumah 1965, 221; Bank of Sierra Leone n.d., 2–3.

tant were some Northern academic experts who provided monetary advice to Southern governments. One of the more prominent was Thomas Balogh, a left-of-center Oxford economist who was very critical of currency boards on the grounds that they served Britain's interests by reinforcing the export-oriented nature of Southern economies, encouraging capital outflows (both official and private), and leaving Southern countries dependent on the judgments of London financiers to determine their creditworthiness (Balogh 1966). His anti-imperialist analysis and his advocacy of powerful central banks in Southern countries appealed to many nationalist politicians in countries seeking to throw off British rule, and he became involved in debates on monetary reform in British colonies such as Malta, Jamaica, and Malaya. For example, in 1958 the Jamaican government invited Balogh to support its arguments for a central bank, arguments that the British government was attempting to counter at the time. He was apparently very effective in this task, leaving one British colonial official to note privately that the "visit by Dr. T. Balogh has probably made it impossible ever to get things properly back."[18] When he intervened in debates in Malaya the next year, a Treasury official warned his colleague, "You may not be aware of the fact but Dr. Balogh has in fact been a considerable thorn in the flesh of the Colonial Office on a number of occasions when Colonial currency systems have been concerned."[19]

As it became clear that they could not resist the creation of central banks, British officials shifted their strategy. They accepted the case for a central bank but insisted that it be managed in an orthodox manner. The national currency should be backed by 100 percent reserves, they argued, and its convertibility into sterling should be guaranteed. They also opposed giving the central bank large powers, such as the power to control capital movements or to force commercial banks to hold funds at the central bank (e.g., Uche 1997). In the words of one British official in the Gold Coast (Ghana) in 1955, the objective was to ensure that the local government "does not set up a Frankenstein."[20]

British officials tried to appeal to nationalist sentiments in advancing these arguments in favor of an orthodox approach to monetary management. In the Gold Coast, Loynes, for example, argued that a stable and internationally convertible currency was crucial because "it is bound up with the international reputation of the Gold Coast as an independent country."[21] Other British officials were encouraged to stress how "the world is strewn with unsatisfactory Central Banks and shaky currencies and the com-

18. PRO CO 1025/123, R.J. Vile to Mr. Marnham, April 30, 1958.
19. PRO T (Treasury Files) 236/5149, C. Lucas to J. Rampton, Jan. 1, 1960.
20. PRO CO 1025/42 59/13/04, "Gold Coast Currency and Banking: Notes for Meeting on Sept. 14, 1955," 4.
21. PRO CO 1025/42 59/13/04, informal report of J.B. Loynes to minister of finance, Feb. 21, 1956, 1.

bination of the two in any country is simply to replace political dependence by economic dependence, exemplified in foreign aid."[22]

When one looks at the kinds of central banks established in many ex-British colonies, it appears that the British were quite successful in advancing these arguments. Most of the central banks set up, with the exception of the one set up in Ceylon, had initially quite orthodox charters when compared with those established under the U.S. Federal Reserve's guidance. They usually had only a limited fiduciary issue, no reserve requirements, strong sterling backing, and often no provisions for the use of capital controls or for direct lending by the central bank (Bangura 1983). This was even true of the central banks set up in countries such as Jamaica, where Balogh initially had had some influence, or Malaysia, where the IBRD had called for more radical measures. Indeed, domestic critics argued that these were not real central banks but just another name for the old currency boards (Gold Coast 1956–57, 705–706). As one Ghanaian critic put it, "If we are going to have a Central Bank we must have a Central Bank with 'teeth' and not a Central Bank which is only a channel for controlling the financial assets of their country by a foreign power" (Gold Coast 1956–57, 711).

The orthodox nature of these central banks partly reflected British pressure. But it also stemmed from the continued dependence of many of these countries on London financial markets and links to the British economy. Policymakers were particularly concerned to cultivate confidence in their new national currencies in order to prevent capital flight and encourage international lending to their country (Bangura 1983; Schenck 1993). A central bank with an orthodox charter served this goal, as did public pronouncements of a commitment to orthodox policies at the time of its establishment. In Kenya, for example, the central bank was set up with what one observer called "the expression of sentiments of impeccable respectability in monetary matters, of which Mr. Montagu Norman would have been proud" (Hazlewood 1979, 146). As President Jomo Kenyatta noted, "One thing cannot be forgotten: currency issues and management is a real business and no magic. The bank cannot make something out of nothing and the Government cannot by order, or 'Fiat' grant to a piece of paper a value independent of the backing which it possesses. Such backing is provided by foreign exchange into which the Kenya currency will be convertible at its established par value" (quoted in EACB 1966, 118).

If monetary reforms were usually quite limited at the time of independence in ex-British colonies, they often moved rapidly in a more nationalist direction in response to fiscal and economic pressures. In Ghana, for example, the government's desire in 1961 to accelerate economic growth and

22. PRO CO 1025/42 59/13/04, "Gold Coast Currency and Banking: Notes for Meeting on Sept. 14, 1955," 4.

government spending led policymakers to allow the central bank to lend to the government more easily, to mobilize the foreign exchange reserves of Ghanaian residents, and to introduce capital controls (Bangura 1983, 99). Similar measures accompanied the introduction of Nigeria's 1962 development plan. Even conservative Kenya had begun deficit financing and tightened exchange controls by 1970. These episodes usually led to the results feared by British officials: the drawing down of sterling reserves, lessened dependence on London financial market, and often a break from the sterling area itself.

FRENCH GOALS: THE SURVIVAL OF THE CFA FRANC ZONE

Not all newly independent Southern countries created national central banks guided by more domestic monetary objectives in the postwar period. One prominent exception among ex-British colonies was Singapore, which maintained a currency board backed by 100 percent reserves (although the Monetary Authority was established in 1970 to do some central banking functions unrelated to note issue). Its unique preference reflected partly its status as an international trading entrepôt, a status that gave it a strong reason to favor a stable currency. Singapore's finance minister from 1959 to 1971 also later made clear that the preference had ideological roots: "None of us [in Cabinet] believed that Keynesian economic policies could serve as Singapore's guide to economic well-being" (Goh 1991, 181).

The more dramatic exception, however, involved the ex-French colonies in West and Central Africa. At the time of independence, most of these countries did not create national central banks and national currencies but instead continued to be members of the two common currency zones that had existed under French colonial rule.[23] The postindependence CFA franc monetary zones functioned in a similar way as had their colonial predecessors (e.g., Chipman 1989, 208–216). The CFA franc was convertible across the entire region, with no capital controls existing among member countries. The notes and coins in use across each zone were also almost identical, with no national emblems on them (with the exception of those in Cameroon, which acquired its own note issue).[24] All external payments from member countries were settled through an "operations account" held

23. The Central African CFA Franc Zone included Cameroon, Central African Republic, Chad, Congo, and Gabon, while the members of the West African CFA Franc Zone in the early years after independence were Ivory Coast, Dahomey, Mauritania, Niger, Senegal, and Upper Volta (as well as Togo after 1963).

24. In 1962, each CFA franc note acquired a small country-identification code (a letter following the serial number), which enabled policymakers to analyze intercountry balance-of-payment situations. These payment situations were important in determining how much credit was allocated to each country by the regional central bank, as noted below (Robson 1968).

at the French Treasury, which continued to cover all deficits emerging in these accounts. Even the name "CFA franc" was the same as the colonial currency, although the meaning of "CFA" had been changed from "Colonies Françaises d'Afrique" to "Communauté Financière Africaine."

How do we explain this anomalous experience among Southern countries? A key part of the explanation is that the French government went to much greater lengths than the British government did to preserve the monetary structures in place in the colonial period. Chipman (1989) argued that French policy was linked primarily to its broader concern with its status as a world power after the war. In his chapter in this volume, Stasavage suggests instead that the French government's desire to maintain the CFA zone reflected the power of specific interest groups who benefited from the zone's existence. Others note that the CFA zone also provided balance-of-payments support for France in much of the postwar period. As in the case of the sterling bloc, the absence of capital controls and exchange rate risk between France and CFA countries encouraged large private capital outflows from the latter to the former, outflows that usually exceeded public and private capital inflows (Joseph 1976; Balogh 1966, 46). Equally important, CFA countries earned continuous foreign exchange surpluses vis-à-vis the outside world in this period, and these surpluses were controlled by the French Treasury, which used them to support the French balance-of-payments position (Joseph 1976).[25] More generally, an official French commission appointed to investigate the future of the CFA zone in 1960 reported that France-CFA trade was bolstered by the zone's existence because CFA francs were convertible only into French francs. Not only did this provide French companies with a protected export market (especially because the CFA franc was overvalued by this time), but also France was able to import raw materials without having to use scarce foreign exchange.[26]

To increase the attractiveness of the CFA zone to African governments, the French government undertook a series of reforms of its operations in the postwar period. The first reform was one that Britain had also introduced in a more limited way in its currency boards: after World War II, the prewar requirement that CFA currencies be backed with 100 percent reserves in gold, French francs, or convertible currencies was changed to allow up to two-thirds of the reserve to be held in local assets (Onoh 1982, 29). The next key reform went much further than the British had contemplated in the sterling area. The French created regional central banks in Central Africa (1955) and West Africa (1959) that provided not only rediscount facilities for local banks but also short-term commercial credit (e.g.,

25. Medhora (1992, 163) noted that an operations account offers an open-ended guarantee of foreign exchange, but that Central African countries had never used the overdraft facility and West African countries used it for the first time only in 1980.

26. BOE (Bank of England Archives, London) OV100/19, "Summary of the Report of the Conseil Economique et Social on the Revision of the Structure of the Franc Zone Published in March 1960," summary by M. Hailstone.

crop finance) and medium-term loans for development projects (Ezenwe 1983; Robson 1968, 201–207). After independence, the French went one step further in 1962 to transform the regional central banks into intergovernmental institutions with a majority of Africans on the board (although the headquarters remained in Paris until 1972 and France retained an effective veto). At this time, each member government was also given more input into the central banks' decisions on the overall level of credit being allocated to their country as well as decisions on how this credit would be distributed to banks and companies within their country.

In these ways, the French attempted to accommodate Southern goals of using the monetary system more actively to promote economic development. The 1960 report of the official commission looking into the future of the CFA zone was explicit in acknowledging this objective; in the words of one British official, the report noted the goal of reforms should be "to allow for the maximum expansion of economic activity in these countries, but nevertheless in such a way as to maintain their allegiance."[27] This last line highlighted the price of these economic reforms: the CFA zone remained a French-controlled monetary system. For this reason, many Africans continued to see CFA franc as "colonial money" and the CFA zone as a form of neocolonialism.[28] The extent of the 1962 economic reforms should also not be overstated. Credit from the central banks was refused to CFA countries that ran a consistent balance-of-payments deficit within the system, and CFA governments were still not allowed to run fiscal deficits (although French aid was available as a partial, albeit politically controlled alternative to finance government spending).[29]

Given these constraints, it may seem surprising that more African governments did not break out on their own and create national currencies and national central banks as governments in ex-British colonies had done. To be sure, some countries such as Guinea and Mali did pursue this option, as I explain later. But the fact that more did not surprised many observers at the time, including this British Foreign Office official who was convinced that the situation would not last: "In the longer term, the very conservativism of the Central Banks, and their inability under the present rules to play the part they ought to be playing in helping the countries they serve to establish their economic independence is, I should have thought, more likely to lead to moves of the kind Guinea and Mali have already taken."[30]

27. Ibid., 3.
28. Quotation is from Joseph Tchunjang (quoted in Guyer 1995, 13). See also Nkrumah 1965, 20.
29. As the French government's Jeanneney Report of 1964 noted, "France in effect renounces the possibility of refusing to finance initiatives taken unilaterally by African governments, in return the States accept a certain monetary tutelage, particularly in the matter of deficit financing" (quoted in Robson 1968, 207). Credit from the IMF and World Bank to national governments also complicated the fiscal arrangements in the CFA zone.
30. BOE OV100/3, R.J. O'Neil (Foreign Office) to W. Pattinson (Treasury), Jan. 16, 1964.

One reason why so many African governments decided to remain in the CFA zone may have been that the French took a very tough stance toward countries that adopted a more independent course. Countries such as Guinea and Mali, which sought to break away from the CFA zone, found their broader security, trade, aid, and other economic links to France severed by the French government in ways that were very costly (Chipman 1989; Joseph 1976). African governments in the CFA zone thus appeared to face a starker choice than members of the sterling area had faced: either accept the CFA currency or face a sharp break in the relationship with France. For many elites, the prospects of losing security ties, aid support, and guaranteed access to the French market (as well as the stable and high prices paid by the French for key exports) were ones they were not willing to consider (Stasavage, this volume).

This explanation is important, but it does not tell the whole story. It neglects the fact that the 1960 French commission examining potential reforms to the CFA actually opened the door to the possibility of France allowing distinct national currencies to be created. The commission even suggested that France would allow these currencies both to be devalued in situations of fundamental disequilibrium and to be defended by capital controls if such controls were necessary for economic development.[31] That African governments did not push more strongly for this kind of reform given French openness to it requires explanation. Indeed, when in 1961 the French government indicated its willingness to consider the creation of distinct national banknotes for each newly independent CFA country in West Africa, the proposal was actually opposed by every African government involved.[32]

To account fully for the choice made by CFA countries, we must look to a domestic explanation: the ideological roots of the decision. Most of the countries that stayed with the CFA zone were headed by conservative governments whose commitment to nationalist ideology was much weaker than that in other Southern countries at this time. Many of their leaders had endorsed the goal of independence from France in only a lukewarm fashion, and they remained wedded to the assimilationist goals that the French had promoted in the colonial period (Chipman 1989). Thus, a national currency and national central bank appeared to hold much less value for these leaders than it had for policymakers elsewhere.

The importance of the ideological orientation of African governments is

31. BOE OV100/19, "Summary of the Report of the Conseil Economique et Social on the Revision of the Structure of the Franc Zone Published in March 1960," summary by M. Hailstone. Other newly independent countries that had been members of the broader franc zone, such as Tunisia and Morocco, had established central banks and national currencies at the time of independence. By the early 1960s, they had also imposed exchange controls on transactions with France.

32. BOE OV100/20, C. M. Le Quesne to Foreign Office, Sept. 19, 1961, 3.

clear when one examines the counter cases of Guinea and Mali. Soon after their independence, each country established a national central bank and national currency (in 1960 for Guinea and 1962 for Mali).[33] They also imposed capital controls, and the central banks were given considerable powers. In Guinea, for example, there was initially no provision for backing the currency whatsoever and no limitation on government borrowing from it. The five French banks in the country were also told to deposit 50 percent of their foreign currency holdings with the central bank, and when four of them refused, they were liquidated.[34]

This radically different approach to monetary reform from the other ex-French colonies was driven by the ideological goals of the two countries' leaders, Sékou Touré (Guinea) and Modibo Keita (Mali). Unlike leaders in other ex-French African colonies, these two leaders were committed to a strong anticolonial nationalism. In the economic sphere, their ideas were in fact much more radical than the nationalist ideas that were prominent in the ex-British colonies and the countries that the United States was advising at this time. Influenced by the French Marxist economist Charles Bettleheim, they sought to build not just a national industrial economy but one that was based on a revolutionary and ambitious form of national economic planning (Touré 1979; Zolberg 1967; Jones 1976). Both leaders saw monetary reform as crucial to their political and economic projects. An independent national currency not only would enable effective capital controls to be introduced but also would allow the country to mobilize the monetary system behind its planning objectives (Touré 1979, 371–379; Yansane 1979; Jones 1976). In broader nationalist terms, Touré (1979, 371) also noted of the creation of Guinea's national currency and central bank, "Its importance is comparable, if not superior, to that of our choice of immediate independence in Sept. 1958. This reform provides the basis upon which we can carry out our economic liberation, previously impeded by a financial system which remained that of the old regime, linked to the economic system of the colonizing country."

CONCLUSION

The pattern of monetary policy making in Southern countries during the early postwar era highlights the themes of this volume particularly well. At the most general level, it demonstrates the centrality of politics in shaping monetary outcomes. If monetary policy were guided by economic effi-

33. See Kirshner 1995. Mali's departure from the CFA zone was not permanent. It reestablished an operations account with France in 1968 and rejoined the CFA zone fully in 1984. Another country that pulled out of the CFA zone was Mauritania. It withdrew in 1973 and created a central bank in 1978 (Yansane 1984, 77).

34. BOE OV106/1, "Guinea" by J. Margetson, March 25, 1960; BOE OV106/1, 103–104.

ciency concerns alone, we would not have witnessed such diversity among monetary policy choices in these countries. The Southern countries examined in this chapter often faced very similar economic contexts and yet chose very different monetary policies. Only by examining political factors can these choices be explained.

One such political factor is the power of dominant Northern states to shape the monetary policy agenda of Southern states during this period. Countries that rejected monetary orthodoxy across the South gained political strength from the fact that their move was endorsed by the dominant financial power after the war, the United States. In a striking reversal of their activities in the 1920s, from the early 1940s through the 1950s U.S. policymakers played a major role in promoting unorthodox monetary reforms through money doctoring missions. This U.S. role stemmed partly from the broad commitment of U.S. policymakers to embedded liberal ideas and partly from geopolitical interests that encouraged them to be sympathetic to the economic nationalist goals of Southern governments.

The importance of U.S. support is made clear when we examine some countries where it was not present. British and French policymakers were opposed to challenges to orthodoxy for different ideological, geopolitical, and interest-based reasons, and they went out of their way to advise their newly independent ex-colonies not to follow economic nationalist policies. In British ex-colonies, this advice was usually unwelcome, but it had some effect in ensuring that monetary reforms would be introduced more cautiously and slowly. In French ex-colonies in Central and West Africa, French advice coincided with the conservative preferences of elite policymakers, resulting in the survival of the colonial CFA Franc Zone.

The roots of the distinct foreign policy preferences of the United States, Britain, and France reinforce the thesis of this volume that politics, rather than economics, determines monetary policy. These dominant powers were not giving advice to Southern countries based on some apolitical calculations of what monetary strategies would be most economically efficient for these countries. Instead, their policy advice was driven by ideological perspectives, interest group pressures, and broader geopolitical desires to maximize each state's power. Political concerns in the Southern countries themselves also drove monetary policy making. In countries that sought to introduce unorthodox monetary reforms, a key appeal of these reforms was an ideological one: they would contribute to the political project of nation building. The absence of this political goal in the CFA zone also helps to explain why their governments showed little interest in these kinds of reforms.

These themes about the specific significance of politics in driving Southern monetary policies during the postwar period are not just of historical interest. Dominant powers continue to play an important role in shaping the monetary policy agenda of less powerful states. Stasavage's chapter in this volume highlights how the French role in the CFA zone remains a key one forty years after the developments I have analyzed. In light of the history outlined in this chapter, even more interesting is U.S. policy toward Southern countries today. U.S. policymakers have often pressed Southern governments during the last decade to consider monetary reforms—such as the creation of independent central banks or the abolition of capital controls—that reduce the possibility of discretionary national monetary policy by their governments. In so doing, they are encouraging the dismantling of interventionist practices that other U.S. officials had helped to build several decades earlier. As Grabel's chapter in this volume highlights, these initiatives today have some ideological roots; in place of embedded liberal thinking, U.S. officials are now often influenced by "neoliberal" ideology that is skeptical of discretionary monetary policy, and of state regulation and national economic planning more generally. In this way, the United States has become a more "orthodox" financial power, a role it also assumed in Kemmerer's era, but one from which it departed in such a dramatic way under Triffin's leadership in the early post-1945 years.

CHAPTER FOUR

When Do States Abandon Monetary Discretion?
Lessons from the Evolution of the CFA Franc Zone

DAVID STASAVAGE

In recent years a number of governments have taken steps to relinquish individual control over their monetary policies. European Union governments have formed a monetary union. Argentina and the Baltic States established currency board arrangements whereby monetary authorities in effect adopted the monetary policy of an advanced industrial country. Ecuador's government has gone a step further by actually using the U.S. dollar as its national currency.

While these decisions to abandon discretion over monetary policy are often advertised as irrevocable, it is important to recognize that actions such as joining a currency union or creating a currency board ultimately are political choices that can be reversed. A look at the past fifty years of monetary history illustrates this basic fact. As one example, upon attaining independence circa 1960, the vast majority of African states participated in currency board systems that denied their governments independent control over monetary policy. By 1970 most of these arrangements had been dismantled. The states of the CFA (Communauté Financière Africaine) Franc Zone are an important exception in this regard, as twelve out of the original fifteen members have continued to participate in a system through which they abandon independent control over monetary policy. What factors account for the CFA Franc Zone's surprising persistence? To answer this question, I focus on two broad periods in the evolution of the union: 1960–73, the years between independence for the African member states and the breakup of the Bretton Woods system, and 1973–94, the years between the breakup of Bretton Woods and the CFA franc devaluation of January 1994. In the end, while events within the CFA zone involve a particular context of decolonization and, subsequently, economic crisis in African countries, the evolution of the union nonetheless provides valuable insights about the willingness of governments to abandon monetary discretion.

Although the CFA Franc Zone is a rarity in terms of its persistence, its recent evolution raises important questions about the factors that determine monetary and exchange rate policy making within a currency union. During the 1960s and early 1970s CFA governments adhered to conservative macroeconomic policies while preserving their fixed and freely convertible peg to the French franc. During the 1980s and 1990s this pattern changed. A series of negative terms of trade shocks left a number of key CFA governments with significant balance-of-payment problems, growing fiscal deficits, and an overvalued currency. African governments faced two adjustment options: either implement deflationary policies involving tight money and budget cuts, or devalue the CFA franc. Instead, they relied on French bilateral aid and credit from the two CFA central banks in order to delay adjustment. This strategy was aided by the fact that the French government turned a blind eye to violations of rules limiting central bank credit to governments, and failed to impose serious conditions in exchange for its bilateral aid. The CFA states finally devalued their currency from one-fiftieth to one-hundredth of a French franc in January 1994. The key question here is, why was France willing to support this delay in adjusting?

The evolution of the CFA zone suggests that considerations of economic efficiency are poor predictors of when countries will abandon discretionary control of monetary policy. Forgoing the opportunity to have a national currency can bring benefits by reducing transaction costs due to nominal exchange rate variability, but it can also have important costs if a country is unable to adjust to country-specific shocks via changes in nominal wages and prices. The theory of optimum currency areas suggests that states should weigh these two considerations (transaction costs vs. adjustment costs) against each other in choosing whether to retain a national currency. If the CFA states had followed this advice, they would certainly have established national currencies long ago.

An alternative economic explanation for persistence of the CFA zone involves its potential to provide policy credibility. It has long been argued that participation in the franc zone brings significant benefits in terms of macroeconomic stability, because the fixed peg of the CFA franc to the French franc with full convertibility obliges the two CFA central banks not to pursue an independent monetary policy. While this theory is a plausible predictor of regime choice, there is no evidence that CFA governments at the time of independence were any more concerned about policy credibility than were other African governments that quickly abandoned rule-based policies.

Given that considerations of economic efficiency or optimality cannot explain why the CFA zone has survived, I develop a political explanation that emphasizes how state strategies with respect to monetary arrangements are influenced by state objectives in other issue areas. Rather than being free to adopt only the forms of international economic cooperation they find optimal, while avoiding those they find costly, governments in many cases find themselves facing two alternatives: either accept an entire bundle of commitments, some of which are desirable while others are less so, or reject the lot. As a consequence, the sustainability of monetary cooperation is strengthened when states also cooperate on other issues, and when those who might consider establishing monetary independence fear this decision would result in losses on other issues.

Other authors have commonly evoked this argument to explain European monetary integration, and Cohen (1993) extended it to other monetary unions.[1] It also parallels the argument made by Abdelal (this volume) to the extent that he considers how choices about participating in the ruble zone have been shaped by the broader goals held by a country's political leaders. However, unlike Abdelal, who emphasizes the goal of national independence for its own sake, I suggest that calculations of Francophone African leaders have had as much to do with preserving the stability of their regimes. For participating African governments, continued membership in the CFA zone has been inextricably linked to their relationship with France in other dimensions of policy, the most important of which are aid and security. Fear of losing privileged aid and security arrangements has raised the costs of exit for a number of governments that would have otherwise sought to establish their own currencies. As a result, even in countries where economic beliefs held by leaders might have argued in favor of establishing a national currency, there was no exit.[2] In contrast, for each of the three countries that exited from the CFA zone, there is strong evidence that their governments were willing to consider exiting only when they sought to loosen ties to France in all relevant areas, including money, aid, and security assistance.

The attitude of successive French governments toward the CFA zone has also been heavily influenced by objectives in other policy dimensions. Monetary cooperation with the CFA states has been part of a broader relationship whereby France provides financial aid, military aid, and intelligence support in order to ensure political stability for key CFA governments. In the same way that U.S. attitudes toward international monetary arrangements during the postwar period were heavily influenced by broader political goals, French policy toward the CFA zone has involved noneconomic objectives.[3]

1. On security goals in the formation of the European Monetary Union (EMU), see Chang 2001.

2. Later I consider how my argument about parallel issue dimensions relates to Helleiner's (this volume) discussion of economic ideas and their importance for the evolution of monetary regimes in the developing world during the 1950s and 1960s.

3. For evidence of the influence of strategic goals on U.S. policy toward the Bretton Woods arrangements, see Gavin, this volume.

However, the French policy toward the CFA zone does not represent a classic case of monetary entrapment, such as the cases presented by Kirshner (1995) and Hirschman ([1945] 1969). The principal reason is that it is difficult to find a clear national interest at stake for France. But maintaining a privileged relationship with CFA governments has been in the individual interests of an influential group of French politicians and administrators whose careers have been built around Franco-African relations. The fact that these individuals place more of a priority on maintaining political stability in the CFA zone than on maintaining macroeconomic stability also helps explain why after 1980, during an unprecedented deterioration in terms of trade for key CFA regimes, the French government decided to overlook major violations of the franc zone's operating rules. Likewise, a weakening in the position of the pro-CFA lobby in France after 1993 helps explain how the CFA devaluation of January 1994 was finally achieved.

OVERVIEW OF EVENTS IN THE CFA ZONE

The CFA Franc Zone is divided into two monetary unions: the West African Economic and Monetary Union (WAEMU) and the Central African Economic and Monetary Community (CAEMC). Each union is based on four main principles. First, the common currency for the two unions, the CFA franc, is freely convertible into French francs at a fixed rate. This exchange rate peg has been modified only once in the last fifty years. Second, interest rates within each union are set by a regional central bank whose primary statutory objective is to defend the exchange rate peg. Third, each central bank's statutes place a strict limit on government borrowing from the central bank, in order to defend the peg. Finally, in exchange for the right to have representatives on the boards of each regional central bank, the French Treasury underwrites convertibility for the CFA franc by providing each central bank in the franc zone with an automatic loan facility. In theory this convertibility guarantee is unlimited.

The implication of these arrangements for participating African countries is that although the convertibility of their currency is backed by an unlimited guarantee, at the same time they do not have an independent monetary policy, and they have a limited ability to finance public-sector deficits through money creation. While these basic principles have remained, two significant modifications have been made. In 1973, at the demand of a number of African governments, the statutes of the two central banks were modified to reduce the degree of direct French involvement in their management and to allow a modest increase in the amount that governments could borrow directly from their central banks. More recently, in 1994 the states of each union signed a treaty that expands their degree of cooperation to include creation of a free-trade area. However, these treaties have been implemented only partially.

Recent policy trends in the CFA zone can be broken down into two broad periods that coincide with trends in the international economy: 1960–73 and 1973–93.[4] Between 1960 and 1973, the monetary policy pursued in each union was fully consistent with the objective of maintaining the peg to the French franc. Interest rates on central bank lending to the private sector were set at or above French levels, the rules limiting government borrowing from the two central banks were scrupulously respected, and the central banks maintained gross foreign reserves well above the minimum of 20 percent of sight liabilities specified by statute (Figure 4.1). Given that CFA governments had limited access to both international capital markets and domestic borrowing from private sources, this policy also necessitated that they run small budget deficits (Table 4.1).

As evidence of the constraint implied by these policies, several governments were forced to scale back public investment projects, and leaders of a number of CFA governments directly criticized the limits on central bank lending. Mali engaged in a lengthy dispute with its regional central bank over credits to public enterprises that would eventually lead to its exit from the union in 1962 (Julienne 1987). Senegal's prime minister pushed for establishment of monetary agreements that would allow greater independence for individual governments. By the early 1970s, leaders in Mauritania and Madagascar also called for greater monetary autonomy, and they would eventually choose to exit the franc zone in order to achieve this goal. Leaders in a number of states that did not ultimately exit, such as Benin, Togo, and Niger, also called for a relaxation of monetary rules.[5] This widespread dissatisfaction with existing lending limits raises the question, why were only three governments actually willing to leave the CFA zone in order to eliminate this constraint?

Following the institutional changes of 1973, the central banks in both franc zones began to pursue more expansionary monetary policies, and this had a direct effect on central bank reserves, as shown in Figure 4.1. This shift in monetary policy coincided with a period of increased volatility in the terms of trade of member states, as seen in Figure 4.2. Following dramatic increases in world prices for export products like coffee, cocoa, and oil during the 1970s, after 1980 a number of CFA states suffered an equally severe deterioration in their terms of trade.

Negative terms-of-trade shocks had two main implications. First, they led to a deterioration in the current account balance of the states concerned and a loss in central bank reserves. This obliged the French Treasury to ad-

4. For a more complete survey of economic policy choices in the CFA zone, see Honohan 1990; Stasavage 1997.
5. Togo's president infuriated President Georges Pompidou of France by publicly criticizing the CFA agreements during a state dinner in Lomé (*Le monde* 11/25/72). The president of Niger called for a thorough overhaul of the WAEMU's monetary policy during a similar occasion (*Le monde* 11/23/72). The president of Benin also called for a revision of his country's monetary arrangements in 1972 (*Africa Contemporary Record* 1972–73, 65–72).

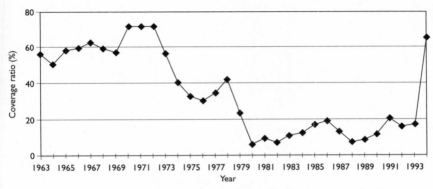

Figure 4.1. Foreign reserve coverage ratio in the CFA zone. Data are for the West African Economic and Monetary Union (WAEMU). *Sources:* Bhatia 1985; International Financial Statistics; Banque centrale des Etats de l'Afrique de L'Ouest.

vance funds to each central bank to ensure continued free convertibility for the CFA franc. What's more, because CFA governments relied heavily on export taxes to generate revenue, the deterioration in their terms of trade also led to a fiscal crisis. The initial response by governments to falling terms of trade was to dramatically increase borrowing from the two central banks, providing a temporary solution to the fiscal crisis but leading to a further deterioration in the position of the two central banks with the French Treasury. Credit restrictions imposed by the French government in 1989 led to a relative improvement in the reserve position of the two central banks, but this measure did not prompt governments to undertake fiscal adjustments because France subsequently increased its level of budgetary assistance, in particular to the governments of Cameroon and Côte d'Ivoire. A definitive solution to the crisis was not decided on until January 1994, when the CFA franc was devalued by 50 percent with respect to the French franc.

Events during the period 1980–94 raise two main questions about the evolution of the franc zone in a period of significant turbulence. First, why was France willing to bear the financial costs of delayed adjustment by the CFA states? Second, why did African governments wait so long to adjust to declining terms of trade?

ECONOMIC EXPLANATIONS FOR THE FRANC ZONE

Optimum Currency Areas Considerations

Economic theory provides two potential motivations for a state to choose not to have an independent monetary policy: reduced transaction

Table 4.1. Macroeconomic Performance in the CFA States, 1960–94 (Annual Averages)

	Inflation (%)			Budget Deficit (after grants, % GDP)			Net Increase in Claims of Banking Sector on Government (% GDP)		
	1960–72	1973–85	1986–93	1960–72	1973–85	1986–93	1960–72	1973–85	1986–93
WAEMU[a]	3.7	10.9	3.9	0.0	-8.0	-6.3	1.5	3.9	3.6
Côte d'Ivoire	3.2	11.6	6.0		-7.1	-12.0	-2.6	-0.4	8.8
CAEMC[b]	4.1	12.2	8.4	-2.6	-2.1	-8.4	-1.2	4.5	8.4
Cameroon	5.4	11.7	5.7		0.7	-8.2	-2.7	1.7	2.9

Sources: (IMF) International Financial Statistics; World Bank, World Development Indicators; IMF 1968, 1970.

Note: Fiscal deficit figures for Cameroon are for 1987–93.

[a] West African Economic and Monetary Union.

[b] Central African Economic and Monetary Community.

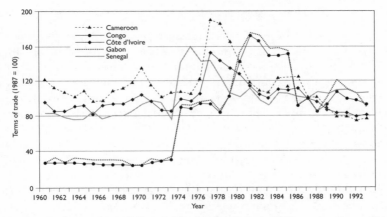

Figure 4.2. Net barter terms of trade for the five largest CFA economies, 1960–93.
Source: World Bank, *World Development Indicators.*

costs for international trade and increased policy credibility. The former idea derives from the theory of optimum currency areas initiated by Robert Mundell.[6] Using a common currency brings benefits in terms of reduced transaction costs on international trade. The size of these benefits depends on how intensively two countries trade with one another. Using a common currency also has disadvantages, because it prevents individual governments from using their nominal exchange rate to adjust to country-specific shocks, such as changes in world prices of export products. The less correlated the economic shocks to which two countries are subject, the more costly it will be for a government to not retain the possibility of changing its nominal exchange rate.

There is little doubt that the CFA Franc Zone does not meet the requirements of an optimum currency area. Less than 10 percent of the total trade of CFA states occurs with other African member countries. When one includes trade with France (since the CFA arrangements also ensure a stable exchange rate with the French franc), this figure for intraregional trade rises to 38 percent, which is still significantly less than the analogous figure for the European Union (EU).[7] Another major reason why the CFA states do not form an optimum currency area is that the economic shocks to which they are subject are only weakly correlated.[8]

6. For a survey of optimum-currency-area theory, see Eichengreen 1994.
7. According to Masson and Taylor (1993), intraregional trade for the European Union (EU) in the early 1990s represented 53 percent of total trade.
8. Bayoumi and Ostry (1997) demonstrated this in a study in which they calculated country-specific shocks by regressing current values of gross domestic product (GDP) growth on lagged values of GDP growth for each country.

Credibility as a Motivation for CFA Zone Participation

Even if considerations of optimum currency areas show that the CFA states lose out by adopting a common currency, it might still be possible to argue that it is in their economic interest to abandon the nominal exchange rate as a policy instrument. This could be the case if it is believed that CFA governments would otherwise face heavy incentives to use expansionary monetary policy and currency depreciation excessively as a means of temporarily stimulating their economies, even in circumstances where no external shock had warranted such a move. The theory of time-inconsistency problems in monetary policy suggests that this temptation may be particularly severe for governments that have short time-horizons.[9]

The theory of time inconsistency in monetary policy provides a plausible explanation for African participation in the CFA zone but one that is ultimately unconvincing. Francophone African governments at the time of independence might arguably have sought to retain their monetary union in order to insure against the possibility that future governments, or they themselves, would resort to high inflation policies. However, credibility theories have two significant weaknesses as predictive theories of monetary regimes. First, work in this area often fails to explicitly acknowledge that institutional changes that are said to improve credibility (such as adopting an exchange rate peg or joining a monetary union) are ultimately always reversible. As an example, if one claims that participation in the CFA zone increases credibility, one needs to develop a theory of when and why it is costly for governments to exit, particularly in light of the fact that there have been four departures from the union. As I argue later, it is difficult to explain costs of exit without referring to political considerations such as sanctions from other states or sanctions from interest groups. The former consideration has been particularly important for CFA states.

The second weakness of credibility theory as a predictor of participation in the CFA zone involves the lack of evidence that establishing credibility was of more concern for CFA leaders at the time of independence than it was for leaders in other African countries that quickly established discretionary control over monetary policy. The writings and speeches by Francophone African leaders from this period reveal two apparent trends. One tendency was to praise participation in the CFA zone but only as a vehicle toward establishing a firm political relationship with France. Nowhere is this more clear than in the writing of Côte d'Ivoire's first president, Félix Houphouët-Boigny.[10] The other tendency was for leaders such as Sékou

9. Following the standard, repeated game version of time-inconsistent monetary policy in Barro and Gordon 1983.

10. In a 1957 article in *Foreign Affairs,* Côte d'Ivoire's first president discussed his intention to retain close political ties with France after independence, and membership in the franc zone is mentioned explicitly as reinforcing this broader political 1957 strategy (Houphouët-Boigny 1957).

Touré in Guinea to call for independence in both monetary and political relations (Camara 1976).

THE POLITICAL SOURCES OF STATE STRATEGIES IN THE CFA ZONE

The weakness of many theories on the credibility-enhancing effects of monetary arrangements is that governments that create a monetary institution ultimately retain the authority to dismantle it. The unanswered questions are, when and why are the political costs of institutional reversal sufficiently high to dissuade governments from choosing this option? One possibility raised by a number of authors is that reversing an institutional decision, such as joining a monetary union, will be more costly in cases where continued participation in the union is linked to benefits in other dimensions of policy. Cohen (1998, 87) suggests that a monetary institution may depend on "the presence or absence of a broad constellation of related ties and commitments sufficient to make the loss of policy autonomy, whatever the magnitude of prospective adjustment costs, basically acceptable to each partner."[11] For participating African governments, membership in the CFA zone has been part of a broader relationship with France that also includes aid and security assistance. These broader ties can help explain how even some CFA governments that pursued a nationalist economic program in other policy areas nonetheless remained in the union.[12] For France, support for the CFA monetary arrangements has also been linked with benefits in other dimensions of policy. While it would be difficult to speak of national strategic interests in the CFA states, a number of top French politicians and administrators have derived personal benefits from the fact that France, through its monetary, aid, and security policies, provides political stability for CFA governments.

The fact that strategies of member states toward the CFA zone have been heavily influenced by goals on other issues has a number of interesting parallels. Nonmonetary objectives have had a significant impact on monetary relations between states in shaping the attitudes of EU governments toward monetary integration, in influencing U.S. government policy with respect to the Bretton Woods arrangements, and in affecting Japan's considerations on whether to promote the yen as an international currency.[13]

---

11. See also Stasavage and Guillaume 2002.

12. I refer to a nationalist economic program as defined by Helleiner (2000).

13. On U.S. policy toward Bretton Woods, see Gavin, this volume; on Japan's international monetary policy, see Grimes, this volume; on EMU, see Chang, this volume; also on EMU, see the contributions in Eichengreen and Frieden 1993.

Benefits for African Governments from CFA Zone Participation

It is not difficult to show that countries in the CFA zone have enjoyed important benefits from their relationship with France in areas other than monetary cooperation. In terms of aid, France has remained the biggest bilateral donor to the CFA states. This aid relationship was important during the 1960–73 period, when CFA governments on average received 2.6 percent of gross domestic product (GDP) per year in bilateral aid from France.[14] After 1973 the annual average increased to 3.5 percent of GDP per year. In terms of the French commitment of aid to the CFA states, the government has been willing to increase aid significantly during balance-of-payment crises.[15] Finally, France has provided indirect aid to the CFA states by lobbying to ensure that a significant share of the French contribution to the World Bank's soft loan arm (the International Development Association) is used for loans to franc zone countries.

The other main benefit that France has provided CFA states is security. Soon after independence, all CFA states except for Mali, Cameroon, and Burkina Faso signed defense assistance accords with France. These provided insurance against both external and internal threats. In addition, France has played an important security role by permanently stationing French troops in the capital cities of Côte d'Ivoire, Senegal, Gabon, Chad, Madagascar, and the Central African Republic. The presence of French troops has helped to dissuade local military officers from launching coups d'état. France's military was particularly active in the CFA states during the first two decades of independence, as French troops intervened on no less than eleven occasions in seven separate states (Nouaille-Degorce 1982).

While France continues to support CFA governments financially, in recent years it has trimmed back its military commitments significantly. French military bases in the Central African Republic and in Chad have closed, as the French government has increasingly supported the use of troops from other African states in regional peacekeeping efforts. French troops remain stationed in Senegal, Côte d'Ivoire, and Gabon, but it seems clear that the French government is now less willing to use these troops to oppose domestic threats such as coups d'état. During the coup in Côte d'Ivoire in December 1999, French troops stationed in the country's capital made no attempt to intervene militarily in support of the existing government. To the extent this decision represents a long-term shift in policy, it

14. Based on OECD (Organisation for Economic Cooperation and Development) Development Assistance Committee figures. The contributions in Michailof 1993 (the published version of an internal French government report) present a thorough review of recent French aid policies. Hayter (1966) presented a review of French aid policies during the initial postindependence period.

15. French bilateral assistance to Côte d'Ivoire during this period also included substantial project aid, as well as World Bank and IMF assistance for which the political support of the French government was critical (Stasavage 1997).

will undermine one of the principal side benefits of CFA zone participation for African governments.

While significant aid and military assistance from France have helped to ensure the continued rule of a large number of Francophone African leaders, it may seem surprising that the maintenance of such close links with a former colonial power did not generate more of a nationalist reaction in the African states.[16] After all, the move to political independence from France had received tremendous support during the 1950s, and in other similar cases, such as the breakup of Great Britain's empire in Africa in the early 1960s and the breakup of the Soviet Union in the early 1990s, political independence often went hand in hand with a nationalist desire to establish autonomy in all areas of policy (Abdelal, this volume). One explanation for the lack of nationalist reaction is that the Francophone African political elite historically has had a very high level of transnational contact with elites in France (attributable to common educational and professional experiences), and therefore, Francophone African governments have, on average, been less motivated by nationalist goals (Stasavage 1995).

This discussion suggests a complementarity between my own argument and that made by Abdelal (this volume) regarding the ruble zone. Benefits in other issue areas such as aid and security can have a significant impact on the viability of a monetary union by increasing the cost of exit. But at the same time, a full explanation of state choices should also recognize that leaders and citizens can have strong preferences for national independence as a goal unto itself, and the stronger these preferences, the greater the cost of *not* exiting.

What Can Explain Exits from the CFA Zone?

The CFA states have clearly relied on France for substantial aid and security assistance, but it remains to be demonstrated that these benefits have been explicitly linked to continued participation in the monetary arrangements. To the extent linkage was a deliberate policy, one would expect the French government to sanction states that exited the CFA zone by cutting off aid and military assistance. In fact, the record suggests that during the 1960s and early 1970s African governments anticipated just such a response from France, and as a consequence, only countries that sought to make a broad diplomatic break from France were willing to exit, simultaneously loosening monetary, aid, and military ties.[17]

16. I use *nationalism* here in the sense used by Abdelal (this volume), meaning a preference for autonomy independent of the material costs that autonomy may imply.

17. Kirshner (1995) noted that if a core state in a currency zone threatens to expel other states that fail to adhere to certain constraints, then a lack of actual cases of expulsion does not necessarily suggest that the threat of expulsion is not credible. States taking actions that would otherwise lead to expulsion may well leave a currency zone on their own initiative precisely because they anticipate that they will otherwise be expelled.

In three of the four cases of departure from the CFA zone between 1960 and 1973, there is firm support for the claim that governments also sought to terminate other types of cooperation with France. This strongly suggests that participation in the franc zone came as part of a package that included aid, security, and commercial ties, and that individual governments had little room to choose to cooperate with France in one area of policy while rejecting cooperation in others.[18] Finally, unlike earlier analyses of Franco-African relations that focused on the "dependency" of the African states, it is important to recognize that Francophone leaders did ultimately retain the choice of whether to accept a "neocolonial" relationship with France or to reject it.

Mali's exit from the franc zone, followed by its reentrance six years later, is particularly interesting.[19] As noted already, in 1962 the government of Mali decided to create its own currency after a series of disputes with its regional central bank over requests for extensions of credit to government and public enterprises. The political problem underlying this dispute over lending was that the French colonial administration had given strong support to an opposition party. Mali was one of the few states that from the outset had refused to sign a defense accord with France. The Malian government at this time made a number of moves to establish close diplomatic and aid relations with Soviet bloc governments, and its decision to leave the franc zone was accompanied by an attempt to reduce aid dependence on France. Mali's reintegration into the franc zone in 1967–68 was an explicit quid pro quo that the French government demanded in exchange for a resumption of French financial aid.[20] Full reintegration did not take place until after a change in regime in Mali following a coup d'état.

Madagascar was another of the three CFA states that chose to terminate both monetary cooperation and parallel agreements with France. In Madagascar, the French government had remained a staunch supporter of President Philibert Tsiranana up to his resignation in 1972. The military government that succeeded him made moves to develop a new political base within the island's growing nationalist movement. Madagascar's exit from the franc zone in 1973 occurred at the same time that the Malagasy government demanded a French withdrawal from military bases on the island.[21] The number of French technical assistants in Madagascar was also dramatically reduced at the request of the Malagasy government (Nouaille-Degorce 1982).

18. It is also important to note that leaders in the four states that exited the CFA zone on average had fewer transnational links with elites in France than did leaders in other CFA states (Stasavage 1995, chap. 5). The fewer transnational links including educational and professional ties may explain why nationalism, as defined by Abdelal, may have been more present in these countries than in other CFA states.

19. The Malian case of exit was considered by Kirshner (1995).

20. Interviews with Jacques Foccart, in Gaillard 1995.

21. Interview with Didier Ratsiraka by Leymarie (1974).

Mauritania's exit from the franc zone in 1973 also occurred as part of a broader political break with France. In the early 1970s a growing nationalist movement in this predominantly Arab-speaking country prompted a change of diplomatic orientation, as Mauritania's ruling party called for the government to "search constantly for a truer independence in all domains" (*Le monde* 11/30/72). The government subsequently terminated its existing aid and military relations with France and negotiated accords with Morocco and Algeria, which had previously not accorded Mauritania diplomatic recognition. France's top official on African policy at the time has since corroborated the idea that broader diplomatic questions motivated Mauritania's renegotiating its existing treaties with France.[22]

The fourth case of exit from the franc zone to consider is that of Guinea, which departed under circumstances different from those in Mali, Mauritania, and Madagascar. Following Guinea's unilateral declaration of political independence in 1958 (independence for other CFA governments was negotiated), to the apparent surprise of Guinean leaders, the French government cancelled all forms of cooperation with Guinea, severing aid payments as well as Guinea's right to participate in the franc zone. While historians have debated whether it was the Guinean government's intention to seek a complete break with France, this outcome nonetheless supports the interpretation that France saw continued cooperation in different dimensions of policy as being linked (Camara 1976; Gaillard 1995).

One common feature for the four states that exited the CFA zone is that their leaders also espoused what one might call a "nationalist" economic ideology. As Helleiner (this volume) noted, economic nationalism in developing countries during the postwar period emphasized the adoption of capital controls and the use of central bank finance to fund development projects, two policies that participation in the franc zone made impossible. In contrast, many governments that remained in the CFA zone, like Côte d'Ivoire, advocated a much more liberal economic program. As a consequence, one might explain state strategies toward CFA zone participation in terms of prevailing economic ideologies.

While economic ideology undoubtedly played a role in pushing some states to exit the CFA zone, it is important to remember that the early 1970s was a period of rising economic nationalism in general in West Africa, and with respect to some policies, several CFA governments (notably Benin and Togo) turned to nationalist economic programs without subsequently exiting the CFA zone. Benin embarked on a state-led development strategy under its new president, Mathieu Kerekou, but it failed to subsequently exit the CFA zone. Ultimately, as I suggested earlier with regard to nationalism of the sort considered by Abdelal, economic ideology is a factor that can raise the cost of remaining in a union for governments that are convinced

22. Interviews with Jacques Foccart, in Gaillard 1995.

that alternative policies would be preferable, but whether exit actually occurs also depends on the perceived benefits from remaining in terms of aid and security.

French Interests in the Preservation of the CFA Zone

We have seen that African governments have tended to remain members of a monetary union in order to enjoy broader benefits of a close relationship with France; but why have successive French governments been willing to provide continued aid and security to a group of former colonies that represents neither a major market for trade and investment nor a significant strategic interest? Even as early as 1969, the franc zone absorbed only 4 percent of total French exports and by the 1990s this figure had dropped to less than 2 percent (IMF, *Direction of Trade Statistics Yearbook* 1972, 1994). While some have argued that support for the franc zone ensures the support of Francophone African countries for French proposals within international forums like the UN, interviews with makers of French foreign policy have demonstrated this not to be the case (Stasavage 1995, chap. 4). This lack of a major strategic or economic interest makes it more difficult to present the franc zone as an example of entrapment, as analyzed by Hirschman ([1945] 1969) and Kirshner (1995), where a dominant state willingly incurs losses from participating in a monetary regime in order to create a sphere of influence comprising a group of smaller states.

As an alternative to explanations involving state interests, several authors have argued that particular interests within the French state have benefited from the continuity of French policy toward the CFA states and from the political stability that it provides for Francophone African regimes (see Bayart 1984; van de Walle 1991; Vallée 1991; Stasavage 1995). It is possible to identify several different types of interests for the French politicians and administrators who are members of this lobby.

At a first level, significant bureaucratic interests in France directly benefit from the continued aid and security commitment to the CFA states. For much of the postindependence period, a number of jobs within the French administration have depended on relations with the CFA states (not with developing countries as a whole). Before it was recently integrated with the French foreign ministry, France retained a separate Ministry of Cooperation, a successor to France's Ministry for Overseas Territories of the colonial period. From 1960 to 1998, the Ministry of Cooperation remained dedicated exclusively to aid and security assistance to CFA states. This was a clear institutional anomaly compared with Great Britain and other former colonial powers, which by the early 1960s had disbanded their colonial ministries and integrated their functions within aid agencies that did not have a particular geographic focus. For the personnel of the Ministry of Cooperation, the continued existence of the ministry as a separate entity was justified by the fact that France has retained privileged monetary, aid, and security relations with the CFA states. One can draw the same conclusion with respect to the personnel who run the Bureau for African Affairs within the French presidency. To this day, the office deals strictly with relations with Francophone African states (no such bureau exists for relations with North America, Asia, or Latin America).

A second type of particularistic benefit also has derived from the maintenance of French policy. The claim of expertise by many members of France's pro-CFA lobby has been based less on training as economists or diplomats than on personal relationships developed with Francophone African heads of state and from specialized training as colonial administrators. This has given them a direct interest in maintaining the privileged nature of France's relationship with the CFA states, because if this relationship were ever reevaluated, there might be a significant reduction in demand for their skills.

Finally, on a third level it has been repeatedly argued that a number of French politicians and administrators have had direct economic interests in Francophone Africa that depend on maintaining cordial relations with Francophone African heads of state.[23] As part of this phenomenon, there have been persistent but unproven rumors that French political parties have been financed in part by African heads of state providing kickbacks on aid contracts.

One of the principal characteristics of France's pro-CFA lobby has been its links to political parties on both the left and the right. Whereas former colonial officials are most frequently associated with the French right, the French Socialists under François Mitterrand also had in their ranks several members of the pro-CFA lobby. This was crucial for the continuity of French policy toward the CFA states after Mitterrand's election in 1981. Although many observers at the time predicted a move away from France's "neocolonial" involvement in Francophone Africa, Mitterrand quickly turned away from career diplomats and toward officials whose expertise tended to derive from personal relationships with African heads of state or from training as colonial administrators (Bayart 1984). In some cases, these officials were associates whom Mitterrand had first met during his tenure as the minister for Overseas Territories in 1950.

The influence of the pro-CFA lobby with the French right is attributable above all to the presence of a prominent faction within the Gaullist Party whose members have had personal interests in Francophone Africa. The faction's creator, Jacques Foccart, was a close postwar collaborator of General Charles de Gaulle, who used links to French commercial firms in Fran-

23. The most notable example here involved the activities of former President François Mitterrand's son, Jean-Christophe, who was a counselor to the French president for African affairs between 1981 and 1992. See Glaser and Smith 1992.

cophone Africa to provide financing for French political campaigns. After the CFA states became independent in the 1960s, Foccart set up the Bureau for African Affairs within the French presidency and directed one branch of the French Secret Services. Foccart continued to figure prominently in French policy making into the 1980s, and many of his former associates played an active role in the Gaullist Party into the 1990s.[24]

French Interests and Macroeconomic Management

The pattern of French interests supporting the continuity of aid and security policy toward the CFA states can help to explain not only the persistence of the CFA monetary arrangements but also their management over time. As noted earlier, from 1960 to 1973 the fixed exchange rate with full convertibility, combined with rules limiting central bank credit, placed a tight constraint on the macroeconomic policies of African member states. At the same time, adherence to a fixed exchange rate did not pose significant problems for real exchange rate adjustment during this period, because of the relative absence of economic shocks. As seen in Figure 4.2, the 1960s was a period of stable prices for the principal exports of CFA governments. Under these conditions there was less threat of a conflict between the stated objective of the monetary arrangements (to promote conservative macroeconomic policies) and the broader objective of French policy: preserving the political stability of CFA regimes. Possibilities of a conflict during the 1960s between these two objectives of French policy were also lessened by the fact that the most vociferous complaints against limits on central bank lending to governments during this period were from the smaller and poorer CFA states such as Mali and Niger.

During the 1980s and early 1990s the two objectives of political stability and conservative macroeconomic policies came into direct conflict, as the CFA states began to suffer from greater instability in their terms of trade. This conflict in objectives was also exacerbated by the fact that the two largest CFA states, Cameroon and Côte d'Ivoire, were among the hardest hit by economic crises. Members of France's pro-CFA lobby advocated use of the CFA monetary arrangements to finance shortfalls in government revenue, in particular for Cameroon and Côte d'Ivoire, in response to a sharp drop in world prices for the principal exports of these two states. After 1986, rules limiting central bank lending to CFA governments were broken, contributing to a loss in reserves for the two CFA central banks and necessitating French financing to maintain the convertibility of the CFA franc. French balance-of-payments support to CFA governments between 1986 and 1993 was noteworthy for the fact that aid to maintain convertibility of

24. The Foccart network has been a frequent subject of interest for French journalists. See Péan 1990; Cohen 1980.

the CFA franc and other forms of French bilateral assistance were extended with little attempt to ensure that CFA governments would take adjustment measures to correct their balance-of-payment problems.

For Cameroon, Côte d'Ivoire, and the other CFA states that suffered from a severe terms-of-trade shock after 1986, balance-of-payment problems necessitated either deflationary policies (including budget cuts and interest rate hikes), a devaluation of the CFA franc, or additional external finance. For a number of years, neither the Cameroonian government nor the Ivoirian government was willing to envisage either of the former two options seriously. Strong support from members of the pro-CFA lobby in France helped ensure that French bilateral assistance continued despite a refusal to undertake macroeconomic adjustments, and despite frequent objections from the officials of the French Treasury, the International Monetary Fund (IMF), and the World Bank. President Houphouët-Boigny of Côte d'Ivoire was able to call on relationships maintained following his period of service as a minister in the French government during the 1950s (Gombeaud, Smith, and Moutot 1992). President Paul Biya of Cameroon made similar use of contacts, notably via France's ambassador to Cameroon, who after his retirement in 1993 would be hired by Biya as a special counselor (Stasavage 1995). The net result was that a number of French politicians and administrators worked at cross-purposes with the agency of their own government that was charged with enforcing aid conditionality.

The fact that the CFA states were finally prompted into devaluing the CFA franc (in January 1994) is attributable above all to the composition of the Balladur government, which took office in France in April 1993. It had fewer members of the pro-CFA lobby within its ranks than had previous governments of either the French left or the French right, and it announced that future French bilateral assistance would necessitate having an IMF program in place (for which devaluation was a precondition). As prime minister, Edouard Balladur was associated with a faction of the RPR (Rassemblement pour la République) party that did not have any members of the pro-CFA lobby as its members, and he replaced several technocrats in key government positions that had traditionally been occupied by members of the pro-CFA lobby.[25]

DISTRIBUTIONAL POLITICS AS AN ALTERNATIVE EXPLANATION

Beginning with the seminal work by Frieden (1991), coherent models have been developed in recent years to establish group preferences on ex-

---

25. On the composition of the Balladur government, see the excellent review article by Marie-Pierre Subtil in *Le monde* 1/20/94.

change rate policy depending on what kind of goods people produce and on whether they buy and sell on international or domestic markets. Here I briefly review several reasons to believe that interest group pressures can provide only a partial explanation for the CFA Franc Zone's evolution. Distributional pressures have clearly been present, and a focus on distributional pressures can complement the argument I have developed about national strategies. However, an explanation that focused on distributional pressures alone would fail to explain why African governments remained in the CFA zone during the 1960s, while it would also provide only a weak explanation for France's continuing commitment to the union during the 1980s and 1990s.

Since the classic work by Bates (1981), it has been acknowledged that economic policies pursued by African governments respond to distributional pressures and in particular to a divergence of interests between urban and rural groups. In most African states rural groups are heavily dependent on exporting commodities, and so have an interest above all in preventing currency overvaluation. But rural producers generally have had little political voice because they are geographically dispersed, ethnically divided, and primarily smallholders.[26] In contrast, urban groups are more concentrated and closer to the seat of power, aiding their ability to organize and influence policy through street demonstrations. Urban groups favor an appreciated real exchange rate to the extent that food imports make up a large part of their consumption basket, while generally they do not produce export products that would benefit from an undervalued exchange rate.

This pattern of distributional politics within African states can help explain why CFA governments during the 1980s and early 1990s fiercely resisted a devaluation of the CFA franc, after the currency became overvalued following a series of negative terms-of-trade shocks (van de Walle 1991). As a result, the interest group view adds to the explanation developed in the previous sections. However, the same interest group theory cannot explain why so many urban-dominated African governments continued to participate in the CFA zone during the 1960s and 1970s, even though participation during this period limited the ability of governments to pursue policies that favored urban groups at the expense of rural agriculturalists.[27] Given that there is no evidence of a general shift in political power within the CFA states from rural areas before 1973 to urban areas after 1973, some other factor must have been responsible for the majority of CFA governments retaining their monetary links with France.[28]

26. This may have begun to change owing to the (re)establishment of competitive elections in many African states during the early 1990s.

27. For example, CFA states could not implement exchange controls that would allow maintaining a higher real exchange rate than would otherwise be possible.

28. For evidence that urban groups were politically dominant in CFA states as early as the 1960s, see Dumont 1966; Berg 1964.

As for the Francophone African states, it has also been suggested that interest group pressures have had a strong influence on French government policy toward the CFA zone. French exporters to the CFA states and certain investors have benefited from a stable nominal exchange rate between the CFA franc and the French franc. During the period when the CFA franc became overvalued (1986–94), these businesses also benefited from the high real exchange rate for the CFA, which in effect subsidized exports to CFA countries. French businesses were quite vocal during this period in opposing devaluation, even forming an association to lobby against such a move.

There is a problem, however, with an explanation that is based on a business lobby. Demonstrating that certain firms had an interest in the status quo is not sufficient to show that they were a major influence on French policy makers. In fact, there is evidence that during the CFA overvaluation of the 1980s, either the French firms that continued to export to the CFA states were too small to have substantial political influence, or in the case of larger firms, the Francophone African countries comprised such a small percentage of their total market that it was not worth spending valuable political capital to lobby against a CFA devaluation (Stasavage 1995).[29] The same can be said with regard to France's continued support for the CFA zone in earlier periods. This lack of a dominant business lobby determining policy toward the CFA zone is, in fact, part of a more long-term historical trend. As one prominent French historian argued with regard to France's initial colonial expansion into Francophone Africa, "The leaders of business or the big banks, oriented towards more profitable markets, did not really involve themselves in this process, and the intellectual elites were hardly associated with it" (Ageron 1978, 267).

CONCLUSION

Many features of the CFA Franc Zone are unique, but its evolution can nonetheless provide several insights about efforts by other states to abandon discretionary control over monetary policy. While today's attempts at rule-based monetary arrangements are often portrayed as technical solutions to a perceived lack of policy credibility, the experience of the CFA zone suggests that whether these arrangements endure will depend heavily on political factors. In the case of multicountry arrangements, when the decision to abandon monetary discretion is linked to benefits of cooperation in other dimensions of policy, such as trade, aid, and security, the decision to abandon discretion will be more durable.

---

29. Major French banks and construction companies continue to have operations in Francophone Africa, but by the 1980s the CFA market made up only a small percentage of their total operations.

CHAPTER FIVE

National Strategy and National Money
Politics and the End of the Ruble Zone,
1991–94

Rawi Abdelal

The Soviet currency union outlasted the Soviet political union, but not by much. In December 1991, when the Soviet Union officially dissolved, all fifteen post-Soviet states shared a common currency, the ruble, and thus comprised the so-called *rublevaia zona,* or ruble zone.[1] This ruble was not yet the Russian currency; it was Soviet, and the notes still bore the traditional picture of Lenin and the fifteen languages of the constituent republics.

The currency union could have succeeded, at least for a while. Many observers thought that it would. A number of post-Soviet leaders wanted it to. The influential industrial lobbies throughout the region supported the union. Russia, by far the most powerful post-Soviet state, intended to keep the ruble zone together to ensure close political and economic ties among the new states. To make participation in the ruble zone more attractive, Russia offered members energy imports at a huge discount. Also, during 1992 officials of the International Monetary Fund (IMF) urged post-Soviet states to maintain their currency union. The proliferation of fifteen new currencies, the officials argued, would lead to the collapse of economic links among post-Soviet states. Even if these links, legacies of Soviet development planning, were arbitrary, they were also deeply institutionalized. IMF officials were sure that their advice was right, and explained that post-Soviet governments would not be entitled to IMF funds if they introduced

1. For insightful comments and suggestions that improved successive drafts of this chapter, I am grateful to Jerry Cohen, Matthew Evangelista, Jonathan Kirshner, Julio Rotemberg, Beth Simmons, Lou Wells, and David Woodruff, as well as the participants in the conferences titled "Power, Ideology, and Conflict: The Political Foundations of Twenty-First Century Money," Cornell University, Ithaca, N.Y. I also thank Lynsey Fitzpatrick for research assistance. The Division of Research at Harvard Business School supported research for this chapter.

their own currencies. Leaving the ruble zone, they insisted, was "economic suicide" (Granville 1995; Åslund 1995).

Despite Russia's initial efforts to hold the ruble zone together, and contrary to the initial advice of international institutions, the ruble zone fell apart completely in the autumn of 1993. In this chapter I explain why. I demonstrate that some post-Soviet governments sought to maintain the currency union, while others never considered their membership legitimate. Post-Soviet governments interpreted the ruble zone in sharply contrasting ways. I argue that the national identities of post-Soviet societies led to these divergent interpretations and, ultimately, to their governments' distinct monetary strategies. My argument departs from the existing explanations for the collapse of the ruble zone, several of which are fundamentally apolitical. Some economists, for example, have speculated that the ruble zone did not comprise an optimum currency area and that it collapsed as a result. Other economists have emphasized the fatal consequences of the institutional flaw underlying the ruble zone's organization. Neither of these economistic explanations is satisfactory.

In this chapter I also demonstrate the insufficiency of the most plausible explanation for the end of the ruble zone that can be drawn from mainstream international relations theory. That the ruble zone collapsed and monetary cooperation failed in post-Soviet Eurasia is no surprise from the perspective of Realist theories of international relations, because their central assumption is that states pursue autonomy and security, despite material costs that result or benefits of cooperation that they forgo.[2] At a minimum, post-Soviet states should have insisted on their own currencies. Yet, even as the ruble zone was disintegrating in the autumn of 1993, five post-Soviet states—Armenia, Belarus, Kazakhstan, Tajikistan, and Uzbekistan—were trying to reconstitute their currency union with Russia. A Realist explanation for the ruble zone's failure can potentially account just for the states that opted out, but not for the states that sought to remain.

The central problem with these three alternative explanations is the *variety* of post-Soviet monetary strategies, a variety which clarifies that the currency union remained viable among a number of post-Soviet states. Some post-Soviet states exited the currency union almost immediately as part of their strategies for autonomy from Russia, whereas others were content to trade monetary sovereignty and economic autonomy for the material rewards of ruble zone membership. Those that left did so in three waves, with the third and final wave coming after Russia itself attempted to destroy the union.

No answer to this empirical puzzle can be satisfactory without explaining how the ruble zone fell apart. That is, a convincing explanation for the end

---

2. On Realist approaches to international political economy (IPE), see Kirshner 1999c; Gilpin 1975; Krasner 1978; Grieco 1990.

of the ruble zone must explicitly address why some post-Soviet states exited earlier and others later, for the currency union collapsed in fits and starts. Only one hypothesis for the variety and timing of post-Soviet monetary strategies currently exists in the scholarly literature on the collapse of the ruble zone: perhaps, some have speculated, the material incentives of ruble zone membership were decisive. The empirical evidence is not merely inconsistent with this materialist hypothesis; the predictions derived from these incentives are, for most of the post-Soviet states, exactly the opposite of what occurred.

I show in this chapter that it was the politics of nationalism and national identity that determined the variety of post-Soviet monetary strategies. In the states where nationalist political parties and their ideologies were accepted by their societies, governments sought the symbolic and real autonomy that monetary sovereignty provided. Where nationalist parties were electorally strong but failed to convince other important political forces, such as formerly Communist elites, governments lacked a coherent strategy and were pushed along by external forces, such as Russia and the IMF. Finally, where nationalists were weak and unpopular, governments dominated by former Communists sought the reintegration of the post-Soviet economic area, and this strategy included monetary union. These domestic political struggles reflected the content and contestation of the national identities of post-Soviet societies, which ultimately were the central influences on the international politics of post-Soviet Eurasia during the 1990s (Abdelal 2001b).

WHY AND HOW THE RUBLE ZONE FELL APART

Russia itself destroyed the ruble zone in the summer of 1993, despite the fact that it had been trying to hold the currency union together since the autumn of 1991. Before Russia's policies changed, however, five states—Estonia, Latvia, Lithuania, Ukraine, and Kyrgyzstan—had already exited (Table 5.1). Four governments—Azerbaijan, Georgia, Moldova, and Turkmenistan—reacted to Russia's destruction of the ruble zone by rejecting the possibility of a new currency union, while the other five—Armenia, Belarus, Kazakhstan, Tajikistan, and Uzbekistan—attempted to reconstitute it.

Early Exit: The Baltic Republics

Estonia, Latvia, and Lithuania exited the ruble zone as quickly as they could (Girnius 1993). Estonia was first out, in June 1992, when it introduced the kroon. Estonians had been discussing an independent currency

Table 5.1. Exits from the Ruble Zone

Country	Date of Exit
Estonia	June 1992
Latvia	August 1992
Lithuania	October 1992
Ukraine	November 1992
Kyrgyzstan	May 1993
Azerbaijan	July 1993
Georgia	August 1993
Armenia	November 1993
Belarus	November 1993
Kazakhstan	November 1993
Moldova	November 1993
Turkmenistan	November 1993
Uzbekistan	November 1993
Tajikistan	May 1995

Source: Adapted from Conway 1995.

since 1987, and Estonian political elites enjoyed a remarkable consensus about the necessity of Estonian monetary sovereignty.

The material incentives to remain in the ruble zone were irrelevant to Estonia's decision. The Russians could not have paid Estonians enough to remain. No one could have. And the IMF and European Community had warned Estonia of the dire consequences of exiting the currency union (Hansson and Sachs 1992; *Financial Times* 6/23/93). Nevertheless, Estonians, who used to say that they would live off potato peelings if that were the cost of independence, celebrated their new currency. On June 22, 1992, at the Viljandi "Ugala" Theater in Tallinn, they held the Kroon Ball to honor the symbol of their monetary sovereignty. Many Estonians bought new wallets to hold their kroons.

Latvia and Lithuania followed Estonia's path out of the ruble zone for the same reason—to achieve autonomy from Russia—and at approximately the same time, during the summer and early autumn of 1992.[3] In all three Baltic republics, political elites nearly unanimously supported new currencies, at whatever economic cost, and rejected the "occupation ruble."[4]

3. See Kukk 1997; Lainela and Sutella 1995. On Latvia, see *Baltic Independent* 7/10/92. The Latvian lat was not officially introduced until 1993. In October 1992 the Bank of Lithuania issued a provisional currency, the talonas, and withdrew rubles from circulation. In June 1993 the Bank introduced the litas, the permanent currency. See *Baltic Independent* 7/2/93; Nauseda 1997.

4. See *Economist* 7/3/93. The industrial lobbies in the three states, however, staunchly opposed leaving the ruble zone. See, for example, Lieven 1993, 356–357.

Out Just in Time: Ukraine and Kyrgyzstan

Ukraine exited the ruble zone in November 1992, later and less decisively than the Baltic states. Ukraine's first government originally had planned to do exactly what the Baltic governments did: introduce an independent currency and reorient the economy away from Russia and toward the West. In March 1992, President Leonid Kravchuk outlined a plan to achieve economic autonomy from Russia, and a new currency was a central component of the strategy.[5] However, internal dissension about the necessity of economic autonomy and an independent currency, including the strenuous opposition of Ukrainian industrialists, delayed Ukraine's exit from the ruble zone until November 1992, when the government introduced the karbovanets as a transitional currency. President Kravchuk significantly scaled back the plans for economic autonomy from Russia primarily because there was not nearly as much public support for breaking ties with Russia as there had been in the Baltic states.[6]

Kyrgyzstan also introduced a new currency before Russia undermined the ruble zone, but its policy reflected a different influence. Rather than popular, nationalist support for an independent currency, the creation of the Kyrgyzstani som, a process led by President Askar Akaev, was part of a sweeping economic reform package designed by the IMF to integrate the country into the world economy. By 1993 the IMF had dramatically changed its approach to the ruble zone (Conway 1995, 40). This policy reversal undermined the institution's credibility among many post-Soviet leaders, and it was able to convince only Kyrgyzstan to introduce a new currency as part of a reform strategy.

Russia Breaks What Remains of the Ruble Zone

By July 1993, nine post-Soviet states—Armenia, Azerbaijan, Belarus, Georgia, Kazakhstan, Moldova, Tajikistan, Turkmenistan, and Uzbekistan—remained in the ruble zone with Russia. None could print rubles, but, for the previous several years, all had been quite generous issuing noncash credit to enterprises within their borders.[7] Price liberalization and Russian stinginess with new notes caused cash shortages that led many of them to introduce ruble supplements, but these coupons were merely temporary measures to create enough money for their economies to function.

5. The plan was reprinted in *Komsomolskaia pravda* 3/26/92. Also see *Izvestiia* 3/25/92; *Financial Times* 3/24/92; *New York Times* 3/25/92.

6. See D'Anieri 1997. Ukraine introduced its permanent currency, the hryvnia, in September 1996. See *Financial Times* 9/27/96.

7. In the Soviet monetary system there were two circuits for money: cash and credit. Cash (*nalichnye*) rubles were used to pay wages and in retail stores. Noncash (*beznalichnye*) rubles were used for credit allocations from Gosbank and transactions between enterprises. This distinction, an institutional legacy of the Soviet economic system, carried over into the post-Soviet period and complicated the monetary transformations of Russia and the other republics.

Beginning in the middle of 1992, Russia attempted to lead the coordination of monetary policies within the ruble zone, in an effort to restrain the profligate credit emission of the other members. The failure of these attempts to organize the region's monetary authority was an increasing source of frustration for some officials in the government and the Central Bank of Russia (CBR).

It is easy to understand why some Russian leaders objected. After Soviet dissolution, all of the region's central banks could loan noncash rubles to their local banks, which in turn could lend to local companies, which then could use the rubles to purchase imports from Russia. Because Russia had a trade surplus with all fourteen of the other post-Soviet states during 1992, these fourteen could finance their trade deficits with rubles that they created themselves. This was quite a good deal for them, and the costs of excessive credit were spread across their economies. Russia, however, paid a price. According to the IMF, the credit and implicit trade subsidy added up to 22.5 percent of Russian gross domestic product (GDP) during 1992 (Åslund 1995, 126).

The Russian government was willing to pay for some of the bill, such as subsidized energy, because those subsidies were under its control and could be used to extract political concessions (Drezner 1999). But many in the government and CBR considered the credit creation of the other central banks to be a problem. Moreover, there were serious internal differences among Russian political elites about whether Russia should expend resources to maintain its sphere of influence, or whether the country should shed the economic burdens of empire.[8]

The Russian government began to reassert authority in the ruble zone in the summer of 1992. On June 21, President Boris Yeltsin warned ruble zone states that they would have to accept CBR control over their credit emissions, and issued a decree that the Soviet-era ruble was now Russian. Then, on July 1, the CBR restrained the power of the post-Soviet central banks to create ruble credit and began keeping separate ruble accounts for each state (*Financial Times* 7/31/92). The other central banks could still issue credit, but the CBR would keep track, bilaterally, of which banks issued how much. In other words, the credit that non-Russian central banks issued was no longer identical to the CBR's: it was still denominated, ostensibly, in rubles, but the CBR now distinguished between its own ruble credit and that emitted by the other banks.

Then in August 1992 the Russian government announced that other post-Soviet states could trade directly with Russian exporters through commercial banks, rather than through their respective central banks. This meant

---

8. These perspectives were epitomized by the political and ideological struggle between Yegor Gaidar, a liberal reformer who argued that the ruble zone complicated Russia's economic reform and stabilization, and Viktor Chernomyrdin, an empire saver who sought to keep the ruble zone together in order to institutionalize Russian regional hegemony and its influence in the near abroad. See Johnson 2000.

that importers of Russian goods needed credit issued by the CBR. After this announcement, credit created by the other central banks was useful only within the state whose bank created it. Each state had its own version of the same currency circulating in banks, though all states had exactly the same currency circulating as cash. Finally, in May 1993, the CBR suspended other central banks' power to create credit altogether (*Economist* 5/22/93).

The beginning of the end of the ruble zone came in July 1993. During the first half of 1993, as the CBR was wrangling with the other banks about credit emission, it was also issuing new, distinctly Russian ruble notes. The CBR refused to include the new notes in its ruble shipments to the other members of the currency area. On July 24, CBR chairman Viktor Gerashchenko announced that all pre-1993 rubles would no longer be legal tender in Russia as of July 26, and that they could be exchanged at a set rate within Russia (*Rossiiskaia gazeta* 7/27/93; *Segodnia* 7/27/93; *Nezavisimaia gazeta* 7/27/93). Because only Russia had the new notes, the other states in the ruble zone were using cash rubles—2.2 trillion of them—that were now worthless in Russia (*Nezavisimaia gazeta* 7/27/93; Åslund 1995).

Thus, only a year and a half after the collapse of Soviet authority, a number of important Russian officials, including some in the administration of President Yeltsin and in the CBR, had obviously changed their views about the political and economic desirability of the ruble zone.[9] Their message to the other ruble zone states was clear. "Russia appears to have achieved the main objective of its currency reform," John Lloyd of the *Financial Times* reported. "Mr. Viktor Gerashchenko, the central bank governor, said yesterday that the forced exchange of pre-1993 rubles had compelled former Soviet republics still using the Russian currency to opt in or out of the ruble zone" (*Financial Times* 7/28/93).

Enough Is Enough: Azerbaijan, Georgia, Moldova, Turkmenistan

Azerbaijan, Georgia, Moldova, and Turkmenistan reacted to Russia's surprise currency reform by introducing independent currencies.

In Azerbaijan there had already been powerful political forces in favor of breaking with Russia and creating a new currency immediately after the dissolution. However, Azerbaijan left the ruble zone much later, in July 1993, just after the Russian currency exchange. The lateness of Azerbaijan's currency introduction reflected the ambivalence of its own internal debate about the political meaning and importance of a national money. Azerbaijan's government made plans to introduce a currency in June 1992, when Abulfaz Elcibey, head of the Azerbaijani Popular Front, by then a political party that had emerged from the nationalist movement, was elected president. President Elcibey withdrew the country from the Commonwealth of

---

9. On Russia's policies toward the ruble zone, see Johnson 2000; Abdelal forthcoming. The best account of Russia's domestic monetary politics is Woodruff's (1999).

Independent States (CIS) and proposed ambitious plans to turn the state's economy away from Russia and toward Turkey and the West. Elcibey's campaign message was nationalist: "Azerbaijan needs to establish an independent state with its own currency and army" (*New York Times* 6/9/92). Toward this end, Elcibey created a ruble supplement, the manat, in August 1992. The country was to switch completely to the manat on June 15, 1993, by presidential decree. On June 13, however, rebels overthrew Elcibey's government and returned the former Communist chief Heidar Aliev to power. Aliev, who remained in power throughout the 1990s, delayed the currency change until late July 1993. The change in Azerbaijan's approach to its currency reflected a broader rapprochement with Russia, as Aliev, to the dismay of the nationalists, returned Azerbaijan to the CIS (*Financial Times* 6/14/93; Swietochowski 1995, 221–227).

The stories of Georgia and Moldova are similar. Georgia had introduced a supplemental currency, the menati, priced at par with the ruble, in April 1992 as a way to deal with cash shortages. When the Russian currency reform of July 1993 left Georgia with the suddenly worthless rubles, the government announced that on August 2 the menati would be the sole legal tender (Conway 1995, 50–54). Georgian nationalists had supported exiting the ruble zone and remaining outside the CIS, but state weakness and civil war kept the state within the Russian sphere of influence. Similarly, the Moldovan Popular Front, after coming to power in parliamentary elections in 1990, had planned to introduce a Moldovan national currency in January 1992 (*Wall Street Journal* 1/24/92). When the Moldovan Popular Front lost power, the plans for a new currency were delayed.

Unlike these other three states, Turkmenistan lacked a powerful nationalist movement urging the country toward an independent currency. Still, Turkmenistan's reaction to the Russian monetary exchange was that it would exit the ruble zone as quickly as possible, and it then rejected the possibility of monetary reintegration (*Financial Times* 8/20/93).

The Failure of the "Ruble Zone of a New Type"

Armenia, Belarus, Kazakhstan, Tajikistan, and Uzbekistan reacted to the July currency reform in Russia by insisting that they would continue to use the ruble, even though they had no way of receiving the new notes (*Financial Times* 7/28/93). For example, the Kazakhstani policy position on the ruble zone was consistent between December 1991 and July 1993: President Nursultan Nazarbaev favored both the currency union and an interstate bank to regulate credit emission among member states and cash distribution from the Russian ruble printing presses.[10]

Similarly, Belarus was committed to ruble zone membership. In 1991 and again in 1992 the Belarusian government introduced the Belarusian

---

10. See, for example, Alexandrov 1999, 65, 67, 156–157.

ruble, nicknamed the zaichik, or bunny, after the image on its face, as a supplement to the Russian ruble to deal with persistent cash shortages. The government and central bank insisted that the zaichik was not meant to become a new national currency. Uzbekistan also remained committed to the ruble zone. And Tajikistan, mired in civil war, was making no plans for an independent currency.

In August and September 1993, these five states, along with Russia, agreed to create a *rublevaia zona novogo tipa,* a "ruble zone of a new type." On August 7, President Yeltsin met with President Nazarbaev of Kazakhstan and President Islam Karimov of Uzbekistan in Moscow, agreed in principle to create a common monetary system, and invited other CIS states to participate (Åslund 1995, 131). Then, on September 7, officials from Armenia, Belarus, Kazakhstan, Russia, Tajikistan, and Uzbekistan met in Moscow and agreed to use the Russian ruble as their common currency (*Segodnia* 9/9/93). The old ruble zone was chaotic and decentralized. The new-type ruble zone was to be orderly and centralized. Russia proposed to solve the problem of cooperation that had plagued the old union with a simple institutional design: all authority would reside in Moscow, at the CBR.

The price of ruble zone membership seemed to be as inflationary as the ruble itself, however. It was not enough, anymore, simply to submit to Russian monetary authority in exchange for the new ruble notes. In November 1993, Russia clarified the terms of membership in the new-type ruble zone. The Russian government declared that the cash rubles would be given to ruble zone members as state credit. In other words, the central banks of the five other states would be obligated to pay interest to the CBR for the rubles as if the notes were a loan. Furthermore, Russia insisted that the ruble zone states deposit at the CBR hard currency or gold worth 50 percent of the value of the ruble "loan." These conditions would hold for a trial period, after which, if Russia deemed the states acceptable partners, the hard-currency collateral and interest would be returned, and the notes would no longer be treated as a loan. In addition, the member states could exchange their old ruble notes for the new, but at a confiscatory rate of approximately three for one. Finally, the members of the new-type ruble zone were required not to introduce an independent currency for a period of five years (*Moskovskie novosti* 11/21/93; *Delovoi mir* 12/13/93; Alexandrov 1999, 172).

These Russian conditions destroyed any chance for the new-type ruble zone to succeed. Russia had changed from a generous leader of post-Soviet monetary cooperation seeking to pay post-Soviet republics for their political acquiescence, to a self-interested hegemon intent on either profiting from the ruble zone or destroying it.[11] Armenia, Belarus, Kazakhstan, and

---

11. In the language of the theory of monetary dependence, in late 1993 Russia sought to extract wealth from member states or expel them; previously it had sought to entrap them, by making membership so attractive. See Kirshner 1995, chap. 4.

Uzbekistan introduced independent currencies in November 1993, complaining all the way out of the ruble zone (*Wall Street Journal* 11/2/93). For more than three months, they had been using rubles that were worthless in Russia, and they could not afford to pay Russia what it asked for new rubles. They were forced to introduce independent currencies. Only Tajikistan, in the chaos of its civil war, continued until May 1995 to use the old Soviet-era ruble.[12]

Belarus, despite having introduced an independent currency, continued to negotiate its return to Russian monetary authority. In January and February 1994 Russian and Belarusian officials made public their intentions to unify the two states' monetary systems, including the significant detail that Belarus would continue to receive Russian energy supplies at heavily subsidized prices (*Izvestiia* 4/14/94; *Segodnia* 2/3/94). Russia and Belarus also announced their future monetary union on the occasion of each of their political integration agreements in 1996, 1997, 1998, and 1999. Their bilateral monetary unification did not take place, however, and at the end of the first post-Soviet decade, only Russia still used its ruble. The ruble zone seems gone for good.

EXISTING EXPLANATIONS FOR THE END OF THE RUBLE ZONE

To date, most research on the ruble zone has focused on the question of why the currency union disintegrated under conditions that many observers had presumed to be conducive to its success. The two most prominent explanations for the ruble zone's collapse are informed by economic theory on the optimal size of currency areas and the appropriate institutional design of a monetary union. Both apply a patina of inevitability to the story of the decline and fall of the ruble zone, but, as the above narrative demonstrates, the end of the ruble zone was not at all inevitable.

An Optimum Currency Area?

Nobel laureate Robert Mundell argued that fixed exchange rates are most appropriate for regions and states that are tightly integrated with regard to trade, business cycles, and factor movements, thus originating an agenda for research into the optimal size of monetary unions—the so-called optimum currency area (Mundell 1961; Kenen 1969; Tavlas 1994).

There are many reasons to doubt that the fifteen states of the former Soviet Union comprised an optimum currency area, despite their extraordi-

12. See *New York Times* 5/15/95. Russia eventually distributed the new ruble notes to Tajikistan for "humanitarian" reasons.

nary economic interdependence.[13] However, the optimality—or lack thereof—of the post-Soviet monetary union is not causally related to its dissolution. That is, none of the standard optimum-currency-area issues (exchange rate flexibility, microeconomic efficiency, and the commonality of economic shocks) had anything to do with the decisions of post-Soviet governments to leave or stay within the ruble zone.

The problem is not merely that the theory of optimum currency areas has virtually no predictive power in general (Cohen 1998a, 83–84; de Grauwe 1993; Goodhart 1995, 452). Concerns about efficiency and exchange rate flexibility were irrelevant to the decision making of post-Soviet governments. Although some observers have assessed the suboptimality of the post-Soviet currency area in order to explain its collapse, Charles Goodhart (1995, 449) still concluded, "No one suggests that the defections from the ruble area occurred because the region was too large an optimum currency area." The material incentives associated with microeconomic efficiency and macroeconomic flexibility were dwarfed by the incentives associated with the institutional design of the ruble zone and the discounted energy imports that Russia linked to currency union membership. Other stakes were much higher.

Institutional Design

There was a striking institutional flaw underlying the ruble zone. The Russian central bank controlled all the printing presses, so it alone could create cash rubles. Prior to 1991, the Soviet state bank, Gosbank, had local branches in each of the republics. After Soviet dissolution, the local branches became the central banks of the newly independent states. These central banks could create noncash rubles by emitting credit. Therefore, at the beginning of 1992, the ruble zone was a currency union with fifteen independent monetary authorities, hardly an effective design to promote monetary stability.[14]

Post-Soviet central banks created large amounts of ruble credit for two reasons. First, each sought seigniorage—the real value of resources transferred to a government through money growth, including that which results from increased private holdings of money and the so-called inflation tax. Seigniorage has inherent limits because there are costs to high levels of inflation. In a currency union, however, the costs are shared by all members. Thus, most post-Soviet states faced incentives to remain in the ruble

---

13. For example, see Orlowski 1994; Gros and Steinherr 1991; Gros 1993.

14. For a focus on this design flaw as the primary cause of the ruble zone's instability and its ultimate collapse, see Sachs and Lipton 1993; Hefeker 1997, chap. 7; Dabrowski 1995; Orlowski 1994; Banain and Zhukov 1995.

zone to gain from seigniorage and push the costs onto other states. Indeed, the unusual institutional structure of the union led to a competition for seigniorage (Conway 1995). As long as post-Soviet governments were relatively indifferent to the union's resulting inflation (and most acted as though they were during 1992 and 1993), they could attempt to take advantage of the other members. Many seemed to try to do just that.[15]

A second reason why the central banks of the successor states created large amounts of ruble credit was to finance trade deficits with other states by issuing credit to local commercial banks, which could extend it to local importers, with the resulting (decreasingly valuable) ruble balances ending up in the accounts of other central banks (Cohen 1998a, 78–80). Thus, governments could orchestrate the transfer of real resources from other post-Soviet republics, and especially Russia, to firms and citizens within their borders simply by emitting more credit.

No doubt the institutional flaw that created excessive credit ultimately would have been fatal to the ruble zone, at least as it was organized between December 1991 and July 1993. But this problem of institutional design is not a sufficient explanation for how, when, or why the ruble zone actually disintegrated. Most importantly, four post-Soviet states—Estonia, Latvia, Lithuania, and Ukraine—introduced currencies while these seigniorage revenues were most available to them, and when they could have transferred real resources from Russia to their economies by emitting more credit. Moreover, the currency reform programs of the three Baltic states emphasized macroeconomic stabilization and, if necessary, deflation. Clearly seigniorage is not what they were after by exiting the ruble zone.

Also, the other ruble zone members were indifferent to the hyperinflation that resulted from the institutional flaw, or at least indifferent enough not to change their policies and exit the ruble zone in favor of monetary stabilization. And even when Russia reasserted control over the ruble zone, at least five post-Soviet states—Armenia, Belarus, Kazakhstan, Tajikistan, and Uzbekistan—were still willing to participate in a currency union in which seigniorage would accrue only to Russia and in which they could no longer finance their trade deficits with Russia by issuing credit.

This institutional flaw is most useful for understanding why the Russian government and central bank ultimately became dissatisfied with the ruble zone members' taking advantage of the currency union, and why they eventually decided to force members to choose either to subordinate their monetary policies to Russia's or to leave the ruble zone. But this institutional flaw offers little insight into the variety of money strategies of the other post-Soviet states.

15. The unusual design of the ruble zone thus altered the usual relationship between seigniorage and currency union membership. That is, the desire for seigniorage is usually a reason to leave a currency union (Fischer 1982).

MATERIAL INCENTIVES AND THE VARIETY
OF POST-SOVIET MONETARY STRATEGIES

Explaining the variety of post-Soviet monetary strategies therefore is crucial because the existing explanations do not provide insight into the timing of and reasons for exits by the post-Soviet states. Although the dissolution of the ruble zone is consistent with the baseline expectations of optimum-currency-area theory and the institutional design approach, the mere fact that the ruble zone fell apart does not confirm those hypotheses. Indeed, the end of the monetary union seems in retrospect to be theoretically overdetermined.

After the collapse of Soviet institutions, Russia continued to subsidize production in the other successor states with energy and raw materials priced at huge discounts, by some estimates at 60 to 70 percent below world prices. In principle, Russia could have offered these subsidies to the other post-Soviet states regardless of whether or not they stayed in the ruble zone, but Russia sought to link ruble zone membership, and political-economic acquiescence to Russian regional hegemony more generally, to the continuation of subsidies. In the early 1990s, post-Soviet governments interpreted monetary sovereignty and continued Russian energy subsidies as a trade-off. The choice was obvious to post-Soviet states, particularly after Russia made examples of the Baltic states, whose societies saw the costs of their energy and raw materials rise from approximately 30 percent of world levels all the way up to world levels after they introduced independent currencies in 1992 (Kramer 1993; Olcott, Åslund, and Garnett 1999, 44–45).

Therefore, one possible explanation for the timing and motivation of exits from the ruble zone is the distribution of costs and benefits from the subsidies implicit in post-Soviet states' trade with each other. An evaluation of the terms-of-trade effects of moving to world prices is a useful way to assess the economic dependence of post-Soviet states on Russia and the Eurasian region (Tables 5.2 and 5.3). As David Tarr (1994) showed, only two states other than Russia—Kazakhstan and Turkmenistan—faced potentially large incentives to move to world prices and to leave the ruble zone, because they were not dependent on energy imports from Russia.[16] Most of the other twelve post-Soviet states were faced with large terms-of-trade losses from independent currencies that, as Russia made clear, would have eliminated Russian energy subsidies. Matthew Evangelista (1996a, 183–184; also 1996b, 175–185) concluded, "It is hard to argue that the policies of the

16. Note, however, that Kazakhstan's refining facilities were quite limited, and its oil pipelines (and train tracks) ran into and through Russia. Goldberg, Ickes, and Ryterman's (1994) analysis of these incentives is based solely on the imports and exports of energy and raw materials.

Table 5.2. Intraregional Share
of Soviet Republics' Total
Commerce, 1990

Country	%
Turkmenistan	93
Estonia	92
Armenia	90
Lithuania	90
Latvia	89
Kazakhstan	89
Uzbekistan	89
Moldova	88
Azerbaijan	88
Tajikistan	87
Belarus	87
Georgia	86
Kyrgyzstan	86
Ukraine	82
Russia	61

Source: Adapted from Michalopoulos
and Tarr 1992.

republics in trying to break away from Moscow were driven strictly by pursuit of economic utility. Virtually all of them stood to lose."

There were clear predictions about ruble zone participation to be made from an analysis of the costs and benefits of membership. Linda Goldberg, Barry Ickes, and Randi Ryterman (1994, 318–319, 313) tallied these costs and benefits and offered a "balance sheet," which included both seigniorage and terms-of-trade effects. In the early 1990s, according to their analysis, Kazakhstan and Turkmenistan faced large incentives to leave the ruble zone and raise their energy prices to world levels and, at the same time, would have incurred small income or output costs associated with a new currency. The three Baltic states "were expected to experience very large immediate income losses," losses that were "unlikely to be compensated." Thus, they concluded, "If there is any prediction to be made from the analysis of the short-term costs and benefits of leaving the ruble zone, it is that [the Baltic states] would try to remain in the ruble zone, while [Kazakhstan and Turkmenistan] would opt for a new currency."

Clearly that is not what happened. Kazakhstan and Turkmenistan—the biggest potential winners from currency separation, according to this analysis—did not leave the ruble zone in 1992. Lithuania, Latvia, and Estonia—among the biggest potential losers from currency separation—did. So, the

Table 5.3. Impact on the
Terms of Trade of Changing
to World Prices

Country	Impact
Russia	+79
Turkmenistan	+50
Kazakhstan	+19
Kyrgyzstan	+1
Uzbekistan	-3
Tajikistan	-7
Azerbaijan	-7
Ukraine	-18
Belarus	-20
Georgia	-21
Armenia	-24
Latvia	-24
Lithuania	-31
Estonia	-32
Moldova	-38

Source: Adapted from Tarr 1994.

problem is not merely that the broadest and most powerful economistic prediction and explanation of the evolution of the ruble zone is incorrect. As Goldberg, Ickes, and Ryterman (1994, 320) summarized, an "analysis of the costs and benefits of independent currencies is yielding opposite predictions from events." Therefore, they concluded, "Politics matter."[17] I take their conclusion about "politics," echoed by other observers of the ruble zone, as a point of departure.[18]

AN ALTERNATE THEORETICAL APPROACH

The politics of national identity were most important in the evolution of the ruble zone. Therefore, the most useful approach to the political economy of post-Soviet money is one that focuses systematically on the influence of national identity on foreign economic policy. I articulate a distinctively Nationalist perspective on international political economy (IPE) elsewhere (Abdelal 2001b, chap. 2), but there are several important theoretical argu-

17. For more on the trade-off between national currencies and continued subsidies, see Spencer and Cheasty 1993.

18. Goodhart (1995, 449) summarized, "Political, not economic events" caused the monetary changes of the 1990s in post-Soviet Eurasia.

ments that can be summarized here and used to understand the diversity of post-Soviet monetary policies.

Most important, a Nationalist perspective on IPE, which explains how nationalisms and national identities affect the economic relations among states, differs from the Realist perspective, which focuses on the effects of statism and the distribution of power. However, there has been considerable confusion on this difference in the field of IPE, because Robert Gilpin equated the Nationalist and Realist traditions of IPE in his classic *Political Economy of International Relations* (1987, 31–34, 41–54). As a result, many IPE scholars have assumed that nationalism is conceptually and empirically equivalent to statism, and that economic nationalism is equivalent to economic statism or neomercantilism. For Realist IPE, statism is a concept and empirical phenomenon that describes the state as an actor with interests distinct from society. In contrast, a Nationalist perspective on IPE is based on the variability of national identities.

The Content and Contestation of National Identity

National identities vary in two primary ways: in their content and contestation. The content of a national identity includes definitions of membership in the nation, of the fundamental purposes of statehood and economic activity, and of the states that threaten those purposes. This content is inherently directional, particularly because nations are imagined to have a most significant "other," against which they are defined.

The other variable, contestation, is closely related, because societies collectively interpret their national identities. Every society has nationalists who attempt to link the symbol of the nation to specific goals and, therefore, who seek to define the content of their society's collective identity. However, not everyone in society always agrees with how the nationalists seek to construct their identity. Sometimes the nationalists cannot even agree among themselves. Specific interpretations of the goals of the nation are sometimes widely shared in a society and sometimes less widely shared. The farther apart the contending interpretations of national identity, the more that identity is fragmented into conflicting and potentially inconsistent understandings of what the goals of the nation should be. Thus, the variable of contestation describes whether the rest of a society agrees (and how it disagrees) with its nationalists.

National Identity and Political Economy

A coherently shared national identity has four primary effects on governments' foreign economic policies. It endows economic policy with a fundamental social purpose related to protecting and cultivating the nation. A shared national identity engenders the willingness for economic sacrifice necessary to achieve societal goals, to realize the nationalists' vision of the future. It lengthens the time horizons of society and government. And a shared national identity specifies a direction for foreign economic policy, away from the nation's "other" and, often, toward another, broader cultural space. In contrast, a contested or ambiguous national identity separates economic activity from national purpose and shortens a society's and government's time horizons.

Economic nationalism, then, is a set of policies that results from a shared national identity; it is economic policy that follows the national purpose and direction. This is clearly different from the Realist understanding of economic statism, which implies neither social purpose nor shared meanings nor a direction derived from historical memory. Finally, a Nationalist perspective on IPE locates the source of economic nationalism in society, rather than in the state. This also means that societies and governments that lack economic nationalism, and whose policies lack social purpose and national meaning, can be explained by the contestation, ambiguity, or ambivalence of national identity. That is, a Nationalist perspective can also explain societies that do not seem very "nationalist."

AN EXPLANATION BASED ON NATIONAL IDENTITY

Nationalist movements rose as the Soviet Union began to come apart in the late 1980s and early 1990s.[19] The levels of nationalist mobilization among Soviet republics were uneven. After the collapse of the Soviet Union, the success of nationalist parties in winning popular support for and implementing their agendas varied as well.

Almost all nationalist movements and parties throughout the former Soviet Union advocated the creation of a national currency for their newly independent states.[20] Frequently, post-Soviet nationalists proclaimed economic "reorientation" as their goal, defined by the reduction of dependence on Russia and economic reintegration with some other group of states, most commonly "the West" or "Europe." An independent money was a fundamental component of nationalists' agendas. Currencies, they tended to argue, would insulate their economies from Russia's turmoil, ensure autonomy from the CBR, and serve as a powerful symbol of indepen-

---

19. The literature on Soviet and post-Soviet nationalisms is quite rich. See especially Suny 1993, 1998, 1999/2000; Beissinger 1996; Laitin 1998; Bremmer and Taras 1997; Szporluk 1994. Post-Soviet national identities are historical outcomes. For a historical-institutional perspective on why they diverged, see Abdelal 2001a.

20. As I discuss later, Armenia was an exception to this rule.

dent statehood. Many nationalists had thought, prior to 1991, that economic autonomy from Russia would bring their nation prosperity. However, after the dissolution, most quickly realized that such a policy would cause economic distress in the short run. The nationalists revised their argument: they claimed that autonomy was worth the costs and that the rewards would accrue to future generations of the nation.

The nationalists' arguments, however, did not consistently convince everyone in society. There were those who demanded that the economic ties of the former Soviet Union be maintained and even strengthened, primarily to avoid economic disaster. Invariably, among the groups that insisted on regional economic cooperation and reintegration were the industrialists and other organized business interests in each state.

These two arguments were clearly incompatible, as were the policies the opposing groups proposed. Post-Soviet societies and politicians were forced to choose: they could side either with the nationalists and exit the monetary union, or with the industrialists and accept regional cooperation under Russian leadership. The political economy of post-Soviet international relations revolved around one basic question: Did post-Soviet societies and politicians agree with their nationalists or not?

As post-Soviet political authority was reconstructed in the early 1990s, the former Communists' reactions to the nationalists were most consequential, and revealing, politically. During the first post-Soviet decade, the defining political difference among the fourteen non-Russian states was the relationship between the formerly Communist elites and the nationalists in each—whether the former Communists marginalized the nationalists, arrested them, co-opted them, bargained with them, or even tried to become like them. These different relationships indicated the degree of societal consensus about the purposes of nationhood and statehood after Soviet rule.

Post-Soviet societies can be divided into three groups based on how they resolved these internal debates, which is a preliminary indicator of the content and contestation of their national identities (Table 5.4).[21] First, there are those societies with national identities whose content, proposed by nationalist movements and parties, was widely shared and, therefore, relatively uncontested. In Lithuania, Latvia, and Estonia, the nationalists came to power and influenced societal debates about economic strategy so that the entire political spectrum, including most former Communists, embraced the nationalist agenda of economic reorientation away from Russia. In Ar-

21. I have coded these societies based on the agendas of their nationalists, the nationalists' electoral success, and the reaction of their other major power center—the former Communists. The nationalists' agendas are proposals for the content of national identity, and the reaction of society—in elections and in the form of the former Communists—is a measure of the contestation of that content.

Table 5.4. National Identities of Post-Soviet Societies: Content and Contestation

Country	Dominant Nationalist Movements, Parties	Nationalists' Proposals for Content	Nationalists' Electoral Success	Reaction of Former Communists	Outcome
Estonia	Estonian Popular Front	Anti-Russian, pro-"European"	High	Cooperative	Clear, widely agreed upon
Latvia	Latvian Popular Front	Anti-Russian, pro-"European"	High	Cooperative	
Lithuania	Sajudis/Homeland Union	Anti-Russian, pro-"European"	High	Cooperative	
Armenia	Pan-Armenian National Movement	Anti-Soviet, anti-Turkic	High	Cooperative	
Azerbaijan	Azerbaijani Popular Front	Anti-Russian, pro-Turkic	Moderate, except Karabakh	Hostile	Contested regionally
Georgia	Georgian Popular Front; Round Table Coalition	Anti-Russian, pro-"European"	Moderate, except Abkhazia, South Ossetia	Ambivalent	
Moldova	Moldovan Popular Front	Anti-Russian, pro-"European," pro-Romanian	Moderate, esp. western Moldova	Hostile	
Ukraine	Rukh	Anti-Russian, pro-"European"	Moderate, esp. western Ukraine	Ambivalent	
Belarus	Belarusian Popular Front	Anti-Russian, pro-"European"	Low	Hostile	Ambiguous, fragmented
Kazakhstan	Zheltoksan; Azat; Alash	Anti-Russian, pro-"Asian"	Low	Hostile	
Kyrgyzstan	Asaba; Ata-Meken	Anti-Russian	Low	Hostile	
Tajikistan	Islamic Renaissance Party; National Revival	Anti-Russian	Low	Hostile	
Turkmenistan	Agzybyrlik	Anti-Russian	Low	Hostile	
Uzbekistan	Birlik; Erk	Anti-Russian	Low	Hostile	

menia, where national identity was also coherently and widely shared, the nationalist agenda also became ascendant, but it was unique among post-Soviet nationalist movements in its generous interpretation of Russia as a historical ally against Muslim neighbors.[22]

Then there were those societies in which the nationalists' proposals for the content of their national identities were regionally contested, with significant variation across space in the mass publics' interpretation of their collective identities. Azerbaijan, Georgia, Moldova, and Ukraine fall into this category, and they demonstrate how the preferences of the first post-Soviet governments after 1991 were insufficient to achieve their goals. This was true, first, because of a failure of societal resolve, since the goals of the governments were not as widely shared as in other societies, for example, on the Baltic littoral. Also, especially in the cases of Azerbaijan, Georgia, and Moldova, internal state weakness and societal contestation of state purpose allowed Russia to influence their domestic politics and affect military and economic outcomes.

Finally, there were those societies whose collective interpretation of their national identities was either ambiguous, incoherent, fragmented, or highly contested: Belarus, Kazakhstan, Kyrgyzstan, Tajikistan, Turkmenistan, and Uzbekistan. In these states, anti-Soviet, anti-Russian, and anti-CIS agendas proposed by nationalist groups were largely rejected by most other societal actors. These six were ruled by pro-Russian, reintegrationist Communist parties (and their successors).

Comparing Tables 5.1 and 5.4 shows that a Nationalist account is largely consistent with the timing of many post-Soviet states' exits from the ruble zone. More specifically, categorizing the post-Soviet societies according to the content and contestation of their national identities corresponds, with a few exceptions, to the three waves of ruble zone departures—early, after the July 1993 reform, and after the failure of the new-type ruble zone. The case of Armenia is comprehensible from a Nationalist perspective only once the specific content of its nationalist ideology is taken into account, and Kyrgyzstan's monetary strategy is not consistent with my argument. The other twelve states fit the pattern quite well, with the exception that Turkmenistan reacted more harshly to the July 1993 reform in Russia than the national identity explanation would have predicted. Thus, the politics of nationalism go a long way toward explaining how, why, and when the ruble zone collapsed. I illustrate these politics with two case studies of post-Soviet monetary policy making: Estonia, the first out, and Kazakhstan, one of the last out.

22. A few nationalist parties were oriented against Russia and the CIS, among them the Free Armenia Mission. However, the most influential Armenian nationalists proposed traditional anti-Turkic content for their society's collective identity. Explicit anti-Russianism was rare. For a review, see Suny 1999/2000, 156–159. Also see Dudwick 1997.

ESTONIA: ECONOMIC NATIONALISM

The agenda of Estonia's nationalists dominated the state's economic strategy during the early 1990s. Its national movement was among the earliest of those that arose during Gorbachev's perestroika. Estonian nationalists enjoyed so much popular support during the late 1980s that many of Estonia's Communists embraced the nationalist agenda as their own. In particular, the Popular Front of Estonia proposed anti-Soviet and anti-Russian content for Estonian national identity, and almost all Estonians shared that interpretation. Just as Estonian national identity was defined in opposition to the Soviet Union and Russia, so was it linked to a "European" identity. Estonian nationalism was pro-European, and the nation's "return to Europe" was one of the dominant themes during this period. The only significant contestation over the meaning of Estonian identity came from the state's substantial Russian-speaking population, which sought at least Estonian citizenship, if not membership in the nation.[23]

Estonian Nationalism

In September 1987, the Tartu newspaper *Edasi* published a plan for increased Estonian economic autonomy within the Soviet Union. The so-called Four-Man Proposal put forward the idea of an independent currency as well. The authors, Edgar Savisaar, Siim Kallas, Tiit Made, and Mikk Titma, went on to play important roles in the development of the Estonian nationalist movement and the first postindependence governments. The Popular Front's first program, published in April 1988, elaborated the theme of economic autonomy, and rather than pushing for outright independence, demanded greater "sovereignty" within the Soviet Union.

At the beginning of 1989, the Estonian national movement consisted of the Popular Front, the nationalist Citizens' Committees, a newly formed Estonian Independence Party, and a number of Communist Party members. All of these groups supported a political agenda of independence and an economic agenda of autonomy from Russia and reorientation toward Europe. The idea of a national currency, especially one that would be "reintroduced" from the years of interwar independence, was a particularly popular component of the nationalist agenda (*Estonian Independent* 9/18/91). In March 1990 Estonians elected new members to their parliament, the Estonian Supreme Soviet. Approximately 70 percent of the newly elected members were affiliated with the Popular Front. The Front formed a new government in April under the leadership of Prime Minister Edgar Savisaar.

---

23. See Laitin 1998. For reviews of Estonian nationalism and politics, see Raun 1997; Taagepera 1993, chaps. 7, 8; Lieven 1993, chap. 8.

The struggle for independence was complete in August 1991, when, after the unsuccessful coup in Moscow, Soviet authorities officially recognized Estonian independence. As the rest of the Soviet Union was coming apart in December 1991, the Estonian government was making plans to reorient the economy away from the Soviet economic space. Even after Prime Minister Savisaar was replaced by Tiit Vahi of the Estonian Coalition Party, which included a number of former Communists, the government planned to exit the ruble zone and "reintroduce" its national money.

The Estonian Kroon and National Autonomy

Estonia introduced the kroon in June 1992 and pegged the new currency to the German mark.[24] Thus, Estonians linked their autonomy from Russia to their shared understanding of the purposes of their statehood; one of those purposes was their "return to Europe" while exiting the Russian sphere of influence. As Siim Kallas (1993, 9), another author of the Four-Man Proposal and the governor of the Bank of Estonia, argued, "In 1992, the Bank of Estonia was accused of knowingly attempting to destroy the current traditional economic relationship with the East. To some extent we did" (also see Sorg 1994). The plan, in other words, was to "break the dominant position of trade with the East" (Kallas and Sorg 1995).

The analysis of Estonia's first president, Lennart Meri, is even clearer. Estonia, President Meri (1993) argued, was rejecting "the last colonial empire in the world." Estonia's money was symbolic: "The kroon is not a piece of paper; the kroon is the flag of Estonian economic and political independence." Of course, the introduction of the kroon was costly, since leaving the ruble zone cut the "umbilical cord" of subsidized Russian energy supplies. But Meri rejected this short-term thinking, deriding "those who would like to be rich today at the expense of our children and grandchildren." A shared vision of the future, derived from national identity and the purposes Estonians ascribed to their new state and economy, lengthened the time horizons of society and government and led Estonians to accept economic deprivation in exchange for their kroon. As Meri concluded, "Money is politics, and politics is money." Estonian scholars who recently reassessed the political foundations of those economic choices recalled, "To have in one's pocket a convertible currency with the pictures of Estonian national cultural heroes on the bank notes, seemed not *less*, maybe even *more* important than to have an Estonian passport" (Lauristin and Vihalemm 1997, 103–104).

24. This decision reflected the ideological context within which the newly independent Estonian state emerged. The choice for Europe implied the embrace of all things European and Western, including the global economy and its normative and ideological foundations. Estonians thus sought to import credibility from the Bundesbank. On this context and how it affected the practices of governments and central banks, see Grabel, this volume.

In Kazakhstan, as in Estonia, a large and vocal Russian-speaking population viewed the rise of nationalist movements in the Soviet Union with suspicion. Both Estonia and Kazakhstan shared a striking demographic characteristic: a large number of these "Russians," many of whom had never been to Russia but who also did not consider themselves Estonian or Kazakh (Laitin 1998). According to the 1989 Soviet census, Kazakhstan's population was 38 percent "Russian," as was 30 percent of Estonia's population. Whereas Estonian political leaders sought to marginalize, and even disenfranchise, their "Russians," Kazakhstani leaders attempted to placate theirs. Estonian nationalists clearly set the terms of debate for their country's political-economic strategy. Kazakh nationalists, in stark contrast, failed to rally Kazakhs (and certainly not Kazakhstanis, or the citizenry as a whole) behind their national vision of a state for Kazakhs first and autonomous from Russia. Kazakh nationalists proposed anti-Soviet and anti-Russian content for their society's collective identity, but the country's political elites rejected it most forcefully. Many of Estonia's former Communists turned into nationalists. Virtually none of Kazakhstan's did.

Kazakh Nationalism

The Kazakh nationalist movement's most salient, recent historical moment was December 1986, when Dinmukhamad Kunaev, an ethnic Kazakh who had been first secretary of the Communist Party of Kazakhstan for more than twenty years, was replaced, on Moscow's orders, by Gennady Kolbin, a Russian with no previous experience in the republic. The dismissal of Kunaev led to what nationalists now call the "Almaty uprising," named for the demonstrations that took place in Almaty (then Alma Ata). Soviet authorities arrested many of the demonstrators, and the Kazakh nationalist movement at that time did not gain the support of the population. Rather than sparking a mass-based movement, the Almaty uprising became merely a rallying cry for the relatively unpopular nationalist organizations that became politically active several years later.

Kazakhstan did not experience a significant nationalist mobilization during the Soviet period. This was not for Kazakh nationalists' lack of trying. Several nationalist groups sought to influence the meaning of Kazakh national identity (Olcott 1995, 279–280). In 1989, Zheltoksan (or December, named for the Almaty uprising) was organized to promote the release of Kazakhs who had been arrested during the 1986 demonstrations. Eventually, Zheltoksan became a nationalist organization with broader political goals, including secession from the Soviet Union. In the spring of 1990, two other nationalist organizations formed. Alash was the more radical, and also more closely linked to Islam. Azat emphasized the development of

Kazakh language and culture and in general supported what it called the "decolonization" of Kazakhstan. In 1992, Azat, Zheltoksan, and the Republican Party, also nationalist, combined to form a broader Azat nationalist organization. In general, these Kazakh nationalists were anti-Soviet and anti-Russian. They sought political, cultural, and economic autonomy from Russia. An independent currency was considered an essential part of the nationalist program.[25]

Kazakh nationalists failed to mobilize popular support for their ideas. Their movement, and its organizations and parties, did not successfully recruit large numbers of Kazakhstanis. Kazakhstan's Communists did not become nationalists and were not pressured to do so by popular support for the nationalist agenda (Olcott 1997a; Verkhovsky 1993). Indeed, Kazakhstan's Communists remained loyal to the Soviet Union, and its single economy, until the end came in late 1991. The outcome of the March 1990 elections to the Supreme Soviet of Kazakhstan, which gave 94 percent of the 360 seats to Communists, indicated that the government would continue to reject the nationalist agenda of independence and autonomy. In April 1990, the Supreme Soviet elected Nursultan Nazarbaev as president. Nazarbaev, who had been made first secretary of the party in June 1989, became the most powerful political leader in post-Soviet Kazakhstan. And Nazarbaev certainly did not support the nationalists.

Indeed, Nazarbaev consistently and explicitly rejected the nationalists' program, calling it dangerous for a state as divided along national lines as Kazakhstan. Nazarbaev promoted the idea of a territorial, civic identity—Kazakhstani, rather than Kazakh—to include all Kazakhstanis, both the ethnic Kazakhs and the large Russian-speaking population. Nazarbaev's administration repressed the nationalists, refusing to allow Alash or Azat to register as political parties. In December 1991, Nazarbaev was elected president of Kazakhstan in an uncontested popular election and held the post throughout the 1990s. His only potential opponent in the 1991 election was Hasan Kozhakhmetov, then the leader of Zheltoksan, who was unable to collect the 100,000 signatures necessary to appear on the ballot. Thus, although the Kazakhstani government clearly discouraged Kazakh nationalism, Kazakh nationalists never appeared to be an influential political force. As a result, there was no compelling national purpose that Kazakhstani society ascribed to its economic activity. The government did not interpret economic dependence on Russia as a security threat. Instead, economic relations with Russia were purely a material issue for Kazakhstan, whose government sought to keep the Soviet economy integrated.

25. On the importance of a national currency in the programs of Kazakh nationalists, see the following sections in Aiaganov 1994: *Grazhdanskoe dvizheniia Kazakhstana* (Social Movement of Kazakhstan) "Azat," 1–3; *Partiia* "Alash," 62–63; *Natsional'no-demokraticheskaia partiia* (National-Democratic Party) "Zheltoksan," 77–79.

Nazarbaev and the Ruble Zone

As a result of his rejection of the nationalist program, in late 1991 and afterward Nazarbaev urged post-Soviet republics at least to maintain the "single economic space" of the Union (quoted in Olcott 1997b, 555).[26] This economic space included the ruble zone, which Nazarbaev and the Kazakhstani government viewed as a convenience and even as a means to benefit from Russian subsidies.[27] Nazarbaev rejected the nationalists' opposition to the ruble zone (Olcott 1996, 63).

In May 1992 Nazarbaev promoted his economic agenda, "Strategy for the Formation and Development of Kazakhstan as a Sovereign State," a plan that did not propose to introduce a national currency. Kazakhstan's sovereign statehood apparently did not require a monetary policy independent from Russia's. Bisenchaly Tadjiiakov, deputy governor of the National Bank of Kazakhstan, insisted, "If we are forced to leave, we will be the last to do so" (*Financial Times* 7/31/92). In February 1993, Nazarbaev explained that ruble zone states "will have to sacrifice some of their sovereignty in this case for the sake of improving the living standards of their peoples and strengthening the ruble" (Alexandrov 1999, 162–163). This way of talking about sovereignty, limited for the sake of living standards, would have been inconceivable in the Estonian political context.

After July 1993, when the actions of the CBR threatened the ruble zone, Nazarbaev finished making arrangements to introduce an independent currency, in case it became necessary. In a speech in August 1993, President Nazarbaev explained, according to Mikhail Alexandrov (1999, 169), that his state was "technically prepared to leave the ruble zone, but that he believed it would be more profitable to stay in it." Thus, the Kazakhstani government continued to support the idea of the new-type ruble zone, despite the CBR's surprise monetary reform in July. As discussed earlier, Russia eventually imposed extremely harsh conditions on prospective members of the new ruble zone, essentially forcing Kazakhstan to introduce an independent currency. Kazakhstan's deputy prime minister, Daulet Sembaev, complained that the Russian conditions were "purposefully designed to be unacceptable," and that Kazakhstan was being "pushed out of the ruble zone" (quoted in Alexandrov 1999, 172).[28] As President Nazarbaev explained to the Kazakhstani parliament, "We made all possible concessions, but now Moscow has asked us to do the impossible—hand over billions of

26. For more on Nazarbaev's support of Eurasian economic reintegration, see Olcott, Åslund, and Garnett 1999, 111–120; Alexandrov 1999, chap. 4.

27. Apparently, in early 1992 Nazarbaev had arranged for a top-secret contingency plan to prepare a new currency in the event that it was absolutely necessary. See Alexandrov 1999, 157–158.

28. See also *Christian Science Monitor* 11/17/93. For more on Kazakhstan's relationship to the ruble zone, see Rutland and Isataev 1995, 97–100.

dollars" (*Financial Times* 11/2/93). Kazakhstan finally, and still reluctantly, introduced its new currency, the tenge, in November 1993.

CONCLUSION

The ruble zone did not simply disintegrate amid the demands for autonomy of newly independent states. Still, some post-Soviet states exited as quickly as they could in their search for autonomy from Russia. The monetary union also was not re-created, though some states, having been ejected from the first currency union, sought to create a second, new-type ruble zone at the expense of their own monetary sovereignty. The region's monetary arrangements were characterized by a complex mix of disintegration, proposals for reintegration, and ultimately the proliferation of fifteen new currencies—some of which were cherished by the societies that chose them, and others of which were treated with skepticism by the societies on which they were forced. The crucial fact about the Soviet and, later, Russian ruble was that post-Soviet governments interpreted it in contrasting ways. The Estonian government considered the ruble a symbol and pernicious mechanism of Russian imperialism. The Kazakhstani government, at the other extreme, interpreted the ruble as a convenience and even as a useful mechanism for economic reintegration with Russia and the rest of the post-Soviet region.

It was the politics of nationalism that led to the Estonians' and Kazakhstanis' contrasting interpretations of the monetary union that they shared at the beginning of 1992. Estonia's nationalists came to power and led the country from the ruble zone. Kazakhstan's nationalists wanted to do the same thing, but they could not convince the rest of Kazakhstani society—or the government—that it was a good idea. So, Kazakhstan remained in the ruble zone until the bitter end, when Russia forced Nazarbaev to introduce a new currency. This explanation can be made general: differences in the national identities of post-Soviet societies led to their governments' contrasting interpretations of the monetary union that they inherited from the Soviets. The success of the nationalists in framing societal debate reflected the content and contestation of post-Soviet national identities. In sum, an explanation based on national identity is the most useful way to account for the variety of monetary strategies of post-Soviet states.

It should not be surprising that post-Soviet monetary integration and disintegration were influenced more by politics than by the variables that economists have identified as the most relevant. The twentieth-century history of regional monetary order and disorder, particularly in the aftermath of imperial collapse, reveals that political motivations always were central. David Stasavage's (this volume) account of the politics of the CFA Franc

Zone emphasizes the strategic considerations of the successor states of the French Empire, including France itself. Eric Helleiner (this volume) shows that ideologies of embedded liberalism and economic nationalism influenced the monetary strategies of Southern states in the years after World War II. An economic perspective on the choices all these states made suggested several plausible alternate outcomes, but the material incentives were never decisive. Indeed, governments frequently disregarded those incentives or interpreted them through distinctive strategic, cultural, and ideological lenses. In the former Soviet Union during the 1990s, those lenses were national.

CHAPTER SIX

The Political Economy of Currency Boards

Argentina in Historical and Comparative Perspective

HECTOR E. SCHAMIS

I t is prevalent reasoning in economics that the salience of distributive conflict is inversely correlated to the level of aggregation. The more aggregate the policy, the less significant the influence of interest groups. Since they cut broadly across sectors, decisions concerning macroeconomic trends thus are not generally seen as responding to particularistic interests but rather as aggregate phenomena that affect equilibria and long-term performance. As a result, these trends are often interpreted as being rather apolitical, that is, issues that do not elicit too much contention in the political arena.

This is usually the case with traditional explanations of monetary phenomena in general—monetary policy, financial regulation, inflation control—and of exchange rate policy in particular—whether focused on regime (fixed parity, bands, floating, etc.) or level (of the real exchange rate). For example, in the optimum-currency-area approaches (Mundell 1961; McKinnon 1962), variation in exchange rate arrangements across countries is seen as the result of differences in the economic profiles of those countries (Edison and Melvin 1990). In much of the trade theory field, in turn, scholars have examined and evaluated exchange rate policy on the basis of its beneficial or detrimental effects on exports and growth (Balassa et al. 1971, Balassa 1984). And, more recently, a wealth of literature in the area of open economy macroeconomics has focused on exchange rate regimes in terms of their effectiveness for inflation control and fiscal discipline (Drazen and Helpman 1987; Calvo and Végh 1991; Edwards 1989; Kiguel 1994; Tornell and Velasco 1995).

As a research program, open economy macroeconomics usually emphasizes the technical consistency and the credibility of economic policy, assuming that inconsistent or incredible programs will generate imbalances or defensive behavior on the part of economic agents, leading, in turn, to weak economic performance and recurrent crises. Concerned with the persistency of inflation in the developing world, a good part of this field has placed attention on the idea that anti-inflation credibility is associated with the adoption of a nominal anchor to the exchange rate. In other words, rules, rather than discretion, and the ability to maintain a precommitment to an established policy course are the best ways to achieve long-delayed stability (Aghevli, Khan, and Montiel 1991).

The problem with this approach (and its language) is that it ultimately masks political implications. These studies for the most part have underestimated issues of political sustainability and its accompanying distributive considerations, as expressed by the behavior of interest groups and the emerging institutional configurations. In other words, this view obscures deeper factors that may explain why exchange rate regimes that lead to imbalances are implemented in the first place; why, once disequilibrium arises, some policies are chosen instead of others; and why binding rules, precommitments, and institutions emerge only under very specific political circumstances, ones not easily transportable from case to case and from time to time.

On this basis, I problematize the idea of optimality in exchange rate policy and highlight the essentially political nature of the institutional devices meant to create policy credibility. I do so by reviewing the political economy of exchange rates in Argentina over the last half-century, leading to the adoption of a currency board in 1991. A number of factors highlight the relevance of the case. First, in the contemporary world characterized by the primacy of monetary phenomena, regimes meant to achieve low inflation by increasing credibility (e.g., central bank independence and nominal anchors) appear to have become the dominant institutional design (Grabel, this volume; Kirshner 2000) as well as the hegemonic ideational blueprint (Blyth, this volume). Seen in this light, the experience of Argentina's Convertibility Program constitutes a relevant case for examining these issues, for the currency board established under this program constitutes a strong version of central bank independence (since the very idea of monetary policy is virtually eliminated) and a strong version of a nominal anchor (since the exchange rate has been fixed by an act of Congress).[1]

Additionally, over the last few decades Argentina has utilized a variety of exchange rate regimes: different types of floating regimes, passive

1. Also, by implementing it in 1991, Argentina sparked academic and policy interest in the currency board. A quick search in the Econlit Database—an index of books, journal articles, dissertations, and articles in books published since 1969 and produced by the American Economic Association—shows more than one hundred titles on currency boards, all published in 1992 or later.

crawling pegs, predetermined crawling pegs, fixed but adjustable rates, multiple rates, and in the 1990s a fixed exchange rate in a dollar-standard currency board.[2] In those regimes the initial values and the evolution of the nominal parity and of the real exchange rate also differed significantly, often between regimes but sometimes within regimes. If nothing else, this record alone highlights the highly controversial nature of exchange rates in Argentina over time, and thus how political this policy can be.

In this chapter, I develop a historical, interest group–based story, where class and sectoral conflict and cooperation are the product of the intensity and directionality of the distributional struggle. To this end, I identify three broad periods. The first one, which covers most of the postwar era until the mid-1970s, is characterized by discrete adjustments of the exchange rate, a reflection of redistributive policies within import-substituting industrialization (ISI) with capital controls. The second period, from the mid-1970s until the early 1990s, is characterized by increasing indebtedness and the acceleration of inflation, driven by the intensification of distributional pressures over fiscal resources, but in the context of openness in the capital account. While exchange rate crises in the first period occurred slowly, the second period shows sudden attacks on the currency through transactions in the capital account, as described by Krugman (1979) and Calvo (1987). Exchange rate crises thus became more unpredictable and the ensuing inflationary episodes more explosive, leading to three hyperinflationary episodes between 1989 and early 1991 (Figure 6.1).

The third period begins in the early 1990s. By that time, hyperinflation, widespread dollarization, prolonged economic slowdown, and mounting indebtedness had reshaped costs and benefits and altered the incentives for coalition building. Preferences shifted decidedly in the direction of monetary stability over real activity and employment, leading to relatively broad support for the Convertibility Program and the currency board. The new approach pegged the peso one-to-one to the dollar and eliminated all discretionary power in the management of the exchange rate, while substantially limiting the use of passive monetary policies to accommodate distributive conflicts. The country's secular distributional conflict, at the roots of exchange rate politics, became more moderate. This moderation was partly due to supporting international conditions and the availability of resources

2. This chapter was written in 2000–2001. While this volume was in press, Argentina's currency board experiment collapsed in December 2001. I decided to maintain the original text, for addressing the failure of the currency board would merit another piece. Nevertheless, in the conclusion to this chapter I address some of the political and economic tensions inherent in this policy arrangement, which provide clues regarding some of the factors that account for the country's currency crisis of 2001–02.

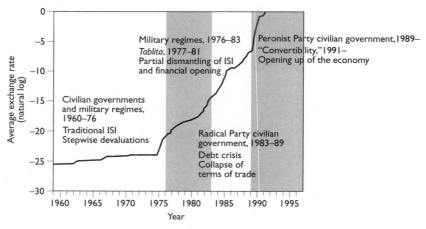

Figure 6.1. Average exchange rate (natural log), 1959–96.

for side payments to some of the affected groups. But mostly it was due to the decreasing power of those who traditionally favored undervaluation of the currency (agro-exporters) and flexible exchange rate regimes (wage earners and producers) relative to sectors who favored exchange rate stability and overvaluation (financiers and groups with dollar-denominated debts).

As a conclusion, I summarize the argument and speculate on the politics of exchange rate–based stabilization more broadly. The stylized facts in exchange rate–based stabilization programs show that the initial consumption boom, appreciation of the real exchange rate, and subsequent difficulties financing the current account balance (which lead to inconsistent fiscal policies) account for the subsequent failure of this strategy. In fact, exchange rate–based stabilization presents boom-bust cycles (Kiguel and Liviatan 1992; Hoffmaister and Végh 1996; Calvo and Végh 1991). While the self-defeating nature of these programs has been amply documented, governments in emerging economies have continued to use them and financial crises have continued to ensue. Trying to draw some generalizable lessons from the Argentine case, I conclude the chapter by discussing three tentative arguments about why this occurs.

INSTITUTIONS, CONFLICT, AND POWER: A HISTORICAL-POLITICAL
ECONOMY OF EXCHANGE RATES

Real Exchange Rate Appreciation under ISI

Despite great political instability, the period from the end of World War II until the mid-1970s shows remarkable continuity in the application of the general policies associated with ISI. In fact, three democratically elected governments, three military regimes, and one civilian but military-controlled government maintained rather closed trade regimes with controls in the capital account. This development strategy was based on the redistribution of the agrarian surplus toward industrialization and the expansion of the state sector, benefiting an urban coalition of domestic-oriented industrialists, wage earners, and public-sector contractors and employees.

The exchange rate moved in steps (Figure 6.2), with periods of more or less stability followed by upward adjustments. Table 6.1 shows the different exchange rate regimes and policies since the end of the 1950s. The stepwise adjustments in the nominal exchange rate were associated with the internal economic limits of the inward-oriented industrialization strategy and its built-in distributional conflict. The exchange rate regime was usually one of fixed (but adjustable) rates, to maintain lower levels of inflation and encourage industrialization. High trade barriers allowed import substitution to be pursued with fixed exchange rates, compensating for real appreciation. A fixed parity was pursued to keep a steady price in industrial inputs and capital goods.

In addition, as Braun and Joy (1968) and Díaz-Alejandro (1963) noted, given that Argentina's exports consisted mainly of food products (or "wage goods" in Ricardian terminology), a devaluation would put pressure on industrial wages. Therefore, under ISI a fixed exchange rate was the preferred alternative for industrialists and urban workers, in contrast to the export-oriented agricultural sector, which supported a competitive exchange rate. The periodic overvaluation of the real exchange rate caused by the fixed nominal parity and the general bias of economic policy toward the protection of industry were meant to provide important disincentives for agriculture (see Little, Scitovsky, and Scott 1970; Balassa et al. 1971).[3]

The limits of ISI recurrently led to balance-of-payment crises and devaluations. The stop-and-go nature of ISI was accompanied by cycles of repression and loosening in the exchange rate. The acceleration of growth led to

3. Relatively high prices for cereals and beef during the 1950s (as a result of the Korean War) and during the 1970s (linked to worldwide stimulative Keynesian policies and the oil crisis) alleviated the impact of an overvalued currency. It should also be noted that different agricultural groups in Argentina during this period had a domestic orientation and, thus, economic incentives similar to those of the urban-industrial coalition.

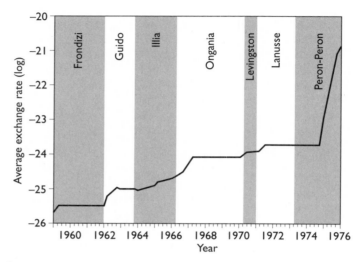

Figure 6.2. Average exchange rate (log), during period of traditional import-substituting industrialization (1959–76). Names indicate reigning presidents.

decreasing exports (because a larger percentage of the wage goods were consumed internally owing to growing incomes) and increasing imports (especially inputs and capital goods to sustain the expansion of the manufacturing sector), generating balance-of-payment crises when official external reserves reached low levels. At times, the constraints inherent in the development strategy were magnified by external shocks, and external crises occurred even when the economy was not expanding fast. In either scenario, owing to existing capital controls, exchange rate crises during most of this period developed at a relatively slow pace, following the decline in reserves caused by the gradual deterioration of the trade balance (Di Tella 1987).

But there was also a political limit, set by the distributive dispute over domestic income between industrialists and wage earners. Under elected governments, especially Peronist ones, labor's influence tended to increase, generally leading to higher wages (Figure 6.3). Frequently, this took place in the context of accommodating monetary policies that fueled inflation and created the conditions for the recurrence of balance-of-payment crises. When the inherent limits of the development strategy converged with growing wage pressures, important industrial groups and part of the middle classes abandoned the original ISI coalition and sided with agrarian interests and the military in the coming coup against the civilian government. High levels of inflation, international reserves insufficient to sustain normal levels of imports and to service the external debt, and growing social

Table 6.1. Exchange Rate Regimes

ISI[a] Period

   1959: important devaluation
   1960–61: dirty float
   1961: fixed exchange regime
   First quarter 1962: important devaluation
   First quarter 1962–first quarter 1967: flexible exchange rate under different
      governments
   First quarter 1967–first half 1970: strong initial devaluation and then fixed ex-
      change rate
   Mid-1970–first quarter 1973: multiple exchange rates with a changing mix of
      commercial and financial rates for different transactions
   Second quarter 1973–last quarter 1974: fixed exchange rate
   Last quarter 1974: strong devaluation
   Second quarter 1975: another strong devaluation (el "Rodrigazo") (transition
      toward the inflationary period)

Inflationary Period

   March 1976–December 1978: passive crawling peg
   December 1978–first quarter 1981: preannounced sliding peg (*tablita*); system
      collapse in 1981
   First quarter 1981–June 1985: floating exchange rate, adjusted passively to in-
      flation, until Austral Plan of June 1985
   June 1985–first quarter 1991: four different attempts at fixing or controlling to
      some degree the exchange rate (Austral and Primavera plans during the Al-
      fonsín administration and programs implemented by Nestor Rapanelli and
      Erman Gonzalez during the Menem administration), all ending in episodes
      of sharp devaluation and very high inflation.

Stability

   March 1991–2001: the Convertibility Plan, which pegged the peso to the dollar
      one-to-one and transformed the central bank into a quasi-currency board.

---

[a] Import-substituting industrialization.

unrest were the reasons often invoked by the military to justify a political intervention that, as was typically claimed, would "reestablish order and clean up public finances."

A paradigmatic illustration of these cycles can be seen in the 1973–76 Peronist government. Its economic program represented the culmination of the ISI strategy of development: it established a fixed exchange rate while at the same time it instituted price controls, increased wages and salaries, and implemented active fiscal and monetary policies to foster in-dustrial activity and employment. This imbalanced mix was helped initially

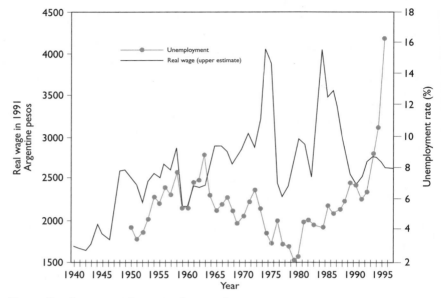

Figure 6.3. Average real wage and unemployment rate, 1940–95.

by an important improvement in the terms of trade, which were at an all-time high (Figure 6.4). During this period the industrial sector reached its largest participation in gross domestic product (GDP), real wages climbed to the highest level for the whole half-century, and unemployment stood below 4 percent (see Figure 6.3).

By mid-1974, however, political and economic conditions began to deteriorate rapidly. The exchange rate peg continued during the third quarter of 1974, but by 1975 the terms of trade had declined significantly and the economy entered into a recession. The government tried stimulative fiscal and monetary policy, but this only fueled inflation, making the real exchange rate decline even further. The deterioration of the external accounts forced sharp adjustments of the exchange rate in the last quarter of 1974 and in the second quarter of 1975, this last one becoming the first of a series of "maxi-devaluations." In a setting marked by deteriorating economic conditions, political uncertainty, and escalating violence, the Peronist government was toppled by a coup in March 1976. From then onward there was a steady decline in the participation of industry in GDP, a fall in real wages, and the termination of the entire ISI experience. With that, a new phase of exchange rate policies and politics began.

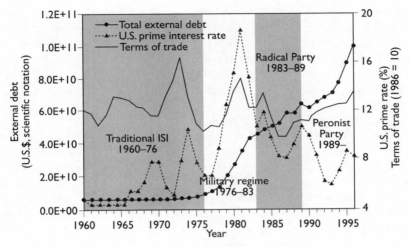

Figure 6.4. External debt, world interest rates, and terms of trade, 1960–96.

Inflation, Indebtedness, and Capital Account Liberalization

Upon coming to office, the military government was expected to deliver economic policies broadly in line with previous authoritarian regimes: pro-agriculture, antilabor, and suspicious of import substituters aligned with Peronism. Simultaneously, the new authoritarian regime advanced a novel interpretation of the country's recurrent political crises: they were seen as the straightforward consequence of protracted ISI. Allegedly, protectionism in the manufacturing sector had swollen inefficient domestic industry and thus artificially strengthened unions, which radicalized their demands in the process. The new minister of the economy, a prominent member of the agro-export and financial elite, persuaded top military leaders of this connection. His approach was appealing for the armed forces: across-the-board liberalization would seek not just to allocate resources more efficiently but also to discipline hypermobilized organized groups, decompose the social base of populism, and restore order (Canitrot 1980).

Accordingly, by April 1976 the authorities had devalued the currency, liberalized prices, frozen wages, and reduced export taxes and import tariffs. In June 1977 additional measures deregulated the banking industry by easing the entry of new financial institutions, reducing reserve requirements, freeing interest rates, and redirecting public-sector borrowing toward private credit markets. As a result, real interest rates became positive, leading to a considerable slowdown in 1978. Although the economic environment was harsh on several sections of the inward-oriented manufacturing sector, the military government nevertheless supported different industrial sectors through increasing military expenditures and public contracts and a generous program of fiscal incentives. This system of subsidies represented a heavy burden on the budget, leading to large fiscal deficits and inflation levels above the historical average (with the exception of the inflationary peaks of 1975–76), all of this compounded by the Tanzi effect on tax collection (World Bank 1988).

With inflation unabated at around 150 percent, the government launched a new program in December 1978, the cornerstone of which was an exchange rate policy based on an active crawling peg (Rodriguez 1982). The *tablita*, as it came to be known, consisted of a series of preannounced devaluations based on a declining rate of inflation. With the *tablita* came the elimination of restrictions on trade and, unprecedentedly, the opening of the capital account. Through these measures the government expected to bring domestic interest rates, deemed too high, in line with international ones adjusted by country risk and the rate of devaluation. This new approach implied important changes in the relationship between broad money and international reserves before and after 1978 (Figure 6.5). While, with capital controls, governments could maintain ratios of 10 to 25 units of domestic money per unit of international reserves, the opening up of the capital account appears to have forced a very specific ratio (about three to one) between these two variables, generating exchange rate crises every time the ratio increased over that value.

The preannounced exchange rate, set at levels below the rate of inflation so as to reduce inflationary expectations, increased real appreciation. With trade and financial liberalization, this new competitive environment put pressure on manufacturing firms, especially those in the consumer-oriented ISI sector. Domestic real interest rates higher than international ones and the exchange rate risk offset by the *tablita* generated massive inflows of capital and drove firms into dollar-denominated debt, either to keep their operations afloat or to engage in arbitrage. Characteristic of exchange rate–based stabilization programs, appreciation and the oversupply of foreign credit financed a consumption boom of imports that was instrumental in gathering support among otherwise castigated middle sectors, precisely during the most coercive phase of the military regime. As a result, private external debt increased from $4 billion in 1978 to $9 billion in 1979, leading to a threefold increase in total (private and public) debt between 1978 and 1981. Most private debt was concentrated among large firms and banks, one-third of it with ten banks and ten industrial firms (Petrei and Tybout 1985).

At the time, Argentina, along with Chile, pioneered the liberalization of cross-border capital flows in Latin America, opening a new chapter in the region's political economy. From 1978 on, attacks on the currency through

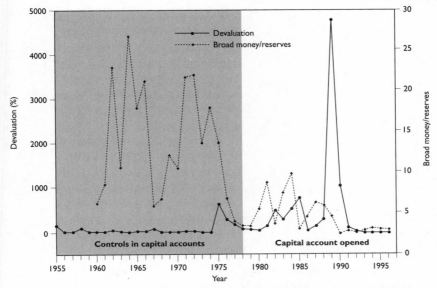

Figure 6.5. Ratio of broad money to international reserves and devaluation, 1955–96.

transactions on the capital account could deplete international reserves suddenly. This began to occur as early as 1980, when the fast deterioration of the balance of payments highlighted the flaws of the predetermined exchange rate and, combined with increases in international interest rates in 1981, led to massive outflows of capital in anticipation of a future devaluation. The government devalued the peso in February 1981 by 10 percent, and again in April and June of that year by more than 20 percent each time.

Given the accumulation of dollar-denominated debt in the private sector, these devaluations exacerbated problems in the real economy, leading to the collapse of several important banks and financial institutions, fifty-nine between March 1980 and December 1981 alone (Giorgio and Sagari 1996). During 1981–82, the central bank enacted a program by which private debtors could transfer their obligations to the state. The government had borrowed in international markets to defend the value of the currency, and when this was no longer possible, it absorbed, under pressure from international banks and domestic financial-industrial conglomerates, an important share of the private external debt. Rescuing the banking sector generated even larger deficits that, when monetized in a context of an open capital account, contributed to wiping out foreign exchange reserves rapidly. Inflation, which had declined to close to 100 percent in 1979–80,

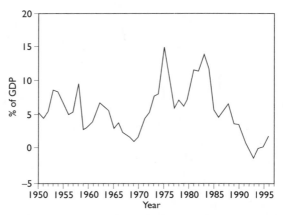

Figure 6.6. Fiscal deficit as percentage of GDP, 1950–96.

jumped back up to about 170 percent in 1981, 163 percent in 1982, and 345 percent in 1983 (see Figure 6.6 for fiscal deficits).

Similar trends in exchange rate management and associated policies were maintained after 1983, when the democratization process brought Raúl Alfonsín to office that December. Though the new government reduced the size of the fiscal deficit, it still remained in double digits. Wages, which had already recovered somewhat in 1983, were raised further in 1984, almost reaching the peak of 1974 in real terms (see Figure 6.3). Consequently, inflation accelerated, reaching 600 percent in 1984 and 1985. In June of that year, a new anti-inflation program was implemented, the Austral Plan. The program included a fixed exchange rate, along with several fiscal and monetary adjustments. The deficit was brought down from 12 percent in 1984 to the 5 to 6 percent range for the next three years. Inflation declined to double digits in 1986. Although advances in fiscal and monetary discipline and inflation reduction were important in comparison to previous years, they did not go far enough to bring the macroeconomy under control. Eventually, the exchange rate had to be readjusted after three quarters from the initial peg, and then it was changed periodically.

The Austral Plan had a political impact. The traditional effect of stabilization plans that utilize the exchange rate as anchors, and lead to consumption booms and sharp declines in inflation, kicked in just in time, helping the party in government to consolidate its position in Congress. However, this bonanza proved short-lived. First, in 1986 commodity prices collapsed, adding pressure to the balance of payments and the fiscal sector. Second, the government was unable, or unwilling, to dismantle the system of subsidies associated with public contracts and the regime of industrial promotion, which by 1987–88 represented 2 percent of GDP and more than half of the nonfinancial fiscal deficit (World Bank 1993a). And third, because of the above, the exchange rate–based stabilization plan moved from the "boom" to the "bust" phase more rapidly than otherwise expected.

Another attempt to recover stability by fixing the exchange rate took place in the second half of 1988 through yet another program, the so-called Plan Primavera, though without much credibility left. As long as the government was determined to maintain the nominal anchor and the capital account remained open, the central bank was forced to intervene in currency markets, eroding its reserves. This process accelerated as of January 1989, when the realization that the macroeconomic imbalances were unsustainable led to massive runs against the currency, flight from money, and other forms of financial adaptation. In early February the situation deteriorated even more dramatically. Central bank authorities suspended foreign exchange auctions, unexpectedly ending their commitment to exchange rate stability. The largest corporations responded to this unforeseen (and unconsulted) decision with a concerted run to the dollar, which caused the virtual collapse of the price system in domestic currency.[4] At that point, the attack on the currency had become a political gesture, to the extent that financial media described it as a "market coup." (See Figures 6.7 and 6.8 for changes in exchange rate and inflation.)

From Hyperinflation to Stability

Plan Primavera collapsed in early 1989 with another maxi-devaluation. The transition between the outgoing Radical administration and the incoming Peronist one was characterized by great uncertainty. The accumulated imbalances of the Alfonsín government, along with doubts about the economic policies of the new government, led to hyperinflation by mid-1989. Chaotic social conditions forced Alfonsín to transfer government well before originally scheduled. The *quarterly* rate of devaluation was 816 percent in the second quarter and almost 370 percent in the third quarter, already in the administration of Carlos Menem, and the inflation rate exceeded 3,000 percent for the year.

The initial economic program implemented by the new government ended up in economic turbulence as well. The pattern of short-lived programs that attempted to fix the exchange rate, only to end in an inflationary explosion, continued during the first eighteen months of the Menem administration. In addition to the hyperinflation of 1989, the new govern-

---

4. In author interviews with members of the Argentine Bank Association (ADEBA) and representatives of large industrial conglomerates at the time, several of them admitted that there was a widespread feeling that "something drastic had to be done in order to make politicians understand that the business community would no longer tolerate unpredictability."

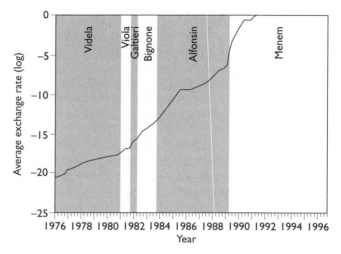

Figure 6.7. Average exchange rate (log) from period of high inflation to stability, 1976–96. Names indicate reigning presidents.

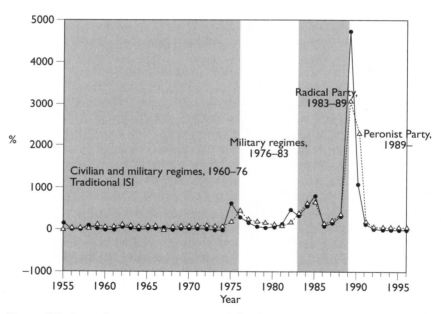

Figure 6.8. Annual average percentage of devaluation and inflation (consumer price index [CPI]), 1955–96.

ment experienced two other similar episodes: one of full hyperinflation in 1990, with a quarterly inflation rate of 334 percent and a devaluation of 267 percent, and another of very high inflation in the first quarter of 1991, with a quarterly inflation rate of 39 percent and a devaluation of 60 percent.

Nevertheless, these failed programs established the foundation for a period of stability that began in March 1991. A few factors need to be highlighted. First, the process of privatization and fiscal consolidation began in earnest. In the second half of 1989 two important pieces of legislation were approved: the Economic Emergency Law and the State Reform Law, which suspended subsidies and fiscal incentives for industrial groups and established the framework for the privatization of public enterprises. Also in March 1990 additional strong measures were taken to reduce public expenditures and increase tax receipts.

Second, in January 1990, the "Plan Bonex" converted short-term assets in the hands of the public (mainly banking deposits and public debt) into a ten-year bond denominated in dollars. Although these measures brought confidence in the financial system down to an all-time low, they helped to reduce interest payments and some quasi-fiscal expenditures by the central bank. Also in March 1990 the central bank was prohibited from issuing rediscounts, in general, and from lending to the government for operational expenditures. Third, the large trade surplus (linked in part to the recessionary economy) and the fact that payments on the external debt were delayed allowed the central bank to replenish its foreign exchange reserves, a key development for the subsequent implementation of the currency board.

In March 1991, the third period in terms of exchange rate behavior began, characterized by exchange rate and price stability. The halting efforts at opening up the economy, controlling fiscal deficits, privatizing public enterprises, and deregulating markets that had been erratically initiated and then abandoned since the second half of the 1970s began to be pursued more firmly after 1989 and were finally implemented in full in 1991. On this basis, the cornerstone of the anti-inflationary program consisted of the exchange rate policy, as defined in the Convertibility Law passed by Congress in March 1991. This plan pegged the peso to the dollar one-to-one, and transformed the monetary and exchange rate functions of the central bank into a currency board. The law directed the central bank to maintain liquid international reserves to cover 100 percent of the *monetary base*. In consequence, the monetary authorities could not increase this aggregate except when international reserves expanded (through trade surplus or net capital inflows). Since then the exchange rate has remained fixed (until the time of this writing, November 2001), by far the longest period of exchange rate stability in half a century. The fixed exchange rate survived the Mexican devaluation of 1994–95 and the financial crises in Asia, Russia, and Brazil, and it was still holding after a change of government and party in the 1999 election.

THE CURRENCY BOARD

Several economic and political factors account for the emergence and sustainability of the currency board. Key questions to bear in mind are why other options, such as a band or a floating regime, were not considered, and how, for the first time in half a century, the current arrangement has become sustainable for over a decade. The main considerations to answer these questions include the emergence of broad-based support for stability; a strong preference among top policymakers for a strong legal-institutional framework that would settle the rules-versus-discretion tension decidedly in favor of the former; and the fact that the distributive disputes over factor returns (capital and labor), sectoral incomes (agriculture vs. industry), and fiscal resources (subsidies), all of which were key elements behind major devaluations in the past, had become more muted toward the 1990s.

The Institutional-Ideational Dimension: Signaling Credibility

The Argentine economic crisis of the late 1980s, whose most visible symptom was hyperinflation, opened a "window for reform."[5] In the market, the crisis had enhanced the structural power of the large industrial conglomerates and mobile asset sectors. In the political arena, in turn, coping with that crisis gave the newly elected president an unprecedented opportunity for centralizing authority in his office. Taking office earlier owing to the magnitude of the crisis, a context that made the period reminiscent of the interval between the election and the inauguration of Franklin Roosevelt between November 1932 and March 1933, Menem moved swiftly toward the expansion of presidential discretion. Accordingly, as already discussed, the first two presidential initiatives sent to Congress were the State Reform Law, which opened the way for the privatization of state-owned enterprises, and the Economic Emergency Law, by which the legislature delegated broad decision-making power to the executive branch. Subsequently, in December 1989, the governing party obtained congressional majority, and by April 1990, the president, appointing six members, had managed to pack the Supreme Court.

In the minds of the main members of the economic team, this period of "extraordinary policy-making" based on increased executive authority was necessary to make a "credible commitment," along the lines described by Sargent (1992), regarding the government's decision to fight inflation. With the memories of the "market coup" still very fresh, the main goal be-

---

5. The term is borrowed from Kingdon (1984) and Keeler (1993). Keeler focused on the effects of deep economic crises in triggering reforms in a number of cases across regions, an argument consistent with that of Hirschman 1985 and Drazen and Grilli 1993.

hind embracing strict macroeconomic discipline to enhance credibility was based on the idea, widely shared by key policymakers, that signaling the largest corporations was necessary to eventually "strike a deal" with them, which in turn was a condition to make disinflation durable.[6]

This setting, however, shows the highly political and self-fulfilling nature of attempts to "create credibility," as Grabel (1997) suggested. To the extent that the largest corporations were capable of resorting again to massive and coordinated capital flight, signaling them in order to become credible was as simple as going along with their revealed preference. The Menem government understood this from day one. Paradoxically, designing rule-based, institutionalized policy-making routines was achieved largely by means of a significant concentration of discretion in the executive branch, particularly in the hands of the president and his finance minister. This may stand in flagrant contradiction with much of the rules-versus-discretion literature, but it was perfectly natural for the Argentine political and policy elites of the 1990s. Furthermore, to the extent that state building by definition implies the centralization of political authority—and much of the marketization drive and its accompanying institutional redesign process qualify as such—this is hardly paradoxical if one uses the analytical tools provided by state formation literature (Schamis 2002).

The decision to adopt a currency board has to be examined in this light. The currency board was established by the Convertibility Law sanctioned by Congress in March 1991. This law, virtually the only piece of the comprehensive reform program of the Menem administration that was not implemented by executive decree,[7] mandates full convertibility between domestic and foreign currency and stipulates that an act of the legislature is required to change the nominal value of the exchange rate. This institutional device locks in the fixed exchange rate regime, for it forces a minister who wants to devalue the currency to face two equally complicated options. One is to ask Congress to sanction the new parity, which risks a rapid loss of reserves while the parliamentary debate takes place. The other option is to stop exchanging dollars for pesos (e.g., through a bank holiday while Congress is deliberating), which opens the possibility of legal charges, given that the law mandates the obligation to exchange dollars and pesos.

The precommitment features of the Convertibility Law, however, went beyond the exchange rate and limited the credit that the central bank could freely create for the public and the private sector. In fact, this strict monetary framework was more important for price stability than the fixed parity itself, to the extent that it did not allow, as had often happened in the past, the monetization of sectoral disputes.

6. Author interviews with high officials of the economy and foreign ministries.
7. See Ferreira Rubio and Goretti 1996.

The Social Basis of Price and Exchange Rate Stability: Politics after Hyperinflation and Dollarization

A look at the institutional configuration of the currency board highlights the need to explore why this strong precommitment device was not used before. The main argument here is that previous peaks of hyperinflation and the ongoing dollarization were conducive to the creation of a broad constituency in favor of stability, providing political support to the currency board.

This constituency included groups that could experience important economic losses in case of depreciation of the exchange rate, such as those indebted in dollars. Table 6.2 shows the jump in dollar-denominated debts. Credit in dollars in the banking system increased by $12.5 billion between 1992 and 1995 and represented about 61 percent of all banking credit. The private sector issued bonds denominated in foreign currencies for almost $9 billion between 1991 and 1995, three-fourths of which had maturities of five years or less.

Debt expansion reached large sectors of the population. Middle- and even lower-income groups had access to consumption loans, most of them in dollar terms, which generated a constituency fearful of a devaluation. On the asset side, equally concerned were the firms in the private sector that had accumulated debts in foreign currency, including the banking system and different domestic economic groups, which, in association with foreign investors, participated in the simultaneous privatization process. Through the divestiture program, in fact, foreign direct investment and foreign investment in the country's stock exchange increased significantly.

The constituency in favor of stability also included the government itself. In the same period (i.e., between 1991 and 1996), the public sector increased its dollar-denominated debt to about $31.8 billion.[8] Accordingly, a devaluation would trigger a fiscal crisis through multiple mechanisms. First, the recession that would accompany a devaluation would reduce tax receipts. Second, the increase in Argentina's payments in pesos of the external public debt would not be compensated by income in dollars, as had been the case in Mexico, with oil-linked public revenues, or in Chile, with copper. Third, the deterioration of the fiscal situation would put downward pressure on public bonds, affecting the recently privatized social security system and the banking system (which had those assets in their portfolios), and any attempt to alleviate the problems of the banking and social security system would compound the fiscal difficulties.

In sum, the dollarization of debts created a broad constituency for exchange rate stability. It should be highlighted, however, that widespread dollarization in the 1980s had not impeded the devaluations and economic

8. By 2000, however, the debt had reached $130 billion, leading to the default of the debt in December 2001.

Table 6.2. Dollarization and External Debt

	1991	1992	1993	1994	1995	1996	1997
1. Banking system (stock; end period)							
Dollar deposits (million pesos)	6,583	10,842	17,532	23,555	23,590	28,405	33,475
Dollar deposits (% M3)	32.9	33.6	36.6	41.9	43.7	43.9	43.3
Credit in dollars (stock, million pesos)							
Private sector	9,198	15,488	20,945	27,382	28,523	31,684	37,992
Public sector	—	4,010	3,270	3,429	3,544	4,432	5,230
Total	—	19,498	24,215	30,811	32,067	36,116	43,222
Credit in dollars (% credit)	50.6	54.2	53.1	58.9	61.2	62.7	64.3
2. Foreign direct investment							
Flows (million US$)	—	4,044	2,556	3,066	4,179	—	—
Accumulated investment	—	14,829	16,476	20,401	24,630	—	—
3. Bond issues, private							
Flows (million US$)	265	1,230	3,902	2,580	952	2,539	—
4. Public debt (stock; billion US$)							
Local currency	1.2	0.7	5.9	7.3	6.7	10.7	—
Foreign currency	57.2	58.4	61.9	72.2	83.0	89.0	—
External debt	57.2	57.4	60.3	69.6	68.2	72.5	—
Internal debt	0.0	1.0	1.6	2.6	14.8	16.5	—
Total	58.4	59.1	67.8	79.5	89.7	99.7	109.4

downturn linked to the debt crisis during that decade. Key elements behind major devaluations in the past had been the distributive disputes over factor returns (capital and labor), sectoral incomes (agriculture vs. industry), and fiscal resources, which generally ended up monetized by passively adjusting monetary policies. The Convertibility Plan established a more disciplined monetary framework, limiting the possibility of the monetization of those distributive struggles. But, perhaps more important, those distributive struggles also appeared to have become more circumscribed in the 1990s (in part due to higher rates of economic growth). In addition, fiscal adjustment advanced more than in the previous decade (although less than what would have been necessary to ensure a better performance when capital inflows dwindled in 1995), and organized labor showed a more passive response to weak wage and employment conditions (a result of a prolonged deindustrialization process that started with the liberalization program in the late 1970s and continued with the debt crisis in the 1980s).

Economic Performance

However broad the support for stability may have been, the ensuing appreciation of the real exchange rate affected different productive sectors. Consequently, the economic program included specific policies aimed at moderating the impact of overvaluation. The agricultural sector received a substantial reduction in export taxes, along with the liberalization of several markets for products, inputs, and auxiliary services that had previously been regulated, helping to improve the price/cost equation for the sector. Industrial producers, though affected by the drastic reduction of import tariffs in place since 1991, received some selective subsidies, including reimbursement of indirect taxes to exporters, expedited antidumping procedures, and special promotion regimes, most notably, though not only, in the automobile sector.

More generally, all productive sectors benefited from the consumption boom associated with the initial phases of the exchange rate–based stabilization. By the time consumption growth began to slow down, the consolidation of the regional trade agreement, MERCOSUR, provided much-needed foreign exchange, as the Brazilian stabilization-cum-appreciation shifted the terms of trade in favor of Argentina, which in turn generated further gains in outward orientation and productivity. It can be argued that three important supply-side factors contributed to the high economic growth in 1991–94, subsequently sustaining the economic reform program through the difficult period of 1995–96 and leading to a significant rebound in 1997: the increase in productivity due to additional investments, the decline in several components of the internal costs linked to deregulation and enhanced competition, and greater opportunities in MERCOSUR.

Yet the acceleration of economic activity was based not only on supply-side measures but also on overstimulative monetary and fiscal policies. Despite the currency board, instead of trying to moderate the expansionary impact of capital flows with tighter monetary and fiscal policies (Calvo, Leiderman, and Reinhart 1996; Schadler et al. 1993), economic policies multiplied their influence through extensive credit creation and increased public expenditures, which further fueled the consumption boom and the high economic growth of 1991–94. As mentioned already, the Convertibility Law mandated only backing of the monetary base with international reserves, not broader definitions of money supply. On this basis, the authorities were able to reduce reserve requirements for the banking system in 1992–93. Capital flows and reduced reserve requirements led to a rapid expansion of credit (IMF 1995), which deteriorated the ratio of monetary aggregates to foreign currency reserves (except for the mandatory coverage of the monetary base). The financial system thus began to experience difficulties well before the Mexican devaluation of December 1994 (Corrigan 1996).

Overall, these expansive monetary and fiscal policies (see below) weakened the banking system and made the country more vulnerable to the 1994–95 external shocks. In addition, combined with a fixed exchange rate regime and trade liberalization, they had a negative impact on the tradable sector, amplifying the impact of the reduction of trade barriers and leading to the bankruptcy of firms that would have been competitive under a different combination of macroeconomic policies.[9] More prudent monetary and fiscal policies during 1991–94 were necessary to avoid some of these problems, leaving the country stronger for the changing economic conditions in 1995.

In addition, the Convertibility Program in the 1990s coincided with improved international conditions. First, in 1989 the administration of the newly elected U.S. president, George H. W. Bush, opened the possibility of debt reductions through the Brady Plan (which Argentina eventually obtained in 1992). Second, the slowing down of the U.S. economy at the beginning of the 1990s led the Federal Reserve to adopt a more stimulative monetary policy, which contributed to lower interest rates in 1991–92. The changed international environment along with a better framework of macroeconomic policies in several Latin American countries generated the return of capital to the region, just at the time the Convertibility Plan was being implemented. In addition, terms of trade, which had collapsed in

9. This discussion is related to two other issues. The first one is the sustainability of the exchange rate peg if the value selected is "too tight." See, for instance, Eichengreen and Wyplosz 1993 and Williamson 1994 on the United Kingdom and the European Monetary Union (EMU). A second issue is that if an initial value that is too tight is combined with a drastic program of trade liberalization, the restructuring of the economy may also harm sectors that would not have been considered inefficient under more adequate levels of the initial peg. See the seminal works of Little, Scitovsky, and Scott 1970; Balassa et al. 1971.

1986–87, initiated a slow but firm recovery that accelerated toward the mid-1990s and lasted until 1998 (see Figure 6.4).

Fiscal Adjustment

A fiscal deficit of about 6 percent of GDP in 1988 was reduced to about 3.8 percent by 1989–90, to 1.6 percent in 1991, and to almost negligible levels in 1992–93 (see Figure 6.6). Fiscal consolidation was helped by better tax administration, the Tanzi effect working in reverse (once inflation declined dramatically), and a comprehensive privatization policy. On the expenditure side, different factors contributed to initially place public accounts under control: the reduction of subsidies to domestic industrial groups, further adjustments in military expenditures, and the decline in world interest rates and the international debt settlement of 1992 under the Brady Plan, among others.

Opposition to cuts in industrial subsidies, the largest single item in the fiscal deficit during the 1980s, was attenuated by the fact that several of the previously subsidized contractors of the state emerged as winners of privatization, producing a process of rent substitution, from fiscal resources to fiscal assets, that served to garner the support of the country's largest and most politicized conglomerates (Schamis 1999). Negatively affected were public-sector employees (particularly those in privatized enterprises) and those, like public school teachers, who saw their real wages decline significantly in the 1990s. Public employees and their unions resisted the policy changes implemented by the Menem administration, but they did not succeed (see below).

The initial success of the adjustment, however, masked the fact that a sizable part of the deficit reduction was based on the divestiture of state-owned enterprises, thus constituting one-time proceeds, and that by 1994 the fiscal deficit had begun to grow again, the result of economic and political circumstances. The economic circumstances included changes in the structure of the GDP toward exports and investments with lower value-added taxes, and the liabilities associated with the privatization of social security. On the political side, Menem's initiative to change the constitution in 1994 so he could seek reelection in 1995 postponed further adjustment, contributing to these fiscal problems, especially in the case of insolvent public banks owned by provincial states. Consequently, IMF estimates for fiscal policy in 1992–93 showed a pro-cyclical effect on aggregate demand, and for 1994 a positive fiscal impulse of about 1.5 percent of GDP (IMF 1998a). This context exacerbated the severity of the economic and banking crisis of 1995–96 (Díaz-Bonilla 1996).

In sum, public accounts improved significantly vis-à-vis the situation in the 1980s, and this proved enough to forestall a Krugman-type exchange rate crisis. However, the government did not take advantage of the favorable initial economic conditions to place fiscal accounts on a more solid footing, to diminish the impact of the external shock.

Organized Labor Politics

The decline of labor unions in Argentina's economic and political arenas had several facets. One was the restructuring and downsizing of the industrial sector that began in the 1970s. Prolonged deindustrialization made an impact on the organizational capabilities of organized labor, especially in the Peronist quarters, where union bosses had historically been the hegemonic clique. This process generated an important renewal, reducing significantly the political clout of unions and increasing the presence of middle-class urban leaders.

The new context allowed Menem to bring a wholesale change in the political leadership of the Peronist Party, promoting outsiders and newcomers better disposed to follow his leadership and his program. This changed the economic and political components of the traditional pro-labor Peronist alliance and led to some disregard of labor's traditional agenda for workers.

In the first main confrontation with unions, over the privatization of the public telephone company, the Menem administration, supported by a strong current of public opinion against the notoriously bad service of the telephone company, first isolated politically and then fired striking employees. At the same time it rewarded groups within the company that did not oppose the privatization process. This action was meant to send a clear signal to different public-sector unions: the economic restructuring of the public sector was for real, and there were tangible costs to opposing it. Later, friendly unions were allowed to participate (or to increase their previous participation) in several profitable activities related to health services, management of pension funds, and even privatizations, opening new economic opportunities for the most business-oriented unions (Murillo 2001). This pattern of selective rewards and punishments was utilized with success to carry on the substantial restructuring of Argentina's public sector. Additionally, the Menem administration maintained for a long time the possibility of wholesale reform of labor laws, including reductions in the legal powers and functions of unions in Argentina, as a bargaining tool in the ins and outs of the relationship between the government and the labor movement.

Although the economy grew at about 7 percent annually between 1991 and 1994, employment increased only by 1.6 percent during a comparable period.[10] Unemployment began to climb, because in addition to lower numbers of jobs created, participation in the job market jumped from 39.5 percent in 1991 to 42.8 percent at the beginning of 1995 (IMF 1995). Also,

10. The cross-currents in job creation and destruction can be seen in the following statistics: between 1990 and 1994, manufacturing and agriculture lost about 380,000 jobs, and the number of public employees in the federal government and public enterprises dropped by about 420,000, because of the privatization and reorganization of the public sector, while commerce, construction, and services gained some 830,000 jobs (IMF 1995) (total average employment for the period was about 12 million people).

because an important percentage of the employment created was related to the unsustainable domestic boom in nontradables, when external conditions changed, unemployment soared. By 1996, levels of unemployment not experienced during the last half-century coexisted with real wages that were below the averages for the two decades between the mid-1960s and mid-1980s (see Figure 6.3). This soft labor market also contributed to mute the response of workers. The struggle over factor returns that had played havoc with previous fixed exchange rate regimes did not exhibit the same intensity this time.

THE POLITICS OF EXCHANGE RATE–BASED STABILIZATION

I have argued that the currency board represents a strong version of central bank independence (since monetary policy is altogether eliminated from the control of governments) and a strong version of exchange rate–based stabilization (since, as in Argentina, the peg is fixed by Congress and can be modified only by Congress). A wealth of literature, however, has highlighted the shortcomings of this type of arrangement for developing economies—basically, that it reproduces boom-bust cycles—and in fact a number of countries have experienced deep exchange rate and inflation crises during the bust phase of the cycle.[11]

On this account, and as a way of conclusion, two questions are pertinent. The first one is whether those crises could have been avoided simply by a stronger institutional configuration—namely, by the currency board. During 1999, moreover, some voices even suggested reinforcing this institutional makeup and embracing full dollarization in order to fend off international financial crises.[12] The decade-long Argentine experience with the currency board, in fact, indicates that widespread financial turbulence was averted until 2001, which explains a good part of the social explosion of late 2001. Given the impossibility of devaluing the currency, implementing typical countercyclical policies, and expanding bank money again through reductions in reserve requirements, the economy has performed sluggishly since 1998, unemployment has been stuck at rates not seen since the 1930s, and real wages have declined to levels seen only under draconian austerity programs that, in the past, required military governments to be sustained.

This unappealing trade-off raises a second question: Why do governments continue to implement nominal anchors? There are some tentative

11. For example, Argentina, Chile, and Uruguay in the early 1980s; Mexico in 1994; the Czech Republic in 1997; several Asian nations in 1997; Russia in 1998; and Brazil in 1999.

12. The Argentine government speculated with full dollarization during 1999 in order to defend the currency when the Brazilian devaluation in January turned the terms of trade against Argentina and financial operators anticipated a devaluation. Ecuador, in turn, adopted a full dollarization scheme in February 2000.

answers. One line of research on the Latin American reform programs, for example, has suggested that persistent inflation has contributed to garnering popular support for comprehensive reform programs in the region (Gervasoni 1997; Gibson and Calvo 2000; Weyland 1998), most of which, in fact, included stabilization based on some kind of nominal anchor. This research has not emphasized, however, that the long-term sustainability of fixed exchange rate regimes seems to depend on a significant increase in the "recession acceptance level" a society is willing to endure and, thus, on the institutionalization of high unemployment as the adjustment variable of price stability. This puts a question mark on the durability and scope of the alleged popular support for these programs, and on the larger question of democratic governance.

Another line of inquiry has brought the government-as-rational-actor into the picture and has revisited traditional notions of the political-business cycle. In high-inflation contexts, the argument goes, stabilization displaces unemployment as the critical electoral issue. It is thus politically rational to stabilize prior to an election. Moreover, unlike orthodox disinflation programs, exchange rate–based stabilizations often lead to a boom in the short run (Guidotti and Végh 1992; Velasco 1994; Stein and Streb 1995). If the typical cycle as devised by Nordhaus (1975) exhibits a "macroeconomic expansion-election-stabilization" sequence, programs based on nominal exchange rate anchors show a "stabilization-expansion-election" sequence, deferring recession until the real exchange rate appreciation builds up unsustainable current account deficits and, thus, balance-of-payment crises.

Whether this form of economic irrationality can be understood as politically rational on the part of incumbent parties and governments remains to be seen.[13] By taking the government as the main actor of the process, however, one may obscure the fact that these scenarios are not distributionally neutral. Capital account openness also facilitates runs against the currency, producing massive reserve losses, and financial sector liberalization, in a context of shallow capital markets and feeble regulatory institutional frameworks, often turns a foreign exchange crunch into a banking crisis. Groups with access to financial adaptation instruments (dollarization, capital flight, currency substitution) tend to transfer the costs of these crises to groups that do not have that capability (Labán and Sturzenegger 1994a, 1994b), and undersupervised and overguaranteed banks often present a monumental moral hazard problem (Kawai 1998), a rent-seeking scenario of a large magnitude. These considerations take us back to the original emphasis of this chapter: the primacy of distributional considerations even in economy-wide policy, as in the Argentine experience with exchange rate policies for the last half-century.

13. Schamis and Way 2000 examines this dynamic.

PART 3
Great Powers and Money Politics

CHAPTER SEVEN

China's Exchange Rate Policy in the Aftermath of the Asian Financial Crisis

Hongying Wang

In the summer of 1997, a currency crisis in Thailand triggered a chain of similar crises in many places throughout East and Southeast Asia.[1] For the next two years, the dark clouds of the Asian financial crisis hovered over the region's economy and threatened to destabilize economies in other parts of the world. As the financial crisis and the ensuing economic meltdown spread to one country after another in 1997 and 1998, the world turned its attention to China.

The concern was not so much that the Chinese currency, the renminbi (RMB), was vulnerable to attack by currency speculators, as the Thai baht, the Indonesian rupiah, and the Korean won were. It was not, because the RMB was not convertible for capital account transactions and investors could not suddenly pull large sums of money out of China. Furthermore, most of the investment going into China was foreign direct investment (FDI), which tends to be far less volatile than portfolio investment. Rather the concern was that the collapse of regional currencies and the downturn of regional economies might force or tempt the Chinese government to devalue the RMB to keep Chinese exports competitive and the Chinese economy afloat.

In early 1998 China-based bankers and economists shared a consensus that the existing RMB-to-dollar exchange rate could last only until the last quarter of 1998 or the first quarter of 1999. Then it would be adjusted down about 11 percent to RMB 9.3 for each U.S. dollar (*Business China* 2/2/98). In mid-1998, as the value of the Japanese yen slid, the market became extremely nervous about an imminent devaluation of the RMB (*Business Week* 6/1/98; *Forbes* 6/15/98). As economic troubles continued in Asia and in other developing areas in late 1998 and 1999, many economic analysts suspected that devaluation of the RMB was just around the corner because

1. I would like to thank Benjamin Jerry Cohen, Allen Carlson, and Jonathan Kirshner for their comments on earlier versions of this article.

from China's point of view "it is the best policy option" (*Barron's* 8/17/98; *Global Investor* 10/98). In the meantime, many Chinese firms and individuals adopted strategies hedging against RMB devaluation (*Economist* 2/14/98; *Global Investor* 10/98; *Business Week* 11/23/98).

However, these speculations notwithstanding, the Chinese government declared early on that it would not devalue the RMB. And to the surprise of many, China indeed kept its promise. The Chinese government lifted the pledge in June 1999. By then the crisis was largely over. The pressure for devaluation had relaxed as many of the crisis-stricken economies were on their way to recovery.

What explains China's decision against RMB devaluation in the aftermath of the Asian financial crisis (1997–99)? The economics of the policy choice was ambiguous. On the one hand, as noted, the instinct of many international analysts was that China would devalue the RMB to counter the pressure of economic competition in the region. On the other hand, Chinese officials emphasized that China could manage such pressure without devaluation. In addition, they were concerned about the negative impact of devaluation on the financial side of the economy. To answer the question, we need to turn to the political factors that shaped China's exchange rate policy.

TO DEVALUE OR NOT TO DEVALUE?

Until the beginning of the economic reforms, which began in the late 1970s, China had a traditional socialist exchange system characterized by central planning and control. The RMB was grossly overvalued (1.7 yuan to a dollar) to segregate a planned domestic economy from a market world economy. Since then China's exchange rate regime has gone through several stages of transformation. By 1994 the Chinese government had adopted a managed float system, with the official exchange rate much closer to the market price (8.4 yuan to a dollar). In December 1996, China announced that it would accept Article 8 of the International Monetary Fund's (IMF) charter and make the RMB convertible for current account transactions. The new exchange system encouraged export and FDI inflows. Until the outbreak of the Asian financial crisis, China's favorable balance of payments along with complaints by the United States and other countries put upward pressure on the RMB. The Asian financial crisis reduced the upward pressure on the RMB, resulting instead in concern about a possible devaluation.

Should China devalue its currency in the aftermath of the Asian financial crisis? From an economic perspective, arguments could be made on both sides. And they were. To simplify the complexity of the issues involved, one could say that considerations of the real economy tilted in the direction of devaluation, whereas those of the financial side of the economy generally pointed in the opposite direction. But even within each set of considerations, the calculations were mixed.

Export, FDI, and Economic Growth

East and Southeast Asia were important export markets for China (Table 7.1). As the currencies of some other Asian economies lost 30 to 75 percent of their value during the financial crisis, their imports dropped sharply, reducing China's exports to those markets. Moreover, their currency depreciation made their products much more price competitive in third countries, adding to China's loss of international markets. According to some analysts, regional devaluation directly challenged $20 to $30 billion of Chinese exports or up to 40 percent of the country's total exports (*Economist* 2/14/98). On this score, China had strong incentives to devalue its own currency so that its exports would remain competitive in and against neighboring economies.

Much of the FDI in China came from other Asian economies (Table 7.2). This flow was likely to dwindle with the depreciation of their currencies, for it made investment in China more costly. Devaluing the RMB could help slow this downturn by making China cheaper to invest in and thus more attractive for new investment from other parts of Asia. Furthermore, many foreign companies were investing in China because of China's cheap labor resource. Devaluation of the RMB would help maintain China's attractiveness as a cheap export platform.

Since exports and FDI had been the twin engines of the rapid growth of the Chinese economy (Lardy 1994), analysts pointed out that China had to devalue its currency to avoid an economic slowdown brought by shrinking exports and foreign investment and to avoid deflation (*Business China* 2/2/98).

While many overseas and some Chinese analysts provided strong economic reasons to devalue the RMB, China's policy makers and policy analysts emphasized that China could deal with the pressure of the regional crisis without devaluation.[2] They claimed that Chinese enterprises could become more efficient and thus remain competitive exporters even with a strong Chinese currency. To the extent that China's exports were losing some competitiveness, the government addressed the issue by increasing

2. China's official position against devaluation was expressed on numerous occasions in 1998 and early 1999 by China's president, Jiang Zemin, and premier, Zhu Rongji. For more detailed economic explanations, see, for instance, Vice Premier Li Lanqing's speech at the World Economic Forum in Davos, Switzerland, in early 1998; press conference by Dai Xianglong, governor of the People's Bank of China, during the first meeting of the ninth National People's Congress, March 1998; speech by Zeng Peiyan, director of the State Development Planning Commission, on September 23, 1998, reported by the China News Agency.

Table 7.1. Chinese Export to Selected Asian Countries (% of Total Export)

	1996	1997	1998
ASEAN[a]	6.4	6.6	5.9
South Korea	5.0	5.0	3.4
Japan	20.4	17.4	16.2
Total	31.8	29	25.5

Source: Almanac of China's Foreign Economic Relations and Trade 1997–98, 1998–99, 1999–2000.
[a] Association of Southeast Asian Nations.

Table 7.2. Foreign Direct Investment (FDI) (Utilized) in China from Selected Asian Economies (% of Total FDI)

	1996	1997	1998
Hong Kong	45.6	49.6	41.4
South Korea	4.7	3.3	3.4
Japan	9.6	8.8	6.9
Singapore	5.8	5.4	7.2
Total	65.7	67.1	58.9

Source: Almanac of China's Foreign Economic Relations and Trade 1997–98, 1998–99, 1999–2000.

the tax rebate from 9 percent in 1997 to 17 percent in 1998. According to one estimate, this was the equivalent of devaluing the RMB by 16 percent (*Barron's* 8/17/98). Additionally, the Chinese analysts warned that devalued Chinese currency would raise the prices of imported goods, including equipment and parts. Since up to 50 percent of China's exports involved imported parts, the rising price of these parts would greatly reduce any gains of a marginal devaluation for China's export competitiveness (Li 1998; *Zhong Guo Jin Rong* [*ZGJR*] 9/98). They argued that the problem posed by a strong RMB for FDI could be compensated by increased domestic investment. In 1998 Beijing began to introduce macroeconomic policies to stimulate the domestic economy. In February 1998 the government announced that it would spend $1 trillion on new infrastructure projects, housing, and high-tech industries over the next three years. This figure was later increased to $1.2 trillion. In addition, in 1998 the government lowered interest rates three times and expanded the monetary base. Banks lowered their lending standards and increased lending. Total lending was 7,491.4 billion yuan in 1997 and grew to 8,652.4 billion yuan in 1998, an increase of 15.5 percent (*China Financial Outlook* 1999). The same trend continued in 1999.

The official optimism notwithstanding, the Asian financial crisis caused troubles for China's economy. As Beijing stuck to its no-devaluation policy, from 1997 to 1999 the growth rate for Chinese exports and FDI slowed down, as did the economic growth rate (Table 7.3). As the economic situation in China worsened, speculations about RMB devaluation continued (*Barron's* 7/26/99; *Business Week* 8/9/99; *Chemical Week* 8/25–9/1/99; *China Trade Report* 9/99).

It is not clear whether the Chinese officials and policy analysts who suggested that there was no need to devalue the Chinese currency genuinely believed their own reasoning. But in retrospect, their reasoning had major flaws. First, it was easy to say that if Chinese enterprises became leaner and meaner, they could stay competitive despite the relative appreciation of the RMB. But the problems causing inefficiency of Chinese enterprises were too numerous and deep-rooted to be tackled in a short period of time (Steinfeld 1998; Smyth 1998). Second, export subsidies were helpful, but they were not cost-free. The Chinese government had used tax rebates to support exports since 1985. After 1994, with the new taxation system in place, all the expenses of the tax rebate fell on the central government. In 1997 and 1998, tax rebates accounted for 11.5 percent and 8.5 percent, respectively, of the central government's total revenues.[3] Given the fiscal problems of the national government and its many other financial burdens, this level of support of export was hardly sustainable. Third, it was plausible that devaluation of the RMB would lead to rising prices of imported equipment and parts, which in turn would reduce China's price advantage in exports. But this fear was exaggerated. Equipment purchased earlier continued to be useful. Some imported raw materials could be replaced by domestic substitutes. And since most of the imports came from other Asian economies, whose currencies had depreciated, a moderately devalued RMB would not lead to significant increases in import prices anyway.

Finally, Chinese officials and analysts were right to point out that China's economic revival ultimately would depend on domestic factors. But the Keynesian policies of the government were not able to reinvigorate the economy in a short time. Fiscal expansion contributed to the artificial realization of the official goal for economic growth rate, but government spending failed to spill over to the private sector. Furthermore, an expansionist fiscal policy increased the government deficit. In 1997 and 1998 the Chinese government deficit was, respectively, 1.5 percent and 2.2 percent of the gross domestic product (GDP). These figures were under the threshold of 3 percent, a widely accepted international benchmark, but they have to be considered in the context of the central government's financial weak-

3. Calculation based on statistics in *Finance Yearbook of China* 1998, 1999.

Table 7.3. Growth Rate of Export, Foreign Direct Investment (FDI), and Economy

	1996	1997	1998	1999
Export	1.5	20.9	0.5	6.1
FDI	11.2	8.5	1	-9.7
Economy	9.7	8.8	7.8	7

Sources: 1996–98 figures: *Almanac of China's Foreign Economic Relations and Trade* 1997–98, 1998–99, 1999–2000; 1999 figures: National Bureau of Statistics of China, www.stats.gov.cn (accessed November 2001).

ness. In the late 1990s, the central government's disposable revenues accounted for not much more than 10 percent of the GDP, lower than even most developing countries in the world. Further deficit spending would be very difficult for the Chinese government to manage.

The government's monetary policy also had problems. First, monetary expansion was undermined by the bad-loan problem faced by the banks. Commercial banks in China follow policy and political needs rather than market principles. By the late 1990s banks had become heavily burdened with deadbeat loans. Many banks had long been technically insolvent (Lardy 1998b, 59–127). Given the prevalence of insolvent state-owned enterprises and the administrative disincentives to lend to other types of enterprises, banks had a hard time finding appropriate projects to invest in. Second, interest rate reduction failed to stimulate demand. The annual change in consumer price index fell from 8.3 percent in 1996 to 2.8 percent in 1997 and-0.8 percent in 1998 (*China Financial Outlook* 1999). People were reluctant to spend money despite lower interest rates because of the reality and prospects of institutional reforms in the 1990s, such as the downsizing of the state-owned enterprises, rising unemployment, and reduced welfare benefits. Moreover, repeated reductions in the interest rate would eventually affect the exchange rate, putting more pressure on devaluation.

On balance, from the point of view of promoting China's exports, FDI inflows, and short-term growth rate in the face of the Asian financial crisis, the Chinese government should have chosen the policy of devaluation. But another set of economic considerations provided a significant counterargument.

Capital Flight, Banking System, and Foreign Debt

Besides exports, FDI, and economic growth rate, China's exchange policy was likely to have consequences for the financial side of the economy. Concerns over these consequences were almost certainly an important part of the policy deliberation, although there was relatively little public debate over these sensitive issues.

First and most immediately, the exchange rate policy would affect public confidence in the Chinese currency. As noted earlier, after the outbreak of the Asian financial crisis, quite a number of companies and individuals suspected that the RMB would be devalued. Any indication from the government that confirmed their fear would lead to widespread panic. In theory, the RMB was not convertible except for current account transactions, and, following the Asian financial crisis, the government had renewed and tightened restrictions on foreign exchange transactions. But in reality, the Chinese regulatory framework had serious loopholes. For instance, companies underinvoiced their exports and overinvoiced their imports. Through these and other means, they transferred large amounts of money out of China. Some estimated that capital flight from China in 1997 and 1998 amounted to $35 to $40 billion a year, or almost as much as the annual inflow of foreign investment (EIU 1999; Zhang 1998; Song 1999). If the government devalued the RMB, it would seriously worsen the problem of capital flight.

Second, the government also had reasons to be concerned about the impact of devaluation on public confidence in Chinese banks. Banks dominate China's financial system. They account for 90 percent of all financial intermediation between savers and investors (Lardy 1998a, 79). As noted earlier, Chinese banks are burdened with bad debts. In fact, the role of banks in China's financial system was even greater and the banks were in even worse shape than were those in the countries swept by the financial crisis. In 1997, nonperforming loans accounted for 16 percent of bank assets in South Korea, 11 percent in Indonesia, 7.5 percent in Malaysia, and 15 percent in Thailand (Noland et al. 1998, 10). Estimates of nonperforming loans in China around that time exceeded 20 percent of the assets of state-owned banks (*Economist* 5/2/98).[4] Devaluation of the RMB could cause a bank run, forcing immediate bankruptcy of many banks and threatening the whole banking system. After all, "it is the willingness of the Chinese people to place their money in the state banks that guarantees the continued viability and stability of the financial system" (EIU 1999, 30).

Third, the exchange rate would have an impact on China's ability to pay its foreign debt. In late 1998, several scandals broke out in the financial sector. Not only did they reveal the fragility of China's financial institutions, but also they showed that China's foreign debt was much greater than it was thought to be. For example, Guangdong International Trust and Investment Corporation (GITIC), the international investment arm of the Guangdong government, went bankrupt with $2.4 billion in foreign debts.

---

4. According to Nicholas Lardy (1998b, 195), nonperforming loans account for roughly 22 percent of the outstanding loans by China's largest banks.

It was just one of the many financial institutions taking on foreign debt without the knowledge of the central government. Moreover, some of the FDI in big infrastructure projects was promised guaranteed returns. It was in effect foreign debt in disguise. If the RMB were to devalue, it would make it harder for China to pay back its foreign debt.

These factors likely gave the Chinese government reasons to avoid devaluing the RMB. But again, the choice was not clear-cut. While the problem of capital flight had become more serious after the outbreak of the Asian financial crisis, it was not caused by the crisis. Instead, it had its roots in China's illiberal financial system and insecure property rights, which would defy an exchange rate solution. As for the fragility of China's banking system, there is no doubt that RMB devaluation would worsen the problem by increasing public anxiety over the value of their savings. But given the lack of a developed capital market at home and strict control of capital account transactions abroad, the public had few alternative destinations for their money besides banks. It was thus not probable for devaluation to lead to a collapse of the banking system. With regard to the impact of devaluation on debt payment, China's debt structure and volume were quite manageable (Table 7.4). Even though financial institutions and enterprises assumed greater amounts of foreign debt than previously known, these additional amounts were not large enough to significantly alter this favorable situation.[5] A moderate devaluation of the RMB would not significantly damage China's debt-paying capacity.

In sum, on economic grounds there were reasons for China to devalue the RMB, especially in light of its impact on the real economy. However, there were also reasons to avoid devaluation, mostly out of consideration of its impact on the financial side of the economy. Overall, the economics were ambiguous and indeterminate. The decisive forces underlying China's policy choice were political.

THE POLITICAL LOGIC OF CHINA'S EXCHANGE POLICY

The main political factors that shaped China's exchange policy were the government's concerns about its own legitimacy at home and the country's image abroad. The latter can be further divided into concerns over China's international reputation and its prestige.

---

5. In January 1999, Governor Dai Xianglong of the People's Bank of China announced that the total foreign debt of the 239 international trust and investment corporations, excluding GITIC, was $8.1 billion, of which $6.7 billion was directly borrowed and the rest represented guarantees (EIU 1999, 32).

Table 7.4. China's Foreign Debt

	1996	1997	1998
Medium–long-term debt (billion US$) (% of total debt)	102.2 (87.9)	112.8 (86.1)	128.7 (88.1)
Short-term debt (billion US$) (% of total debt)	14.1 (12.1)	18.1 (13.9)	17.3 (11.9)
Total debt (billion US$)	116.3	131	146
Debt-to-GDP ratio (%)	14.2	14.5	15.2
Debt-to-foreign exchange income ratio (%)	75.6	63.2	70.4

Source: Finance Yearbook of China 1999.

Legitimacy

Since the beginning of the economic reform, the communist regime had become increasingly reliant on delivering economic goods to maintain public support. With the decline of the communist ideology and in the absence of democratic political reforms, the government's economic policy had emerged as its main basis of legitimacy (Ding 1994). Faltering in a highly visible way on economic issues would seriously undermine the public confidence in and endorsement of the government.

Devaluation of the RMB, especially after the government declared that it was not going to do so, could be seen as such faltering. As noted earlier, the Chinese government managed to devalue the RMB in 1994 without evoking public panic. But that was carried out in normal times. To devalue the RMB under pressure during a crisis would be much more difficult. The public had a lot to be anxious about, including, ironically, economic problems worsened by the high value of the RMB.[6] The perception of the government's being unable to manage the exchange rate of the RMB would add to that anxiety and undermine public confidence in the government. The collapse of the Suharto government in Indonesia after the outbreak of the financial crisis there seemed to be a particularly sobering lesson (Jin 1998).

In addition, Chinese officials feared that devaluing the RMB would increase the prices of imported products. Among other things, this would lead to higher inflation. Such a consequence would be politically unacceptable to the government, which had struggled with the problem of inflation throughout the reform period. Indeed, by 1996 the government had just cooled down an overheated economy with a painful austerity program, and it was not about to let inflation raise its ugly head again. In retrospect, the

6. Some estimate that unemployment reached 20 percent for urban areas and 35 percent for rural China in 1998 (*Global Investor* 10/98).

fear of inflation was grossly exaggerated. As both deductive and empirical research shows, there is hardly any evidence that moderate inflation (below 10 percent and some argue below 20 percent) is negative for economic growth (Kirshner 2000, 428–432). Furthermore, by the late 1990s, inflation was no longer a serious problem for China. To the contrary, because of the relative saturation of the consumer goods market and because of the reforms of the state-owned enterprises and the reduction of welfare benefits, people grew reluctant to spend money. The major challenge for China had become deflation.

However, rationality had to succumb to the official ideology against inflation. In the minds of Chinese policymakers, inflation was closely associated with political instability. This mentality was rooted in the historical precedents of political crises resulting from high inflation. In the late 1940s, hyperinflation played a major part in the downfall of the Kuomintang government. In the late 1980s, rising inflation contributed to the political turmoil that climaxed with the massive protests around Tiananmen. The Chinese government of the late 1990s saw inflation control as essential to maintaining public support and political stability. In light of this political consideration, it was quite sensible for the government to opt against devaluing the RMB.

International Image

Besides domestic legitimacy, a strong desire to improve China's international image was another main reason why the Chinese government chose not to devalue the RMB. In 1997 and 1998, as the crisis swept through the region, the world watched China nervously, fearing the devaluation of the RMB and its disastrous consequences for other economies. The Chinese government was well aware that under such an intense spotlight, China's policy choice would have a magnified impact on how the world viewed China. By holding the value of the RMB, the Chinese government sought to demonstrate to the international community that China was a "responsible great power" (*fu zeren de daguo*). This theme dominated the government's statements of the policy of no devaluation throughout the period.[7]

Embedded in the phrase of "a responsible great power" are two components of China's desired image—being responsible and being a great power. The former stresses China's willingness to act according to international norms and to contribute to the public good. It is a reputation that China sought to establish. The latter emphasizes China's status and prestige in the international hierarchy.

---

7. For example, see official statements cited in fn. 2.

Reputation

Reputation is an important part of international relations. As Robert Keohane (1984, 116) pointed out, "To a government that values its ability to make future agreements, reputation is a crucial resource; and the most important aspect of an actor's reputation in world politics is the belief of others that it will keep its future commitments even when a particular situation, myopically viewed, makes it appear disadvantageous to do so." In the aftermath of the Asian financial crisis, the Chinese government was keen to establish a reputation for being a cooperative and trustworthy team player. Not only did China declare its policy of no devaluation early on, but also it carried out this promise throughout the period. Chinese officials stressed to foreign governments and media that this policy meant economic risks for China, but in the interest of the greater public good, China was willing to stick to its commitment.[8]

Why did the Chinese government so desire a reputation of being responsible—so much so that it was willing to sacrifice the country's short-term economic interests? To understand this, we need to briefly review China's existing reputation and how it affected the country's interests.

Before the Asian financial crisis, China's international reputation was quite unfavorable. The negative image was partly due to the lingering effect of the government's bloody crackdown of peaceful demonstrators around Tiananmen in 1989. China's image was also damaged by its uncompromising position with regard to Taiwan, Tibet, and the South China Sea; its arms sales to so-called rogue states; and the apparent rise of militant Chinese nationalism. Through the lens of this overall image, China's problems were magnified, whereas its progress was overlooked.

As the Chinese economy grew rapidly, so did anxiety in certain parts of the world. For instance, in the 1990s in the United States and Southeast Asia, the perception of China as a threat to the region and the world was gaining influence (Bernstein and Munro 1997; Whiting 1997). This unfavorable image caused serious difficulties for China's foreign relations and, in turn, harmed China's political and economic interests. For years after the Tiananmen incident, the U.S. Congress subjected China's normal trading status to an annual review, making it conditional on satisfactory progress in human rights development. This procedure was humiliating for China, given China's growing dependence on the U.S. market for exports; in addition, the U.S. threat of trade sanctions brought a great deal of political pressure and economic uncertainty. Likewise, before and since Hong Kong's return to Chinese sovereignty in 1997, the Chinese government has faced unrelenting international scrutiny over its every move regarding Hong

---

8. According to President Jiang Zemin, although the economic problems it created for China were not serious enough to force RMB devaluation, China's exchange rate policy was not cost-free (*Washington Post* 6/21/98).

Kong.[9] In the meantime, China's (often clumsy) efforts to unify Taiwan with the mainland met with international resistance.[10]

After the mid-1990s, the Chinese government and policy analysts became increasingly concerned about repairing China's international image. Policy analysts pointed out that great power status could not be built on power alone. It had to be based also on other countries' acceptance and recognition. To achieve the latter, China needed to convince the world that it would integrate into the existing international system, abiding by its rules and following its norms (Xi 1996; Yan 1996; Shi 1999).[11] As the world's attention turned to China after the outbreak of the financial crisis in Asia, Chinese leaders saw a valuable opportunity to show the world that China was not a rogue state determined to upset the existing international order, but a cooperative partner willing to sacrifice self-interest and live up to its commitment.[12] The policy against devaluation was especially aimed at showing the credibility of China's commitment to Hong Kong's continued economic prosperity under Chinese rule and China's readiness to be a responsible member of the World Trade Organization (WTO).

In 1983 Hong Kong adopted a linked exchange rate system, pegging the Hong Kong dollar to the U.S. dollar at the rate of HK\$7.8 to US\$1 with a small band of fluctuation. The monetary policy of Hong Kong had one clear goal: to maintain a stable exchange rate. This system, which was basically a currency board, served Hong Kong well, making it one of the most credible and attractive trading partners and financial hubs in the world. After the outbreak of the Asian financial crisis, when pegged currencies in the region fell one after another, the Hong Kong dollar came under tremendous pressure from currency speculation. When international money managers attacked Hong Kong's currency as well as its stock market, the Hong Kong monetary system became quite vulnerable. The Hong Kong government took unprecedented actions to stabilize its currency and economy. For instance, in August 1998, the government injected \$15 billion into the stock market and saved the stock market and the Hong Kong dollar from attacks by international hedge funds.

9. In 1992, the U.S. Senate passed the U.S.–Hong Kong Policy Act, obliging the U.S. government to monitor and report the situation in Hong Kong, especially regarding judicial independence and civil liberties. The media has been watchful of any signs of declining political freedom in anticipation of or following Hong Kong's return to Chinese sovereignty.

10. In contrast, Taiwan, with its carefully cultivated image of a new democracy facing the threat of a communist giant, enjoys widespread sympathy from the international community.

11. Some Western observers noted an immense gap between China's rhetoric of cooperation and its actual conduct based on a high dose of realism (Yahuda 1999). But there is no doubt that China has become more cooperative with other countries in the last two decades.

12. One analyst pointed out specifically that the policy of no devaluation would lead other countries to be friendly to China. It would win China great intangible assets (Yang 1999, 22).

However, there was a consensus among the international financial community that if China devalued the RMB, Hong Kong would have to abandon its currency peg. Although there was no systematic linkage between the RMB and the Hong Kong dollar, as shown by the fact that when the RMB depreciated significantly against the U.S. dollar in 1994, the value of the Hong Kong dollar remained unchanged vis-à-vis the U.S. dollar, the prevailing international perception after the outbreak of the Asian financial crisis did not follow this logic. It was widely believed that if the RMB went down in value, fund managers would renew their attack on the Hong Kong dollar, making it impossible for Hong Kong to maintain the present value of its currency.[13] The Chinese government recognized this danger and was determined to uphold the RMB in order to avoid undermining Hong Kong's currency peg.

The reason why Beijing was so firm in its support of Hong Kong's currency system had largely to do with China's reputation. The Asian financial crisis began at a very sensitive time. The Thai government gave up defending the baht on July 2, 1997, one day after Hong Kong ceased to be a British colony and returned to Chinese sovereignty. Having promised the people of Hong Kong and the world of its readiness to ensure Hong Kong's continued prosperity under Chinese rule, the Chinese government could not let Hong Kong fall victim to the currency crisis. By holding the value of the RMB, China made it possible for the Hong Kong dollar to stay pegged to the U.S. dollar. This was crucial to Hong Kong's financial stability and its status as an international financial center. Indeed, Beijing's effort paid off. After the Asian financial crisis, Hong Kong citizens recognized their dependence on China more than ever before. In the summer of 1998, a well-known Hong Kong commentator, who was often critical of Beijing, pointed out, "If in the run-up to the handover Hong Kong citizens were eager about erecting barriers against 'interference' from Beijing, a radically different mind-set reigns today" (Lam 1998). Beijing's exchange rate policy played an important role in enhancing the credibility of its commitment to the economic well-being of Hong Kong.

As the Chinese government calculated its exchange policy, another salient consideration was the impact of the policy on China's accession to the WTO. China became interested in becoming a member of the General Agreement on Tariff and Trade (GATT), the predecessor of the WTO, in the mid-1980s. In the 1990s China's pursuit of GATT/WTO membership gained urgency, so much so that since the mid-1990s it had been a top policy priority for the Chinese government. The reformers in China had been

13. According to Donald Tsang, Hong Kong's finance chief, the argument that RMB movement would automatically lead to Hong Kong dollar movement was "the scare mongering of people who wish to speculate against the Hong Kong dollar and are unable to come up with some solid argument why the Hong Kong dollar needs to move" (*Euromoney* 7/99).

pushing hard for China to become a member of the global trade body. Membership would bring prestige and political influence and would help further domestic economic reforms. After more than a decade of reforms, China's economic system had reached a critical point by the mid-1990s. The relatively easy steps, such as the decentralization of power and the expansion of the private economic sector, had exhausted their potentials. It was time to take more difficult measures, such as restructuring the state-owned enterprises and the banking system according to market principles. Since these reforms would threaten powerful domestic interests, including government officials and labor, they faced formidable obstacles. As the domestic sources for change weakened, it was necessary to look elsewhere for alternative stimulants. Reform-minded leaders hoped that China's membership in the WTO would provide a new catalyst for change.[14] Thus, the stakes of China's WTO entry were high.

A major obstacle for China's joining the WTO all along was the question of whether China would play by the rules after becoming a member (Mastel 1997). It was imperative for the Chinese government to convince the major players that it was willing to abide by the rules and to be a cooperative partner in the international economic system. By holding the value of the RMB after other currencies in the region fell, the Chinese government sought to demonstrate to the rest of the world that it was willing to sacrifice short-term self-interest to maintain system stability (Zhu 1999).

China's bid for the WTO was especially dependent on the support of the United States. Thus, it was particularly important from a Chinese perspective to counter the prevailing fear in the United States that China, just like Japan before it, was a mercantilist trading power seeking to enrich itself at the expense of its trading partners. Such fears had grown in the 1990s with China's growing trade surplus with the United States.[15] Devaluation of the RMB after the Asian financial crisis would only worsen the United States's perception of China in this regard. Instead, if China refrained from devaluation as urged by the United States, it would help improve China's image and increase the prospect for U.S. support of China's bid for the WTO.

In this area, China seems to have achieved its policy goals. China's cooperative behavior during the financial crisis was recognized by the major gatekeepers of the WTO. For example, during Premier Zhu Rongji's visit to Europe in April 1998, leaders of the European Union pointed to China's continued determination not to devalue its currency as a highly responsible position (*South China Morning Post* 4/13/98). U.S. officials expressed similar views. In the years after the Asian financial crisis, China reached trade

---

14. In the language of Chinese officials, this is "letting in rushes of water to wash away the sand" (*fangshui chongsha*) (Sheng 2000).

15. According to U.S. government statistics, the U.S. trade deficit with China rose from $39.5 billion in 1996 to $49.7 billion in 1997 and $56.9 billion in 1998.

agreements with one country after another, including the United States. In November 2001 China was officially accepted by the WTO as a member.

Prestige

As mentioned earlier, the phrase "a responsible great power" had two connotations. In addition to creating a reputation of being responsible and cooperative, China's exchange rate policy was motivated by a desire to improve its international prestige as an influential great power.

States, like individuals, pursue prestige as well as material interests (Thucydides 1972, 80; Morgenthau 1967, 36). National greatness has long been a cherished goal for the Chinese. The combination of pride in ancient Chinese civilization with the humiliations of the nineteenth and early twentieth centuries produced a particularly strong desire by the Chinese for international recognition. The pursuit of a respectful place in the family of nations inspired revolutionaries from Sun Yat-sen to Mao Zedong. When Deng Xiaoping took power in the late 1970s, this ambition remained as strong as ever.

However, Deng adopted a more pragmatic strategy to achieve this goal. In sharp contrast with Mao, whose foreign policy was characterized by high drama and confrontation with the major powers of the world, Deng emphasized the need for China to keep a low profile in international affairs, so that China could concentrate on modernizing its economy (Chen 1997). Accordingly, Chinese foreign policy in the 1980s was quite conservative, concentrating on a limited number of issues directly affecting China's national interest. In Deng's own words (1994, 363), "We are not going to be the head [*bu dangtou*] no matter what. This is a fundamental national policy."

As China's economy grew and the living standards of the people rose rapidly, Chinese confidence in their national power and destiny also grew. Around the mid-1990s, this new confidence found sensational expressions in the popular media (Song, Zhang, and Qiao 1996; Li and Yong 1997). Official rhetoric also indicated subtle changes. There was less emphasis on Deng's principle that China should bide its time and cultivate strength (*taoguang yanghui*). Instead, the new leadership under Jiang Zemin moved toward an emphasis on China's status as one of the great powers in an emerging multipolar world. China, alongside other great powers, should be a manager of the international system (*People's Daily* 12/15/97). "Great power strategy" (*daguo zhanlue*) and "great power relations" (*daguo guanxi*) have become central concerns for Chinese policymakers and analysts (Yu 1998; Zhu, Pu, Tang 1999).[16]

16. Western scholars, however, are doubtful of China's great power status (Kim 1997; Segal 1999; Yahuda 1999).

Economic statecraft, including exchange policies, can have an impact on nations' prestige. First of all, regardless of whether or not it makes economic sense, the strength of a currency is often associated with the strength of a country. As Charles Kindleberger (1970, 204) pointed out, "A country's exchange rate is more than a number. It is an emblem of its importance in the world, a sort of international status symbol." Given China's self-perception as a rising power and its desire to convince the world of this perspective, it is not hard to imagine that Chinese policymakers might have seen the devaluation of the Chinese currency as bad policy, especially with the whole world watching. Although there was little public debate at that time over how a devaluation of the RMB might diminish China's international status, the near-patronizing rhetoric used by the Chinese media toward countries whose currencies had collapsed was an indirect reflection of such considerations.

Second, exchange policy, like diplomatic gesturing and military posturing, can be used to demonstrate a country's prowess and boost its prestige. In the aftermath of the Asian financial crisis, the Chinese government saw an opportunity for the country to show its ability to make a difference through its action.[17] In particular, it was eager to contrast the growing clout of China to the decline of Japan's status.[18] In the aftermath of the financial crisis, Japan came under international criticism for its paralysis. The U.S. government praised China's policy while it criticized Japan's slow pace in reforming its financial institutions and ensuring the stability of the Japanese yen (*Washington Post* 6/27/98). Businesspeople in the West expressed the same sentiment. An op-ed article in the *New York Times* (6/26/98) declared that the Asian financial crisis made clear that "the economic and geopolitical leader of the region is no longer Japan but China." Given China's determination to compete with Japan for regional leadership, this contrast made the policy of no devaluation especially appealing to the Chinese government.

China's exchange rate policy seems to have been quite successful in improving the country's status as a consequential power. In May 1998, U.S. Assistant Secretary of State Stanley Roth said that China should be treated as a "major power" on virtually every big international issue from the Asian crisis to the Middle East peace process (*Strait Times* 5/14/98). During his summit with President Jiang Zemin in June 1998, President Bill Clinton praised China for its "statesmanship and strength" (*Strait Times* 6/28/98).

17. In this context, it is interesting to note that the Chinese government was very sensitive to any political gains Taiwan might get from the crisis. The Chinese government warned Taiwan not to take advantage of this crisis to improve its international status (*Banker* 2/98).

18. In addition to its exchange rate policy, China contributed roughly $4 billion to the rescue fund shortly after the crisis broke out, which, according to one analyst, was "the first evidence of China taking an international stance. . . . The amount of money was not that great, but psychologically China played the role that you would expect Japan to play in this crisis" (*Euromoney* 5/98).

Similarly, the Singaporean minister of information and arts praised China for not devaluing the RMB and for its efforts to stimulate its domestic economy. He pointed out that China's role had to be seen in relation to other big powers, namely, the United States, Japan, and the European Union. He warned that the role individual nations played during the Asian financial crisis would determine how much say they had after the crisis was over (*Strait Times* 4/23/98). Chinese policymakers and analysts were quite frank in their expression of satisfaction in this regard (*Washington Post* 6/21/98; Chen 1999). Some analysts explicitly cheered China's gain as "another point scored in its hard struggle to catch up with and surpass Japan to become the economic leader of Asia" (Hua and Huang 1998). Some went so far as to declare that owing to its stand on the RMB, China had become an equal partner of the United States in the world, a status that otherwise would have taken another two decades to realize (Yang 1999; Zhang 1999).

CONCLUSION

In the aftermath of the Asian financial crisis, the Chinese government faced a choice in its exchange rate policy: to devalue or not to devalue the RMB. From a purely economic perspective, arguments could be made on both sides. On the one hand, devaluation could ease the pressure faced by China in exports, FDI inflows, and economic growth rate. On the other hand, devaluation could worsen China's problems with capital flight, bank fragility, and foreign debt payment. Overall, the economics was ambiguous and indeterminate as to what policy China should choose. A number of political factors, however, provided strong incentives for the decision against devaluation. Holding the value of the RMB was important to maintaining the Chinese government's legitimacy at home. It was also seen as greatly contributing to China's international reputation and prestige. While economic theory sheds little light on the path taken by Chinese decision makers, a political analysis turns out to be quite illuminating.

Contrary rhetoric notwithstanding, governments do not make monetary policies on the grounds of economic efficiency. Instead, they are motivated or constrained by all kinds of political considerations—power, ideology, and conflict. Of these three broad categories of political factors, this case about China is primarily a story of power.

This is not to say that ideology and conflict of interests play no role in policy making. They do, and they did. As Jonathan Kirshner points out in the first chapter to this volume, ideology can be a powerful force shaping policy choices. This point is made clear by Eric Helleiner's study of the paradigm of "embedded liberalism" in the post–World War II era and Ilene Grabel's examination of the theory of policy credibility in recent years. Both chapters show how some ideas can take on the quality of faith, despite ambiguous economic grounding, and influence policymakers across the world. In the case of China, the importance of fighting inflation has been such a faith-like idea. For reasons of historical experiences, Chinese leaders have long been obsessed with a fear of inflation. Even though there is little evidence that moderate inflation is harmful to the country's economy, throughout the reform period the government has made it its mission to keep inflation low. In the aftermath of the Asian financial crisis, the major problem faced by China's economy was deflation rather than inflation. But in the early months after the Asian financial crisis broke out, Chinese policymakers continued their familiar preoccupation with controlling inflation. The government's ideological commitment to low inflation was in part responsible for its decision against RMB devaluation.

Conflict of interests is another important political source of monetary policy, as Kirshner notes in chapter 1. In the case of China, the exchange rate policy had distributional consequences for different groups. The policy against devaluation was very costly to township and village enterprises and foreign-invested enterprises, which were largely dependent on exports. These enterprises, along with local governments that relied on them for tax revenues and employment, lobbied hard for devaluation of the RMB. But they simply did not have enough political clout in this policy area to feature prominently in the decision-making process. This lack of influence forms a sharp contrast to the strong influence of interest groups on monetary policy in Argentina as described by Hector Schamis, in Japan as discussed by William Grimes, and in Germany and France as studied by Michelle Chang (all in this volume). This lack of influence on the part of interest groups is testimony to the remarkable and somewhat surprising resilience of state autonomy and capacity in China despite the trend of decentralization.[19]

Compared with ideology and conflict, power—though power of a soft kind—was much more important in shaping China's policy making in this case. As Kirshner (1995; this volume) has argued, states use monetary policy to enhance their own autonomy and influence. Indeed, the pursuit of state power both at home and abroad was a central element underlying China's policy choice. At the domestic level, Beijing's primary motivation to hold the value of the RMB was to prevent the ripples of the Asian financial crisis from weakening public confidence in the government and undermining the government's legitimacy.

On the international front, the most important driving force behind China's policy choice was to improve China's image in the world community. This image-building effort involved two related but distinctive aspects.

---

19. Much has been written on the weakening of the Chinese state as a result of decentralization (Goodman and Segal 1994). However, as this case indicates, the weakening of the state has not happened evenly across different policy areas. In some areas, particularly those having to do with foreign relations, the central government remains quite autonomous and strong.

One aspect was reputation. The Chinese government sought to use its policy to demonstrate that China was a trustworthy partner rather than a rogue state. It was particularly keen to show its willingness to carry out its commitment to Hong Kong's continued prosperity under Chinese rule and to convince major trading partners of its readiness to become a responsible member of the WTO. This runs parallel with Francis Gavin's analysis (this volume) of U.S. monetary policy, which shows that U.S. commitment to the Bretton Woods system during the 1960s was guided, among other factors, by concerns over U.S. credibility in the eyes of allies and rivals.

The Chinese government also saw the crisis as an opportunity to raise China's international prestige both as a country with a relatively strong currency and as a powerhouse whose policy choices had profound consequences for the region and the world. The connection between monetary policy and national prestige is a latent theme shared by a number of other cases studied in this volume, but most of the authors do not explicitly use the concept of prestige. Grimes's study of Japanese monetary policy comes close to it by suggesting that a major motivation of the internationalization of the yen is the issue of Japan's position in the international system, including gaining respect for Japan on the world stage.

Insofar as the past is the best predictor we have for the future, the present study suggests that political motivations and constraints will continue to shape China's monetary policy in the twenty-first century. Just as the Chinese government based its exchange rate policy in the late 1990s on political rather than economic grounds, China's future monetary policies are likely to continue to be shaped by political factors such as power, ideology, and conflict of interests.

CHAPTER EIGHT

Internationalization of the Yen and the New Politics of Monetary Insulation

WILLIAM W. GRIMES

Since 1997, the "internationalization of the yen" has been a hot topic among Japanese policymakers, politicians, and pundits.[1] While the debate has been largely ignored outside Japan, within the country it is seen to touch on fundamental questions of Japan's role in the world, the direction of change in its financial system, and the future of its economic system as a whole. The internationalization debate offers differing ideas on the utility and desirability of having one's own currency be an international or regional "key" currency, and helps us to understand Japan's role in the international monetary sphere and perhaps the roles of other major players.

The debate not only has addressed fundamental issues of power and vision but also has contributed to changes in important Japanese policy stances. In what may be the most important and controversial practical ramification for international political economy, the yen internationalization debate has become closely connected with the more widely controversial proposal for an "Asian Monetary Fund" or its equivalent. The two goals are complementary in a number of the specific policies they imply, and even though they do not have precisely the same practical meaning, the problems they are meant to address are largely identical.

One of the major problems for which yen internationalization and regional monetary arrangements have been proposed as possible solutions is the desire to insulate domestic economic policy making from globalization pressures. The breakdown of the postwar Keynesian compromise of "embedded liberalism" in the era of globalization has significantly reduced the possibility of economic policy pluralism for countries that are full participants in the global economic system.[2] The reduction in choices available to

---

1. I would like to thank Shinju Fujihira, Paul Habeshaw, Peter Johnson, Peter Katzenstein, Beth Simmons, and all the authors in this volume for their helpful comments on various drafts.
2. On embedded liberalism, see Ruggie 1982, 1993. Regarding the challenge that globalization poses for embedded liberalism, see, among others, Strange 1998b; Kirshner 2000; Gilpin 2000; as well as Grabel's and Helleiner's chapters in this volume. Polanyi's (1944) warnings about unfettered capitalism remain relevant to this point of view.

states in their macroeconomic (and to a lesser extent, microeconomic) management eliminates the possibility of using such policies as a political safety valve if global economic forces lead to destabilizing swings or disparities in relative wealth, income, or power, either within or between economies. As Eisuke Sakakibara, a former Japanese vice-minister of finance for international affairs, warned, "While we cannot deny the reality of globalization, if we do not curb the ferocity of fundamentalist capitalism, world order may collapse with a crash in the near future" (Sakakibara 1998, 180).

Inevitably, international power is also at issue. The issue of insulation is not purely economic—it is also political. The strong U.S. and Chinese opposition to Japan's initial proposal of an Asian Monetary Fund reminds us that differing visions of regional leadership run deep. The tensions caused by the challenge to a U.S.-dominated international financial architecture are not purely technical, as Grabel (this volume) makes clear. On the other hand, Chinese policymakers' visions of their own role in the world made for a very suspicious initial response to Japan's leadership in trying to reshape the regional monetary system (Wang, this volume). Japan's ability to take the lead in that regard (and thus in insulating its own economy from the effects of rapid global capital movement) depends finally not only on its powers of persuasion and co-optation of potential participants and opponents but also on its vision of a future global or regional system. In this respect, the currency debate is embedded in the broader issue of Japan's appropriate role in Asia and the world. Thus, the role of ideas is important, even as those ideas remain contested.

Although in its particulars this chapter may appear unrelated to the others in this volume, in fact it addresses the same problems. Along with Grabel and Blyth, Japanese policymakers are grappling with the problem of determining an appropriate framework for global capital movements and economic management. Like the developing and transitional economy policymakers described by Wang, Schamis, Stasavage, Helleiner, and even Abdelal, Japanese policymakers simultaneously seek insulation and engagement through the external stabilization of their currency. But like Chang's Europe of the 1980s and 1990s and Gavin's United States of the 1960s, present-day Japan finds itself in a position where it can actually shape its external—or at least regional—environment. Moreover, in dealing with these fundamental issues of financial architecture and economic management, Japan must make choices based on ambiguous economics and contested politics.

AMBIGUOUS ECONOMICS

It is possible to define internationalization of the yen, or of any other currency, in the following manner: "An international currency is . . . a currency that is used as a measure of value or for settlements in international trade of goods and services and in international capital transactions, or a currency that is held in the international currency reserves of private economic bodies or national currency authorities" (FEC 1999, appendix, p. 5). Nonetheless, the concept remains slippery in many ways (Cohen 1998a, 98–109). One issue is that of measurement. What is the geographic or economic sphere in which it is meaningful to measure the international use of a currency? What level of use is high enough to prompt the description "international currency"? Which of the functions mentioned—settlements, unit of account, or store of value—is most important to the international status of a currency? None of these questions has a clear answer in theory, although we can use them to delineate the *comparative* international use of a currency.

In the case of Japan, the low use of the yen as an international currency does seem striking. Despite Japan's large share of the international economy (in 1999, 14 percent of total production, 7 percent of trade), the yen is used in only about 5 percent of world trade and comprises only about 5 percent of world foreign currency reserves (FEC 1999, Exhibit I-1; SGPIY 2001, Exhibit 1). Thus, it stands in marked contrast to the U.S. dollar, which is used for about 50 percent of world trade and comprises 65 percent of reserves, and the European currencies, accounting for about 17 percent of reserves (30 percent of trade and 20 percent of reserves prior to the introduction of the euro) (SGPIY 2001, Exhibit 6; FEC 1999, Exhibit I-1). Even looking at Japan's own trade, yen-denominated trade accounts for only between 20 and 25 percent of all imports and around 35 percent of all exports. These shares are lower than own-currency-denominated trade shares for France and Italy before monetary union, let alone the United Kingdom and Germany (FEC 1999, Exhibits I-2, I-3). (The U.S. dollar is in a different class altogether because of the large number of internationally traded commodities that are customarily invoiced in dollars.) In finance, where Japan is the world's largest net creditor, the picture is perhaps even more dismal: as of March 2001, only 7.2 percent of outstanding international bonds and 6.2 percent of outstanding international bank loans were yen-denominated, and in the 1990s only about 20 percent of overseas lending by *Japanese* banks was denominated in yen (BIS 2001a, 14, 17; FEC 1999, Exhibit I-5). The only place where yen-denominated transactions are a large share of total world transactions is in foreign exchange markets, where the yen held a 20 to 25 percent share in the 1990s, compared to a 90 percent share for the U.S. dollar and 38 percent share for the euro (BIS 2001b, Table 3). (Foreign currency trades naturally involve two currencies, so the total is 200 percent.) The yen's share is not very high even if we look only at Asia, presumably Japan's most likely sphere of influence. These facts are particularly striking given the many predictions for Japanese economic predominance in the late 1980s and early 1990s, as well as the international prominence of Japanese firms and financial institutions. The question of why is one that many Japanese observers and policymakers have asked themselves.

But while Japanese policymakers fret over the yen's modest international role, the economic costs and benefits of yen internationalization are actually quite ambiguous. Standard benefits of having an international currency include seigniorage (implicit government "revenues" created by paying for fiscal purchases with currency whose value will be eroded by inflation), the ability to finance current account and budget deficits in the home currency, increased market liquidity, and reduced volatility of costs and revenues for traders in goods and services.

In Japan's case, seigniorage is not really a major part of the debate—indeed, with Japan's current deflation, seigniorage might actually work in the opposite direction. There have been some half-hearted attempts to calculate potential seigniorage benefits, but they are seldom cited.[3] The only time seigniorage really makes an appearance is in complaints about the seigniorage that accrues to the United States from international use of the dollar.

Financing of current account deficits is similarly not an issue for the medium term for Japan, which is after all the world's largest creditor nation. Financing of budget deficits is potentially more important. The Japanese government is now running the largest deficits in the world, at exactly the same time that the structure of government bond (JGB) purchases is changing. Government trust funds are moving away from automatic purchases of government bonds, the Bank of Japan no longer purchases short-term financing bills at below-market interest rates, and banks are increasingly being urged to diversify their assets. In these circumstances, increased foreign purchases might reduce the danger of sudden increases in JGB yields such as those seen in December 1998–January 1999 (although that is by no means assured). Fear of increased borrowing costs presents a clear rationale for the state to benefit from more liquid markets with greater foreign participation.

As for reduced volatility of costs and revenues in international transactions, here again the benefits are ambiguous. Certainly that is the conclusion of a spring 2000 study of top executives of leading Japanese firms (Keizai Dōyūkai 2000). The study found that very few firms were worried about the effects of short-term volatility in exchange rates on their profits. While some government-affiliated reports have explained this lack of concern as "inertia," the Keizai Dōyūkai study emphasized the advanced hedging capabilities of the major Japanese multinational companies. If a Japa-

---

3. The Ministry of Finance, for example, has made no attempt to calculate seigniorage from expanded use of the yen. Kwan (2001) explicitly dismissed its importance. The only mention I have come across that seigniorage is a major benefit for Japan of internationalization of the yen is from Kihon Seisaku Kenkyūkai (1999, 16), on the basis that Japan's aging society will in time lead to low savings and the need for seigniorage revenue.

nese firm is capable of hedging currency risk at a lower cost than its counterpart in a transaction, then there are gains to be made by having the Japanese firm take on that risk. Some Japanese multinational companies apparently have also become adept at shifting production among their various global affiliates even in the short term, in order to lessen the effects of currency volatility.

The major potential costs of currency internationalization can be found in the responsibility for system maintenance—acting as international lender of last resort, providing a market for distressed goods, and in the case of a nominal anchor, being unable to adjust by altering the value of the home currency in an autonomous manner (Gilpin 1987, 75). Like the benefits just discussed, these apparently economic costs are essentially unmeasurable because of the difficulty of assigning values to political variables. For example, even if one could accurately gauge the risks and direct costs of a currency crisis on a lender of last resort (a task made even more doubtful by the impossibility of gauging strategic interaction effects or predicting contagion effects), that would go only a short way toward assessing the costs and benefits of carrying out such a function. The costs of saying no to a neighbor in crisis are also unmeasurable. How, after all, do states value economic and political stability of their neighbors, their bilateral and multilateral relations, and their reputations on the world stage?

Similarly, providing a market for distressed goods or being a nominal anchor may mean subordinating domestic economic goals or fundamentals such as the savings-investment balance. Japanese policymakers have also spent a considerable amount of time thinking about how tax policy and financial regulation affect yen internationalization. Needless to say, the politics of these issues goes far beyond a simple cost-benefit analysis and inevitably means differential benefits and costs for different sectors of society. For example, some of the tax policy debates center on the dilemma that easing rules to promote internationalization of the yen can also make tax evasion easier for wealthy individuals or corporations (Grimes 2002).

Finally, it is widely feared that a more internationalized yen will mean a stronger yen. While this equation is economically indeterminate, greater international availability and overhang of any currency probably will make it harder for domestic authorities to target a given exchange rate (Kwan 2001, 118). Even if internationalization were to strengthen the yen, this would clearly have benefits for some economic actors and costs for others; however, in Japan, popular discourse is predominantly afraid of a strong currency because of the country's perceived vulnerability as a trade-dependent economy. Nonetheless, such concerns represent more of a short-term issue because exchange rates should be more stable *within* the Asian region, which already accounts for about 40 percent of Japan's total trade, a share that might be expected to rise with stabilization of regional currency values (IMF, various years).

Turning to the broader issues of insulation and stabilization, it is impossible to discuss yen internationalization at this point in history without referring to the Asian financial crisis of 1997–99. It is widely believed in Japan that the crisis might not have occurred were it not for Asian currencies' implicit or explicit dollar pegs (FEC 1999; Nihon Keizai Chōsakai 1998; IIMA 1999a, 1999b; Pempel 1999c, 75–76). If one accepts this argument, then internationalization—or at least regionalization—of the yen is of huge importance to the Asian region and to Japan. Moreover, it is also widely believed that rapid and massive provision of capital to ailing currency authorities early in the crisis could have stopped the crisis short and contained its contagion effects. This argument is the basis for proposals for Japan to expand its regional responsibilities as lender of last resort.

Despite the certainty with which these arguments are sometimes asserted, however, here too the economics are ambiguous. The argument goes like this: Most of the East and Southeast Asian currencies other than the yen were on an implicit or explicit nominal dollar peg in the 1990s. The rapid appreciation of the yen against the dollar in 1994 and 1995 created current account benefits for the countries in question—either because they increased their exports to Japan (Thailand, Indonesia) or because their products became more competitive on world markets relative to Japanese products (South Korea). However, when the strong yen trend was reversed after the summer of 1995, these countries rapidly found themselves running trade deficits. The accumulation of trade deficits meant outflows of foreign exchange and ultimately led to currency crises. If currencies had been pegged to a basket of currencies that included the yen more prominently (and thus the dollar less prominently), shifts in the yen-dollar exchange rate would not have had such huge effects on the economies (Kwan 2001; FEC 1999; Nihon Keizai Chōsakai 1998).

While the story appears plausible, there are several problems with it. The three main ones are that it does not distinguish between real and nominal exchange rates, it does not take into account the recession in Japan, and it does not account for domestic financial problems in Thailand and South Korea.

The first point is the most obvious. The Thai baht and other currencies that ended up in crisis were appreciating in terms of their real effective rates, regardless of what the yen-dollar exchange rate was doing. Financial liberalization—particularly in Thailand but also elsewhere—had led to massive capital inflows, leading to domestic inflation—particularly in asset prices—when productivity gains could not keep up with new investment. With a nominal peg to the dollar and low U.S. inflation, the inevitable result was deterioration in international competitiveness and excess demand at home—in other words, a worsening of the trade account. Once international investors came to see Thai assets as overvalued, capital flows reversed and a currency crisis ensued. In other words, the attachment to a nominal peg in the face of significant inflation differentials with the outside world, rather than the currency composition of that peg, was the key to the deterioration of the real effective exchange rate for Asian currencies (Ohno 1999a).[4]

Second, Japan's economic stagnation had important effects beyond the exchange rate dynamic. Through the trade channel, stagnant demand in Japan meant that it was taking in fewer imports (Japan is the number one or two importer of goods from virtually every East or Southeast Asian economy), and that its exports were competing with those of the other Asian economies, particularly South Korea and Taiwan. Meanwhile, the domestic problems of Japanese financial institutions meant that by 1995 many were cutting back their international operations and lending, which hit Asian economies disproportionately hard. And investment from other Japanese firms was also drying up. These effects help to explain the lack of "cover" for Asian current account deficits but are not related either to the choice of exchange rate regimes or the role of the yen as an international currency.

A third problem with the currency basket composition story is that it ignores the role of policy and structure *within* the crisis economies (Goldstein 1998, 7–14, 23–26, 65–72; Council on Foreign Relations Task Force 1999, 44–51; Eichengreen 1999, 38–51). I have already noted capital liberalization as an element in the mix; in retrospect, it is hard to argue that capital account liberalization was not premature, given the development of local financial systems. The problems of the financial systems included inadequate regulation as well as low levels of sophistication (and sometimes high levels of corruption) among financial institutions that were mediating rapid inflows of money.

Thus, while it is evident that better-composed currency baskets (whether in terms of trading share or competition) are preferable to poorly composed ones, the case for the role of the yen in and of itself as a brake against regional currency crises is at best ambiguous. However, a good argument can certainly be made for the benefits *to Japan* of better currency baskets in regional economies. Whether that will necessarily lead to greater internationalization of the yen is somewhat questionable. There is statistical evidence that monetary authorities in Korea and some other Asian economies began to give a greater weight to the yen in their currency management in

---

4. There are at least two possible ways out of the problem of the nominal peg. The more orthodox approach is sterilization of capital inflows to maintain a fairly constant price level—a tall order given the magnitudes of capital inflow relative to the economy as a whole. The second, perhaps more practical way is through capital controls. While capital controls are never perfectly effective, Wang (this volume) shows how China faced a fundamentally different level of threat to its currency values compared to the other major Asian developing economies, owing to its ability to prevent capital flight. Malaysia's experience with currency controls is also suggestive.

2000–2001, even though there was no dramatic change in the use of yen as a vehicle of exchange, means of invoicing, or store of value.[5]

A final issue of ambiguous economics is to be found in the whole idea of transforming a national currency into an international one. That is, what policies will make a currency attractive enough to economic partners in other countries that they will choose to use that currency in place of another? There are very few clear historical examples of states consciously choosing to make their currencies "key" currencies and succeeding, but there are clearly certain characteristics that make some currencies more attractive for international use. These characteristics include currency stability and highly liquid financial markets, but they do not seem to be sufficient. Some Japanese authors (e.g., Kaneko 1999, 9–10) have also pointed to explicitly political factors, such as military hegemony and leadership in other areas, that support the key currency status of a national currency. In the absence of a clear guide, then, the practicality—let alone the benefits and costs—of promoting internationalization remains in question.

THE CHANGING DEBATE IN JAPAN

In addition to theoretically measurable issues, another source of ambiguity in the discussion of international currencies is the meaning that is assigned to international currency status by policymakers and market participants. Here we cannot just let economics be our guide. It is around these ambiguities that the Japanese debate over the implications of yen internationalization has circled for over twenty-five years. In particular, the justifications and proposed methods of promoting yen internationalization have changed through the years.

The earliest references to internationalization of the yen date to the mid-1970s (Ginkō Tsūshinsha 1976; Kondō 1979). Policymakers expected that the declining role of the U.S. dollar in the world economy would mean a commensurate increase in the role of the currencies of the major surplus economies—the German mark and the Japanese yen. Warnings of the potentially severe disequilibrating effects of the "dollar overhang" added to fears that the yen would become an international key currency and that Japan would thus become unable to prevent its rapid appreciation.[6] Thus, the issue of yen internationalization in the 1970s was fundamentally identi-

---

5. According to data supplied by Kenneth Courtis, vice chairman of Goldman Sachs Asia, in December 2001. This trend developed after 2000. Indeed, a semi-official Japanese report from June 2000 found that "Asian countries' exchange rate regimes are thus reverting to the regimes—virtually pegged to the dollar—that existed prior to the crisis" (SGPIY 2000, 12).

6. For a contemporary worst-case scenario regarding the dollar overhang, see Bergsten 1975. Hayami (1995, iii) argued that the dollar overhang has increased over time and is continuing to destabilize the international system.

fied with fears of losing control over international competitiveness, as well as over domestic monetary policy.

By the early 1980s, floating exchange rates were largely accepted as legitimate or at least inevitable, and the world had already managed to survive the dreaded plunge in the dollar, as seen in the dollar support package of autumn 1978. Thus, the driving force for the debate on yen internationalization no longer focused on Japan's responsibility for maintaining the endangered international monetary system. Rather, it involved the need to deal with the rapidly changing status of Japanese financial institutions (Frankel 1984; Rosenbluth 1989). High savings and declining investment opportunities for investing those savings increased the "costs of closure" for Japanese financial institutions and created great pressures to make capital outflows easier.[7]

In the face of these various pressures, reformers in the Ministry of Finance and the financial world turned their rhetoric to the benefits of internationalization of the yen. In the 1980s, the connotation was of taking advantage of opportunity rather than of just responding to exogenous events. The measures advocated went beyond small openings in the capital account or increased activity in international fora. These decision makers called for Tokyo itself to become a major hub of international finance, and for Japanese financial institutions to take a leading role in providing financial services throughout the world. This new agenda recognized for the first time the potential of finance to be a leading economic sector in its own right, rather than just an adjunct to manufacturing.

The efforts of this forward-thinking group were only partially successful, but by the late 1980s the concept of yen internationalization had changed again. This time, Japan's economic rise, and America's apparent economic descent, had raised the question of how Japan could convert its economic power into political power and defend itself against unreasonable demands from the United States. One answer was to promote internationalization of the yen, particularly in the Asian region. By forming a de facto trading and financial "yen bloc," it would be possible to gain cooperation from neighboring states and to develop exclusive markets that were beyond the reach of U.S. policy. While financial reformers continued to try to use yen internationalization as a justification for greater liberalization, they were limited in their successes. Instead, the policies of yen internationalization focused on aid, recycling of current account surpluses through government financial institutions such as the Export-Import Bank (now merged into the Japan Bank for International Cooperation), and encouraging the expansion of Japanese manufacturing networks throughout East and Southeast Asia.

---

7. The concept of "costs of closure" is from Frieden and Rogowski (1996, especially 34). Rosenbluth (1989) made a similar argument for Japanese capital liberalization in the 1980s.

The debate over yen internationalization and how to promote it largely disappeared between the years 1993 and 1997, as Japanese policymakers focused more and more on dealing with the consequences of the deepening financial crisis at home.[8] But in 1997, two major events revitalized the whole concept: the Asian financial crises that began in Thailand in early July, and the announcement by the European Union of the first set of states that would participate in monetary union as of January 1999. The twin fears of financial contagion and of becoming a "local currency in a local market" brought internationalization of the yen back onto the national agenda, while transforming its meaning yet again.

The new debate is fundamentally one about *insulation* (Grimes 2000, 2002). This is somewhat paradoxical: in the 1980s, a Japan that was far less integrated into the world economy (in terms of intraindustry trade, inward foreign investment, transnational corporate alliances, etc.) sought a more prominent role in the world economy, whereas insulation in the late 1990s and early twenty-first century is a goal that must coexist with much greater integration. The terms of the debate are just as interesting and paradoxical. In the 1980s, discussion of internationalization of the yen focused on increasing the role of the yen *within* the existing framework of monetary relations. The current debate looks more broadly, considering new means to make the world safe for economic policy pluralism (Sakakibara 1998; LDP-SIY 1998). In other words, Japan has toyed with becoming a major advocate of a return to a kind of embedded liberalism, as demonstrated by a variety of official position papers and speeches from the Ministry of Finance. To use the language of Grabel and Blyth in this volume, Japanese policymakers are trying to alter the dominant "paradigm" or "trope" that has been institutionalized in the International Monetary Fund (IMF) and the ideological triumph of capital markets.

I have already considered arguments concerning the role of the Asian currency crisis in restarting the debate on yen internationalization. The importance of the role of European monetary integration is also straightforward. Japanese analysts have made the reasonable assumption that the euro—a new currency that represents 21 percent of global production and 30 percent of global trade (FEC 1999, Exhibit I-1)—will be used widely throughout the world for trade, finance, and exchange rate intervention. While eventually the euro will probably eat into the dollar's share, erosion of the yen's much smaller share is likely to reduce its international role much more decisively.[9] This explains why policymakers expect the yen's international role to decline, but it does not explain why that international role matters. I will return to this question later.

8. Two exceptions that I have found are Hayami 1995; Oka 1996.

9. The short-term impact of euro introduction has been less dramatic. As of April 2001 "the main impact of the introduction of the euro appears to have been through the elimination of intra-EMS [European Monetary System] trading" (BIS 2001b, 2).

For many Japanese policymakers, the current situation presents a clear rationale for internationalization of the yen. Taking the next step, advocates have come up with systematic programs for enhancing the yen's international—or at least regional—role. Policies fall into two general categories: liberalizing measures, and what I call "active measures" (Grimes 2002).

Liberalizing measures are based on the premise that given enough knowledge, market participants and foreign governments will use the international currencies that make the most economic sense in a given situation. Thus, these measures concentrate on increasing the attractiveness and liquidity of the yen as an investment instrument by eliminating disincentives to its use. Broadly targeted measures include the elimination of the Securities Transaction Tax (formerly levied on all securities trades) and the elimination of the withholding tax for foreigners on government securities purchases.[10] Other measures are more narrowly targeted. For example, since currency authorities need access to default-risk-free, highly liquid securities in order to ensure their ability to carry out rapid and effective interventions in the exchange market, yen internationalization advocates pushed for—and won—a substantial liberalization of the short-term government securities market.

Proposed and enacted active measures show less confidence in the invisible hand of the market. They include, for example, the provision of credit insurance on yen-denominated sovereign bonds issued by Asian nations, the expansion of yen-denominated lending by government financial institutions, the proposed Asian Monetary Fund, and even some fairly elaborate schemes to increase trade in yen-denominated commodities between Japan and its neighbors (Grimes 2002). Unlike liberalizing measures, active measures depend much more on positive government intervention and harken back to preferences for a developmentalist state over a regulatory state.

Advocates of liberalizing measures and of active measures are not necessarily in opposition to one another—indeed, they are often the same people. This is at least partly because there is no accepted economic or political theory that addresses the issue of intentionally becoming a key currency state. For many, active measures are an essential complement to liberalization, and it is at least plausible that they could work together as a seamless whole, even though their philosophical roots diverge seriously. (Indeed, a number of Ministry of Finance bureaucrats and others refer to internationalization of the yen and Asian integration as a "package.") Nonetheless, different actors seem to assign different costs and benefits to actual policies, even where they agree on the likely results.

10. See FEC 1999; Grimes 2002. To be exact, the withholding tax has not been eliminated across the board but only on purchases registered in the Bank of Japan's book-entry system and held in trust by a qualified "custodian" bank. This restricts the actual impact of the change on the attractiveness for foreign bondholders.

Finally, a commonality among most advocates of yen internationalization is the premise that the process should focus first on Asia. Despite some grandiose public statements by pundits about challenging the hegemony of the dollar (Kikkawa 1998; Ishihara 1998), most serious writers and policymakers see the primary benefits of yen internationalization as accruing in the Asian region, and any prospect for a more central global role emanating from strength in the region.

INTERNATIONALIZATION OF THE YEN AND INTERNATIONAL POWER

One of the major motivations for internationalization of the yen involves the issue of Japan's position in the international system. Posited benefits take both economic and political forms and are seen in terms of both absolute and relative capabilities.

One of the most popular and controversial arguments is posed in the 1998 book *Defeat in the Money Wars,* by a banker-turned-professor named Mototada Kikkawa. Kikkawa saw both absolute and relative costs. He argued (1998, 6–12) that Japanese savers have lost hugely by virtue of holding so much U.S. dollar–denominated debt—by his calculation, more than was lost in the implosion of Japan's financial bubble in the 1990s.[11] This loss of wealth has been possible because Japanese investors have been willing to lend to the U.S. government and private investors in dollars, thus making themselves vulnerable to unilateral changes in economic policy. In other words, the U.S. government has had the power to transfer the costs of its own economic mismanagement and adjustment to Japanese savers. Kikkawa also added a moral element to the mix. In an afterword entitled "The Grasshopper's 'New Economy,'" he argued that the dollar's dominance has rewarded the profligate U.S. economy (Aesop's grasshopper) and penalized Japan's diligent savers (the ant). Moreover, in so doing, the U.S. appetite for unproductive investment and consumption has cheated poor countries out of sufficient capital for development (Kikkawa 1998, 200–205).

Needless to say, there are immense holes in Kikkawa's argument. Nonetheless, his work does raise the question of whether it is the creditor or the borrower who should be expected to bear currency risk in a transaction. Kikkawa and other authors of similar works (e.g., Ishihara 1998) seem to have missed the obvious economic point that if a Japanese creditor can handle the resulting currency risk more cheaply than its foreign partner in a transaction, it can be mutually beneficial to denominate in yen. However, there may be a political angle to such decisions, at least in the aggregate.

---

11. *Calculation* may be too strong a word. Kikkawa completely ignored any differences in interest rates between dollar- and yen-denominated assets.

Properly speaking, this issue should be stated in terms of currency *volatility* rather than the expectation of a long-term trend of devaluation of the dollar—after all, the latter would presumably be reflected in interest differentials. The only way in which the threat of devaluation per se makes sense is if one utilizes a political argument: that the U.S. government would choose to manipulate exchange rates in order to injure Japanese (or other foreign) creditors in a specific instance, a reverse form of what Kirshner (1995, 46–47) termed "predatory currency manipulation." It is not necessary to adopt the minority position of McKinnon and Ohno (1997)—that U.S. policy has forced a long-term "syndrome of the ever-higher yen" on Japan—to believe that the U.S. government has engaged in some degree of predatory currency manipulation. There is, of course, no good reason to believe that rational economic actors will not make some sort of reasonable effort to charge a risk premium in the case of anything that even approaches a "syndrome." However, it does appear to be the case that U.S. economic authorities have made efforts to shift the burdens of macroeconomic adjustment to other countries, and that at least on occasion "talking down the dollar" has been as heavily practiced as aggressive trade policies (Strange 1987; Helleiner 2000; Hiwatari 1996).[12] (Japan's willingness to accept such burden shifting can be seen in its economically inefficient accumulation of over $390 billion in foreign exchange reserves as of October 31, 2001, in efforts to prevent yen appreciation.)

If we take seriously the problem of U.S. currency manipulation as a means of leverage against the Japanese state, as at least some observers do, then the type of insulation that we are discussing offers interesting parallels and contrasts with the problematiques of Grabel's and Helleiner's chapters in this volume. One of the most striking points about the debate on currency internationalization and regionalization in Japan is the disquiet concerning financial globalization (Grimes 2000). If globalizing forces provoke feelings of anxiety in the world's second largest economy—and indeed efforts at the global level to regulate the dangerous effects of globalization—then there is very little hope for the ability of small economies to insulate themselves. Moreover, the Japanese government's inability to put its concerns on the global agenda speaks powerfully to the political power of the globalization paradigm. Even the language used in official protestations—which has followed dominant discourses about moral hazard for bondholders and "highly leveraged institutions" (hedge funds), for example—differs from the language of much of the domestic debate, which is about national systems of capitalism.[13]

---

12. On talking down the dollar, see, for example, Destler and Henning 1989, 51.

13. This is even true of the official statements of Sakakibara, although he has made no effort to disguise his personal feelings concerning the importance of economic policy pluralism. See his 1998 and 1999 policy statements at http://www.mof.go.jp/jouhou/kokkin/system.htm and http://www.mof.go.jp/english/if/if.htm.

Authors such as Kikkawa (1998) also presented counterfactual arguments. While these counterfactuals are often rather simple-minded, they raise several questions. First, would the United States have been able to run such large current account deficits from the 1980s onward if international lenders had insisted on denominating large portions of debt in their home currencies rather than in dollars? Second, even if U.S. borrowers had been willing to do so (and risk premiums were not prohibitive), would the U.S. government have been able to maintain its position of predominance in international monetary politics? And would Japanese banks have had to pay the so-called "Japan premium" in international markets in 1997–98 if the vast bulk of Japan's accumulated foreign assets had not been denominated in dollars and other foreign currencies (Kihon Seisaku Kenkyūkai 1999, 13–15)?[14] Regardless of how well or poorly these questions are answered, they do point out the fundamental issue of Japan's vulnerability to the whims of its most important partner as long as most of its accumulated overseas assets are denominated in dollars.

A Strategy of Insulation

In the face of such vulnerability, the classic realist response is insulation (Gilpin 1987, 31–34). Actually, the political power story of pursuing yen internationalization can be told either as an attempt to insulate Japan from the effects of U.S. monetary power or as a means of pushing forward a positive policy agenda. There is a difference in connotation—insulation is primarily a defensive strategy, whose extreme logical extension is disconnection, whereas a positive policy agenda suggests engagement. But in practice, or at least in the short to medium term, they are identical. There is also little practical analytical leverage to be gained by distinguishing between economic and political goals of insulation, so I will treat them as one.

The main goal of internationalization of the yen is to stabilize Japan's international economic environment. It is hoped that greater use of the yen will reduce the volatility and risk of international transactions involving Japanese firms or government. One way in which that would work would be through shifting currency risk to others. But nearly universally among poli-

14. There are several reasons why I label the counterfactuals simple-minded. First, as even Kikkawa (1998, chap. 6) noted, one of the major reasons why Japanese financial institutions went into the highly liquid U.S. Treasuries market was that the Japanese financial markets were heavily regulated and uncompetitive. Second, one can only imagine the nationalist U.S. reaction in the 1980s to any attempt by Japanese financial firms to force the U.S. government and firms to borrow in yen—to some extent, Japanese purchases of dollar-denominated U.S. debt and securities prevented bilateral trade frictions from getting out of control. (Ironically, populist American authors like Burstein [1988] and Fallows [1989] suggested that Japanese purchases of dollar-denominated U.S. government debt were a powerful lever over U.S. government behavior.) Third, in regard to the "Japan premium," it is by no means clear that prudent lenders in any denomination would not have done the same thing. In any event, if sufficient political will had existed, the Japanese government had at its disposal sufficient funds in either yen or dollars to relieve the banks' "Japan premium" woes.

cymakers, one also finds a hope that greater regional use of the yen will lead to less volatility in exchange rates (FEC 1999; Kwan 2001; personal interviews).[15]

One part of the stability story is the assumption that regional currency stability will promote trade, as some argue it has done in Europe (Frankel and Rose 1998).[16] If Japan's trade and finance with a more yen-based Asian region were to grow more quickly than with dollar- and euro-dominated zones, the overall stability of its exchange rate environment would also improve. (This would be true even if the region did not move toward a true yen peg but if monetary authorities just increased the weight of the yen in their exchange rate management—as noted earlier, there is preliminary evidence that this is happening already.)[17]

But advocates mean currency stability not only within the Asian trading area but also with regard to the dollar and the euro. They argue that this might be accomplished through two avenues. First, the more viable alternatives there are to dollar-based financing, the less the United States will be able to ignore the destabilizing international effects of high current account deficits. At the same time, some participants in the debate argue that with a more fully internationalized yen and a unified euro, Japanese and European finance authorities will have greater bargaining power to force the United States to act to stabilize exchange rates (Utsumi 1999). In this respect, even though internationalization of the yen will not lead to much Japanese-held U.S. debt being held in yen (and thus not to a weapon that can be used directly against the United States), yen-euro stability might force the United States to modify its policies in order to prevent erosion of the dollar's position as the global economy's central currency (Cohen 1998a, chap. 7). (Generally speaking, however, given the relatively low shares of external trade of the United States, Japan, and the euro zone, it is hard to see the justification for large-scale sacrifice of domestic goals for the sake of currency stability, if it came to that.)

A final point to be made with respect to the idea of yen internationalization as insulation is the way it fits into Ruggie's (1982) concept of "embedded liberalism." As Ruggie argued, the postwar economic system was constructed to allow a maximal level of openness in international transactions (primarily trade at the beginning) *given that states themselves had the autonomous right to decide their own domestic macroeconomic and adjustment policies.*

15. Between 1999 and 2001, I discussed yen internationalization with more than two dozen of the key participants in the debate in Japan, including current and former officials of the Ministry of Finance and the Bank of Japan, Diet members, academics, and financiers.

16. Chang's chapter in this volume presents a more critical view of the certainty of trade promotion as a result of currency stability and unification.

17. Several studies demonstrated that the correlations of regional currency and yen values were extremely low in the 1980s and 1990s. Onishi (1999) offered an overview of some of these studies. The SGPIY (2000) showed that those correlations were again low in 1999 and 2000, following a brief increase during the 1998 weak yen episode.

The very aggressive financial deregulation and globalization strategy followed by the United States in the 1990s seems to threaten that principle of autonomy (Ruggie 1993; Kirshner 2000, 432–436; Helleiner 2000, this volume; Grabel, this volume), but more stable regional currency relations could improve Japan's ability to choose its own pace and style of adjusting to global pressures. In this respect, internationalization of the yen is partly a defensive response to globalization (Grimes 2000).

JAPAN'S ROLE IN THE ASIAN MONETARY SYSTEM

The Asian financial crisis of 1997–98 reignited debate in Japan (and in Asia generally) over the proper configuration of the regional monetary system and of Japan's role in it. While creating feelings of insecurity, it also provided an opportunity for Japan to take an enhanced leadership role in the region. Indeed, the actions of the Japanese government during the crisis appeared to many to have been far more responsible and prescient than those of the U.S. government or the IMF.

Despite speculation in the late 1980s and early 1990s that Japan would take a greater leadership role in the region—perhaps even leading a "yen bloc"—Japan's economic stagnation through most of the 1990s had largely eliminated any such expectations. But official pronouncements and actions in the midst and aftermath of the crisis served as a reminder that Japan had two attributes as a regional monetary leader that could make it attractive to its neighbors. First, Japan had money and was willing to use it for regional stabilization. Its willingness to take a leading financial role in the bailouts of Thailand, Indonesia, and South Korea stood in sharp contrast to the limited IMF and U.S. responses. Second, Japan's interpretation of the crisis—that Asian economies had been the victims of sudden, inexplicable shifts in capital flows rather than of their own mismanagement—was a much more attractive one to economies that were caught up in the crisis than was the U.S.-IMF alternative. (Subsequent events essentially showed that Japan was right, at least as seen in some influential postmortems such as Stiglitz 2000 and Yoshitomi and Ohno 1999.)

Starting with Japan's material abilities, evidence abounds. Japan contributed $4 billion, $5 billion, and $10 billion, respectively, to the bailouts of Thailand, Indonesia, and South Korea. Even these substantial amounts were dwarfed by estimates attached to the aborted Asian Monetary Fund plan in the fall of 1997—according to journalistic reports, proposed funds were to total $100 billion, with $50 billion being put up by Japan. After the Asian Monetary Fund plan was taken off the table, it was replaced by the more aid-focused, $30 billion New Miyazawa Plan. Although even these massive amounts did not make up for the money withdrawn from the region by Japanese financial firms in the late 1990s, they far exceeded any other serious proposals and they certainly made policymakers in and outside Asia take notice.

At the ideational level as well, Japan offered a potentially attractive alternative. Not only did Japanese policymakers and prominent analysts argue from early on in the crisis that the problem was due to the new reality of globalized capital and unregulated hedge funds, but also top Ministry of Finance officials took that analysis to G-7 and IMF meetings. In a series of extraordinary policy statements issued in 1998 and 1999, Finance Minister Kiichi Miyazawa and then Vice-Minister for International Affairs Eisuke Sakakibara

1. Argued for international authorities (mainly the IMF) to move to a system of rapid and massive credit provision without immediate conditions for countries that were facing sudden outflows of capital in spite of responsible fiscal and monetary policy;

2. Explicitly supported the right of developing economies to impose capital controls, thus attempting to reverse one important element of the 1990s Washington Consensus;

3. Explicitly supported managed exchange rate regimes, in defiance of the Washington Consensus "two-corner solution";

4. And called for international regulation of the hedge funds that some governments in Southeast Asia had prominently accused of capriciously triggering the crisis for their own gain.[18]

This intellectual agenda of insulation and economic policy pluralism, hedged though it was in standard neoclassical language, constituted a potentially powerful challenge to the Washington Consensus.[19]

In this regard, one of the more eye-opening contrasts is that of Japanese versus U.S. reactions to Malaysia's decision to impose controls on repatriation of capital. The U.S. government called on markets to discipline Malaysia's actions and made clear its preference that Malaysia not receive any official support for its strategy from other nations or international organizations.[20] Japan, on the other hand, made Malaysia the first recipient of a bridging loan under the New Miyazawa Plan.

18. Ministry of Finance policy statements on "Internationalization of the Yen" and "International Financial Architecture" on the Ministry of Finance Web site at http://www.mof.go.jp/jouhou/kokkin/system.htm; for English version, see http://www.mof.go.jp/english/if/if.htm.

19. I use the term *potentially* not only because of the difficulty of overturning a dominant policy paradigm in general (as Grabel demonstrates in this volume), but also because several of the broad proposals were never effectively spelled out. Technical problems inevitably remained severe in determining reasonable criteria for rapid and massive capital provision, as well as the conditions under which capital controls and currency pegs and baskets might be maintained, and the mechanics of regulating hedge funds. Thus, the Japanese proposals never constituted a paradigm challenge.

20. The U.S. position calls to mind Grabel's argument (this volume) about how the IMF has tried to enforce its preferred policies.

Difficulties of Regional Leadership

Despite the potential attractiveness of Japanese money and ideas in the Asian region, however, any attempt at establishing leadership faced serious political, economic, and even ideational difficulties.[21] The most immediately evident of the political hurdles was the strong opposition of the United States. Although it was presented as a principled opposition to potential moral hazard, few in Japan saw the U.S. position as anything other than an attempt to thwart Japanese regional leadership. Nonetheless, the U.S. position carried serious weight due to not only Japan's considerable dependence on the United States in both economic and political senses, but also the dependence of other Asian countries such as South Korea and the Philippines that refused to publicly support the Asian Monetary Fund plan. Moreover, the fears of many countries of losing access to U.S.- and European-dominated global capital created a clear incentive not to go along with a plan that was not fully ready to be put in place.

Japan's plans also met with opposition from China. Chinese authorities had good reason to be suspicious of an unexpected Japanese démarche, and owing to China's extensive system of capital controls, it had the luxury of not needing external help in the early heat of the crisis. As Wang (this volume) makes clear, Chinese leaders also valued the opportunity later on to stand as the region's most responsible leader when the country maintained the value of its currency even in the face of a 20 percent drop in the value of the yen from fall 1997 to mid-1998. Finally, the World Trade Organization accession debate in the United States provided added incentive for China to reject Japanese plans that the U.S. government publicly opposed.

Economically, very few states in the region were willing to take a chance at forgoing access to global capital markets, which had been instrumental in their rapid growth. Rather, their main goal was to regain the confidence of international markets, as seen in particular in the cooperative attitudes of Thailand and South Korea to IMF demands. In retrospect, the apparent success of the Malaysian policy of limited capital controls suggests that such fears may have been overblown, but the risk could not have been very attractive for most leaders (Pempel 1999b).

Finally, the plan contained logical problems as well. Most prominently, it is hard to imagine a regional order built on economic policy pluralism when external finance has been such an important part of most states' development strategies. Moreover, the fragmented financial markets of East and Southeast Asia would necessarily be too limited in terms of both scope

---

21. These difficulties are in addition to the somewhat half-baked nature of the Asian Monetary Fund idea. Based on extensive interviews with Japanese policymakers, it appears to be universally agreed within the Ministry of Finance and political worlds in Japan that Vice-Minister Sakakibara introduced the idea without gaining even the support of his own government, let alone that of other states in the region.

and scale to be a challenge to the dominant paradigm of financial globalization—what Sakakibara and others were calling for was not an integration of a single financial market, but a partial disintegration.[22]

Continuing Efforts toward a Regional System

While the Asian Monetary Fund proposal was quickly withdrawn, and formal currency baskets with a higher yen component have yet to catch on anywhere in the region, other moves toward a regionalization of monetary affairs go forward, apparently reflecting China's recalculation of the costs and benefits of financial cooperation. While few specifics are available (or even decided), we can now see the contours of a return to a sort of Asian Monetary Fund. The funds in the New Miyazawa Plan ($15 billion worth for short-term stabilization uses and $15 billion worth for longer-term uses) can be seen as a statement of Japanese commitment to regional stability.[23] Institutionally, two other initiatives loom large—the establishment of multilateral surveillance under the Manila Framework and the so-called Chiang Mai Initiative (Bergsten 2000).

As of November 2001, the Manila Framework surveillance regime (which includes the United States, Canada, Australia, and New Zealand, in addition to most of the major East Asian economies) was still at a relatively undeveloped stage, with little agreement even over what types of indicators should be subject to surveillance and discussion. The Chiang Mai Initiative, based on "ASEAN+3" cooperation among the ten members of the Association of Southeast Asian Nations (ASEAN), plus Japan, China, and South Korea, had developed somewhat further. The initiative called for the establishment of a set of bilateral and multilateral swap lines (agreements between governments to lend foreign exchange reserves to one another for short periods) among the countries.[24] The intention is to provide countries with expanded access to foreign exchange reserves in the event of a speculative attack on one or more regional currency. However, not all of the lines had yet been formalized in late 2001 (only the intra-ASEAN, Japan-

22. As opposed to Helleiner's (2000, 238) point about the economic and political implications of integrating European financial markets.

23. Funds in the New Miyazawa Plan are explicitly to be disbursed in yen, at least partly for the purpose of promoting internationalization of the yen as a major regional currency. Ironically, however, the plan's magnitude has been defined in dollars. In fact, the $30 billion total was not just a current calculation of the dollar equivalent at the time of the plan's announcement; the plan explicitly called for the yen equivalent of $30 billion dollars, a number that would obviously be expected to change over time, since the funds were not all disbursed at once.

24. ASEAN members include Brunei, Cambodia, Indonesia, Laos, Malaysia, Myanmar, the Philippines, Singapore, Thailand, and Vietnam. The multilateral swap line is an intra-ASEAN agreement, while Japan, China, and South Korea agreed to establish bilateral lines with each other and with each of the ASEAN states.

Malaysia, Japan-Thailand, and Japan-Korea lines), and these were relatively small when compared to the needs of economies in a crisis as in 1997–98 or even the actual Japanese contributions in that crisis.

Moreover, institution building is always hard, and ASEAN+3 cooperation faces major difficulties. Two of the most severe of these difficulties lie in ideas and leadership. Surveillance regimes make sense only where there is a clear sense of what factors need to be monitored, and there remains much confusion about this question. (Surveillance criteria logically need to go beyond indicators that are already subject to IMF surveillance; otherwise, the Manila Framework exercise would be redundant.) Ideas about how to prevent another Asian financial crisis while also maintaining access to global financial markets and fostering economic policy pluralism are as yet insufficiently developed to make Manila Framework discussions anything more than just talk.[25]

Similarly, the problem of analysis will inevitably plague any regional liquidity-provision regime that actually gets off the ground. At what point should collective action kick in to prop up a declining currency? How can participants distinguish between crises caused by contagion and those caused by bad policy? Surveillance based on clear criteria is a necessary first precondition of such collective action, but it is not necessarily determinative.

Perhaps a larger problem is that of leadership, particularly during crises. Put baldly, the question is, how can one state or group of states say no to a partner that is in serious economic trouble, even if surveillance has already made clear that its policies are irresponsible? Put even more baldly, what if the troubled economy were China? No Japanese writers of whom I am aware have any appetite for controlling the politics of neighboring or participating states (unlike France and Russia, as Stasavage and Abdelal, respectively, describe in this volume). Nonetheless, Japan's uncomfortable position as lead fund provider but ambiguous leader means that it may well find itself facing a choice between political showdown and economic loss in the case of crisis. At least for the moment, two factors reduce this risk, however. First, as noted earlier, the amounts of money are relatively small (indeed, much smaller than the funds that Japan actually put up for bailouts in 1997). Second, following the initial blowup over the Asian Monetary Fund proposal, Japan and other potential participants have been careful to emphasize that ASEAN+3 arrangements would complement, not supplant, standard IMF procedures. In particular, Japan's current agreements make ASEAN+3 liquidity provision a short-term, stopgap measure carried out in

25. The Tokyo-based Asian Development Bank Institute (headed by a retired Japanese economic bureaucrat) has been involved in trying to come up with an understanding of "capital-account crises." See Yoshitomi and Ohno 1999.

consultation with the IMF and only available until either the crisis fizzles or the IMF is able to assemble a rescue package (SGPIY 2001, 22–23).[26] Future developments or contingencies may alter the equation, however.

Looking to the Future

One of the most important economic and foreign policy debates in Japan in recent years has been over the broader issue of Japan's role in Asia.[27] With the Cold War over, and as Asian economies have grown in size, vibrancy, technological sophistication, and interconnectedness with the Japanese economy, serious debate has developed over whether Japan's future lies in Asia or in the West.

One of the visions that motivates a number of thinkers on the subject is that of an Asian analogue to the European Union (Kishimoto 1999; Inoki 2000; Kobayashi 1997). A regional economic union is clearly a long-term goal, but the debate over it does create the idea of a *process* of increasing engagement and integration. While the concept of "open regionalism" remains attractive, this line of thought suggests a move away from the more established Asia-Pacific Economic Cooperation (APEC) forum, thus suggesting a partial disengagement from the economic leadership of the United States.

More practically, the goal of an Asian economic union or even just increased economic integration calls for certain intermediate steps, all of which have important practical significance even if more ambitious integration ideals are not achieved. These intermediate steps include continued economic aid and investment from Japan, the possibility of regional or subregional free trade areas, and internationalization (or more accurately, increased regional use) of the yen (Kishimoto 1999; Kwan 1997; Ohno 1999b; Miura 2000; Miyoshi 1999). Internationalization of the yen in this case is not primarily for the purpose of insulating Japan's economy or reinvigorating its capital markets, but is presented as a means of stabilizing regional currencies and reducing barriers to financial and trade transactions. The yen itself is important not because political leadership is expected to come from Japan; rather, the yen is the only currency in the region that has international status. Also, the Japanese private sector is one of the major unifying forces in the region, having contributed to a complex regional division of labor through corporate investment and trading networks (Hatch and Yamamura 1996; Ernst 1994; Pempel 1997). Nonetheless, a regional

26. This assessment also reflects extensive interviews with Japanese policymakers and economists in August and September 2000 and July 2001, as well as news reports. See also Miura's (2000) summary of Japanese and other Asian think tank views on the matter.

27. Saori Nishida provided important research assistance for this section. Some of this debate has been addressed in English in Katzenstein and Shiraishi 1997; Funabashi 1995.

monetary system based at least initially on the yen also presupposes the Japanese government's underwriting of the system in case of trouble.

The importance of currency basket pegs in this point of view is considerable. Japanese policymakers have been quite enthusiastic about currency baskets as a means of reducing the effects of movements among the major global currencies on regional economies—in other words, calling for exchange rate management based on a weighted average of the dollar, yen, euro, and perhaps other currencies.[28] Over time, those weights may well change and the baskets may come to include the Chinese yuan among other currencies, thus reducing the essential (hegemonic) role of the yen. Moreover, if currency baskets are a good means of stabilizing individual currencies versus the major currencies, they may also be good for stabilizing regional currencies against each other—in other words, the optimal currency basket may be a *regional* one rather than a variety of country-specific ones.[29] The possibility of a regional currency basket clearly draws on the example of the European Monetary System and its Exchange Rate Mechanism and suggests the possibility of long-term evolution toward a unified Asian currency—but without spelling out the potentially troublesome division of responsibilities among Japan, China, and other states.

THE YEN IN THE WORLD POLITICAL ECONOMY

The push for internationalization of the yen is meaningful for Japan, Asia, and the global political economy at a number of levels. It is deeply connected with the sense of vulnerability felt in many areas of the world in the face of globalization and the ongoing demise of embedded liberalism in the financial sphere.

Despite the enthusiasm for financial liberalization on the part of some participants in the yen debate in Japan, at its core yen internationalization is about insulation and stabilization. By increasing the weight of the yen in the global and regional financial systems, Japanese policymakers hope to reduce their economy's susceptibility to currency volatility and to capricious

28. Kwan (2001) presented a way of calculating appropriate weights based on elasticities, while the analysis of the FEC (1999) presupposes another method based on trade weights. This technical debate is meaningful for actual management of exchange rates but is not directly relevant to the overall argument about the *type* of exchange rate system a given state follows.

29. Optimum-currency-area theory presents some possibilities about which state groupings (if any) would be most rational. See Kwan 2001 for such an analysis dividing Asia into two separate currency areas (developing countries such as Thailand and Malaysia versus more industrialized economies such as Japan, South Korea, and Taiwan), and Ohno 1999a for a somewhat skeptical view of the importance of regional baskets from an empirical vantage point.

changes in U.S. exchange rate policy. Insulation also comes with the political benefits—and potential price tag—of greater regional integration, and thus internationalization is increasingly seen as a "package" with formal attempts at integration.

Necessarily, the debates and decisions that follow have profound meaning for Japan's own vision of itself in the world and in Asia. The Chiang Mai Initiative (and the concept of the Asian Monetary Fund that preceded it and still lies dormant within it) constitutes the first time that Japan has actively sought out and helped to lead regional cooperation that explicitly excludes the United States. This alone is significant, even more so because it builds on ideas that have been percolating among Japanese policymakers and opinion leaders about Japan's future role. The effort is clearly not meant to close Asia off from the rest of the world, as evidenced by the gingerly and cautious way in which it has proceeded. Nonetheless, it both reflects and supports a reduction in Japan's perceived dependence on the United States.

Also important at the level of ideas is that national and regional insulation based on currency leadership can be seen as a call for a return to a kind of embedded liberalism, or what I have called "economic policy pluralism." In this sense, some of the efforts to internationalize the yen can be seen as at least a tentative challenge to the dominant Washington Consensus and financial globalization. Ironically, however, a number of the practical measures to promote greater international use of the yen—such as liberalization of Japan's government debt markets and financial system—presuppose the triumph of globalization, or at least a global competition among currencies. Whether it is possible to achieve both (or indeed either) of these apparently contradictory goals remains in doubt. We can similarly question whether it is desirable or even possible to intentionally "internationalize" a currency. Japanese policymakers are embarking on an experiment with little theory to guide them, and strong political and economic checks on many of the instruments they have considered using. In the end, however, even if financial globalization appears to prescribe fatalism, worries about power, interests, and ideas ensure continuing efforts by Japan to shape its external economic environment.

CHAPTER NINE

Ideas, Power, and the Politics of U.S. International Monetary Policy during the 1960s

Francis Gavin

> We are at a most important moment in postwar history. Both the Communist world and the non-Communist world are in considerable disarray. The outcome—whether in Vietnam or the gold crisis—depends on how free men behave in the days and weeks ahead.
>
> —Walt Rostow to President Lyndon B. Johnson[1]

In 1964, the James Bond thriller *Goldfinger* was released in movie theaters throughout the United States and Great Britain. In the Ian Fleming novel on which the film was based, the sinister Goldfinger, ably assisted by Pussy Galore, plots to steal the U.S. gold supply from Fort Knox.[2] But in the film, Bond is understandably skeptical that Goldfinger could physically remove tons of gold from the most secure building in the world. Goldfinger tells Agent 007 that he does not have to *physically* remove it. Instead, he only needs to get inside Fort Knox and explode a timed nuclear device supplied by the People's Republic of China, which would instantly increase the value of Goldfinger's private hoard. And with the U.S. gold supply rendered unusable, international liquidity would seize up and the Western trade and monetary systems would collapse. The Chinese would exploit the collapse of the free world economy to achieve an easy victory in the Cold War without firing a shot. Fortunately, this calamity is averted by a timely combination of Bond's usual quick thinking and an un-

---

1. Walt Rostow's memo continued in the same frightening tone: "If the free nations of the world fail to cooperate intensively and if the Congress fails to vote a tax increase, we could set in motion a financial and trade crisis which would undo much that we have achieved in these fields and endanger the prosperity and security of the Western World." Rostow to the president, March 19, 1968, National Security File (NSF), Files of Walt Rostow, box 16, Lyndon Baines Johnson Library and Museum (hereafter, LBJ Library), Austin, Texas, 1.

2. Ian Fleming, *Goldfinger* (New York: Signet, 1959).

likely last-second shift in political (and sexual) sentiments by Ms. Galore. Together, James and Pussy save the free world from chaos and disaster.

The target chosen by the film for the economic decapitation of the West is revealing. It was not a large factory or a valued natural resource that fueled machinery, transportation, or a weapons system. It was not even a financial center, such as Wall Street or the City in London. It was a pile of heavy, yellow metal, a regulated commodity with a fixed price and few non-monetary uses, expensive to guard and difficult to move. Would destroying this resource really paralyze the free world economy?

Policymakers and economists of the time certainly thought so, as memos detailing scenarios as grim as Goldfinger's plot were circulated within the Johnson administration throughout 1968. In a memo to the president entitled "Explanation of Possible World Financial Crisis," Council of Economic Advisors (CEA) Chairman Arthur Okun laid out just how he thought such an economic catastrophe might happen. Okun argued that unless Congress passed the president's balance-of-payments program, the world would believe that "the United States is *not serious* about preserving the dollar." Foreign investors would cash in their dollars, driving the price of gold skyward and forcing central banks to demand "huge quantities of gold for their dollars." Sterling would collapse, the United States would be forced to suspend gold convertibility, and the gold-exchange standard would crash. "Thus, we would expect tremendous havoc and uncertainty in world finance." Okun argued that this would be "a *major world political defeat for the United States.*" International trade would founder, employment would drop, and stocks and bonds would plummet. U.S. leverage at a world monetary conference would be "pathetic." "Reactionaries at home would have a field day *attacking all Government programs.*" The Federal Reserve would be trapped between the traditional policy to fix a balance-of-payments crisis— "very tight money"—and the need to calm panicked financial markets with easy money. "Perhaps the most long-lasting consequence would be in the international political sphere. Our financial disaster would create pressures to *renege on our worldwide commitments.*"[3] Troops would be called back home, the Paris Peace talks would collapse, and a dangerous power vacuum would come into being. And all without Goldfinger or the People's Republic of China doing a thing.

This alarmism was even more surprising because the administration had believed, months earlier, that it had solved the gold outflow and payments deficit issue. After extraordinary political pressure, the United States's closest European ally, West Germany, had publicly announced that it would hold its surplus dollars and not turn them in for U.S. gold. Similar, less formal reserve management policies were made with other allies, most notably

---

3. Okun for the president, May 21, 1968, White House Central Files, Ex Fi 10/11/66, box 2, LBJ Library, 1–3.

Japan, in the hope that other surplus countries could be "persuaded" to follow a similar no-gold policy and accept a de facto dollar standard. Negotiations to create a new form of liquidity to supplement gold and the dollar, the Special Drawing Rights, had resulted in the Rio accords of September 1967. These agreements had been hard won and were expected to ameliorate the gold drain that had plagued the United States since 1958.

But things didn't go as planned. When the British government devalued sterling in November 1967, the dollar weakened and the demand for gold rose sharply. The U.S. balance-of-payments deficit ballooned at the end of 1967, driven by the inflationary strains of the Vietnam War and the Great Society programs. A program to improve the balance-of-payments deficit through restrictions on capital, trade, and tourist accounts met with harsh resistance from the U.S. Congress. Instead, pressure rose for massive troop withdrawals from Europe, the most obvious candidate for balance-of-payments relief. But a major redeployment of U.S. troops could initiate a chain of events with outcomes inimical to U.S. strategic interests, including the nuclearization of the West German military, a Franco-German alliance to shut the United States out of Europe, and an intensified conflict with the Soviets over the status of Germany.

As surprising as it may seem now, during the 1960s the primary objective of U.S. foreign economic policy was to find a way to control the U.S. balance-of-payments deficit and stem the loss of gold from the U.S. Treasury. Even more surprisingly, many of the policies that were enacted or considered in order to solve the payments problem and ease the gold drain conflicted with the larger goals of U.S. foreign policy and made little sense when viewed under the lens of macroeconomic efficiency. These policies created enormous tensions within both the U.S. government and the Western Alliance and affected a whole range of policies, from U.S. troop deployments overseas to U.S. investment in Europe. Despite these political tensions, U.S. policymakers feared an economic catastrophe if the balance-of-payments deficit was not reduced and the gold outflow ended. Many policymakers, correctly or not, drew parallels with the international monetary conditions of the 1930s and feared that a failure to correct the problem could unleash an international economic collapse and political disaster.

In retrospect, most of the Johnson administration's fears were wildly misplaced. In March 1968, the administration separated the private and intergovernmental gold markets, essentially putting the world on a dollar standard. In August 1971, the Nixon administration ended dollar-gold convertibility. And the United States abandoned any attempt to return to fixed exchange rates by 1973. None of these events produced the economic or political calamity that had been widely predicted. In fact, monetary relations became far *less* politicized when fixed exchange rates were abandoned. Yet the story of U.S. international monetary policies during the 1960s is revealing nonetheless and can tell us much about how policymakers make trade-offs between wealth, power, and ideology. Why did the United States choose the types of policies that it did—trade and capital controls, restrictions on tourists, taxes on foreign borrowings in the United States—in order to maintain a monetary system that was breaking down? And, most important, why were U.S. leaders willing to threaten key elements of their foreign policy because of the dollar and gold problem?

In fact, the episodes detailed in this chapter reveal that monetary relations were guided by anything but concerns about efficiency and wealth creation. The United States and its partners lurched from crisis to crisis. U.S. policymakers frantically worked to avoid ending dollar-gold convertibility and allowing the dollar to "float," and instead went to extraordinary lengths in a desperate attempt to maintain a system that was collapsing. Capital controls, trade restrictions, massive multilateral interventions to stymie currency markets, the creation of a new "international" money, troop withdrawals, and threats to end security commitments were all considered more attractive policies than allowing currency markets the power to determine the value of the dollar. These policies strayed so far from traditional concerns about efficiency, and so distorted real macroeconomic issues, that Milton Friedman (1968, 240) complained:

> How low we have fallen! The United States, the land of the free, prohibits its businessmen from investing abroad and requests its citizens not to show their faces or open their pocketbooks in foreign ports. The United States, the wealthiest nation in the world, announces that its foreign policy will no longer be determined by its national interest and its international commitments but by the need to reduce government spending abroad by $500 million.

This story reveals that in international monetary relations, the economic issues are often ambiguous, making politics—both domestic and international—determinant. There was no economic inevitability to the policies chosen. The choices that were made during the 1960s were largely driven by ideas and political (as opposed to efficiency) concerns. The ideas about economics, which framed policy choices, were the product of historical circumstance and context and would eventually be replaced by another set of ideas. International political concerns were even more important, as issues such as the United States's troop commitment to Europe, the German question, and nuclear policy dominated debates over the U.S. international monetary policy.[4] The new archival evidence presented here affirms the findings of the essays in this volume by Stasavage, Helleiner, and Grimes—

---

4. For earlier works recognizing that international monetary relations, particularly under the Bretton Woods system, were thoroughly politicized, see Bergsten 1975; Block 1977; Hirsch, Doyle, and Morse 1977. For excellent, more recent works, see Helleiner 1994; Johnson 1998; Kirshner 1995.

namely, that state power and international political concerns often were the key forces driving monetary arrangements. Furthermore, this chapter, like Grabel's, demonstrates that where the policy choices offer only modest or ambiguous macroeconomic outcomes, ideology (particularly demonstrated in a policymaker's understanding of the past) can be determinative.

IDEAS AND MONEY DURING THE 1960S: THE SDR AND STERLING CRISES

Economic historians have never fully recognized that the Bretton Woods system was broken well before the U.S. escalation in Southeast Asia, and that U.S. policymakers had been obsessed with ending the U.S. payments deficit and gold outflow since the late 1950s. In 1960, for example, President Dwight D. Eisenhower became so panicked over the dollar and gold outflow that he suggested the monetary system could be fixed if uranium was "substituted for gold" as the reserve metal of the international monetary system.[5] And in 1962–63, the Kennedy administration considered making drastic changes in U.S. international monetary policy, including gold standstill arrangements, long-term funding of overseas dollar liabilities, and even a unilateral suspension of dollar-gold convertibility.[6] But a dramatic shift in U.S. monetary policy became more urgent when in early 1965 French President Charles de Gaulle denounced the Bretton Woods monetary system and suggested that other countries should follow France's example and turn in their surplus dollars for gold. While the French policy was not a surprise, the severity and public nature of de Gaulle's attack caused great concern.[7]

President Lyndon B. Johnson rejected de Gaulle's call for a return to a pure gold standard. "To go back to a system based on gold alone—to the system which brought us all to disaster in the early 1930's—is not an answer the world will, or should, accept."[8] In July 1965, Secretary of the Treasury

---

5. Memorandum of November 9, 1960, *Foreign Relations of the United States (FRUS)*, vol. 4, 1958–60, 131. For an example of how several years earlier the Eisenhower administration had used explicit threats of monetary coercion against the British during the Suez Crisis, see telegram from embassy in Washington to British Foreign Office, dated December 2, 1956, Prime Minister's Private Office (PREM) 11/1826, XC 7840, Public Records Office, England. See also Kirshner 1995, 63–82.

6. For the intense debate over international monetary policy within the Kennedy administration, particularly discussions over plans for reform, see Gavin and Mahan 2000.

7. Because of the large "overhang" of dollars already in European central banks, de Gaulle's actions forced the Johnson administration to make international monetary reform a higher priority than ending the U.S. payments deficit. By mid-1967, the amount of surplus dollars overseas was $27 billion, $12 billion in the hands of central bankers. If all other dollar holders had followed de Gaulle's policy, the U.S. gold supply could have been quickly run down.

8. "International Monetary Negotiations and the SDR Plan," chap. 12 of Administrative History, U.S. Department of the Treasury, in *The National Economy under President Johnson* (Bethesda, Md.: University Publications of America), microfilm, 52.

Henry Fowler announced "that the United States now stands prepared to attend and participate in an international monetary conference which would consider what steps we might jointly take to secure substantial improvements in international monetary arrangements."[9] Fowler warned his audience that any unilateral attempt by the United States to end its dollar and gold outflow could choke off international liquidity. Many European central bankers and politicians, particularly the French, disagreed, arguing that the influx of overvalued dollars since the late 1950s was exporting inflation to their countries and allowing U.S. firms to dominate Western Europe's economy. But Fowler warned that failure to provide a new form of liquidity would undermine growth and stable exchange rates just as trade and capital movements were rapidly increasing, and urged international negotiations to create a new, globally accepted reserve asset.

To alleviate the reserve burden on the dollar, in 1965 the United States proposed the creation of a new international asset, called the Special Drawing Rights (SDR), allocated according to a ratio based on gold and dollar holdings. The United States envisioned it not as a credit but as a real store of value that could be transferred like gold or dollars but not convertible into gold or dollars on demand. The French protested vigorously, arguing that any new instrument should be a credit that eventually would be paid back, or "reconstituted," into real money such as gold.[10] The French saw the SDR plan as a U.S. ploy to force Western Europe to finance even more U.S. balance-of-payment deficits. The dispute was an acrimonious test of wills. But the U.S. position prevailed when the administration pointed out that its monetary problems were the direct result of its commitment to defend Western Europe. Because of this pressure, the Federal Republic of Germany (FRG) agreed, albeit reluctantly, to reject the French and support most of the U.S. policy. But it remained to be seen when and how the SDR would be activated and whether they would be widely used.[11]

There was something unreal about the SDR debate. By 1967, many academic economists, especially in the United States, were pointing out that the balance of payments and gold problem would disappear overnight if currencies were allowed to adjust naturally in a freely floating exchange rate system. But both the U.S. and European policymakers feared that float-

9. "Remarks by the Honorable Henry H. Fowler, Secretary of the Treasury, before the Virginia State Bar Association at the Homestead, Hot Springs, Virginia, Saturday, July 10, 1965, 6:00 p.m.," Papers of Francis Bator, box 7, LBJ Library, 10. For the origins of the administration's shift in policy, see memo from the president, "Terms of Reference for Study of Monetary Arrangements," June 2, 1965, Declassified Documents Reference System (DDRS) 1993, 2373, 1. See also memo from the president to the secretary of the treasury, "Forward Planning in International Finance," June 16, 1965, DDRS 1993, 2375.

10. Memo, "Informal Report on Ministerial Meeting of the Group of Ten," September 7, 1967, NSF, Files of Edward Fried, box 1, LBJ Library.

11. For an account of the SDR negotiations, see "International Monetary Negotiations and the SDR Plan."

ing exchange rates would create instability, disrupt trade and capital flows, and deflate the world economy. In addition, the U.S. officials disliked a floating exchange rate system because they feared it would undermine the dollar's role as a "key" currency, which allowed the United States to finance its deficit in ways nonreserve currencies could not. The Europeans didn't want a free-floating exchange rate system because that would amount to a devaluation of the dollar, which would decrease the value of their large dollar reserves and, more important, make U.S. exports far more competitive in Europe.

Still, by 1967 the United States had finally seemed to be on the road to monetary stability. The public pledge by the Bundesbank, under the threat of U.S. troop withdrawals, to hold dollars provided protection for the U.S. gold supply. A tough balance-of-payments program that would shrink the U.S. deficit and restore confidence in the dollar among European central banks was being prepared. And the United States had largely defeated the French by winning approval of SDR. It was hoped that in time the SDR would supplement gold and dollars as reserve assets and remove the risk of a dangerous run on the U.S. gold supply.

But it was not to be. The weakness of the dollar was largely hidden by the weakness of another currency, sterling. The British balance-of-payment difficulties were far more crippling, and British gold reserves stretched far thinner. When sterling finally collapsed, the dollar was left dangerously exposed. Speculators moved quickly from sterling to the dollar, and then from the dollar to gold. The protective framework for gold and the dollar was undermined by the sterling devaluation. The November 1967 collapse exposed the contradictions in the dollar-gold monetary system, contradictions that had been largely hidden for ten years through creative management of the system. It also reveals that traditional economic concerns, such as efficiency and wealth creation, were far less important than ideas and politics in determining monetary policy.

The U.S. Response to the 1967 Sterling Crisis

Though the dollar was weak, British sterling was weaker. Sterling had long been the most fragile link in the fixed exchange rate system. The British had devalued sterling in 1949 by 30.5 percent, from $4.03 to $2.80, in open violation of the rules of the International Monetary Fund (IMF). But this massive devaluation did not bring sterling any closer to full current-account dollar accountability, and Great Britain withstood serious monetary crises in 1957, 1961, and 1964, saved only by U.S.-led bailout efforts. If sterling were devalued again, international confidence in the ability of the United States to hold the par value of the dollar and maintain convertibility of dollars into gold would be weakened. Massive capital flows out of the dollar and into gold and stronger European currencies might deplete the U.S. gold supply. If the administration could not prevent sterling devaluation, what could it do to prevent international monetary disorder?

During the summer of 1966, the Division of International Finance at the Federal Reserve produced a top-secret study arguing that a sterling devaluation would be a "severe crisis with dire consequences for the international economy." The "foundations of the existing international monetary system would be shaken at best" with "far-reaching implications for the stability of international commerce and finance, for domestic policies, and for economic welfare at home and abroad."[12] What policies could be developed to meet this threat? The preferred choice was for the United States to adjust to the new situation without any change in par value for the dollar or other major currencies and without changing the role of gold. But this would require the United States to impose capital controls, to order the IMF to invoke the "scarce currency clause," and to pressure the European surplus countries to revalue their currencies upward. The second option was to end the practice of selling gold to foreign central banks without necessarily abandoning the dollar's par value or its convertibility into other currencies. The United States could also design a "defensive ring" of cooperative central banks that would manage gold convertibility among themselves while denying gold to unfriendly countries. Additionally, the administration could ask London to close its gold market, separate the private and central bank gold markets, or raise the official price of gold.

The third option—the one that made the most sense from an economic standpoint—was to establish a new par value for the dollar, either through negotiations with the leading industrial countries or by allowing the dollar to float. This option, called "Plan X," was "a ready-made, welcome opportunity to get the gold and the balance of payments monkey off our back" by forcing "the Europeans to fish or cut bait."[13] The United States would force the Europeans to decide whether they would support their currencies at the old exchange rate, and accumulate more dollars, or let their own currencies appreciate against the dollar. The "full-blown floaters" who would support Plan X believed that the IMF/Bretton Woods system was deeply flawed and wasted valuable resources. In a floating exchange rate regime, liquidity, exchange rate adjustment, and par values would cease to be an issue for the United States.

Predictably, politics and ideas determined which of the three policies was chosen. Regardless of what trained economists told them, no one in the Johnson administration saw the sterling devaluation as an opportunity for a

12. Division of International Finance, Federal Reserve Board, "Contingency Planning—Sterling," September 20, 1966, Papers of Francis Bator, box 8, LBJ Library.

13. Division of International Finance, Federal Reserve Board, "Contingency Plan X: A Proposal to Force Major Surplus Countries to Support the Dollar at Present Parities or to Allow a Relative Appreciation of Their Currencies," September 21, 1966, Papers of Francis Bator, box 8, LBJ Library, IX-2.

bold new course in international monetary policy. In November 1967, Special Assistant to the President Walt Rostow warned that the risks of a sterling devaluation "are just too great to be worth the gamble."[14] Henry Fowler told the president that "if sterling falls, there will be great monetary unrest. The dollar will be affected strongly."[15] Great efforts were made to put together yet another massive, multilateral bailout package for sterling, even if it made little macroeconomic sense.[16]

When the Wilson government eventually devalued sterling, the United States had little choice but to accept the new exchange rates and calm the currency markets to avoid flight from the dollar. On November 18, 1967, after devaluation of the pound sterling from $2.80 to $2.40 was announced, Johnson declared that the new parity would allow the United Kingdom to "achieve the needed improvement in its ability to compete in world markets." The president reaffirmed the U.S. commitment to "buy and sell gold at the existing price of $35 an ounce."

But could the United States, with the help of the gold pool, supply enough gold to the London market to keep the price of gold around $35 per ounce? The European members of the gold pool were unprepared to accept an unlimited amount of dollars and lose gold to the London market at the same time. Complicating matters was the fact that the French appeared to be conspiring to unsettle the currency markets with rumors. Although France had dropped out of the gold pool during the summer of 1967, this fact was never publicly announced, and the United States just picked up France's share. But Paul Fabra, a financial writer for *Le monde* who had close ties to de Gaulle's government, chose the week after the devaluation to write that France had dropped out of the gold pool. Other items that were discussed in top-secret G-10 meetings also appeared in French newspapers at the time.[17] A top-secret Central Intelligence Agency (CIA) report claimed that in the weeks following the devaluation of the pound, "French government attitudes, and the actions of some French officials, were important factors contributing to the massive speculation against the dollar and gold." But as the gold crisis intensified and the United States seemed more prepared to take drastic action, the French backed off. "By mid-December . . . the French government had become

14. Rostow for the president, November 13, 1967, NSF, Gold Crisis, box 53, LBJ Library.

15. Fowler for the president, "The Gold Situation," November 13, 1967, NSF, Gold Crisis, box 53, LBJ Library.

16. Memo for the president, "Additional Assistance to the U.K. in Support of Sterling," October 19, 1967, NSF, 1968 Balance of Payments Program, box 54, LBJ Library; Rostow for the president, "Contingency Support for Sterling," October 19, 1967, ibid.; Fowler for the president, "Sterling Crisis," November 12, 1967, NSF, Gold Crisis, box 53, LBJ Library.

17. Memo, "Paris Press on Gold Situation," December 8, 1967, NSF, Gold Crisis, box 53, LBJ Library. See also Central Intelligence Agency (CIA), Directorate of Intelligence, "French Actions in the Recent Gold Crisis," March 20, 1968, CIA, Information and Privacy Coordinator, Washington, D.C.

concerned about the deepening crisis and subsequently has generally refrained from unsettling actions."[18]

The Europeans rejected a new U.S. scheme to replace gold with "gold certificates," and in the weeks after the devaluation, there was a strong feeling among European central bankers that the gold pool should be terminated before their losses got out of hand.[19] An agreement negotiated by Fred Deming, under secretary of state for monetary affairs, collapsed in an atmosphere of rumor, speculation, and massive gold losses.[20] Only a dramatic, last-minute intervention by Federal Reserve Chairman William McChesney Martin saved the gold pool. Hubert Ansiaux of Belgium, speaking for the Belgians and the Germans, Italians, Dutch, and Swiss, told Martin in a December 15 phone call that "we were strongly of the opinion until yesterday night, when you got in touch with all of us, to recommend that we should stop our intervention in the market." But Ansiaux agreed to continue the pool with two conditions: the United States must reimburse the Europeans in gold for "excessive accumulations of dollars" and announce a strong balance-of-payments program within the next few weeks. "We very much hope that the program will be really very fundamental and substantial; not just a stop-gap measure; something really affecting the root of the matter."[21]

The Johnson administration had been working on a serious balance-of-payments program throughout the fall of 1967, but now the stakes were much higher.[22] The available options were not inviting. The trade account could be adjusted with export rebates and import surcharges, but that would not produce the immediate results the Europeans wanted. Moving from voluntary to mandatory capital controls would strike many as overly intrusive, and the banking and business community would protest loudly. Restricting tourism would seem like an assault on a fundamental freedom. Reducing military expenditures would require an important policy shift—either ending the war in Vietnam or cutting the number of U.S. troops stationed in Europe. In late 1967, it was hard to imagine that the Johnson ad-

18. "French Actions in the Recent Gold Crisis."

19. "Some Questions and Answers on the Gold Certificate Plan," November 24, 1967, NSF, Gold Crisis, box 53, LBJ Library; Board of Governors of the Federal Reserve System, "Talking Paper on the Relationship between the Gold Certificate Plan and the Financing of the U.S. Balance of Payments Deficit," December 5, 1967, NSF, Gold Crisis, box 53, LBJ Library.

20. Ackley for the president, "The Gold Situation," November 24, 1967, NSF, Gold Crisis, box 53, LBJ Library; "The Gold Crisis: Nov. 1967–March 1968," 1967, NSF, Gold Crisis, box 53, LBJ Library, 4.

21. Memo, December 15, 1967, NSF, Gold Crisis, box 53, LBJ Library, 1. See also Rostow for the president, December 15, 1967, NSF, Gold Crisis, box 53, LBJ Library.

22. For earlier discussions, see Winthrop Knowlton, "1968 Balance of Payments Program: Status and Strategy," October 12, 1967, NSF, Files of Edward Fried, box 1, LBJ Library; Robertson to the Cabinet Committee on the Balance of Payments, October 19, 1967, ibid.; Cabinet Committee on the Balance of Payments, November 8, 1967, ibid.

ministration would simply end the Vietnam War for balance-of-payment purposes. That meant that U.S. expenditures in the NATO area were the most attractive targets for balance-of-payment cuts. But any significant troop reduction in Europe could unleash a political crisis over the complicated and delicate German problem. Would the United States completely alter its European security commitments in order to solve its international monetary problems? As we will see, the proposal to withdraw troops from Europe to end the dollar and gold outflow was not new. The question of the United States's international monetary policy would center on questions of politics and security, not economic efficiency.

POWER, POLITICS, AND MONEY DURING THE 1960s

In September 1966, Under Secretary of State George Ball sent President Johnson a memo detailing his views on how the president should approach the international monetary negotiations during his upcoming meeting with German Chancellor Ludwig Erhard. Erhard, whose political survival depended on a successful meeting with the president, sought a drastic reduction in the current offset agreement and a complete and public decoupling of future monetary arrangements from the issue of U.S. troop levels in Germany. Several of the president's advisors, including Secretary of Defense Robert McNamara and Secretary of the Treasury Henry Fowler, insisted that the FRG had to fulfill the agreement in full. Furthermore, they urged the president to reaffirm the link between full West German monetary cooperation—especially with the offset agreement—and U.S. troop levels. German military purchases were a critical part of the administration's policy to reduce the U.S. balance-of-payments deficit. To the United States, any reduction in German offset purchases had to be met with corresponding U.S. troop withdrawals. Ball strongly disagreed and contended that such a hard-line stand over the offset agreement would prove short-sighted.

Ball's memo, which was declassified recently, warned the president that the atmosphere surrounding Erhard's visit would be "electric and ominous."[23] The U.S.-German monetary dispute would pose "a major challenge to American statesmanship." Unless it was handled with understanding and sensitivity, the offset issue could "produce a crisis in our relations with Germany—and hence with Europe." A failed meeting would finish the Erhard government and might encourage forces that could lead Germany "down a dark and dangerous road." Ball pointed out that both German politicians

23. Memo, Ball to the president, "Handling the Offset Issue during Erhard's Visit," September 21, 1966, Papers of Francis Bator, Erhard—9/66, box 21, 1. Quotes that follow are from pp. 1–2a.

and the German people were showing worrisome signs of "malaise . . . malaise which has been an early warning signal in German history on earlier occasions." The coupling of monetary policy and troop withdrawals made Germans deeply suspicious of U.S. leadership and led to a growing conviction that "de Gaulle is right and that the U.S. cannot be trusted." The U.S. demand for full weapons offset made Germany feel that it was "singled out" despite its support for a number of unpopular U.S. policies, including the war in Vietnam and the Kennedy Round of trade negotiations. Ball explained that as a result of their "unequaled capacity for feeling sorry for themselves," the Germans "have come to regard our demands as nagging and resentment against us is deepening. . . . They can easily develop neuroses that can be catastrophic for all of us. They did it before and they can do it again. . . . A neurotic, disaffected Germany could be like a loose ship's cannon in a high sea."[24]

Because of the enormous political stakes for U.S. policy in Germany and Europe, Ball recommended that Johnson accommodate Erhard by softening the money-security link and reducing the current offset obligations. The under secretary of state thought that this was a small price to pay to avoid a public rupture with the United States's closest ally, especially at a time of great uncertainty within NATO. Despite his dark warnings, Ball was overruled, and the president followed the hard line on monetary policy recommended by McNamara and Fowler. The chancellor, who had often been characterized in Germany as the United States's "errand boy,"[25] was ridiculed in Germany for being so naive in his dealings with the Johnson administration and suffered a barrage of attacks and insults at home until his government fell in November. The public atmosphere surrounding his collapse was marked by widespread demands for a "reassessment" of Germany's relationship with the United States.

Why were monetary relations between these two close allies so politically explosive? The most important point to make is that there was far more at stake than a simple financial arrangement. The monetary agreement, which included but went well beyond the issue of offset purchases, was a critical part of a larger security framework that had important political, strategic, and military components. This security framework was a series of largely tacit understandings that kept U.S. troops in Germany, nuclear weapons out of the hands of Germans, and the Soviets out of West Berlin. A crucial part of this arrangement was the commitment by the FRG to help strengthen the dollar and protect the U.S. gold supply by offsetting and neutralizing the foreign exchange cost of the U.S. forces stationed in Ger-

24. Ibid., 2a.
25. Memo, State to the president, "Visit of Chancellor Erhard, September 26–27, 1966," DDRS 1993, 3191.

many. If this offset arrangement unraveled, the U.S. payments deficit would balloon and gold losses would increase. This could force the Johnson administration to withdraw troops from West Germany, increasing pressure on that country to get its hand on a nuclear trigger and scaring the Soviet Union into a far more hostile posture. The détente and relative stability that had been created in Central Europe would be shattered.[26]

President John F. Kennedy first linked the continued presence of U.S. troops in Europe to a resolution of U.S. payment difficulties. During a 1963 National Security Council meeting, Kennedy declared that the payments deficit "must be righted at the latest by the end of 1964," and the Europeans must be prevented from "taking actions which make our balance of payments worse." The president contended, "We cannot continue to pay for the military protection of Europe while the NATO states are not paying for their fair share and living off the 'fat of the land.'" When formulating its monetary policy, the United States had to "consider very hard the narrower interests of the United States."[27] It no longer had any source of financial pressure it could exert on the Europeans and had to exploit its military power before the Europeans became nuclear powers. "This sanction is wasting away as the French develop their own nuclear capability."[28] "I know everyone thinks I worry about this too much," he told his speechwriter, Ted Sorensen, but the balance of payments "is like a club that de Gaulle and all the others hang over my head." In a crisis, Kennedy complained, they could cash in all their dollars and then "where are we?" (quoted in Reeves 1993, 431). The United States would be forced off the Continent in the most humiliating way.

The administration weighed a wide variety of possible responses, including dramatic monetary reforms. George Ball, Dean Acheson, and James Tobin recommended policies ranging from gold standstill arrangements to a decision to let the dollar float. Acheson surprisingly concluded, "The Bretton Woods arrangements have been outgrown; outdated."[29] But in the end, Kennedy eschewed international monetary negotiations and decided to pursue power politics, pure and simple. The president and his administration put tremendous pressure on the Germans to accept the link between international monetary cooperation and the maintenance of six U.S. divisions in West Germany. McNamara told Kennedy that it was vital for the

26. The origins of this monetary-security framework are elaborated in greater detail in Gavin 2002. For the link between monetary policy and the so-called strategy of flexible response, see Gavin 2001.

27. Remarks of President Kennedy to the National Security Meeting, January 22, 1963, *FRUS*, vol. 13, 1994, 486.

28. Summary Record of National Security Council (NSC) Executive Committee Meeting, no. 38 (part 2), January 25, 1963, *FRUS*, vol. 13, 1994, 486–487.

29. Acheson oral history, John F. Kennedy Presidential Library (hereafter, Kennedy Library), Boston, Mass.

administration to "get the dollars out of them."[30] The president told the Spaniards that "the question of the American balance of payments constituted one of his greatest concerns." If he did not resolve the dollar and gold problem, then Kennedy would be forced to "change his whole policy" and "dismantle the military support of Europe."[31]

Bundes minister Heinrich Krone was explicitly told that the United States would be forced to withdraw because of its international monetary problems.[32] During a tense meeting, President Kennedy warned German Chancellor Konrad Adenauer that "economic relations, including such matters as monetary policy, offset arrangements and the Kennedy Round of trade negotiations" were "possibly even more important to us now than nuclear matters" because the nuclear position of the West was strong enough to deter any attack. West German cooperation was expected for all of these economic initiatives. "Trade was important to us only because it enabled us to earn balances to carry out our world commitments and play a world role."[33] During a meeting with West German Foreign Minister Gerhard Schroeder in September, the president warned that "the U.S. does not want to take actions which would have an adverse impact on public opinion in Germany but does not wish to keep spending money to maintain forces which are not of real value."[34] And McNamara told his German counterpart, Kai-Uwe von Hassel, "America cannot carry this burden any longer if it couldn't reduce this deficit." Maintaining the troop commitment to Europe would be "impossible if the offset is not found for this. . . . The Americans have no choice whatsoever here."[35]

In the end, the threat to withdraw troops forced the West German government to both a NATO policy based on U.S. leadership and U.S. international monetary policies.[36] It also meant full and public support for the United States's international monetary policy. There could be no more hints of monetary collaboration with the French and no more rumors that surplus dollars would be turned in for gold, and most importantly, the offset arrangement had to be fulfilled and renewed. The U.S. demands for

30. July 30, 1963, meeting, Kennedy Library tape no. 102/A38, second side of cassette no. 1, right after first excision (43, 26).

31. Gesprach des Botschafters Freiherr von Welck mit Staatsprasident Franco in Madrid, May 29, 1963, *Akten zur Auswartigen Politik der Bundesrepublik Deutschland* (Munich, 1994), vol. 1, no. 185.

32. Ibid., no. 185, fn. 9.

33. Memo of conversation, "Trade and Fiscal Policy Matters," June 24, 1963, *FRUS*, 1961–63, vol. 9, 1995, 170.

34. Memo of conversation, "U.S. Troop Reductions in Europe," September 24, 1963, *FRUS*, 1961–63, vol. 9, 1995, 187.

35. Gesprach des Bundeskanzlers Adenauer mit dem amerikanischen Verteidigungsminister McNamara, July 31, 1963, *Akten zur Auswartigen Politik der Bundesrepublik Deutschland* (Munich, 1994), vol. 2, no. 257.

36. For a document showing the Germans analyzing and weighing all their foreign policy options, but suggesting that the FRG had little choice but to follow the American line, see "Aufzeichnung des Staatssekretars Carstens," August 16, 1963, ibid., no. 306.

German monetary cooperation would have to be met. In October 1963, Secretary of State Rusk told Defense Minister von Hassel in West Germany, "If our gold flow is not brought under control, the question could become an issue in next year's elections. The continuation of Germany's payments under the offset is vital in this respect."[37] The new West German government understood what was at stake and with few other options, accepted these conditions. Flanked by Rusk, the new chancellor, Ludwig Erhard, gave a major speech in Frankfurt in which he publicly acknowledged that the U.S. payments deficit arose from the U.S. "rendering the major portion of economic and military aid to the free world."[38] In December, a full offset arrangement was reached, and the settlement was announced as an agreement of "great value to both governments" that should be "fully executed and continued."[39] To underscore the importance of this objective, Erhard was told by the new administration in December that offset was an "absolute necessity" if six divisions were to remain in Germany.[40]

Perhaps even more importantly, the U.S. pressure compelled the supposedly independent West German central bank to hold its surplus dollars in interest-bearing securities instead of buying gold or selling them to others who might buy gold. When Secretary of the Treasury Douglas Dillon warned Johnson that "we have recently had numerous first-hand reports that the Bundesbank is considering the purchase of very substantial quantities of gold from us" that would be "most damaging to the dollar,"[41] Under Secretary of the Treasury Robert Roosa was dispatched to lean on Karl Blessing, head of the Bundesbank. Blessing informed Roosa that Erhard had intervened to make sure that the Bundesbank would hold its dollars and not buy gold.[42] By linking U.S. security policies to West German monetary cooperation, the United States essentially forced the FRG into accepting a pure dollar standard.

37. Memorandum on von Hassel Rusk talks, October 10, 1963, Papers of George McGhee, 1988 add, box 1, Georgetown University, Washington, D.C.

38. Background Paper, "Germany and the U.S. Balance of Payments," December 20, 1963, National Security Files, Country File, Germany, box 190, LBJ Library, 1. See also Georges-Henri Soutou, *L'alliance incertaine: Les rapports politico-stratégiques franco-allemands, 1954–1996* (Paris: Fayard, 1996), 265. This was an important shift for Erhard, who had previously stated that the American payments deficit could only be reduced through basic internal adjustments in the U.S. economy.

39. McNamara to the president, September 19, 1966, Papers of Francis Bator, box 21, LBJ Library.

40. Brief Talking Points on Offset Agreement, December 26, 1963, NSF, Country File, Germany, box 190, LBJ Library, 1.

41. Memo, Dillon to the president, "West Germany and Our Payments Deficit," December 13, 1963, NSF, Country File, Germany, box 190, LBJ Library, 3.

42. Memo, Dillon to the president, "Late Report on Germany and Our Payments Deficit," December 20, 1963, NSF, Country File, Germany, box 190, LBJ Library, 1. Apparently there had been some confusion in the Bundesbank over reserve management policy because of Blessing's absence in the last half of 1963; he had suffered a heart attack and apparently those below him were not aware of the arrangements with the United States.

Not surprisingly, the monetary-security link created problems and mis-understandings between the United States and West Germany almost im-mediately. In a memo written six months after the December meeting, Mc-George Bundy told the president that Erhard did not want "a formal bargain that offset payments are a condition of our 6-division presence" al-though he knew that "the connection exists." Bundy suggested that the president "firmly but always privately" underline the linkage, but Bundy re-ported that "Dean Rusk wishes you wouldn't."[43] The arrangement became completely unglued in late 1965, when Secretary of the Treasury Fowler warned the president that the FRG was seriously behind in its payments:

> If the FRG should seek to withdraw from its present offset commitments, it would be logical to assume that the FRG no longer considered it necessary to maintain U.S. combat troops in Germany at present levels. Such a con-clusion seems reinforced by the fact that senior U.S. officials have repeat-edly made clear to the FRG the relationship between German fulfillment of its offset commitments and U.S. ability to maintain present levels of forces in Germany.[44]

The issue was confused even further in May of 1966, when McNamara and von Hassel publicly disagreed with each other in a meeting. McNamara reiterated the direct link between full offset and U.S. combat troop levels in Germany. Unless a full offset was forthcoming, now and in the future, the "U.S. would be required to reduce its forces to the level of the offset goals." Von Hassel replied that it was the view of his government that the agree-ments entered into "only applied to specific periods of two years each"; any further agreements, which were unlikely to contain full offset through ar-maments purchases, would have to be negotiated.[45]

By 1967, the severity of the monetary crisis seemed to make such a mas-sive troop withdrawal unavoidable. Months before the crisis, Fowler had been furious that the financial and monetary aspects of U.S.-European re-lations had not received more scrutiny. In a May 1967 meeting called to dis-cuss problems in the U.S. relationship with Western Europe, Fowler com-plained that no mention was made of what he felt was the most important issue of all, "the financial problem." Fowler had told the president that "the financial problem" with Western Europe "is our Achilles heel, which more than any of the specific problems listed in the State Department paper" is a "threat to our position in Western Europe and the effectiveness of our for-eign policy in dealing with it."

43. Bundy to the president, "Check List for Your Talk with Chancellor Erhard," June 12, 1964, NSF, Country File, Germany, box 191, LBJ Library, 1.

44. Memo, Fowler to the president, "Erhard Visit: Military Offset Agreement," Decem-ber 9, 1965, NSF, Country File, Germany, box 190, LBJ Library, 3.

45. Background Paper, "U.S./German Military Offset Relationship," November 5, 1966, NSF, Trilateral Negotiations and NATO, box 51, LBJ Library, 5.

The primary cause of this problem was the "disparities in burden-sharing relative to *financial* strength which result from political, diplomatic and military arrangements."[46] It was bad enough that the West Europeans were uncooperative. Some of them, led by France, were following overtly hostile actions aimed at harming the economic and political interests of the United States. By standing idly by without trying to stop the French, the rest of the Common Market, according to Fowler, was complicit in these destructive policies. The Common Market countries had "made less contribution to the common defense" than they should have; they had "continued to pile up international reserves," instead of embracing policies which promoted international payments equilibrium; they had been "overly cautious" when considering U.S. proposals for international monetary reform; and they had allowed their balance-of-payment receipts to be swollen from "U.S. military expenditures."[47] The devaluation of sterling, the upward pressure on gold in the London market, and the flight from the dollar added urgency to all of Fowler's arguments.

This line of argument was not new—the two previous secretaries of the treasury, Douglas Dillon and Robert Anderson, had produced their own, almost identical proposals to do something about the balance-of-payment costs of the U.S. military commitment to Europe. But the circumstances in the second half of 1967 were changing dramatically. First, this monetary crisis was far worse than the ones faced by Eisenhower and Kennedy. Second, tensions with the Soviet Union over Europe had receded dramatically since 1963, while U.S. relations with Western Europe were increasingly strained. France pulled out of the NATO organization, Great Britain was rejected from the Common Market for the second time in four years, and there were almost universal misgivings in Europe about a whole range of U.S. policies, from the balance of payments to Vietnam. Even West Germany was quietly demonstrating its discontent with the U.S. commitment and the utility of NATO by striking out with its own initiatives toward East Germany and the Soviet Union.

Did this mean that the administration would order a massive withdrawal of U.S. troops? The administration had already removed one and one-third divisions in 1967 for balance-of-payment reasons. This reduction, which was a result of the trilateral negotiation between the United States, Great Britain, and West Germany, had already caused great bitterness in West Germany and the rest of Europe. John McCloy told President Johnson that any cuts beyond this risked "the collapse of the alliance" and Europe returning to "the old world of dog-eat-dog—each nation for itself."[48]

46. Fowler for the president, "Problems Ahead in Europe," May 25, 1967, NSF, NSC Meetings File, box 51, LBJ Library, 1.

47. Fowler for the president, "U.S.-European Relations," May 23, 1967, NSF, NSC Meetings File, box 51, LBJ Library, 1.

48. Ibid., 5.

How would further troop withdrawals inspired by the balance-of-payments issue be seen in Europe? A November 16, 1967, report entitled "Implications of a More Independent German Foreign Policy" claimed that "the mood underlying present FRG policies is, to a much greater extent than prior to 1966, one of uncertainty, resentment, or suspicion regarding the direction of U.S. policy." This was largely because the United States was threatening troop withdrawals from West Germany at the same time that it was initiating a conciliatory policy toward the Soviet Union. "Many Germans fear deeply that the United States will either progressively reduce its forces in Europe and thus make the Germans vulnerable to Soviet pressure, or strive increasingly for accords with the USSR at the expense of FRG interests, or both."[49]

Another policy-planning paper, written three months later, was even more pessimistic. "The Germans are convinced that the United States will in the relatively near future make further substantial and unilateral reductions in its forces in Germany." This report, entitled "Germany and the Future of Western Europe," predicted that FRG policy would be increasingly willing to make dangerous concessions to the Soviets to win liberalization in East Germany. The report suggested that such liberalization, let alone progress toward unification, was against Soviet interests. FRG security concessions would purchase nothing but disappointment and eventually resentment within West Germany. "Disillusion in West Germany might well set in and produce radical movements of the right and left." The fear of U.S. troop withdrawals would make the West Germans feel "intensely isolated." They would also feel that they were being impelled toward acceptance of a neutralized status in any event, and probably one in which the division of Germany would be permanently institutionalized, in effect, by East-West security control arrangements. In this frame of mind, almost any FRG government would be inclined to believe it must try to purchase confederation with the East Germans from the Soviets at the price of neutralization and of perhaps even more far-reaching concessions, as a desperate last chance for progress toward reunification and assurance of some security.[50]

In the end, this was too high a price to pay in order to strengthen the dollar and staunch the outflow of gold. But that such dramatic security reductions *were even considered* reveals to what lengths U.S. policymakers were willing to go to maintain a dysfunctional system. It is no coincidence that the

49. Department of State Policy Planning Council, "Implications of a More Independent German Foreign Policy," November 16, 1967, Papers of Francis Bator, box 22, LBJ Library, 3. See also Department of State Policy Planning Council, "The Future of NATO: A Pragmatic View," November 1, 1967, Papers of Francis Bator, box 22, LBJ Library; memo, no author, "Key Issues in U.S.-European Relations," November 8, 1967, ibid.

50. Department of State Policy Planning Council, "Germany and the Future of Western Europe," February 23, 1968, Papers of Francis Bator, box 22, LBJ Library, 1.

whole question of offsetting the foreign exchange costs of U.S. troops in Europe (as opposed to budgetary concerns behind "burden sharing") disappeared during the 1970s. In a flexible exchange rate system, the whole question of surplus dollars acquired through U.S. military expenditures and used to purchase U.S. gold ceased to exist.

But if the administration would not consider floating the exchange rate and could not further reduce its security commitments abroad, then other, more extreme measures would be needed if dollar-gold convertibility was to be maintained at $35 per ounce.

The 1968 Balance-of-Payments Program and the March Gold Crisis

Politics prevented further troop withdrawals from Europe or Vietnam. The influence of ideas kept the administration from pursuing the solutions, such as ending dollar-gold convertibility and letting the dollar float, that made the most economic sense. If the supposed disaster many feared was to be avoided, what monetary policies would be chosen?

On December 23, 1967, presidential aide Joseph Califano sent a telegram to President Johnson summarizing the findings of the cabinet committee on the balance of payments. The recommendations were severe and included capital controls, border taxes and export subsidies, steep travel taxes, and increased offset payments from allies. For an embattled president entering an election year, this plan was politically disastrous, angering everyone from banks and multinational firms to average U.S. tourists and close allies. The Atlantic Alliance, strained to the breaking point in 1966 and 1967 by internal crises, would be pressured further by the committee's policies. Furthermore, the plan reversed the cardinal tenet of postwar U.S. foreign economic policy: to promote open markets and free trade around the world, even if accomplishing this goal meant accepting unfair discrimination against U.S. goods and capital.

Johnson blamed his monetary problems on the United States's political responsibilities abroad. "Our role of world leadership in a political and military sense is the only reason for our current embarrassment in an economic sense on the one hand and on the other the correction of the economic embarrassment under present monetary systems will result in an untenable position economically for our allies."[51] But his advisors told him that if he failed to act, the world monetary system would collapse, with untold economic and political consequences.

The program was announced on New Year's Day 1968, and the administration dispatched groups of high-level officials to Europe, Japan, and Canada to explain the plan and seek further concessions on trade, tourism, and

---

51. Telegram, Joseph Califano to president, December 12, 1967, "The 1968 Balance of Payments Program," NSC History, box 54, National Security File, LBJ Library.

offsets for military expenditures.[52] But there was a certain strangeness to the whole effort. Here was the world's largest economy—representing 40 to 45 percent of the world's total output, with more than $110 billion of assets overseas, and possessing 20 percent of the world's gold reserves—forced to seek approval for a politically unpopular plan from countries like Italy and Japan. There was a growing sense that these problems were to some extent *unreal,* more a product of an ineffective monetary system than a reflection of a broken U.S. economy. This feeling moved to the foreground as it became clear the program would not stem the gold outflow problem.

The gold markets had responded enthusiastically to the program at first, and gold pool losses were dramatically reduced in January. But the Tet offensive in Vietnam, which began on January 31, shattered the calm on the London gold market. The tax increase—which the Europeans believed was absolutely necessary to stem U.S. inflation—had not been approved, the domestic gold cover had not been lifted, and the trade and capital accounts were weakening despite the 1968 program. Worse, the U.S. government was forced to draw on the IMF and sell gold in order to settle swap arrangements with gold pool countries.[53] As Rostow told the president in February, "The situation could turn into a crisis of confidence and feed on itself— much like a run on a bank. The end result could be a serious contraction of international liquidity and pressure on all countries to adopt restrictive economic policies—at home and abroad—to preserve their gold holdings."[54]

Clearly, the severe balance-of-payments program was not working. Economist and Johnson confidante Barbara Ward Jackson argued, "A situation is brewing up in the world economy with some dangerous overtones of the 1929/31 disaster." The collapse of international trade would unleash "depression," leading the Russians to "scent the long-hoped-for failure of capitalism and revert to hard-line adventurism and hostility."[55] Johnson's chairman of the Council of Economic Advisers, Gardner Ackley, warned that "surely there is a *risk* of a critical deterioration of the world economic situation—one that could even lead to a world depression if prompt action were not taken to reverse it."[56] Rostow claimed that "international financial problems could get out of hand with very serious deflationary consequences for the world economy."[57]

Then why not simply end dollar-gold convertibility and allow the dollar

---

52. President, "Message to the Nation on the Balance of Payments," December 21, 1967, NSF, 1968 Balance of Payments Program, box 54, LBJ Library.

53. History, "The Gold Crisis," undated, NSF, Gold Crisis, box 53, LBJ Library, 7.

54. Memo, Rostow for the president, February 14, 1968, NSF, Gold Crisis, box 53, LBJ Library, 2.

55. Undated memo, Barbara Ward Jackson, NSF, Gold Crisis, box 53, LBJ Library.

56. Memo, Ackley for the president, January 1, 1968, NSF, Gold Crisis, box 53, LBJ Library.

57. Memo, Rostow for the president, January 23, 1968, "The Gold Crisis," NSC History, box 53, National Security File, LBJ Library.

to float, as many economists were suggesting? Rostow did not think the Europeans would allow this without instituting exchange controls and trade and capital restrictions against the dollar. This would be the first step on the road to ruin. "In the end world trade would decline and many countries would be under pressure to follow deflationary policies."[58] Treasury Secretary Fowler was even more concerned about the impact of a move off gold toward a dollar float, claiming that there was a strong possibility that a "gold embargo would lead to exchange rate wars and trading blocs with harmful political as well as economic effects."[59]

But by the end of the second week in March, it was clear that the gold pool operation would not hold. On March 13, Rostow told the president, "Strong and dramatic international action is required to end the hysteria. . . . Unless we can take convincing international action to this effect very, very soon, we shall face a choice among even more difficult and disagreeable alternatives."[60] After high-level discussions on March 13 and 14, the administration settled on a plan to close the London gold market and convene an emergency meeting of select central bankers on the weekend of the March 16–17 to hammer out new rules on gold and reserves. The administration pressured the Europeans to accept new international monetary rules, including a separation of the private and intergovernmental gold markets, measures to keep order in the financial markets, and a timetable for early activation of SDR. If the Europeans did not accept the plan, the administration would "have to suspend gold convertibility for official dollar holders, at least temporarily, and call for an immediate emergency conference."[61]

The administration went to work on two tracks, domestic and foreign. The State Department sent out an urgent wire to the European embassies ordering them to contact the most important central bankers, waking them from sleep if necessary. "You must track down these men at all costs."[62] Rostow complained that Congress was less cooperative, since the legislators had no idea that the gold crisis went "to the heart of the nation's capacity to carry its external commitments; maintain the world trade and monetary system; and avoid a serious domestic breakdown in our economy."[63]

Under enormous political pressure from the United States, the European central bankers accepted a new system they had little faith in: the two-price scheme for gold. The gold pool would be dissolved, but the central

---

58. Ibid., 6.
59. Ibid., 2.
60. Rostow, "Next Steps in International Monetary Policy," March 13, 1968, NSF, Gold Crisis, box 53, LBJ Library, 1.
61. Memo, Rostow to the president, "Gold," March 14, 1968, NSF, Gold Crisis, box 53, LBJ Library, 1.
62. State to American consul in Frankfurt, Embassy in Brussels, Rome, Bern, and Bonn, dated March 15, 1968, NSF, Gold Crisis, box 53, LBJ Library.
63. Memo, Rostow to the president, March 14, 1968, NSF, Gold Crisis, box 53, LBJ Library, 1.

banks involved would declare that the gold they possessed was sufficient for monetary purposes. This meant that they would neither buy nor sell gold on the London market—in effect, demonetizing new gold production. If the global trading system needed more liquidity to achieve payment equilibrium, then SDR would be activated. There was also the problem of central banks outside of the gold pool. The gold pool countries agreed not to sell gold to those countries that continued to sell gold in the private market.[64] The United States also sent telegrams to all the world's central bankers, warning of severe consequences unless they refrained from exploiting any arbitrage situation made possible by the two-tier market.[65] The one country that could cause problems, France, was experiencing balance-of-payment difficulties of its own and was in no position to buy gold from the United States.

The United States managed to avoid devaluation or a formal repudiation of dollar-gold convertibility, and the separation of the gold markets was hailed as a great success. But the two-tiered gold market and the SDR liquidity measures were—from a macroeconomic standpoint—obvious gimmicks. In retrospect, it is clear that these measures could not have saved the Bretton Woods system. The rules of international monetary relations had become completely divorced from economic reality and, hence, thoroughly politicized.[66] Whether responding to de Gaulle's attacks, the devaluation of sterling, questions surrounding the foreign exchange costs of U.S. troops abroad, or international monetary reform, U.S. policy was driven far less by concerns of macroeconomic efficiency than by forces that could broadly be defined as "ideological" or political. The administration was willing to consider and at times enact the most drastic political and economic policies in order to maintain a monetary system that was dysfunctional. The fact that U.S. policymakers feared that a 15 percent devaluation of sterling could start the world on the road to a second Great Depression reveals how divorced America's foreign economic policy was from macroeconomic reality.

CONCLUSION

Historical research often reminds us that actual policy making rarely conforms to social scientific generalizations or models. Nor are particular

64. History, "The Gold Crisis: Nov. 1967–March 1968," undated, NSF, Gold Crisis, box 53, LBJ Library, 12–13.

65. These telegrams are located in NSF, Gold Crisis, box 53, LBJ Library.

66. The reprieve only lasted as long as it did (three and a half years) because of American political pressure on the biggest surplus countries, West Germany and Japan, to hold dollars. Other traditional surplus countries of Western Europe, particularly France, suffered balance-of-payment difficulties in 1969 that prevented them from purchasing American gold.

policy choices inevitable. This is especially true with international monetary policy, where, as Jonathan Kirshner argues (chap. 1, this volume), the aggregate economic benefits of particular policies are often ambiguous and overshadowed by their political impact.

Nowhere is this more obvious than in the history of U.S. monetary policy during the 1960s. We are often told that the Bretton Woods system functioned in an economically optimal way during this period. Robert Gilpin (2000, 67) recently argued that Bretton Woods was successful in the 1960s because it "solved the fundamental problems of the world economy." "Distribution" issues were settled at both a national and an international level, "national autonomy" questions never arose, and the "international regime" functioned effectively because the United States behaved responsibly and the issues the system faced "were relatively simple."[67] But this was not the case at all. National autonomy, or "politics," drove international monetary relations throughout the decade. The issues involved were quite complex, the distribution questions unclear and unsettled, and the international regime was powerless to resolve disputes.

In other words, the history of monetary relations during this crucial decade cannot be explained by reading a macroeconomics textbook. The most important forces driving U.S. monetary policy during this period surrounded questions of security and alliance politics in Europe. We cannot understand the monetary history of the 1960s without a detailed knowledge of the German question, alliance nuclear politics, de Gaulle's vision of organizing Europe, and Great Britain's relationship with the Commonwealth, to name just the most important issues. Politics, power, and ideas, and not concerns about economic efficiency, drove the key policy choices during the 1960s.

---

67. It is fair to say that Gilpin's assessment is representative of a large conventional wisdom surrounding international monetary relations during the 1960s.

CHAPTER TEN

Franco-German Interests in European Monetary Integration

The Search for Autonomy and Acceptance

MICHELE CHANG

I s there any room left for politics in European monetary policy?[1] In the 1990s central bank independence came into vogue as the solution to the problem of inflation. The idea was that monetary policy, freed from self-interested politicians with short time horizons, could credibly be geared toward price stability rather than votes (Cukierman 1992; Alesina and Summers 1993). Moving toward this goal over the last two decades, the countries of the European Monetary System (EMS) emulated the independent German Bundesbank, mimicking first its policies and then its institutions (McNamara 1998). In addition, as part of the monetary union process, governments freed national central banks from political control, and in January 1999, the highly independent European Central Bank assumed responsibility for monetary policy making. Indeed, the conversion of the European states to monetary orthodoxy seems complete given the institutional changes required by the Maastricht Treaty and the willingness of the member states to adhere to the rigors of its convergence criteria.

Despite the numerous academic treatises that advocate the separation of politics from economic policy making, the experience of European monetary integration demonstrates that such a separation is illusory. As Ilene Grabel notes in this volume, the implementation of central bank independence rests on power relationships that its proponents try to mask under an air of theoretical "truth." But the truth is, economic logic cannot explain monetary union. Economic justifications are based on the benefits of central bank independence and the efficiency and trade-creating effects of an

---

1. I thank Jonathan Kirshner, Peter Johnson, Benjamin Cohen, Peter Katzenstein, Rawi Abdelal, Mark Blyth, Ilene Grabel, William Grimes, Hector Schamis, David Stasavage, Hongying Wang, Jeff Frieden, David Andrews, and Joseph Foudy for their helpful comments and suggestions.

optimum currency area. These arguments, however, fail to offer a compelling explanation for why monetary integration took place in Europe.

Rather than the raw pursuit of price stability or trade benefits, European monetary integration can best be understood as a political compromise involving divergent ideas and preferences within Europe, specifically between France and Germany. France used monetary integration to enhance its power and autonomy in both an international and a regional context. Since the Bretton Woods era, France has fought against U.S. power derived from the dollar's role as the international anchor currency. Indeed, the desire to mitigate the effects of the dollar's fluctuations on Europe contributed to France's and Germany's desire to create regional exchange rate stability. Both countries attempted to counterbalance the power of the dollar through the promotion of first their own currencies and now the euro. U.S. financial dominance and the alleged mismanagement of U.S. monetary policy provided both actors with powerful incentives to escape from the dollar's grasp and enjoy greater monetary policy autonomy.

But before tackling the United States, France had to first contend with Germany, a country subscribing to ideas and policies antithetical to the French republican tradition that regards state involvement in the economy as both a right and a duty. Successive French governments chafed under the restrictions demanded by Germany and participation in the EMS. The solution to this problem rested with a process of monetary integration that would incorporate elements of both French and German economic preferences and would embed the monetary integration process within European political integration. From this platform of an integrated Europe with a single currency, France could continue its quest to differentiate itself from the prevailing liberal orthodoxy on an international scale. Monetary integration would provide France with greater autonomy from both German and U.S. power.

In contrast to the French drive for autonomy, Germany's interest in monetary union rested with its need for acceptance by Europe in the wake of its rapid reunification. Initial European trepidation at the prospect of a united Germany provided Chancellor Helmut Kohl with yet another opportunity (perhaps even obligation) to tie Germany's future with that of Europe's. Despite some unease on the part of the Bundesbank and German business and financial interests, monetary union along with enhanced political cooperation became the foundation of the post–Cold War European order. Linking German unification to European integration conforms to Germany's postwar foreign policy pattern of "exaggerated multilateralism" (Anderson 1997, 85) and removes doubts about whether a united Germany would turn away from the European Community and face either inward or eastward.

It was not economics but Franco-German political interests that drove monetary integration. As Eric Helleiner writes in this volume, when countries (in this case, France and Germany) possess different beliefs about monetary policy making and currency cooperation, the economic path chosen depends on political imperatives rather than on economic logic. Despite France and Germany's common interest in European monetary integration, their divergent motivations led to conflict over the pace and content of monetary union. Contrary to theories emphasizing German dominance in this process, both France and Germany showed a willingness to compromise in order to achieve their desired goals, and these compromises determined the timing, content, and composition of EMU.

THE ALLEGED BENEFITS OF MONETARY UNION
AND CENTRAL BANK INDEPENDENCE

The economic rationale for monetary union is that the transaction costs of trade will be lowered as the region forms an optimum currency area. European monetary union based on an independent central bank has been justified on the grounds that such an institution offers lower inflation and provides greater credibility against exchange market speculation. However, neither theories on optimum currency areas nor those on central bank independence provide a compelling explanation for Europe's monetary union.

Optimum-currency-area theories (Mundell 1961; Kenen 1969) explicate the best conditions for a currency union to be constructed. A region of countries affected symmetrically by economic shocks, with high labor mobility and with fiscal harmonization, is a good candidate. When an economic shock affects the subregions symmetrically, a single monetary policy can be used effectively to handle the crisis for the whole region. In the absence of the symmetric distribution of such a shock, high labor mobility and the possibility of fiscal transfers offer alternative methods of dealing with the shock.

Studies have shown that Europe does not currently constitute an optimum currency area. Shocks affect the countries in Europe more idiosyncratically than they do the individual states of the United States, and Europe is slower to respond to them (Bayoumi and Eichengreen 1992; Dibooglu and Horvath 1997). In addition, labor mobility between European countries remains low, and countries have steadfastly refused measures geared toward fiscal harmonization (Eichengreen 1992b). Yet nothing in the Maastricht Treaty or its convergence criteria takes steps toward rectifying this situation.

Proponents who continue to emphasize optimum-currency-area theory to justify monetary union argue that it is possible for the countries in the European Monetary Union (EMU) to become an optimum currency area in the future if business cycles become more similar as trade and financial integration between the countries increase (Frankel and Rose 1998). In addition, automatic fiscal stabilizers may be adequate in offsetting shocks (Verdun 1999). But this speculation about rationalizing Europe as an "optimum-currency-area-in-waiting" obscures more than it clarifies. First of all, it switches optimum-currency-area theory from a prescription to a goal. Rather than providing an economic rationale as to why a region should switch to a single currency, it makes the set of conditions for that rationale a goal in itself. But to what end? Second, it does not explain the exclusion of the central ideas behind this theory in the Delors Report, on which the EMU was based, and subsequent European agreements (Chen and Giovannini 1994). What is even more surprising is that though some countries in the Europe Union could benefit from monetary union, France is not among them (Bayoumi and Eichengreen 1992; Garrett 1998). Yet France was the most ardent proponent of monetary union. If optimum-currency-area benefits do not explain French support for monetary union, can another theory account for this?

The second set of economic theories used to justify European monetary integration involve the alleged benefits of central bank independence. Central bank independence is simply the latest in a series of economic orthodoxies that, as Eric Helleiner (this volume) notes, change over time. Conventional wisdom posits that a consensus has emerged in Europe (and elsewhere) concerning the benefits of central bank independence, including bestowing greater credibility on governments with such institutions. The success of Germany since 1945 in sustaining strong growth with low inflation, even when other countries were mired in recession, made the German model the one to emulate in the 1990s (McNamara 1998).

But what sort of benefits would institutional mimicry actually confer? While countries with independent central banks tend to have lower inflation (Cukierman, Webb, and Neyapti 1992; Grilli, Masciandaro, and Tabellini 1991), this relationship is not necessarily causal (Alesina 1988). In addition, the purported outcomes of central bank independence are not robust when different variables are used to measure and interpret central bank laws, even though these variables may be the same in principle (Eijffinger and De Haan 1996). Collins and Giavazzi (1993) showed that monetary union is neither necessary nor sufficient for bolstering price stability.

Moreover, lower inflation is not billed as an end in itself. Proponents of central bank independence claim that it would lead to a virtuous cycle of low inflation and investment and growth. But Alesina and Summers (1993) demonstrated that central bank independence "has no measurable impact on real economic performance." In addition, if a consensus regarding the desirability of low inflation for its own sake really did exist, what would be the point of institutionalizing it at an international level? In the run-up to monetary union the participating states had already made their central banks substantially more independent. And the benefits of central bank independence on an international scale were uncertain. Therefore, monetary union itself must have offered something else that is valuable; as we will see later, political interests were of greatest concern.

In regard to central bank independence offering greater credibility (Sandholtz 1993) and allowing countries to reduce inflation with lower economic costs (Melitz 1988; Grilli, Masciandaro, and Tabellini 1991), the empirical evidence does not lend overwhelming support. Instead of institutional fixes at the international or domestic level conferring automatic credibility, governments must still earn credibility over a period of time (Burdekin, Westbrook and Willett 1993). According to Posen (1993), countries with independent central banks do not enjoy lower disinflation costs (Eijffinger and De Haan 1996). They may even aggravate short-term adjustment problems and increase unemployment as the trade-off to reduce inflation (Walsh 1995). The predictions based on the theory of politicians' delegating authority to independent central banks also fail to bear fruit; there is no correlation between delegation to an independent central bank and countries with higher government debt, political instability, or employment-motivated inflationary bias (De Haan and van Hag 1995).

The economic explanations for European monetary integration are ambiguous at best. Optimum-currency-area theory has played no role. The benefits of central bank independence also fail to explain the incentive for European Union member states to participate. Central bank independence neither confers credibility nor improves economic performance. Economic theory also cannot explain the timing of monetary union, for member countries had neither reached a state of optimum currency area nor suffered from high inflation by the late 1980s. In addition, it cannot explain the content: the convergence criteria did not include measures to increase labor mobility or fiscal transfers between states, as optimum-currency-area theory would suggest. The convergence criteria also demanded that states reduce inflation in advance of participation, making an independent European central bank superfluous if its major accomplishment was to lower inflation. Lastly, economic logic cannot explain the composition of the EMU, which contains some countries that neither form an optimum currency area nor conform to the demands of the convergence criteria. Another explanation must be found to account for such discrepancies, and that explanation lies in the ideas and interests of the two most powerful members of the European Union, France and Germany.

EXPLAINING MONETARY COOPERATION

Power

Economists and political scientists have naturally turned to Germany, Europe's wealthiest country, when trying to explain European monetary cooperation. Germany's ability to set policy more independently than its European partners has led some economists to conclude that Germany acts as a regional monetary hegemon (Kutan 1990; Wyplosz 1989). But the economic evidence for dominance is mixed. Some have found that Germany alone exercises monetary independence (Giavazzi and Giovannini 1989). Others reject the German dominance hypothesis and argue that the EMS was not hierarchical but rather interactive (Fratianni and von Hagen 1990; Hafer and Kutan 1994). Another economist described the situation as a bipolar one between Germany and France (Weber 1991).

The evidence for German political hegemony also varies. A hegemon provides public goods, defines a regime's objectives, solves collective action problems, and eases the adjustment process. Germany's behavior, however, was relatively passive. Its economic policies and institutions provided models that other countries emulated, but Germany did not provide active leadership (McNamara and Jones 1996).

The existing theory of hegemony describes two types: a coercive hegemon versus a benign one that provides public goods (Lake 1993). I suggest an additional distinction for hegemons: those that aspire to it and those that find hegemony thrust upon them.[2] Which type of hegemon a state is will determine the extent to which it will be willing and able to assume the mantle of leadership. Both types possess a certain amount of power and influence, but what they do with this power differs greatly. A state that welcomes the prospect of hegemony, even pursues it actively, undertakes leadership in a manner that one typically associates with a state that possesses a preponderance of power. Such a state uses its power to create regimes that allow it to pursue its interests or provide public goods. A reluctant hegemon, one on which hegemony presents itself by virtue of the state's power and strength, will not push forward cooperation. Germany's use of power resembles Britain's in the nineteenth century more than the United States's active wielding of monetary power in the twentieth. If Germany is a hegemon, it can only be defined as a reluctant one (McNamara and Jones 1996).

Whereas the EMS, once in place, could have been characterized as a "followership" (Abdelal 1998), monetary union required more leadership. France, an aspiring hegemon, provided the necessary impetus for monetary integration to go beyond the existing fixed-but-adjustable exchange rate system. France would likely have acted as sole hegemon if it had possessed the means. But France could not dominate Europe. With Germany, however, France could spur action within the European Community. Together they succeeded in fulfilling the most ambitious project the European Union has ever undertaken.

Thus, the pursuit of monetary cooperation in Europe was also a pursuit

2. I thank Peter Johnson for this point.

of power, as France sought to increase its position within Europe and potentially internationally. Historically, France has often used monetary policy to advance its interests internationally. According to Kirshner (1995, 148), "throughout the history of the modern international economy, France has been the most politically sensitive nation with regard to international monetary affairs." France tried to establish monetary hegemony in Europe in the 1860s and in French Africa during the twentieth century (Kirshner 1995, 148–156; see also Stasavage, this volume). Kindleberger (1985) wrote of France's attempts as a "near-great power" to shift the international balance of power in its favor during both the interwar and the Bretton Woods periods. Gavin (this volume) tells a similar story in which the French sought to overturn the Bretton Woods system because of the privileges it bestowed on the system's hegemon, the United States. Monetary union was the continuation of a policy that Dyson and Featherstone (1999, 63) described as "a project that engaged the status, power and prestige of France."

In order to enhance its power at the international level, France had to first wrest power from Europe's monetary leader, Germany. France had made various attempts to make European monetary cooperation more symmetric. The design of the EMS promoted more symmetry in the system than did its predecessor, so that both strong currencies (like Germany's deutsche mark) and weak currencies (like the French franc) would be obligated to intervene (Ludlow 1982; Ungerer, Evans, and Nyberg 1983).[3] When states declined to make use of institutional innovations such as the divergence indicator, France tried reasserting symmetry in other ways. After the rancorous currency realignment in January 1987, the French government took further steps to rebalance power in the EMS. In February 1987 French Finance Minister Edouard Balladur proposed a macroeconomic surveillance council to improve policy coordination between the member states. The Basel-Nyborg agreement that same year recognized the need to reconfigure the burden of adjustment for member states, calling for greater use of intramarginal interventions; renewed the European Community's commitment to automatic financing; and expanded the ability to pay off debts in European Currency Units rather than a hard currency like the deutsche mark (Dominguez and Kenen 1992; Boche 1993; Loedel 1999). The French government later that year advocated the creation of a Franco-German Economic Council for the coordination of medium-term policy objectives (Oatley 1997; Heisenberg 1998). In February 1988 Balladur proposed the construction of a common currency and a European central bank (Gros and Thygesen 1992, 312). All of these attempts failed to rebalance the asymmetry in the franc–deutsche mark relationship.

---

3. The main innovation of the European Monetary System was the introduction of the divergence indicator; see Ludlow 1982.

But in April 1989 the Delors Report was published, and it was soon followed by negotiations that resulted in the Maastricht Treaty. Was monetary union the result of a long-term convergence process based on economic and financial interests (Frieden 1998; Moravcsik 1998)? These interests might partially explain France's long-term enthusiasm for monetary cooperation with Germany, but not Germany's acquiescence. As Moravcsik (1998, 391) wrote, "The EMS status quo was also relatively attractive, perhaps even more so than EMU was." German reunification acted as a catalyst, at the very least accelerating and possibly even enabling monetary union to occur. On the German side reunification gave Kohl an incentive to alleviate doubts about German commitment to the European Community and multilateralism and gave the French a window of opportunity in which to gain German acquiescence to a goal that it had previously resisted. As Katzenstein (1997, 8–9) explained, "The acceleration of the European integration process . . . was, among other things, also a self-conscious French attempt to harness the enhanced power of a united Germany to an international institution that promised to grant France partial control and thus keep the European power balance from shifting too rapidly against France."

France's longstanding attempts to make monetary cooperation in Europe more symmetric finally gained German consent in the late 1980s, in part as a result of the politics surrounding reunification. While Germany demanded adherence to strict economic criteria, France made the adjustment to monetary union easier and more feasible for a larger group of states by requiring politicians rather than central bankers or even finance ministers to make the decision regarding membership. Finally, French and German negotiators disagreed over how politicized the institutions of the EMU would be.

Ideas and Interests

Though France and Germany agreed on the principle of monetary union, substantial disagreements about its terms remained. Conflicting preferences existed within and between these two countries regarding both the nature of the government's role in the economy and the character of integration. These preferences can be divided into three types of interrelated interests about which the adherents disagreed: growth versus price stability, central bank independence versus a government-dominated monetary policy, and monetary union as a goal in itself versus as a step toward political union.

Though the coherent institutional structure of France's monetary policy making, in contrast to the divided nature of Germany's, may have contributed to France's policy consistency in regard to monetary union (Kaltenthaler 1997), divisions within France made an agreement with Germany possible. Different sectors of the French government were associated with either conservative liberalism, social Catholicism, or social radicalism, and the outcome of EMU negotiations reflected these divisions. Conservative liberals predominated in the French Treasury, the Banque de France, and the Foreign Ministry. Officials in these institutions pursued monetary integration as a credibility and disciplinary device to make the French economy more competitive. Many of the German criteria for monetary union were acceptable, even desirable, to conservative liberals, as they meshed with their own views on making the French currency more credible and the economy more competitive.

In contrast, proponents of social Catholicism viewed monetary union as a means toward modernization while allowing government intervention to ease economic adjustment. Adherents of social radicalism likewise equated monetary union with European social policies that would promote equality at the same time as efficiency and modernization. They believed that the government must not lose its ability to intervene in economic policy, for governments are the sole sources of legitimacy, according to the French republican tradition (Dyson and Featherstone 1999, 67–71, 85–94). These factions viewed the primary French interest in monetary union as wresting control over the formation of monetary policy from Germany (Marsh 1992; Connolly 1995). France has had a long tradition of government intervention in the economy in the pursuit of higher growth (Hall 1986), and the centrally controlled government has been able to use various instruments, including its central bank, to pursue its goals. Despite the monetary integration process, elements within France clearly have wanted to continue to experiment with alternative economic models that would allow for elements like a shorter official workweek and a greater emphasis on growth and equity.

Moreover, the republican tradition in France and emphasis on legitimacy emanating from the people as embodied by the government (as opposed to independent, unaccountable institutions) made a wholehearted acceptance of German ideals and institutions problematic. Such concerns contributed to the argument over diversity and accountability versus centralization and efficiency. Meunier (2000, 112) reported that in October 1999 some French socialists argued that the European Union should "play a leading role in defending a 'civilization model' that *would respect economic, social, and cultural differences*" (emphasis added). European integration has not ended France's ideological pursuits, nor has it erased France's belief in its exceptionalism.

Ultimately France decided to work with Germany within the system rather than outside of it, and to increase its influence through the institutions of the EMS and eventually monetary union. As Katzenstein argued, "France has thus begun to follow what had become Germany's postwar foreign policy strategy: seeking to regain national sovereignty through international integration" (1997, 31), allowing France to alter the "normative context that constitutes actors" (1997, 12–13). France hopes to expand what Bulmer (1997, 73–5) called "indirect institutional power." By influencing the structure and the norms of monetary policy making within the EMU, France can promote its interest in pursuing growth-oriented policies. This is why it was so important for France to make monetary union as encompassing as possible and to include like-minded countries such as Italy.

France's republican tradition, which focuses on a highly centralized state, contrasts with Germany's federalist nature, which gives more autonomy to its Laender and to institutions like the Bundesbank (Kennedy 1991). The Bundesbank's statute prioritizes price stability, in contrast to the French preference for growth. This interest in price stability exists not only within the Bundesbank but also within areas of the government and society, financial interests in particular. The Bundesbank's priority at times came into conflict with French objectives, most famously with the French socialist experiment of the early 1980s.

As in France, various factions in Germany held different perspectives. The chancellery under Kohl and the Foreign Office pushed for monetary union with the goal of political union underlying the negotiations (Woolley 1994; Loedel 1999). Monetary integration served as a way for Germany to tie itself more closely to Europe, assuage fears of German strength, and ultimately allow Germany to pursue policies within a European framework that might trigger alarm in a unilateral context. German power has long been associated with German aggression, and throughout the postwar period Germany has been constrained in its foreign policy decisions. The prospect of German reunification exacerbated problems associated with the "German question" and made it a propitious time to pursue monetary union (Bulmer and Paterson 1996).

In contrast, the Bundesbank and Finance Ministry retained a considerable amount of skepticism toward monetary integration and focused more on the mechanics of monetary union to ensure that it did not compromise the goal of price stability. Despite the convergence of inflation rates in the late 1980s, the Bundesbank and financial interests killed the aforementioned Balladur proposals for greater monetary coordination on the grounds that they would threaten German price stability (Kaltenthaler 1998, 62–65).

The pace of monetary integration quickened considerably, however, with the fall of the Berlin Wall in 1989. Moreover, the process did not stall despite difficulties such as the onset of major currency crises in most of the European Union countries; previous attempts at integration had always faltered during such distress. A new political imperative had clearly taken over the process and empowered the foreign policy contingent of German policymakers over those concerned with price stability.

Thus, on the one hand, some French interests expressed the desire for greater policy-making autonomy on the domestic level than what had been permitted under regimes that were strongly influenced by German (and U.S.) economic interests. Monetary union based on a wide membership of European states would allow France to alter the norms of monetary policy making in Europe from within. Germany, on the other hand, wanted to protect the value of the deutsche mark through a monetary policy that prioritized price stability (an endeavor supported by some French actors). To ensure that countries with conflicting preferences did not intrude on Germany's pursuit of price stability, German policy makers believed that monetary union should happen only after economic convergence. These priorities were subject to negotiation, however, with the prospect of other German goals like political union on the table. France's drive for autonomy, which was directed both within Europe and for Europe, coupled with Germany's quest for acceptability found their expression in monetary union.

THE MAKING OF MONETARY UNION

Timing

Less than a decade after the inception of the EMS, the participating governments began negotiations for monetary union. The rapid pace of monetary union was the result of French negotiating tactics that overcame the division within Germany over the desirability of monetary union. During this period Germany equivocated on making any firm commitments, as France strongly pressed forward with its agenda until reaching its goal. Once monetary union was accepted as inevitable, Germany concentrated on its content, eager to make it resemble German policy making as closely as possible.

Most of the plans for monetary union resulted from French initiatives rather than German ones. Despite the benefits that Germany had enjoyed as the result of monetary stability brought about by the EMS, monetary union was a different matter. Though it appeared that some industrialists and exporters might benefit from the greater exchange rate stability and lower interest rates resulting from monetary union, the "hard" EMS period, after 1987, during which no realignment occurred, indicates that these objectives were already largely achieved. In 1988 the annual report from the Bundesbank stated that monetary union was unnecessary because "the EMS in its present form would then provide sound underlying conditions for the internal market to function smoothly," contradicting arguments on the necessity of monetary union to complement the single market (Heisenberg 1998, 105). Exchanging the Bundesbank for a European central bank that might not control inflation as well as its German predecessor presented German interests with a risk, despite the potential gains that a single market with a common currency could offer.

Shortly before the Strasbourg summit in December 1989, Kohl wrote a letter to François Mitterrand in which he argued against setting a firm date for the beginning of monetary union. Ultimately, Kohl agreed to an EMU conference in the second half of 1990, after the German parliamentary elections. In return, the member states of the European Community expressed their support for German reunification during the summit. At the European Council meeting in April 1990, Kohl and Mitterrand issued a joint letter to the president of the European Council that called for an intergovernmental conference on political union to parallel the monetary union talks (Katzenstein 1997, 26).

Though the German political establishment had been won over to the idea of monetary union in exchange for German reunification and enhanced political cooperation, the Bundesbank remained skeptical. In September 1990 the Bundesbank issued its own paper on monetary union that essentially demanded that its anti-inflationary priorities be superimposed on the rest of Europe. A tough series of convergence criteria would have to be fulfilled before the second stage of monetary union was to proceed; all members would have to relinquish their capital controls; inflation would have to be reduced along with budget deficits; and the European Central Bank would be modeled after the Bundesbank (Kaltenthaler 1998, 80). The Bundesbank enjoyed the backing of the governors of other European central banks (including the Banque de France) who had largely accepted that monetary union would be predicated on the German model. Germany's economic success and the strength of the mark made it difficult to conceive of an EMU that did not incorporate major elements of the German model.

When the conference on monetary union in Maastricht began, the French government came in with the following priorities: (1) establish an intergovernmental forum by which the European Council would set economic and monetary policy for the union, (2) create a European central bank and begin stage 2 of monetary union in January 1994, and (3) pursue monetary union in a series of progressive steps with a fixed timetable. These preferences reflected the French government's desire to lock in Germany (and the other European nations) to the process of monetary integration, thus giving France the role of agenda setter in monetary union.

The German Finance Ministry and Bundesbank, however, became concerned with the details of monetary union once the process was set in motion. Germany's primary concern was that candidates for monetary union adhere strictly to the convergence criteria that would limit inflation, budget deficits, public debt, and interest rate differentials. German representatives also opposed a monetary union that would automatically come into force at specified dates. Instead, they believed it should occur after economic integration had occurred and the member states had come to a unanimous agreement. By proposing rigid standards that many EMS countries presumably would be unable to meet, and by trying to explicitly allow the possibility that monetary integration would sputter out and die as it had before, Germany clearly did not act as a leader in the initiation of monetary union. If anything, Germany came closer to derailing it than to bringing it about.

But the Germans made some significant concessions at the Maastricht summit. First, the treaty allowed for a multistage process despite Germany's formal rejection of it. French insistence on this provision helped ensure the continuation of the monetary integration project, even in the face of setbacks. Second, the German delegation acquiesced to requests to establish dates for progression to the third stage of monetary union. If a consensus were not reached in 1996 on the beginning of the third stage of monetary union, in 1998 the European Council would make the decision by a simple majority. Such demands illustrate the political rather than the economic or technocratic nature of monetary union. By insisting that a major decision be made at the level of the European Council and not by central bankers or finance ministers, France ensured that monetary union was more likely to include a larger number of members (Mazzucelli 1995, 121). Therefore, the possibility existed that political decisions would override any obstacles to monetary union posed by participants not strictly meeting economic convergence criteria (Kaltenthaler 1998, 82). Not only had France led the way in reinvigorating monetary integration in Europe, but it also began influencing the EMU's composition to go beyond the deutsche mark zone.

Content and Composition

If France won the battle in terms of the timing of monetary union, Germany is perceived as having won the issue of its content. The convergence criteria would ensure that the more inflationary countries would not be admitted to the final stage of monetary union, and the European Central Bank would be granted statutory independence. But what is considered less often is the various safety valves that reduced the pressure exerted by the rigorous criteria. The loose interpretation of the convergence criteria of the Maastricht Treaty allowed a maximum number of countries to participate, which was in the interests of the French. Including countries that were expected to be weaker in the fight against inflation and would prefer growth could only help France's pursuit of more domestically oriented economic policies. For example, according to Article 104 (c) of the Maastricht Treaty, a country's budget deficit would be evaluated on its ability to meet the stated numerical criteria unless "the ratio has declined substantially and continuously and reached a level that comes close to the reference value." As for government debt, participation was permissible if the country was approaching the 60 percent cutoff "at a satisfactory pace." In addition, France and Italy were able to engage in short-term solutions that would qualify their economies (privatization payment by France Télécom and a repayable euro tax, respectively).[4] Spain also used receipts from privatized companies to reduce its deficit (*Economist* 11/30/96). These measures did not go against the letter of the treaty, but they did go against its spirit if the intent was to ensure fiscal austerity.

Contrast the relatively loose interpretation of the convergence criteria with the draft treaty on monetary union that Germany proposed at the Intergovernmental Conference in February 1991, which demanded strict compliance with the convergence criteria (Mazzucelli 1995, 112). As early as 1994 members of the Bundesbank expressed concern that the convergence criteria were being softened when Ireland's government debt was approved by the Monetary Committee as satisfactory even though the debt was still 90 percent of gross domestic product (GDP). These fears were renewed in 1996 when the European Union failed to reprimand Denmark for excessive deficits when its debt ratio was 71.9 percent (Heisenberg 1998, 156).

Indeed, had the convergence criteria been strictly enforced, monetary union would look very different. Belgium and Italy, for example, suffered from debt-to-GDP ratios that were double the Maastricht criterion of 60 percent of GDP. The Bundesbank and the Dutch central bank attacked Belgium's debt-to-GDP ratio, which is not expected to meet the 60 percent convergence criteria until at least 2011, and demanded that the Belgians make some sort of "binding commitment" on debt reduction. Dutch politician Frits Bolkestein, parliamentary leader of the free-market Liberals (VVD), voiced his concern that the convergence criteria were not followed for political reasons, complaining, "I voted for an economic euro and I'm getting a political euro."[5] The Dutch central bank governor, Dutch Prime Minister Wim Kok, and Dutch Finance Minister Gerrit Zalm echoed this disapproval of admitting countries that did not seem ready for monetary union, based on the Maastricht criteria. The Dutch traditionally have allied themselves with Germany on issues of monetary policy, having surrendered any pretense of monetary autonomy long ago. This like-minded approach to monetary policy made Dutch interests virtually indistinguishable from German ones, and perhaps the Dutch were in a better position politically to vocalize what the Germans could not.

Even the Stability and Growth Pact, which imposes fines on countries whose budget deficits exceed 3 percent of GDP, is not as onerous as it initially appears. The fines are not imposed automatically; they first must be approved by a majority of the euro members. Once the euro members approve the penalty, the country has at least two years to pay it, and if the

4. Even Germany tried to engage in creative accounting by revaluing the Bundesbank's gold reserves and applying the new value to the 1997 deficit. The Bundesbank refused to allow Germany to sidestep the criterion, and the revaluation was to be applied to the 1998 deficit (*New York Times* 6/4/97).

5. Quote, from May 1998, is from the Reuters Web site at www.reuters.com/emu.

country enters a recession, it need not pay at all. Prominent economists have already questioned the Stability Pact's ability to prevent profligacy (Eichengreen and Wyplosz 1998). At the Edinburgh summit in 1992 the European Council even agreed to increase the structural funds in order to ease the fiscal adjustment process for the weaker countries.

Though Germany clearly won many of the demands made in terms of the content (and composition) of monetary union, France made use of a wide variety of mechanisms to ensure that its preferences would be instituted. Most important, the inclusion of like-minded members such as Italy in the EMU has given France a better chance of altering the political culture from within. Just months after the third stage of monetary union began, the French and Italian governments were issuing documents calling for an employment pact to increase growth (*Financial Times* 4/21/99). Despite the strides made in spreading the culture of price stability across Europe, the preference for growth persists and may stand a better chance within the context of a monetary union.

THE SYMBOLISM AND SUBSTANCE OF EMU'S INSTITUTIONALIZATION

France also attempted to alter the nature of European monetary cooperation through the manipulation of political symbols. The debate over the nature (and even name) of the Stability and Growth Pact, the development of the Euro-11, and the controversy surrounding the selection of the president of the European Central Bank highlight the differences between France and Germany despite their shared commitment to monetary union. Though the symbolic battle that France has waged may be dismissed as window dressing to the monetary integration process, it does indicate conflicting ideas and provides a normative validation of them. The use of these symbols gives official recognition of their importance and provides a launching pad for further reform.

The surveillance program of the Stability and Growth Pact consists of the member states submitting stability and growth convergence programs to the European Council and the European Commission of the European Union. This annual consultation may indicate the need to reconfirm common interests, intents, and policy priorities when differences in preferences continue to exist. In another indication of diverging policy preferences, German Finance Minister Theo Waigel insisted on the creation of the "Stability Pact." French Finance Minister Dominque Strauss Kahn, however, contended that their countries were "entering into a new phase of European politics . . . [and a] policy mix that supports growth" (Reuters 11/16/98), and demanded the incorporation of the word "Growth" in the title.

In response to creation of the independent European Central Bank,

France tried to obtain a political counterweight.[6] The closest thing France could get was the Euro-11, an informal group within the Economic and Finance Committee (Ecofin) of the participants in the first wave of monetary union (to the chagrin of Great Britain).[7] The group meets monthly and is free to discuss any matter that affects the euro, which effectively means any economic policy issues. While some have argued that the Euro-11 is an insufficient counterweight to the European Central Bank, its very informality may eventually become a source of its strength. The group has no legal basis in any European Union treaty, and thus it is not required to report to any specific groups, nor must it operate along a particular degree of consensus. This group or a sizable portion of this group therefore could have a substantial impact on Ecofin meetings and push forward its interests. It potentially can use a greater claim to legitimacy as an institution composed of elected government officials, and in an age where words move massive amounts of capital almost instantaneously, the Euro-11 will likely prove a potent force in shaping market expectations.

The other new institution created by monetary integration is the European Central Bank. It had long been a foregone conclusion that the position of president of the bank would go to Wim Duisenberg, the Dutch central banker who had presided over the European Monetary Institute. Duisenberg's original acceptance of the position at the EMI had been on the condition that he would be the first president of the European Central Bank, an arrangement that all countries except France and Italy agreed upon.

In November 1997, however, just six months before the final decision would be made, France nominated its own candidate, Jean-Claude Trichet. French President Jacques Chirac sought this position for a Frenchman to temper the Germany-influenced institutional structure of the European Central Bank, which would also be located in Frankfurt (*Financial Times* 5/2/98). Though Duisenberg is not German, the Netherlands has closely followed German monetary and exchange rate policy for years and was the closest member of the deutsche mark zone to Germany. Duisenberg and Trichet enjoyed similar reputations and credentials as central bankers. The conflict turned into a political dogfight between Germany and France.

In May 1998 negotiators reached a compromise in which Duisenberg would assume the presidency of the European Central Bank but would "voluntarily" step down midway through his term, allowing Trichet to direct the bank for the remainder of the term. Rumors also floated that this was part of a package deal that would give a German, Horst Köhler, the presidency

6. This is a goal supported by Thomasso Padoa Schioppa, a member of the executive board of the European Central Bank (*Handelsblatt* 1/30/2000).

7. Euro-11 included Germany, France, Italy, Belgium, the Netherlands, Spain, Portugal, Finland, Austria, Luxembourg, and Ireland. The admission of Greece in 2000 made it Euro-12.

of the European Bank for Reconstruction and Development (*Libération* 5/2/98). Köhler did become its president, but whether or not Chirac had actually achieved his concession is unclear. After the compromise was made, the German press and various German politicians expressed their dissatisfaction. Finance Minister Waigel even publicly confirmed that there was nothing to legally block Duisenberg from refusing to step down during his term (*Financial Times* 5/5/98). And in an interview with a French newspaper, Duisenberg himself confirmed that he would not step down (*Le monde* 12/30/98). In early 2002 Duisenberg did announce his retirement, though as of this writing his successor has not been officially named.

The choice of central bank president was important on a symbolic level and potentially on a substantive level as well. By achieving the commitment that a Frenchman would share the position of the first president of the European Central Bank, Chirac reaffirmed France's primary role in the monetary union. Chirac extracted this concession after Duisenberg's candidacy was already considered a "done deal," underscoring France's ability to renegotiate the terms of monetary union. In doing so he indicated that a Frenchman might have different ideas of how the bank should be run, despite the similar reputations of the two candidates for president of the bank. This also offers yet another example of France's using European institutions to amplify its own power and promote its interests.

CONCLUSION

Politics and the regional distribution of power played an important role in European monetary integration. France and Germany exhibited different preferences regarding the evolution of monetary integration, with France continually advocating a bigger role for political actors in order to pursue greater economic growth and social stability, and Germany defending the independence of economic institutions in order to achieve price stability. These differences signal potential conflict in the functioning of EMU in the twenty-first century. Conservative liberals within France and in Germany have not converted those who prefer economic growth and social justice to price stability. France achieved the objective of German participation in a monetary union consisting of a wide membership, but it remains to be seen if France can provoke a shift within the stability-oriented culture of European monetary politics.

In regard to France's other objective of freeing Europe from U.S. monetary influence, the euro may one day challenge the dollar for international preeminence. Though the impact of the euro on the dollar will depend on how it develops as a currency and affects policy making within Europe (Henning and Padoan 2000), the stage is set for a more independent European monetary policy.

Finally, the origins and institutionalization of monetary union in Europe should banish notions that monetary policy is now based on economic rationale rather than political interests. Winners and losers appear at the national and international level when some policies are chosen over others, and the EMS status quo benefited Germany and financial interests disproportionately. France adjusted the monetary balance of power in Europe despite the wide acceptance of the German model. This case and the others covered in this volume emphasize that monetary policy does not function according to economic theories. States use monetary policy to manipulate the existing power balance, to spread their ideas on policy making (and not just monetary policy making), and to enhance their own prestige and capabilities. Politics and policy still go together, even in an integrated Europe.

PART 4

The Politics of Ungoverned Capital

CHAPTER ELEVEN

The Political Power of Financial Ideas
Transparency, Risk, and Distribution in Global Finance

MARK BLYTH

W hy do states, regulators, and market participants continue to hold that the current international financial regime of liberalized and integrated markets is the optimal way to organize the world's payments system? The persistence of such a regime constitutes a puzzle since it is both inefficient and increasingly crisis-prone.[1] Given such problems, one would expect demands for its replacement to be commonplace. Yet, instead of such calls, both states and regulators deem the current regime satisfactory, and reform initiatives resolve to a single call for greater transparency. I explain these puzzles in this chapter.

To do so I highlight two interrelated phenomena: transparency-enhancing reforms and the political power of financial ideas, with the former being illustrative of the latter. I argue that the promotion of transparency enhancement as a governance solution derives from erroneously viewing information failures as the primary cause of financial market instability. Building from this discussion I analyze the political power of financial ideas and the institutions such ideas have made possible. The politics of such ideas is important. Not only do the ideas that underpin these markets dictate specific governance solutions, but also such ideas are valuable political weapons. Both financial interests and states have used these ideas to defend and extend the current regime *despite* the volatility and asymmetric distributions it produces. In sum, I explain the *political sources of support* for the current regime, and why such a regime is likely to persist despite the disorder it creates.

---

1. By the East Asian crisis of 1997 there had been three waves of crises in the 1990s, or one major currency crisis every nineteen months. In contrast, Kindleberger (1989) showed that from 1780 to 1980 there was an average of one financial crisis every seven years.

THE EMERGENCE OF LIBERALIZED FINANCE

To understand the magnitude of the changes international financial markets have undergone in the past twenty years, it is necessary to briefly recall the previous regime. The key lesson Keynes and his U.S. counterparts took from the experience of the 1930s was that an "unregulated international monetary system [that] . . . impose[d] a contractionary bias on all domestic economies" caused the collapse of the interwar years (Kirshner 1999b, 323). Such reasoning called for a new type of financial regime in which trade was "in" but arbitrage and speculation were "out." The postwar Bretton Woods system was specifically designed to allow states to achieve this balance—that is, to attain domestic policy autonomy through capital controls without having to keep an eye on the exchange rate.

The Bretton Woods regime worked as long as European economies were financially dependent on the United States. In such an environment, the United States could essentially "pump-prime" the global economy by exporting dollars to promote recovery. However, as Milton Friedman reminded us, there's no such thing as a free lunch. Acting as "banker to the world" had a cost, as Robert Triffin (1960) pointed out. If U.S. capital exports were the only thing that was priming the pump for the "rest of the West," then if the United States ceased to run a deficit, the world's money supply would contract, and deflation would follow. Although "Triffin's dilemma" did identify a fundamental weakness in the Bretton Woods regime, what ultimately destroyed it was the independent growth of capital mobility (Helleiner 1994).

Beginning in 1958 with a deposit of Russian oil dollars in London, the Euromarkets came into existence. Being neither in the United States nor the "coin of the realm" of the United Kingdom, these Euro-deposits fell beyond the domestic regulations of both states. Because of this regulatory permissiveness, surplus dollars flowed into these markets, where they were lent out without regard for such controls. Unfortunately, these new markets also had a hidden cost. They enabled private financiers to engage in exactly the type of destabilizing hot-money transactions that the Bretton Woods regime had sought to eliminate. As predicted by Triffin's dilemma, the opportunity for arbitrage profits against the dollar and other major currencies was overwhelming. Speculation consequently worsened, and ultimately the system collapsed.

In its place a regime of free-floating exchange rates emerged, shifting foreign exchange risk from the public sector to the private sector (Eatwell 1996). In this volatile environment corporations needed new ways to hedge risk and turned to the financial sector for answers. During the economic slowdown of the 1970s, states were unwilling to do anything that would worsen economic performance, and so they allowed the private sector to pick up the new market in risk that was necessary for trade to continue. Consequently, financial deregulation on both a domestic and an international level was pursued, and the states that deregulated first had a strategic advantage in the delivery of these new and lucrative products of risk management: futures, swaps, and other derivatives. After the United Kingdom's trials with the International Monetary Fund (IMF) in 1976 convinced the British that Keynesianism was bankrupt, and after Paul Volcker's "Saturday night massacre" in October 1979 started a global recession, the two main centers of financial power, the United Kingdom and the United States, deregulated their markets, and over the next decade countries from Chile to Sweden followed suit. Thus, by the mid-1990s, a new system of integrated capital markets characterized by high mobility and capital account convertibility had reemerged, as Helleiner (1994) argued, to replace the Bretton Woods regime.

THE BENEFITS AND SHORTCOMINGS OF LIBERALIZED FINANCE

The rationale for these new institutions was that they would supply economically superior outcomes because they were free from the "financial repression" of controls. Specifically, three main benefits were expected. First, savings would be directed to where they would receive the highest return, which in turn would increase competitive pressures and reduce the cost of finance overall. Second, long-run growth and investment would be higher as the threat of exit facilitated by liberalization would enforce "a healthy discipline on governments which [would] encourage better economic policies and performance" (Eatwell 1996, 11). Third, in such an environment, serious financial crises would be more easily avoided, as policy would be both more "sound" and more transparent.

As Eatwell and Taylor (1998) documented, however, these claims have little empirical support. First of all, domestic savings tend to be correlated with domestic investment (Feldstein and Horioka 1980; Sinn 1992). As a result, even if markets are increasingly integrated, they do not seem to allocate capital more globally.[2] Second, in comparison with the previous regime, long-term interests rates throughout the Organisation for Economic Cooperation and Development(OECD) have been *higher* since liberalization began. Consequently, it is difficult to make the case that either borrowers or lenders are better served in the aggregate (Eatwell 1996, 15–17). Third, liberalization and integration have not resulted in higher long-run growth. As Davidson (1999, 11) noted, the annual average growth rate of

---

2. There is an important caveat here concerning states with well-developed financial sectors. I return to these issues in the conclusion.

per capita gross domestic product (GDP) in the OECD since 1973 was "approximately half of what it was during the Golden Age [1950–73]."[3]

Finally, the current regime seems to be more crisis-prone than its antecedent and carries with it far bigger costs. As Williamson and Mahar (1998, 52) noted in their survey of financial liberalization, "Almost all of the thirty-four economies in our panel experienced . . . systematic financial crisis between the beginning of the 1980's and July 1997." Most worryingly, the effects of integration and liberalization in exacerbating financial crises are apparent in the data. Even after they excluded the countries affected by the 1997 East Asian crisis from their panel, Williamson and Mahar (1998, 53, 57–58) found that of nine countries in their sample experiencing "severe crises," six were open to short-term capital flows, and in nine of fourteen identified as "crisis countries," large capital inflows appeared "in the years leading up to the crisis or during the crisis itself."

While explanations of these crises range from the cultural (crony capitalism) to the quixotic (self-fulfilling rational manias), their increasing frequency and cost are not in doubt, nor is the potential for systemic risk arising from localized shocks. Specifically, the derivative instruments invented by the private sector to manage risk may themselves be a new source of instability, a theme I return to later. In sum, the empirical benefits of the new system of finance are, by any measure, far lower than what the regime's proponents have claimed.[4] Given that the case for the new regime cannot be made on empirical grounds, one has to ask why such a regime persists. A large part of the answer lies, as Kirshner (2000) noted, in the fact that monetary regimes differ greatly in their distributional effects, with the current regime creating a far more asymmetric distribution than the former one.

While the financial services sector in the developed world has greatly benefited from the liberalization and integration of financial markets, and while such sectors contribute ever larger shares of GDP in certain states, the wealth derived from such transactions "tend[s] to flow to people at the top ends of national distributions [of income] and contribute to an ongoing trend in worldwide inequality" (Eatwell and Taylor 1998, 9). As in any other situation where there are concentrated benefits and diffuse costs, one would expect those who benefit the most from these asymmetries to be the most politically active in defense of the institutions that make them possible. Moreover, such sustained inequality must be *legitimated,* and it is this issue that draws attention to the ideas underpinning the current regime. Examining the ideas of finance is necessary since the ability to consistently

3. Similarly, in a comparison of investment-to-GDP ratios in a sample of fifty-four countries for the periods 1960–71 and 1982–91, Felix (1995) found that thirty-five countries had suffered investment-to-GDP declines in the latter period, compared with thirty-two that gained in the former period.

4. This is not to say that there have been no benefits. There have been, but their attendant costs are often not factored into the overall balance sheet of liberalization.

portray the current regime as both "the only way" and indeed the "best way possible" to organize the world's payments system is an important political weapon for those who benefit most from the regime's distributions.

THE MODERN THEORY OF MARKETS

Since the fall of the Bretton Woods regime, the theory of financial markets has undergone a revolution. In brief, since the mid-1970s macroeconomic theory has argued that causal accounts of the behavior of aggregates such as "financial markets" must be grounded in causal accounts of the behavior of individuals. Specifically, "credible" theories must be supported by models generated from the two main assumptions of neoclassical economics: that individuals are self-interested maximizers and that markets clear. It was argued at the time that such a move was necessary because existing Keynesian models assumed that "people had no knowledge of the economic system and did not perceive any interrelationships between the (hypothesized) variables" (Bleaney 1985, 142). Consequently, individuals in some sense must be "deluded" all the time. Since being deluded all the time is very expensive, especially when making margin calls, one would expect agents operating in such markets to correct these mistakes.

Modern macroeconomic theory argues that people do indeed invest in being correct—to the point that "economic agents are assumed [to be] completely aware of the 'true' structure of the economy, that is, the form of the equation and the size of the coefficients in the econometric model which govern it, and make full use of this in forming their expectations" (Bleaney 1985, 143). Thus, while *individual market participants* can be expected to make mistakes, systematic mistakes *by markets* are impossible since the structure of the market itself is invariant and known to all agents. Moreover, if all agents share the same model of the economy, and if there are no large informational asymmetries, then agents' expectations about possible future states of the economy should converge and promote a stable and self-enforcing equilibrium.

Part of the theoretical backing for this rediscovered belief in the efficiency of financial markets is the idea that asset prices follow a "random walk in continuous time" (Merton 1975). This insight suggests that *even if* different agents respond to new information such that prices move in an essentially random direction, this randomness can nonetheless be predicted. Developing these insights, Fama (1970) formulated the efficient markets hypothesis. He argued that asset prices followed a random walk because any informational advantages agents had regarding asset price discrepancies would be revealed in their market decisions. Thus, market outcomes would be efficient because asset prices would be driven by competition into equilibrium (cf. Friedman [1953] 1988).

As Eatwell (1996, 10) noted, however, the efficient markets hypothesis is just as important politically as it is theoretically, for it holds that "financial assets embody the true value of their real counterparts, creating an environment in which individuals trading in these assets can make Pareto efficient decisions." This claim, plus the "rational expectations" of investors, dictates that liberalized markets will yield superior economic performance than will regulated markets, with employment and output being produced up to the "natural rate" possible. The "modern theory of markets" therefore "present[s] a picture of economic efficiency being dependent upon free markets for goods, labor, and finance, and a minimalist state. Market liberalization is accordingly beneficial because it involves the removal of market distortions, which are *by definition* inefficient" (Eatwell 1996, 10).[5] Liberalized markets therefore are not merely the only way to organize finance; they are indeed the best way possible.[6]

THE POLITICAL POWER OF FINANCIAL IDEAS

As the foregoing discussion shows, the modern theory of markets contains a strong ideological element since it is partly an explanatory theory and partly a filter that prevents contrary data from being interpreted as invalidating it. Specifically, the modern theory of markets provides market agents with an interpretive framework that describes the workings of the economy, defines its constitutive elements, and denotes their "proper" (and therefore "improper") interrelations. Such a framework provides agents with both a "scientific" and a "normative" critique of the existing economy (regulated markets) and a vision that specifies how these elements *should* be constructed (the current regime). Financial ideas therefore not only provide an explanatory theory and a legitimatory framework but also supply, as Daniel Bell noted, "a way of translating ideas into action" (quoted in Geuss 1981, 11). That is, as well as offering an interpretation of how the economy "should" work, such ideas comprise "a program or plan of action, based on an explicit, systematic model or theory of how society works . . . aimed at the . . . transformation or reconstruction of the society as a whole . . . [that is often] held with more confidence than the evidence for the theory or model warrants" (Geuss 1981, 11).

The modern theory of markets does seem to operate in exactly this way—as both explanation and ideology. The arguments for liberalization and integration are indeed "a way of translating ideas into action." Such programs are clearly "based on an explicit, systematic model or theory of

5. A few economists have begun to question the efficiency of financial markets. See, for example, Willett 2000.

6. As ex-U.S. Treasury Secretary Lawrence Summers put it, "The logic of efficient markets is compelling" (quoted in Davidson 1999, 54).

how society works," and as the previous discussion highlights, they are most certainly "held with more confidence than the evidence for the theory or model warrants." Indeed, as Grabel (this volume) argues, such theories are ideological along two particular dimensions: "First, the theory is elevated to the status of singular truth. . . . [Second,] the theory and the policies inspired by it are fundamentally untestable and empirically irrefutable." As the regulatory responses to recent financial crises have made clear, the modern theory of markets is indeed elevated to the status of a singular truth, and no amount of contrary ex post evidence can refute the fundamental belief in the efficiency of markets.[7] After all, an efficient market, by definition, cannot produce a crisis.

Given this acceptance of the theory of markets as corresponding to the actual condition of markets, regulation is effectively reduced to a call for greater transparency. After all, if equilibrium is built into the system, then disequilibrium can only occur through informational imperfections. And with information defined as the only possible problem facing such markets, more and better information—greater transparency—becomes the only possible solution. Indeed, the dominance of such ideas is exactly why international regulatory authorities have seized on transparency as a governance panacea. For example, the IMF repeatedly has argued that the goal of financial reforms should be "to promote transparency and accountability, . . . to develop, disseminate and monitor implementation of better standards and best practices, . . . [and] to pay greater attention to the orderly liberalization of capital markets" (IMF 1999, 1). Similarly, Federal Reserve Chairman Alan Greenspan (1998a) testified to the U.S. House of Representatives that "a market system can approach an appropriate equilibrium only if the signals to which individual market participants respond are accurate and adequate to the needs of the adjustment process." In short, as far as regulation is concerned, transparency enhancement seems to be the only game in town.

There are, however, good reasons to see such a choice as less logical and more ideological. For *even if* one accepts the full-blown efficient markets hypothesis as the true condition of markets and better information as the solution to most problems, it is still possible to argue that increasing transparency in and of itself will not create stability, nor will the consequences of such a policy be distributionally neutral. To substantiate these claims I now examine both the likely and the actual effects of transparency enhancement within foreign exchange, stock, and derivatives markets. Doing so not only allows us to better understand the fragility of the current system. It also

7. As attested to in the responses of the IMF, the U.S. Treasury, and the U.S. Federal Reserve to the East Asian crisis, where the actual efficiency of integrated financial markets was never questioned. Nor was the proposition that integrated markets themselves may have been to blame for precipitating the crisis taken seriously by regulatory authorities (Fischer 1998c; Greenspan 1998b).

allows us to understand why pursuing such a strategy may in fact make greater political rather than economic sense, for such a strategy threatens to make the distributional effects of the current system even more asymmetric. This is why the politics of ideas is important—because of the distributions they make possible.

TRANSPARENCY AND MARKET KNOWLEDGE

A major logical problem facing transparency enhancement is the familiar "common-knowledge" problem found in games of incomplete information (Weber 2000). From this basis Winkler (2000, 5) argued that transparency alone is insufficient to promote market stability because "transparency hinges on a shared mode of interpretation." Such a "mode" is not guaranteed, however, by simply increasing information. He further stated (2000, 8) that transparency is a multifaceted concept that must be broken down into its four components: openness, clarity, understanding, and honesty. *Openness* refers to the amount of information released to the market. *Clarity* refers to the degree to which such information needs to be processed. Such processing is made possible by the third term, *understanding,* which is "a common interpreting device for encoding and decoding a message" (Winkler 2000, 8). However, given the inherent ambiguity of the term *understanding,* this gives rise to issues of *honesty,* which is seen here as "the degree to which the framework for reasoning and analysis adopted [by market regulators] internally corresponds to the presentation adopted for . . . external communication" (Winkler 2000, 8).

From such a perspective, transparency can offer no panacea for financial reform because these different facets of transparency oftentimes can work against each other. For example, increasing information may serve to lower clarity if understanding is imperfect, while honesty may become a problem if understanding is not common between the sender and the receiver. Moreover, different actors may want a different quality of signal from the same institution. Bond markets may want a simple monetary rule from the central bank, whereas derivatives traders may want full disclosure of the deliberations by the central bank. Conflicting demands may not be reconcilable by simply providing more information. In short, stability supposes a "common knowledge" that all agents receiving signals share the same "understanding." Yet, if agents can respond to the same piece of information in different ways, then rather than promote stability, such a policy may encourage greater instability (Rivlin 1998). Regardless of whether one deems markets efficient or not, there is no endogenous solution to this problem once it is recognized that transparency is multifaceted.

TRANSPARENCY AND TRADING

Further problems for transparency-based reforms are encountered in foreign exchange and stock markets. According to Watson (2000, 13), the Bank for International Settlements calculates that "less than one in five foreign exchange market transactions are conducted with a non-financial customer." If this is the case, then the ultimate determinants of behavior must rest more on the momentum of trades than on economic fundamentals. In theory, this should not be possible, nor should such speculative transactions be either destabilizing or persistent. Buying above the equilibrium price should be punished by other traders shorting their positions. Consequently, the market must clear at the "efficient" price (which reflects the fundamentals) because of competition. There is, however, strong evidence that such an equilibrating process does not actually occur and that speculative dynamics predominate in such markets.

First of all, if 80 percent of the trades made in such markets are simply attempts to make money from price discrepancies, then, as Watson (2000, 15) argued, such markets cannot clear at the equilibrium price because the supply and demand schedules for such assets are codetermined by the same players. Including both buyers and sellers at the same time, the market is moved by the momentum of trading itself, while the underlying value of the currencies themselves becomes irrelevant and simply a vector of trading. In short, such dynamics do not merely cause "overshooting"—they create trends in the market that have little or nothing to do with fundamentals.

Second, such a pattern of trading suggests that buying above the equilibrium price may not be punished but actually may be rewarded as traders attempt to follow trends. Given sufficient leverage, such momentum trading strategies can push the market as a whole toward a position that may be far from equilibrium but very profitable for those who set the trend. Again, as Watson (2000, 16) argued, "Each market actor knows that, should flows . . . be organized . . . with the specific aim of embedding a certain trend, then this will always become the dominant trend . . . [which is] sufficient to act as a further incentive for momentum trading." As a consequence, information about fundamentals becomes irrelevant since "investors devote far less [attention] . . . to fundamentals than they do to identifying the dominant market trend" (Watson 2000, 16; Grossman and Stiglitz 1980). Such momentum trading creates a competitive dynamic that reinforces rather than eliminates destabilizing speculation and herd behavior since "a trader [not following a trend] . . . will reason that the probability of losing his job is close to 100 percent if he does not take the . . . [same] position [as other traders]" (Eatwell and Taylor 1998, 12). Thus, the incentive to "follow the trend" becomes self-reinforcing.

A similar pattern is apparent in stock market behavior. As Shiller (2000,

185; 1986) argued, if stock markets operate as the modern theory dictates, then volatility in stock prices should be positively correlated with volatility in dividends, with movements in the dividend present value positively correlating with the notional stock price. Unfortunately, argued Shiller (2000, 186), when looking at the data, "we see no tendency for the stock price to forecast the dividend present value: the dividend present value is not doing anything especially dramatic while the [stock] price is jumping around a great deal." Given such evidence, one conclusion follows: financial assets in fact do not reflect their real counterparts, and trading in them is primarily determined by speculative dynamics. If market participants can generate and profit from strategies such as momentum trading, or if there is simply no relationship between the perceived value of an asset and underlying fundamentals, then providing better information flows will prove utterly irrelevant for producing stability. Transparency enhancement may prove to be, at best, a futile exercise.

Moreover, the ability to engage in speculative strategies depends in large part on instruments of leverage and credit creation. Indeed, the liberalization of finance has itself created instruments that facilitate the type of trades just noted. While derivatives such as repurchase agreements, swaptions, and the like undoubtedly help companies hedge risk, there are nonetheless two major problems with such instruments. First, the systemic risk that derivatives transactions pose by the nature of their composition and trading characteristics means that their effects can be amplified throughout the system in an unpredictable way. Second, and most important, transparency enhancement may prove to be more than simply a futile exercise. The recent experience of transparency-enhancing technologies in derivatives management suggests that reliance on transparency enhancement to promote stability may prove to be positively dangerous.

TRANSPARENCY AND DERIVATIVES MANAGEMENT

A series of high-profile losses during the early 1990s made the effective management of derivatives trading a must for both regulators and individual firms.[8] Part of the problem facing financial institutions was that the technology of derivatives trading was so complex that traders lacked proper oversight. Hence, when traders got into trouble, their parent institutions simply had to pay the piper. In an effort to monitor agents better, reduce

---

8. For example, Metallgesellschaft lost $1.34 billion and Kashima Oil lost $1.45 billion in 1994. Public authorities such as Orange County lost similar amounts shortly thereafter, while the Queen of England's private bankers lost an estimated $2.4 billion in similar circumstances (Millman 1995, 159).

such losses, and put some certainty back into trading derivatives, a technology called "value at risk" (VAR) analysis was invented.[9]

VAR analysis generates a figure for the exposure of an individual trade, and by summing VAR figures, one can estimate the total exposure of a firm and thus the total amount a firm is likely to lose given its current positions. If one then takes the total returns to a firm's portfolio divided by the volatility of those returns, one can calculate the "risk-adjusted rate of return on capital" (RAROC). These technologies allow risk managers to make their positions more transparent by closely monitoring VAR numbers, thus avoiding future Nick Leesons. VAR and RAROC were heralded as bringing control and stability to derivatives markets. Indeed, the banking regulators in Basel were so impressed with VAR and RAROC that they decided they "would permit the use of [these] internal models in allocating capital for a derivatives business. In other words, the biggest banks would be able to regulate themselves" (Dunbar 2000, 140).

There was, however, a quid pro quo to go with this self-policing, a variant of the Basel capital adequacy accords. Firms were to establish calculable "VAR limits," and if these were breached, then the firm in question would have to liquidate positions, bring down exposure, and reduce its VAR numbers (Dunbar 2000, 146–147). While this self-policing seemed to have a reassuring automaticity that convinced the regulators, as Keynes had argued sixty years earlier, what was to prove individually rational at the level of the firm was to prove collectively disastrous at the level of the global capital market. What got VAR analysis into trouble was the sequence of the East Asian and Russian financial crises.

As Dunbar (2000, 176–180) noted, the effects of the East Asian crisis filtered through to Western banking institutions in an unexpected way. As the crisis shifted from one economy to the next, overall volatility rose in Western stock markets. Short-term stock options, a favorite derivatives hedge, rose in price. This created a problem because under VAR analysis a firm's exposure is calculated as "mark to market." That is, all positions are calculated in terms of what they would fetch upon immediate sale. Consequently, with the cost of hedging rising, VAR limits were being breached without anyone's actually engaging in riskier-than-average trades. Given the need to reduce VAR numbers, more liquidity had to be found to bring the VAR numbers down. At this point, what happened to a hedge fund called Long Term Capital Management (LTCM) is emblematic of what happened to the markets as a whole.[10]

LTCM made its money on the so-called convergence trade, which in-

9. For an overview of VAR, see Jackson, Maude, and Perraudin 1998; Jorion 1997. While it may be unusual to call VAR a transparency-enhancing technology, it is defensible. If the goal of risk management is to see the risks coming, then VAR enables risk managers to do this better by making trades more transparent.

10. For overviews of LTCM, see Dunbar 2000; Lowenstein 2000.

volved betting that interest rate spreads in major bond markets would narrow.[11] In early 1998 on capital of $4.8 billion, "LTCM managed . . . total gross notional off-balance sheet derivative contracts amounting to about $1.3 trillion"—approximately 270 times its base capital (Eichengreen and Mathieson 1999, 10). LTCM, like other large derivatives players, needed such leverage to make money from the quantitative arbitrage models they operated, which were designed to extract profit from very small price discrepancies between assets.[12] LTCM, like other players, took heavily leveraged positions in order to profit from these "convergences."

An opportunity for all derivatives players to engage in such a strategy occurred when, on the heels of the East Asian debacle, the Russian government offered a 40 percent return on a new ruble-denominated security called the GKO. LTCM and several banks bought large quantities of GKOs and hedged them with forward contracts on the ruble. Hence, if the bonds fell in value, the forward contract on the ruble would cover the losses—in theory. However, the Russians defaulted on their debt, thereby devaluing their bonds, and the Russian central bank "forbade domestic banks from honoring foreign exchange contracts" (Dunbar 2000, 201). In other words, the futures contract became worthless, firms' exposures shot up, and so did their VAR numbers. Such a mass breaching of VAR limits in an already volatile market meant that either "more capital would have to be allocated [to cover exposure] or positions had to be cut" (Dunbar 2000, 203). At this juncture, Keynes's collective irrationality hit home with a vengeance.

With so many players cutting back positions at the same time, liquidity became scarce and derivatives traders such as LTCM suddenly found themselves without the necessary capital to make their trades. This led to a cascade effect: in order to find liquidity to cover exposure in one area, positions were cut in other areas. Unfortunately, this simply served to transmit the liquidity crunch across unrelated markets, and widened rather than narrowed bond spreads.[13] Caught in the midst of all this, LTCM's capital base shrank to $600 million, with outstanding liabilities of $100 billion in a matter of days. Eventually a consortium of fourteen major banks were called in by the New York Federal Reserve Bank to rescue LTCM before it became completely illiquid, with total losses at the time of the bailout estimated at $4.6 billion.[14]

---

11. As a hedge fund they are also not required to use VAR. They apparently used individual collateral hedges as an equivalent risk-reducing strategy.

12. The account of LTCM's collapse is gleaned from various sources, but especially Eichengreen and Mathieson 1998, 1999; Dunbar 2000.

13. As Dunbar (2000, 207) remarked concerning the European bond market, "The difference between German and Norwegian bond yields was trying to say that Norway had broken free from the North Sea and drifted down to the South-eastern Mediterranean."

14. What is seldom mentioned, however, is that other major derivatives players were similarly affected: Merrill Lynch lost $1.8 billion, Salomon lost $1.3 billion, and Goldman Sachs lost close to $1 billion by using the same quantitative arbitrage strategies. See Dunbar 2000, 225–226, on total players' losses.

The paradox of VAR is that it was a technology specifically designed to make trading *more transparent* and therefore *less risky*. Instead, it made trading much more dangerous by tying unrelated markets together in the search for liquidity. VAR analysis was indeed a logical, or perhaps better, an *ideological*, choice for risk management—ideological insofar as the ideas that made these derivatives markets possible were also the same ideas that made the VAR crisis unavoidable. By assuming that efficient markets, rational expectations, and all the rest accurately describe how markets work, regulators, with a singular focus on transparency enhancement, were blinded to sources of instability that were endogenous to the markets themselves. By relying on VAR analysis as a way to minimize risk, market participants ended up precipitating a crisis that had massive dislocative effects across the financial system as a whole. Thus, rather than providing an exercise in futility, transparency-enhancing reforms in derivatives markets actually jeopardized the entire financial system.

Taken together, these three examples throw the utility of transparency-based reforms into doubt. First, as the common knowledge example showed, simply providing more information may be perversely destabilizing if agents interpret that information differently. Second, as the examples of foreign exchange and stock market trading made clear, actual market behavior diverges quite drastically from what the modern theory of markets dictates. With the majority of trades following trends rather than fundamentals, increasing transparency over such factors as corporate balance sheets and governments' forward positions may prove to be utterly irrelevant in shaping trading behavior. Third, as the VAR crisis demonstrated, focusing on informational imperfections as the sole problem of risk management in fact may risk far more than it secures. Designing a technology to manage risk that assumes that markets behave as they do *in theory* is useless when complex derivative positions interact in such a way as to create crises that have nothing to do with informational imperfections. In fact, such a focus on transparency enhancement may make instability more commonplace as local shocks are translated into global events. So, one might ask, why are these policies pursued, and institutions supported, in the face of such contrary evidence?

THE POLITICS OF FINANCE: RENTIERS, STATES, AND DISTRIBUTION

Answering this question requires a focus on the two sets of actors who benefit most from the current regime: financial interests and states. As authors such as Helleiner (1994) have argued, states were at the forefront of the creation of the new financial regime. Yet many states, particularly those in the developing world, have fared worse under the present regime than under its predecessor. Similarly, while the current system offers benefits to financial intermediaries, it also contains great risks for them. Why then does the current system have such vociferous backing from both sides despite the risks? The analysis presented here suggests one possible answer: a coalition between states with large financial sectors and global financial interests, a coalition united for very different but mutually beneficial reasons.

Financial interests—even when seen as an undifferentiated whole—clearly have the most to gain from the current regime. Putting it bluntly, the more integration and liberalization proceed, the more profit these interests make. However, such an analysis is too simplistic. Instead, a more sophisticated answer lies in the risk and reward structure the current regime has established. Here the example of losses in derivatives markets is illustrative. In a straightforward bank loan, the bank assumes the risk of default and thus has an incentive to monitor the borrower, with the interest earned being the risk premium. In the case of derivatives markets, the complex leveraged positions taken by firms and the unpredictable interconnections of such trades threaten to become so destabilizing of the system as a whole that the moral hazard problem is reversed. The customer cannot effectively monitor the supplier because of the complexity of the assets in question, while governments cannot allow the suppliers to fail since their systemic exposure is so great. Given this inversion, the risk that these interests are supposedly managing in fact is thrown back on the public sector in the form of ad hoc government-sponsored bailouts anytime something goes awry, which seems to be happening more frequently. Perhaps even more dangerously, such a risk structure may well encourage firms to "gamble on resurrection." That is, when such firms do get into trouble, their ability to leverage huge amounts of capital, and thereby become "too big to fail," may paradoxically encourage them to take *more* exposed positions in the expectation that they will either succeed or be bailed out because of the systemic risk they threaten.

The case of LTCM is exemplary of this dilemma. Had this been simply a bunch of rich investors placing bets, one could have argued, "Without risk there is no reward," and let LTCM go under. However, given its exposure, letting LTCM go under could have turned a liquidity *problem* into a serious liquidity *crisis* in the entire global payments system. Alternatively, another scenario could have unfolded. Although derivatives are exempt from bankruptcy provisions, they could have been "sold off en masse by their creditors as LTCM was liquidated" (Eichengreen and Mathieson 1999, 12). Had this occurred, such a volume of contracts hitting the market at once could have increased liquidity too much, relaying different but equally destabilizing shocks throughout the whole system. Either way, LTCM, like other major players, received all the reward for managing risk but paid none of the costs of generating it.

Consequently, while the costs of crisis bailouts have been rising exponentially, market participants seem to be relatively unconcerned—for reasons that are equally easy to fathom.[15] With such crises becoming more frequent, the role of international institutions in responding to these crises grows in importance. However, recent IMF-sponsored bailouts tend to be costly for the affected country while offering a free lunch to financial interests. First of all, bailouts are not grants to crisis-hit countries. Rather, they are loans that must be paid back with interest. While such loans may stabilize the "shocked" economy, they must ultimately be paid back from the taxes of local inhabitants. Given the precedent of such a policy, these bailouts effectively collateralize the exposure of private investors. As long as a state in crisis can raise taxes over the long run, then bailouts are credible. Consequently, financial interests can invest without regard for risk, since the risk premium is effectively socialized by domestic taxpayers' future ability to pay.

However, financial interests' position of strength is not merely based on playing a game of chicken with the world economy. Once again the ideas of finance are important in this regard. As previously noted, the ideas of finance legitimate a particular distribution of risk. Representing the current system as the "only way" to organize capital flows ensures that the financial sector itself becomes largely immune from criticism and protected against calls for more fundamental reforms. For example, because of the modern theory of markets' singular truth status, any financial disruption cannot be, by definition, the fault of the markets themselves. Borrowing states, domestic "cronies," local banks, and all the rest must be to blame instead. The ability to operate under such an ideational shield gives these markets tremendous political power. For if things go well—that is, countries grow, markets are relatively stable, and so on—then this is taken as proof that the current regime is optimal. However, if things go wrong, then, since the theory dictates that such markets can only fail when there are informational failures, the hunt for post hoc problems with the fundamentals begins while the markets themselves remain above reproach. The political power of such ideas is to allow market participants to blame the victim: to take the reward and disavow responsibility for generating any of the costs.[16]

Regulation-cum-transparency provides an interesting example of this. It is worth recalling that at the time of the collapse of the Bretton Woods regime, many commentators expected the IMF, as the handmaiden of capital controls, to go out of business. It did not. Rather, it retooled itself with the new ideas of finance and turned from the regulator of markets into the regulator of governments on behalf of markets. Again, ideas served as critical

15. For example, the cost of the Mexican bailout was estimated at $50 billion, while the cost of bailing out the East Asian region as a whole was estimated to be as much as $170 billion (Solomon 1999, 142).

16. As Watson (2000, 24) put it, "At the same time as Asian populations paid the costs of adjustment . . . the international investors whose actions created the speculative bubble . . . were able to rely upon institutional guarantees to ensure their debts were repaid in full."

resources in this regard. By constantly affirming the efficiency of the new regime in line with the new theory of markets, international regulatory authorities effectively became captured regulators. Working wholly within the modern theory of markets, and thereby accepting the diagnosis of any crisis as a function of either bad local policy or imperfect information, regulation becomes reduced to attempting to produce a perfect capital market through transparency enhancement.

Yet as I demonstrated in my examples, even if such a strategy proves to be disastrous for the system as a whole, such reforms rather obviously suit financial interests. First of all, regulation-cum-transparency reaffirms the idea that market agents can never be wrong unless they either suffer government-engineered inflationary surprises or are informationally shortchanged, which thereby puts them beyond reproach. Second, if transparency is defined as the sole and proper regulatory strategy, then regulation under such ideas is best done, logically at least, by those who carry the risk—financial interests themselves.[17] However, as the VAR example demonstrated, even if markets are efficient, it is in each firm's self-interest to monitor only its own risk. With regulation being carried out at the level of the firm, the possibility of *systemic* risk arising out of individually rational actions is de jure discounted as impossible—yet this is exactly what the VAR crisis illustrates.

Given these benefits, it is simple to understand why, despite the risks of the current regime, financial interests wish no fundamental alterations to it and why transparency enhancement is such an attractive policy. After all, they get to run their own regulation, they cannot be blamed if it goes wrong, and when it does go wrong, they are not expected to pay for the damage because of the risk they carry. In sum, by using a set of ideas to legitimate an asymmetric distribution and resocialize risk, financial interests have achieved an enviable position. They can take all the profits from the private management of risk and yet suffer none of the losses associated with it.

Such a regime may suit financial interests, but why do states, particularly leading industrial states, favor it? Why do states support a regime that provides skewed distributions, low growth, and instability? Posen (1995b) once hypothesized that independent central banks can exist only where there is a sizable political coalition in favor of the policies such institutions would produce. By analogy, it is possible to extend this argument to demands for a liberalized global capital market in states where such a coalition of interests exists. However, if one assumes that states are somewhat more than simple reflections of interest group preferences, then accepting such a re-

---

17. Moreover, by continually affirming the importance of transparency enhancement, market agents such as investment managers and regulators can shift the blame from "not doing their homework" to a more generic and unaccountable "lack of information."

gime constitutes a puzzle. Watson provided an intriguing solution that has implications beyond the single case he discussed.

Watson (2000, 20–21) argued, in the context of an analysis of the United Kingdom, that states with chronic balance-of-payment problems, specifically long-run current account deficits, are both those most in favor of and those most integrated into international financial markets. The logic behind such a claim is simple and elegant. States with chronic structural imbalances in the current account face two choices: let the currency depreciate or deflate the domestic economy to achieve equilibrium. Apropos Posen, however, states with large financial sectors, especially those with reserve currency status, will be very wary about letting the exchange rate depreciate too far because *such an action* would devalue their holdings. Realizing this, states must defend their exchange rate or risk capital flight. The other alternative, domestic deflation, has little chance of success in a modern democratic polity. As the European Exchange Rate Mechanism crisis of 1991 demonstrated, not only will politicians fear being voted out if they deflate too far, markets themselves may regard the commitment to deflate as "incredible." If market agents do make such an estimation, then they can short the currency and create a very profitable one-way bet.

In addition to these two rather unappealing choices, states with chronic current account imbalances and large financial sectors have a third, and mutually beneficial, alternative: to finance their deficit through running a capital account surplus—that is, to import capital from the rest of the world. Evidence that this argument has salience for both the United States and the United Kingdom is straightforward. First, both states have huge long-term structural imbalances and are the main promoters of the current regime. Second, both states have the world's most developed financial sectors and are more integrated into the new regime than are other comparable states. For example, while the findings of Feldstein and Horioka (1980) cited earlier suggest that domestic saving tends to be correlated with domestic investment, Sarno and Taylor's data for the United Kingdom suggest that the United Kingdom "has the highest measure of international capital mobility of any G7 country" (Watson 2000, 20).

Similarly, U.S. capital imports have consistently made up the current account deficit since liberalization began. So much so that by "1999, the United States [had] . . . a merchandise trade deficit of $347 billion. However . . . for the financial account . . . foreign investors acquired $751 billion of assets in the United States, yielding a net financial and capital account surplus of $378 billion."[18] Data concerning the global pattern of capital flows confirm this pattern. By 1996, even though total capital flows to the developing world reached $244 billion, "the US continue[d] to ab-

18. Quote from "Fedpoint 40: Balance of Payments," www.ny.frb.org/pihome/fedpoint/fed40.html.

sorb two-thirds of the rest of the world's surplus savings, even though real rates of return . . . are well below those in the developing world" (Eatwell and Taylor 1998, 9; see also Solomon 1999, 113). Given this situation, the potential for a mutually beneficial coalition between "structurally challenged" states and international finance exists. Just as the Euromarkets allowed states to avoid hard choices over Triffin's dilemma in the 1960s, so the current regime allows states with large financial sectors to avoid hard choices over their structural deficits in the new century.

Such an explanation reveals why the United States and the United Kingdom are so determined to both support and extend the current regime. Again, ideas matter. The constant promotion of the current regime and the downplaying of its costs are necessary for these states and their financial allies to reap their rewards. As in any situation where there are concentrated benefits and diffuse costs, the greater the number of agents pooling risk, the smaller the risk for any individual. However, in this case, some "individuals"—specifically the United States and the United Kingdom—count more than others. Consequently, the more the United States and the United Kingdom manage to extend the current system, the more they asymmetrically benefit.

Again, the East Asian crisis is illustrative. When London and New York were falling over themselves to pour capital into East Asia in the early 1990s, they reaped the rewards of having such deep capital markets. When the crisis hit, however, they were similarly blessed. Capital flight *benefited* these states because there was a "flight to quality" that pushed up the price of U.K. and U.S. equities and bonds as the Asian markets fell. Such a situation is "win-win" for these states. By spreading the gospel of liberalization and extending the regime, leading states reduce their risk as the pool of available capital and risk bearers increases, and as the potential returns increase. Costs in this case are somebody else's problem—by definition they cannot be the market's—and leading states, like financial interests, can take all the benefits without exposing themselves to many of the costs.[19]

In sum, this is why the current regime persists: it provides states with chronic structural imbalances and large financial interests a way of avoiding painful domestic trade-offs by rent seeking from the rest of the world. This analysis demonstrates not just the politics of finance but also the power of financial ideas—specifically, how such ideas legitimate the current regime and allow such patterns of regulation and reform to persist. As Keynes knew nearly seventy years ago, such ideas are the cornerstones of financial governance, but for reasons vastly different from the ones given by the modern theory of markets. Such ideas not only legitimate current practices but also are at a most fundamental level what makes market stability possible.

---

19. This is hardly an exaggeration when one considers that after the outbreak of the East Asian crash, City of London bonuses for 1997 still topped $1 billion.

CONCLUSION: WHAT KEYNES KNEW AND SOME CHOSE TO FORGET

Arguably, the most fundamental insight of Keynes's *General Theory* (1936) was that financial stability is largely a function of expectations. However, for Keynes, such expectations were nonrational, myopic, and the very opposite of the self-stabilizing and rational expectations found in the modern theory of markets.[20] Keynes (1936, 148) arrived at this conclusion because for any market participant, "the most probable forecast we can make . . . depends upon the *confidence* with which we make this forecast" (emphasis added). The problem here is that this "state of confidence" rests on expectations that are neither rational nor naturally convergent. Rather than assuming both convergent expectations and that agents know what the "fundamentals" actually are, Keynes assumed that individual investors were myopic and looked to each other for signals. However, such signaling, as my common knowledge example demonstrated, is far from unambiguous. Market confidence is then an intersubjective construction that has a tenuous relationship to market fundamentals but does not have any precise, calculable metric.[21] Once again, ideas matter, but this time for the production of order itself. Specifically, to explain how order is possible in such a random world, Keynes united financial ideas and expectations in the concept of "conventions."[22]

Conventions are intersubjective understandings shared by market actors that specify how markets are supposed to behave. Such conventions are neither naturally apparent focal points nor simply produced by accurate information. Instead, they are sociological constructs. Market behavior therefore rests on the coordination of agents' expectations through the maintenance of conventions. So long as such intersubjectively held conventions regarding the economy are adhered to, then the economy will perform within the parameters of the expected "conventional judgment." In sum, there is no truth about markets "out there" apart from the prevailing wisdom markets have about themselves (Keynes 1936, 136–147; Putnam 1981, 103–126; Parsons 1981). Change occurs when expectations diverge and conventions falter; only then do markets ultimately fail. Given this rather different understanding of how financial markets operate, the im-

---

20. As Keynes (1937, 213–214) put it, "We have, as a rule, only the vaguest idea of any but the most direct consequences of our acts . . . [and] the fact that our knowledge of the future is fluctuating, vague, and uncertain renders wealth a peculiarly unsuitable topic for the methods of classical economic theory. . . . About these matters there is no scientific basis on which to form any calculable probability whatever. We simply do not know."

21. This is different from contemporary "cascade" and "mimicking" hypotheses, as these are strategies employed by rational agents to overcome information problems.

22. As Keynes (1937, 214) put it, "Knowing that our own judgment is worthless, we endeavor to fall back on the judgment of the rest of the world . . . that is, we endeavor to conform with the behavior of the majority or average . . . to copy the others . . . [to follow] a *conventional* judgment" (emphasis added).

portant task for governing the economy becomes shaping expectations so that they conform to expected parameters. This in turn suggests an important point about what institutions actually do.

If, as institutionalists argue, behavior is shaped by participation within institutions, then institutions must be designed to structure the "conventional judgment" necessary for the coordination of agents' expectations.[23] In terms of my analysis, during the Bretton Woods era regulators saw agents' expectations as divergent and in need of institutional coordination that would allow the formation of the conventional judgment so important for producing market stability. This is why Keynes sought the extension of "the traditional functions of government," to create the common baseline of expectations necessary for stability to become endogenized (1936, 379). Similarly, under the current financial regime, conventions are also coordinated by institutions, albeit institutions of a very different type.

As financial liberalization gained momentum, the institutions that had previously provided expectational coordination—the Bretton Woods exchange rate mechanism, capital controls, and so on—were dismantled. The problem with dismantling these institutions is that they were based on the assumption that *investor myopia and expectational divergence were the norm,* and sought to rectify this state of affairs by supplying expectational coordination institutionally by reining in certain market practices. The problem now is that the new institutions that replaced those of the old regime and that make global finance possible—the IMF, which promotes capital account convertibility; independent central banks; deregulated and integrated markets; and so on—take *long-sighted behavior by market participants and convergent expectations as a given* and seek to coordinate expectations "as if" they were in accord with the modern theory of markets.[24] However, as I have demonstrated, the current regime neither produces the outcomes it is supposed to nor acts in accordance with theory. Thus, the more financial integration continues apace, the less institutional protection there will be against an expectational coordination failure.

This is what Keynes knew and what modern finance chose to forget— that as global financial integration proceeds, it may increasingly affirm a set of conventions, transparency enhancement chief among them, that are singularly inappropriate given the way that markets actually behave.[25] Guided by such conventions, "if the markets believe that higher fiscal deficits result

23. That is to say, institutions do not socialize behaviors; rather they structure expected states of the future.

24. As an example of changing conventions, consider that twenty or thirty years ago better employment figures were seen as a macroeconomic "good." Now, whenever better employment figures are released, markets regard this as bad news and demand an inflation premium or higher interest rates.

25. To list a few of these new conventions: market stability is generated by rational market participants, instability can only come from government interference, macroeconomic stability is best achieved by demonstrating credibility, deficits cause higher interest rates.

in higher real rates of interest, then so they will," regardless of whether the fundamentals demand this or not (Eatwell 1996, 32). Unfortunately, with "beauty-pageant" dynamics determining market outcomes, market opinion will be prone to sudden shifts in that all too fragile "confidence." As a result, market meltdowns will become increasingly frequent, and the more the current regime spreads, the more likely it is that it will fall, from time to time, into panics and crashes. If this scenario is correct, then none of the transparency-enhancing reforms currently underway will make a blind bit of difference to any of the underlying problems such markets actually engender. Nor will such policies alter the distributions such a regime makes possible in the first place.

Explaining Choices about Money
Disentangling Power, Ideas, and Conflict

JONATHAN KIRSHNER

The main theme of this volume is that politics, not economics, largely explains the choices made about monetary policies and reforms in the world today.[1] This is at odds with the prevailing conventional wisdom, which rests on two widely shared conclusions. First, there is a broad consensus among mainstream theorists and influential decision makers about the policy implications that derive from economic theory. As a result, there is a working understanding on which economic policies are "correct," regardless of any interests that might be at stake. Second, the contemporary influence of market forces on economic policy—especially in the macroeconomic sphere—is enormous, perhaps greater than it has ever been. Since certain policies are correct and others unsound, given the power of markets, it is the immutable force of economic logic, not the vagaries of the political process, that dictates the nature of policy choices about money.

But these foundations on which the conventional wisdom is built are hollow. As I argue in the first chapter of this volume, while there is a broad consensus on issues such as inflation policy, central banking, and capital deregulation, the evidence is inadequate to support the conclusions drawn. Vigilance to ensure low inflation is considered to be the fundamental task of monetary policy, but an enormous amount of empirical literature has failed to yield clear evidence that moderate levels of inflation have a negative effect on real economic performance. The economic justification for central bank independence (CBI) also rests squarely on the idea that inflation is harmful. The case for capital account deregulation (which I explore further below) is even shakier than that for very low inflation. On this issue, the logic is largely assumed—very little empirical evidence exists on either side of the debate.

1. I thank Rawi Abdelal, Rachel Epstein, Ilene Grabel, Charles Kindleberger, and two anonymous referees.

In sum, there is good reason to challenge the idea that the existing policy profile of the conventional wisdom is singularly correct. In fact, there may be a range of policies that are plausible and sustainable, from a purely economic perspective. This is true for the "settled" issues regarding domestic monetary policy just mentioned. It is clearly also true to an even greater extent for the issues recognized as "unsettled" even from an economic perspective, such as the international use of money, basic aspects of monetary geography (which currencies are used where), the choice of exchange rate regime, and the adjustment mechanism. In these areas the economic debate is still open, and therefore the choice of one policy over another must be influenced by noneconomic forces.

The existence of a plausible range of policies directly undermines the second pillar of support for the conventional wisdom—that the disciplining role of powerful market forces ensures that policies are selected on economic rather than political grounds. If there is more than one plausible policy choice—that is, more than one policy that is sound and coherent from the perspective of economic reasoning—then the power of market forces cannot explain why one policy is chosen over another. The power of market forces, in theory, should only rule out those policies outside of the plausible range.

Thus, the challenge posed by the essays in this volume is not that market forces are insignificant or incoherent. On the contrary, such forces powerfully affect basic choices about money, and the logic of such forces will effectively rule out certain options. Rather, the competing claim offered here is that economic theory is very often indeterminate—the difference between many plausible policies is of ambiguous or, in some cases, reasonably clear but very modest economic effect—and thus economics will have little to tell us about which policy is chosen from that plausible set. Even in cases where the difference between the aggregate economic consequences of one choice over another is discernable, those consequences typically will be dwarfed by the considerable differential and political effects that the choice of one policy over another will have.

The chapters in this volume have examined policy choices about money from every corner of the globe—but they have shared a basic analytical structure. The contributors have demonstrated—regardless of whether they were explaining the internationalization of the yen, participation in the CFA Franc Zone, or the dissolution of the ruble zone—that the power of market forces or the conclusions of economic theory are insufficient to explain the observed outcome. In all of the cases considered, economic forces offered either no unambiguous choice (as to which policy or outcome is "better") or a clear choice of little absolute significance. Rather, each of the authors concluded, the observed policy choices were attributable to political forces. The ambiguous, relatively broad, and modest economic pressures provide clues to which policies will fall within the plausible

set, but political factors—ones that tend to produce powerful, more narrow, and divergent interests and preferences—provide the missing link between the plausible set and the outcome observed. These findings are summarized in Table 12.1.

Those political factors derive from three sources: ideas, conflict, and
power. Ideas are enormously important in the study of money because of
the fact that money, especially in the modern era, derives its value solely
from the fact that people think it is valuable. Thus, what people think about
money matters, in a unique and consequential way. Further, the power of
ideas in the monetary sphere can also obscure some of the more basic interest-based conflicts over money. Macroeconomic policies and other
choices about money, typically conceptualized in aggregate terms, have
markedly differential economic consequences for various groups and actors
within societies. This takes on much greater significance if there is a plausible range of policy choices, rather than one unique and unambiguously
"correct" choice. Finally, power—state power—is another important political source shaping policy. As states seek autonomy, attempt to pursue their
strategic interests, and negotiate over sharing the burdens necessarily
borne to facilitate international adjustment, they shape the pattern of monetary practice.

In this concluding chapter, I first review the three political foundations
of monetary phenomena—ideas, conflict, and power—and draw together
lessons from this volume about how they influence policy choice. This discussion points to an important future direction for research—the challenge of disentangling the roles that these factors play in explaining observed outcomes. For while the contributors to this volume argue
convincingly that it is impossible to understand money without focusing on
its political foundations, we do not yet have an understanding of how those
forces interact. Although the underlying interest-based conflicts are usually
readily identifiable, the interplay between ideas and power inevitably plays
a crucial role and complicates the analysis. I then give an example of this
challenge with an exploration of a pressing contemporary policy debate—
the motives behind continued pressure for capital account deregulation.

IDEAS, CONFLICT, AND POWER

As I noted in the first chapter, it is widely acknowledged that ideas, even
if they are introduced instrumentally in the service of interests, can often
play a significant role in policy debates. With regard to money, there are
three principal mechanisms through which ideas can profoundly shape policy in ways divorced from the economic logic or merits of those ideas. The
first is beliefs—that is, assumptions about causal relationships. Beliefs, especially when they harden into an ideology (defined here as beliefs that are

Table 12.1. Choices about Money: Ambiguous Economics, Ubiquitous Politics

Chapter	Issue Area	Standard Economic Explanation	Assessment of Economic Explanation	Political Explanation
1. Kirshner, "Inescapable Politics"	Low inflation	Best practice (inflation has real costs)	Cost ambiguous; any effects modest	Distributional conflict; ideology
2. Grabel, "Monetary Institutions"	Monetary management in emerging economies	Depoliticize management; assure credibility	Credibility constructed, self-fulfilling	Ideology; distributional conflict
3. Helleiner, "Postwar Monetary Policy"	Central bank design in Southern states	Best practice (given state of knowledge)	Indeterminate; varied structures	Geopolitics; beliefs
4. Stasavage, "Monetary Discretion"	Persistence of CFA Franc Zone	Establish credibility; facilitate trade	Inconsistent with evidence; modest effects	Security cooperation; narrow interests
5. Abdelal, "National Money"	Collapse of ruble zone	Optimum currency area; trade, transactions costs	Uninformative; inconsistent with pattern of dissolution	National identity; international politics
6. Schamis, "Currency Boards"	Exchange rate policy in Argentina	Market pressures; need to establish credibility	Credibility endogenized by well-positioned interests	Interest group bargaining; distributional conflict
7. Wang, "Exchange Rate Policy"	Valuation of RMB by China	Best practice (maintain at equilibrium rate)	Ambiguous; cases for and against devaluation	Responsible great power; domestic legitimacy
8. Grimes, "Internationalization"	International use of yen	Costs and benefits to issuer; attractiveness of currency	Costs/benefits ambiguous, modest; predictions vague	Search for autonomy; international politics
9. Gavin, "International Monetary Policy"	Management of dollar, 1960s international reforms	Market pressures require changes in policy, system	Indeterminate, esp. regarding nature of change	Beliefs; power politics; conflicts over adjustment
10. Chang, "Monetary Integration"	European monetary integration	Optimum currency area (OCA); trade, transactions costs	European Monetary Union not OCA; transactions gains trivial	Broader political goals of dominant partners
11. Blyth, "Global Finance"	Open, integrated financial markets	Best practice (transparency, stability efficiency)	Poor practice (volatile, unstable)	Ideology; financial interests
12. Kirshner, "Choices about Money"	Pressure for capital deregulation	Best practice (discipline, efficiency)	Benefits unclear; theory ambiguous; evidence thin	Ideology; interests; international politics

held as articles of faith and thus resistant to change even in the light of evidence), can skew the ways in which policymakers understand and react to problems. This can create severe constraints even when those beliefs turn out to be wrong, as Francis Gavin illustrates in chapter 9 regarding the adjustment and payments crises the United States faced in the 1960s. While there were economic problems that demanded attention, from a contemporary perspective, some of these crises were crises of the mind. Eric Helleiner also illustrates the powerful formative influence of beliefs in chapter 3. As he shows, the distinct beliefs held by the U.S., French, and British advisors largely determined the pattern of different rules and institutional structures of central banks established in the South after World War II.

The second mechanism through which ideas can shape monetary practice is norms—ideas that contribute to normative understandings about "appropriate" behavior. Such norms can create artificial yet powerful constraints on policy. (*Artificial* here means not derived from any economic "truth.") One prominent example of this is attitudes toward devaluation. From an economic perspective, devaluation or revaluation of a currency is a step taken to restore external equilibrium—it cannot be said that one direction for currency adjustments is "better." All prices—like those of autos or computers—change up or down in response to market conditions. But in practice, devaluation (and depreciation) is associated with weakness, while a "strong" currency affords prestige to its issuer. These sentiments, however widespread they may be (and history suggests a remarkably broad consensus on this issue), have no basis in economic logic. But they can guide policy. As Hongying Wang illustrates in chapter 7, China's decision not to devalue its currency was not based on the potential economic costs and benefits of the measure (which were ambiguous, though suggestive of devaluation). Rather, China's leadership chose not to devalue in order to enhance its prestige—it was behaving as a "responsible great power." Responsible great powers don't devalue—they maintain strong currencies because they are powerful and stable.

The role of beliefs, ideology, and norms is important, indeed at times determinant in shaping monetary practice, even when, as in the examples given, the forces of interests and economic pressures are also at work. These ideational variables have identifiable parallels to other issue areas such as trade policy. What is special about ideas in money, however, is the third mechanism, the unique link between ideas and "market sentiment" in money matters, and the overwhelming influence of that sentiment on the ability to practice macroeconomic policy. Because market actors can essentially "vote with their currency"—that is, abandon some currencies in exchange for others—policies are sustainable only if they are credible. "Credible" policies are those that the market (market actors collectively) thinks are right. Policymakers need to understand what the market demands and to respond appropriately. As Gavin shows, officials were gravely concerned that unless specific policy measures were adopted, the United States would be perceived as "not serious" about preserving the dollar, which in turn would seal the dollar's fate.

In theory, this phenomenon could be optimal from an economic perspective—the market selects out those policies that are inefficient and rewards proper practice. But in fact, this is too thin a reed to stand on. Market sentiment can be "wrong," as Milton Friedman and Anna Schwartz (1963, 111, 133) suggested it was in its preferences regarding the U.S. monetary standard in the late nineteenth century (see also Rockoff 1990). Or, rather than one "correct" policy, there may be (in theory) several plausible policy options. The power of market sentiment, however, exacerbates rather than corrects problems that emerge from these two factors. As Ilene Grabel argues in chapter 2, "policy credibility" is often expressed as a "singular truth," and one that is not supported by evidence but "demands to be taken on faith." Thus when the market is wrong, it does not self-correct—rather, its influence is unyielding. In the example mentioned above, not only was the United States inhibited from exploring other options such as expanding the monetary role of silver, but also the knowledge that such options were even debated forced the introduction of contractionary policies to assure "the market" that the United States remained credibly committed to the (dubiously optimal) gold standard.

The potentially pernicious effects of market discipline about money do not come simply from the claim to "truth" about the correct policy, but rather, in Grabel's terms, from the claim to "*singular* truth." As Mark Blyth observes in chapter 11, given the fact that money has value because it is believed to have value, everything depends on the "state of confidence"—which is the result of a "coordination of agents' expectations." The value of a currency, then, is not determined by actors' expectations about its future value. Rather, as Keynes (1936, 156; 1937, 114–118) suggested, it is determined by actors' expectations about the expectations of others. This creates a convergence toward the "singular" policy that is credible, and makes others unsustainable. Even if there were, in theory, five policies that were each plausible from the standpoint of economic theory, if three were *perceived* to be illegitimate, they would not in fact be sustainable, *solely for that reason*. In sum, resting exclusively on market discipline to rule financial markets is a dicey proposition. When the market is wrong, it does not self-correct. Even when it is right, it will invalidate other plausible policies, some of which may be even more appropriate for the particular circumstances that some states find themselves in.

These conclusions are of great significance because they are at odds with the conventional Darwinian understanding about which policies survive and which must be discarded. By this reasoning, good policies succeed because they are the right policies—at least the best-possible policies that can be established, backed by progress in economic theory and by their ability to deliver superior economic performance. Bad policies are discarded because, built on a foundation of poor (or superseded) economic reasoning, they simply do not deliver the goods. The right policies, therefore, the policies chosen by the market, derive legitimacy from their theoretical and practical superiority.

If policies are chosen because they are unambiguously the best practice, it is understandable how the legitimacy they enjoy can mask, or at least mute and undermine, debates about policies that call attention to their differential economic effects on various groups within society. Legitimacy clothes the banker's call for inflation fighting in righteousness, while the sugar producer stands naked when advocating for protection. But if the "legitimacy" bestowed on some monetary practices rather than others is not the inevitable revelation of optimality but a path-dependent self-fulfilling prophecy, then it becomes necessary to revisit the distributional consequences that result from the choice of one monetary policy over another.

As I argued in the first chapter, monetary politics are inescapable. There is no "neutral" policy. Rather, every macroeconomic phenomenon and monetary policy has significant and inevitable differential and political implications. This is currently underappreciated, partly because macroeconomic theory focuses on aggregates, and most macroeconomic models impose strict homogeneity assumptions on their models. While these abstractions and assumptions are appropriate for many of the inquiries undertaken by macroeconomists, they effectively preclude the consideration of the differential effects of macroeconomic phenomena.

In particular, looking at aggregate data, such as national income, obscures the fact that most of the time different income groups, regions, and sectors may indeed experience markedly different rates of income growth. Attention to the *composition,* rather than the *rate* of economic growth, calls attention to the political stakes on the table when choosing between macroeconomic policies. Given that the income of some actors will be rising at a faster rate than others, there may be divergent perceptions about what policies should be pursued—some might urge caution while others agitate for expansion. More pointedly, conflicts of interest can emerge not simply because the distribution of growth affects macroeconomic policy choice but because of the converse: macroeconomic policies shape the distribution of growth.

In the absence of (justifiable) claims to exclusive legitimacy, choices about money—such as low inflation, CBI, capital regulation, and sensitivity to "market discipline"—the differential effects of various policies must be put back on the table. Economists may generate models of the costs of inflation that do not address "the distributional consequences of the disinflation or of the reduced inflation" (Feldstein 1997, 153; 1999a, 38), but in order to explain monetary policy other scholars need to focus on the fact that low inflation, and the policies required to sustain low inflation, will have marked distributional consequences (Kirshner 2001). Similarly, the absence of clear findings of real economic gains from central bank independence provides support for the argument of Adam Posen (1995) and others (Piga 2000) that CBI is best understood as an outcome of political conflict rather than economic reasoning.

There remains little evidence to support the claim that CBI enhances economic growth. Sylvia Maxfield (1997), in her careful study of central banks in developing countries, noted that existing studies support the notion that greater central bank authority is associated with lower inflation, but no conclusions can be drawn about the relationship between central banks and growth.[2] Maxfield's argument is that developing countries increase central bank authority when they need to signal credibility to international capital markets. The implication of this argument changes markedly, and is arguably of even greater significance, if there is a shift from a "singular truth" model to a conflict-of-interest model. Under the former model, developing states are attempting to signal a credible commitment to "best practice." In the latter model, where there are a number of plausible "good practices," an additional, more politically pointed, question is raised: *credibility of what, to whom?*

As Blyth argues in this volume, in international capital markets, credibility is best understood as part of the collective behavior that yields a self-fulfilling (and legitimating) prophecy. He explains that to some extent, if markets think *a* will lead to *b*, then it will. This takes a sharper political character when interests are attached more explicitly to the story. As Hector Schamis illustrates in chapter 6 in reference to Argentina, large corporations are "capable of resorting again to massive and coordinated capital flight practices." As a result, signaling credibility in this case is reduced to little more than "going along" with the preferences of those capable of moving capital.

Conflict over money, then, often cloaked by legitimacy and executed by anonymous market forces, is also an exercise of power by purposeful actors. This is always the case, but it is especially clear in the realm of international relations, where states are usually presumed to advance their narrow self-interests with less regard for the collective good. Here most plainly, choices between plausible alternatives about money are shaped by power and interest, not simply by market pressures. States desire wealth and growth, but unlike private interest groups they are also motivated by noneconomic goals, such as power and security, and they also often seek autonomy from destabilizing market forces. When no unambiguous economic course presents itself, the interplay of states pursuing these goals will determine the pattern

---

2. It should be noted that Maxfield does seem to support the idea that greater central bank authority in developing countries is a good thing.

of international monetary practice. Even in the cases where the economic message is plain, states will typically be willing to bear some material sacrifices to advance their political goals.

The contributors to this volume show that state power and international politics almost always have an important role in explaining policy choices about money—even in the contemporary environment where states need to be more sensitive to the constraints presented by international market forces. Rawi Abdelal illustrates how neither the forceful suggestions of the International Monetary Fund (IMF) nor the logic of currency unions—whether derived from prior trading patterns, transactions costs, or pooled expertise—can explain the pattern of the monetary strategies chosen by the states of the former Soviet Union. Rather, that pattern by which new national currencies were introduced depended directly on each state's preferences regarding its future relationship with Russia. Wang shows how China's leadership focused on a variety of political concerns—domestic legitimacy, conducting itself as a "responsible great power," establishing a reputation for cooperation with an eye toward future participation in the World Trade Organization—as the basis for its decision not to devalue its currency. William Grimes demonstrates how concerns for power and autonomy—the international political implications of yen internationalization and the ways that it might insulate the Japanese economy from global financial instability—were the cornerstones of the debate on this issue in Japan.

Other authors highlight more basic security and geopolitical concerns. Gavin illustrates how discussions about the fate of the dollar were inseparable from questions about the Vietnam War and the United States's security relationship with Europe. David Stasavage shows how economic pressures and motives were poor predictors for explaining participation in the CFA Franc Zone. Rather, African states were motivated by access to privileged aid and security arrangements that accompanied membership. The states that did withdraw did so not because the costs of following the rules were too high but rather as part of a broader political split with France. This explanation fits neatly with Helleiner's account of how the geopolitical concerns of the great powers (in concert with their economic beliefs) explain the pattern of central banking practice in the South after World War II.

State power and the pursuit of security also shape the pattern of international monetary cooperation. Any effort at monetary cooperation must confront "the adjustment problem": to resolve disequilibria as they arise in the international economy, states must accommodate their macroeconomic policies. Cooperation can be sustained only if there is agreement about how such adjustments are to take place, and, most important, about who will bear the burdens of monetary retrenchment and deflation.

Monetary cooperation is inherently difficult, therefore, because to adhere to agreements, states will routinely be called on to engage in deflationary economic practices—regardless of whether they seem appropriate in the moment—for such cooperation to be sustained. Obviously, leaders will often face enormous domestic political pressure to break free from the constraints presented by adhering to monetary agreements, and for this reason such agreements are likely to be fragile. Security concerns can help overcome this problem. When national security is perceived to be at stake, the costs of monetary cooperation (the adjustment burden) remain the same while the benefits are increased to the extent that monetary cooperation supports valued allies or facilitates and enhances overall political cooperation.[3] Additionally, states may refrain from abrogating monetary agreements owing to the fear that such action might cause a larger set of political understandings to unravel, or signal dissension to common adversaries.

Appealing to the role of security to explain the pattern of international monetary cooperation fits the broad contours of twentieth-century history. Introducing security concerns, for example, unties a vexing knot about the 1930s: Why did the 1933 London economic conference end in complete failure, whereas just three years later Britain, France, and the United States were able to reach the Tripartite Monetary Agreement? While there was little time for material factors to change, perceptions about security did. The United States and Britain shifted their assessment of the German threat in the brief but eventful three years that followed the collapse of the London conference. Now focused on that shared threat, they were willing to bear whatever adjustment costs were required to facilitate French devaluation (Kirshner 1995, 91–95; Oye 1992, 128, 131). This perspective is also consistent with the rise of the Bretton Woods system. The United States, in the shadow of the Cold War, was willing to tolerate a disproportionate share of the costs of the system; it allowed for widespread deviations from the rules of the IMF, most obviously with the postponement of generalized convertibility until 1958 (Hinshaw 1958; Ikenberry 2000). Finally, as Michele Chang illustrates in chapter 10, European monetary cooperation is not easily attributable to economic forces. Rather, it reflected the larger international political ambitions of the dominant players—Germany's search for acceptability within Europe and France's desire for greater autonomy, both from Germany and for Europe vis-à-vis the United States.

Security concerns clearly must be a part of any explanation of choices about money. But the security approach offers an incomplete picture. In each of the examples above, ideational variables were also in force. The Tripartite Monetary Agreement was forged by international politics but also signaled the end of a bitter ideological conflict about money between France and Britain, and was accompanied by the election of the first social-

---

3. Of course, there may be times when actors are willing to forgo the benefits of cooperation. As seen in Abdelal's chapter, many of the former Soviet republics were willing to make considerable economic sacrifices by eschewing cooperation in order to get farther away from Russia.

ist government in France.[4] U.S. power ensured that the establishment of Bretton Woods institutions and the structure of the IMF were much closer to the U.S. vision than that of the British. But the monetary order that emerged after World War II reflected the immense intellectual influence of Keynes and a broad consensus on the basic contours of an "embedded liberal" monetary order (Ikenberry 1992; Ruggie 1982; Kirshner 1999b). Finally, while power and interests are clearly an important part of any explanation of the European Monetary Union, once again ideas cannot be ignored. As Kathleen McNamara (1998, 2) argued, European monetary cooperation was the result of "a neoliberal policy consensus"—one that "redefined state interests in cooperation . . . and induced leaders to accept the domestic policy adjustments needed to stay within the system."

Ultimately, conflict, ideas, and power all play important roles in explaining monetary phenomena. The complex interrelationship between these factors is captured neatly in Gavin's chapter. To be sure, Gavin shows that there was a clear material conflict: Who would bear the burdens of the adjustments necessary to address problems that emerged in the international monetary system in the 1960s? But that conflict was played out in the arena of international politics: the use of power to shape the outcome, and concerns about how monetary politics would affect security relationships. And the tactics employed and reforms proposed were further circumscribed by beliefs—about how the international monetary system could function, about what behavior was appropriate for the issuer of the "key currency," and about expectations concerning market reactions.

Markets matter, perhaps more than ever. But monetary choices can only be explained by attention to the roles that conflict, ideas, and power play in creating motives and empowering actions. This is illustrated by a brief discussion of how to explain the continued drive for capital deregulation in the wake of the Asian financial crisis.

THE CONTINUED DRIVE FOR CAPITAL DEREGULATION

As I discussed in chapter 1, there are conflicting deductive claims as to whether completely unregulated capital is optimal from an economic perspective. Further, there has not been a great deal of empirical work on this issue. Therefore, it continues to be an excellent example of a case where the economics are both ambiguous and, to the extent that findings can be established, of modest overall significance. Results of recent studies only add further support to this conclusion (e.g., Edwards 2001). There are also

---

4. For an illustration of the sharp disagreements about the appropriate monetary system, see the contrasting comments of Gregory (1931) and Aftalon (1931).

a number of reasons to err on the side of caution with regard to capital flows. As Dani Rodrik has pointed out, his finding (1998) that there is no association between capital controls and real economic performance might understate the case for controls, since only countries that are confident in the underlying soundness of their economies would eliminate such controls. Or, as Richard Cooper (1998) noted, after sifting carefully through competing claims, even if the case for universal capital account convertibility were clear (which he does not conclude), it does not necessarily mean that states should be pressured to adopt it.[5] Most pointedly, the evidence suggests that capital account liberalization is associated with an increased risk of financial crisis, suggesting yet another reason to be cautious about the deregulation of capital flows.[6] Blyth emphasizes this link and its causes in his discussion of global finance, and the relationship is further supported by recent studies. Not only is liberalization associated with an increased likelihood of financial crisis, but also such crises may occur even when the government is following "sound" policies. And even when the market's response does reflect an identifiable need for discipline, the market correction is likely to be inefficient—that is, "too much too late" (Williamson and Mahar 1998; Buria 1999; Willett 2000).[7]

Skepticism—or at least caution and reevaluation—about the benefits of unlimited capital mobility would appear to make more sense with the unexpected spread and depth of the Asian financial crisis. Moreover, efforts by many states to defend their currencies in an environment of mobile capital required deflationary measures that only exacerbated economic distress, while countries that had retained their capital controls were largely spared the worst of the crisis. And the crisis was, to say the least, unanticipated. In September 1996, the IMF asserted that "international capital markets appear to have become more resilient and are less likely to be a source of disturbances" (*IMF Survey* 9/23/96, 294). Two months later the institution touted "ASEAN's Sound Fundamentals Bode Well for Sustained Growth," in a banner headline of its newsletter (*IMF Survey* 11/25/96).[8] As late as May 1997, Managing Director Michel Camdessus of the IMF would

5. As Rodrik (1998, 57) noted, "Where knowledge is limited, the rule for policymakers should be, first, do no harm."

6. As mentioned in the introduction, the argument about capital mobility is a qualified one: It is not that mobile international capital is assumed to be harmful—on the contrary, it is assumed to be beneficial, even essential. Rather, the argument is that completely unregulated capital will contribute to an inefficiently high and unstable level of capital movements.

7. All three studies cited are also in accord with the general view that the aggregate economic effects of fully unregulated capital are modest and ambiguous.

8. Under the headline "International Capital Markets Charting a Steadier Course," the IMF also noted that "although the scale of financial activity continues to grow, market participants—including high-risk high-return investment funds—are more disciplined, cautious, and sensitive to market fundamentals" (*IMF Survey* 9/23/96, 293). On ASEAN's (Association of South-East Asian Nations) sound fundamentals, see *IMF Survey* 11/25/96.

remark that "global economic prospects warranted 'rational exuberance.' " In addition, economic prospects were "bright," and "overheating pressures have abated in many emerging market economies, especially in Asia— where growth has stayed strong for several years" (*IMF Survey* 5/12/97, 129–130).

In fact, while it remains a minority position among economists, the Asian financial crisis did spark a much broader consideration about the costs and benefits of capital controls.[9] Some highly respected mainstream economists such as Benjamin Cohen, Barry Eichengreen, and Paul Krugman have come to favor some forms of control.[10] But those who have pushed the hardest for the elimination of controls on international capital—the IMF, the United States, and the financial community more broadly—have not paused to consider that their faith should be reviewed. Stressing the "fundamentals" of an economy, their credo remains "get the pricing right and hot money will take care of itself" (*Far Eastern Economic Review* 7/16/98, 29). In particular, the IMF's retrospective analyses of the crisis make clear that it has not been shaken in its beliefs, remaining focused on the domestic sources of the crisis and highly suspicious of any forms of capital control (1998b, esp. 6, 11, 57, 63, 73, 148–150; 1998c, esp. 16–18, 101–102).[11]

Stanley Fischer, first deputy managing director of the IMF, has articulated on numerous occasions the two pillars that provide the foundation for the IMF's view on capital mobility and the Asian crisis. First, unlimited capital mobility remains the only appropriate policy. The IMF's decision to amend its Articles of Agreement in order to promote deregulation was correct and should not be reversed. Second, while there are some technical international factors to address, such as the choice of exchange rate regime, the Asian financial crisis was largely the result of structural flaws within the affected countries themselves. In particular, "weak financial institutions, inadequate bank regulation and supervision, and the complicated and nontransparent relations among governments, banks and corporations were central to the economic crisis" (1998b, 105; 1999; 1998a; *IMF Survey*

9. The crisis thrust the issue into the public policy debate. See, for example, Paul Krugman, "Saving Asia: It's Time to Get Radical," *Fortune* 9/7/98; Jonathan Kirshner, "Culprit Is Unregulated Capital," *Los Angeles Times* 9/13/98; Robert Reich, "The Real Policy Makers," *New York Times* 9/29/98; and analyses in *Asian Wall Street Journal* 9/7/98 and *Business Week* 9/28/98.

10. Krugman (1999) proposed controls on capital outflows, while Eichengreen (1999) emphasized controls on inflows. Cohen (2000) sifted through both sides of the debate and emerged sympathetic to the idea of controls. Some have questioned whether capital controls could ever be effectively introduced, even if they were appropriate in theory. See, for example, Edwards 1999.

11. It should be noted that in the wake of the crisis the World Bank has been willing at least to address the issue of the possible benefits of some control over short-term capital flows (1999, xi–xii, xxi, 4, 123–124, 128, 142–152; 1998, 9–10, 16, 34).

1/26/98).[12] These views are representative of top-level policymakers in both the United States and the IMF.[13]

The puzzle is not with the items on Fischer's list—weak financial institutions and problems that derive from inadequate transparency need to be addressed. Rather, it is with the stubborn unwillingness to consider other—in particular international—sources of crisis. As Blyth argues, there are good deductive reasons to believe that perfect transparency will not eliminate the problem of financial crises. The balance of evidence currently available supports Blyth's perspective, which is consistent with the view that the crisis was more of an international financial panic than the result of deep structural flaws in the domestic economies of the countries affected. The recent rebound, a "V-shaped" recovery, is more in accord with the panic view. The "U-shaped," or much slower, recovery predicted by the IMF was derived from the assumption that recovery would be sluggish and only occur after the required and thorough domestic economic restructuring had occurred (Sachs and Woo 2000). This and other questions relating to the IMF's management of the crisis, however, are not of central concern here.[14] Rather, the issue is why the IMF (and the United States) continues to cling tenaciously to the idea of dismantling capital controls, in the face of competing deductive arguments, ambiguous empirical evidence, and an apparent increase in the rate of international financial crises.[15] Once again, this requires taking a closer look at ideology, interest, and power, which conflate to a confounding extent in the case of capital account liberalization.

Clearly ideology—ideas held as articles of faith to the extent that they are highly resistant to change even in the light of new evidence—plays an important role. This role can be seen in the reaction by many to Malaysia's decision to impose capital controls in response to the crisis. In contrast to its neighbors, when the financial crisis reached Malaysia, rather than going to the IMF and imposing austerity measures, Malaysia introduced strict con-

12. See also Dornbusch 1998 for the argument that the market pressures created by unregulated capital impose discipline on governments and force them to pursue appropriate economic policies.

13. According to U.S. Federal Reserve Board Chairman Alan Greenspan, "The root of the problems is poor public policy." He discussed eight possible measures to prevent future crises, all of which are aimed at domestic reform in the affected states (Greenspan 1998a); see also similar testimony before the Senate Foreign Relations Committee (Greenspan 1998b).

14. There is a voluminous debate on the IMF's handling of the crisis, in particular the extent to which its initial contractionary programs made things worse. Eichengreen, in an article largely sympathetic to the IMF, reviewed the principal points of contention. He argued that the errors of the IMF have been somewhat exaggerated, and that the worst mistakes were quickly reversed. He concluded, it should be noted, that "the IMF should not be a rigid advocate of capital account liberalization" (2000, 178, 183, 191).

15. The number of such crises in the past twenty years is considerably higher than the historical norm (Kindleberger 2000).

trols over capital movements on September 1, 1998. The idea was to allow for an aggressive pro-growth policy and interest rate cuts, measures that would not have been sustainable in the absence of controls (*Asian Wall Street Journal* 9/2/98; 9/3/98; *Business Week* 9/21/98; *Far Eastern Economic Review* 9/17/98, 9/24/98).

Malaysia's economy performed well after the imposition of controls. Reflationary policies were introduced, and short-term interest rates fell, from 11.1 percent in July 1998 to 6.6 percent in December of that year, and stood at 3.17 percent in December 1999. There was a steady rise in the stock market, exports surged, and economic growth rebounded. Importantly, the control measures were designed to make a sharp distinction between short-term capital controls and foreign direct investment (FDI), which the government did not wish to discourage. These efforts were also successful, and FDI continued to flow into Malaysia. In February 1999 the government was able to loosen some of the controls imposed. This relaxation was not followed by a surge in capital outflows, further supporting the view that controls provided a useful circuit breaker in the context of international financial panic (Zainal-Abidin 2000, 143, 145; Noble and Ravenhill 2000b, 17; Perkins and Woo 2000, 241–244; Toyoda 2001).

The current conventional wisdom, however, holds that it is difficult to attribute much of Malaysia's economic recovery to the imposition of capital controls. Rather, from this perspective Malaysia's economic recovery must be seen in the context of the broader recovery in the region, including countries like Thailand and South Korea whose economies also rebounded, in the absence of controls and under IMF-style orthodox programs. But this view understates the performance of the controls in Malaysia. As Ethan Kaplan and Dani Rodrik (2001) argued, the performance of other states is not the relevant counterfactual to assess the Malaysian controls. Rather, the question is how the Malaysian economy would have performed in the absence of controls. In September 1998, South Korea and Thailand were under IMF programs, did not face a new financial crisis, and were not following unsustainable policies. Malaysia, on the other hand, refused to go to the IMF, opting instead for reflationary policies. The country could not have continued on that course; the package of refusal and reflation would not have been sustainable, and the choice was either to reverse course and adopt an IMF-style program, or to impose capital controls. The conventional view implicitly assumes that pressure on Malaysia would have abated and the economy would have rebounded in the absence of any policy change. Kaplan and Rodrik (2001, 7) also compared the performance of Malaysia after the imposition of controls with the performance of South Korea and Thailand in the period following their IMF-led stabilizations, and concluded that "the Malaysian controls produced better results than the alternative on almost all dimensions" (see also Zainal-Abidin 2000, 137).

But more important than the resolution of the economic debate about the Malaysian controls is the way that ideology colored the analysis of the case. The agnostic conclusion of the current conventional wisdom—that all one can say is that controls apparently did no harm—fails to reconcile the performance of the Malaysian economy under controls with the predictions made by opponents of controls and other mainstream officials at the time the controls were introduced. The imposition of the controls was widely criticized and even condemned in the international community. The IMF's *World Economic Outlook* in October 1998 stated that controls might "be an important setback . . . to that country's recovery." Over time, the IMF updated its assessments, first cautiously noting the following May that "domestic demand is expected to strengthen only gradually," and finally conceding five months later that "a strong economic recovery is now underway" (Kaplan and Rodrik 2001, 11; see also Zainal-Abidin 2000, 135). Two weeks after Malaysia imposed its controls, U.S. Federal Reserve Board Chairman Alan Greenspan (1998e) gave rather pointed testimony in expressing his opposition, quickly equating capital controls with "borders closed to foreign investment," leaving states that implement capital controls "mired at a sub-optimal standard of living and slow growth rate." Greenspan did acknowledge that during the 1950s and 1960s most advanced industrialized retained capital controls, and that those controls reduced both instability and contagion of financial crisis. He was quick to add, though, "presumably, however, at the cost of significant shortfalls in economic growth"—a clear illustration of how an ideological commitment to one's beliefs can allow the faith to run ahead of the facts.[16]

That ideological commitment, in this case to capital deregulation, has meant that the fact that the Malaysian capital controls, at a minimum, greatly outperformed expectations has done nothing to allow the measure to be considered or even evaluated. Thus, Michel Camdessus initially called the Malaysian controls "dangerous and indeed harmful" and has not subsequently reevaluated his position (quoted in Wade 1998a, 368). On the contrary, years later he stated that no one at the IMF doubts the benefits of capital deregulation—the issue is not even discussed.[17] This may explain some of the motives behind those in Washington who "quietly expressed the hope" that the introduction of controls in response to the financial crisis "would fail so spectacularly that the smoldering ruins of the Malaysian economy would act as a caution to other countries" (*New York Times* 9/9/98; see also *Asiaweek* 9/18/98). Clearly, once people start rooting for their theories, belief systems have hardened into ideology. And as Grabel argues in chapter 2, such ideologies "demand to be taken on faith."

16. See also Greenspan 1998a; 1998b, fn. 13.
17. Michel Camdessus, comments made at breakfast seminar, Einaudi Center for International Studies, Cornell University, 4/10/01. Fischer also refused even to put capital controls on a lengthy menu of possible reform measures (1998b, 105; 1999; 1998c; 2000; *IMF Survey* 1/26/98).

There is, of course, a sharper interpretation of the motives of those rooting against the Malaysian reforms—that they are rooting for their interests, not their ideologies. In Malaysia the role of (foreign) narrow material interests is not superficially apparent. But interests are at least as visible as ideology when one examines the Korean financial crisis. When South Korea met its share of the Asian financial crisis, in the autumn of 1997, it approached the IMF and reached an agreement that provided enormous emergency assistance. In exchange, it agreed to a comprehensive list of domestic economic reforms (Heo 2001; Hong and Lee 2000). Some of these were clearly related to the crisis. For example, considerable attention was paid to restructuring, prudential regulation, and transparency of the banking and financial sector. But among the dozens of measures required, many were just as clearly unrelated to the risk of financial crisis. South Korea was forced to abolish restrictions on foreign ownership of land, eliminate ceilings on foreign equity ownership, relax limits on FDI, and dismantle trade barriers in both goods and services, including insurance and securities dealings. The agreement also pushed capital account liberalization, calling on the country to "accelerate liberalization of foreign exchange transactions."[18]

These measures require explanation, even in the light of two important qualifications. First, important aspects of the Korean economy, especially in the banking and financial services sector, did need reform. Second, as mentioned already, the question of note for this volume is not whether the IMF's medicine was "too strong" (though at first it clearly exacerbated the deflationary effects of the crisis). Rather, it is whether the measures were ideologically skewed, or worse. W. Max Corden (2001, 59), who offered a careful and balanced assessment of the IMF's performance during the crisis, reported "surprise" at many of the measures contained in the letter of intent. Many of the required measures might make sense in broad economic perspective, but it is "hard to see how they would either help resolve the crisis or prevent a future one." In particular, fluctuations in FDI were not a cause of the crisis, and it "is not sensible that IMF crisis programs include conditions that require further opening to such direct investment." Most pointedly, Corden stated that the provision to relax restrictions on corporate foreign borrowing, including foreign borrowing, "amazes me," since one of the causes of the Korean crisis was excessive short-term private international borrowing (see also Pempel 1999a, 236).

The IMF's program only makes sense if one understands the ideological interpretation of the crisis. Rather than a financial panic, for some true believers the crisis was proof that the "East-Asian model" of capitalist develop-

---

18. Chol-Hwan Chon (governor, Bank of Korea) and Kyu-Sung Lee (minister of finance and economy), Letter of Intent of the Government of Korea, 5/2/98, www.imf.org. external/np/loi/050298.htm.

ment was fundamentally flawed. The Asian way featured marked divergences from the idealized neoclassical model, and thus interfered with the working of the market. Such an approach was doomed to ultimate failure, and the end was hastened by globalization, which accelerated the influence of market forces. Thus, as Camdessus explained, although some of the capital liberalization measures required of South Korea would appear to exacerbate the proximate cause of the crisis, this misses the point. The IMF program was targeted instead at the root cause of the crisis: a failed economic model and the need to fundamentally remake Korean capitalism.[19] According to Greenspan (1998c), "One consequence of this Asian crisis is an increasing awareness in the region that market capitalism, as practiced in the West, especially in the United States, is the superior model." Thus, preventing future crises requires much more than regulation, reform, and transparency in domestic banking and financial sectors—it requires breaking up *chaebol* conglomerates, eliminating restrictions on FDI, in essence, changing the culture of Korean business. Again, in Greenspan's words, the crisis led to "an increasing awareness, bordering in some cases on shock, that their economic model was incomplete, or worse, has arguably emerged in the region."[20]

The ideological position on the Korean reforms provides a problem for analysis, because it overlaps so neatly with interest- and power-based explanations. The measures required by South Korea's letter of intent, as Robert Gilpin (2000, 157, 159) observed, "included specific items that the United States had long demanded of Asian governments, and that the latter had rejected." South Korea had always restricted FDI and had protected its financial service sector from foreign competition, in both cases over the strenuous objection of the United States. Similarly, many of the measures served to benefit U.S. export interests, which had been lobbying for years to gain greater access to the Korean market (Corden 2000, 59–60; Pempel 1999a, 237). This interpretation is also consistent with the way in which the Korean reforms were supervised over time. The IMF successively—over the course of five reviews—relaxed the macroeconomic constraints imposed on South Korea, as it realized the extent to which those measures were strangling the Korean economy. But none of the more politically charged measures were reevaluated. Instead, complete capital market decontrol was accelerated, and most restrictions on foreign equity and land ownership have already been eliminated (Hong and Lee 2000, 211–223; Eichengreen 2000, 178).

The economic interests of U.S. business provide only one of several political sources that are consistent with the Korean stabilization. Looking more narrowly, domestic politics within South Korea also played an impor-

19. Michel Camdessus, breakfast seminar, Cornell University, 4/10/01.
20. See also Greenspan's (1998d) similar testimony before the House Agriculture Committee; Hamilton 1999.

tant role, providing political interests that were receptive to the conditions required by the letter of intent. Consistent with one of the principal themes of this volume, while the hard evidence available suggests that aggregate economic benefits of the stabilization package were modest and ambiguous at best, the differential effects were quite dramatic. In particular, President Kim Dae Jung, a reformer challenging established centers of power within Korean society, embraced some parts of the IMF reforms because they would undercut the entrenched interests of his opponents. This explains why some IMF conditions, resisted elsewhere, were embraced in Korea (Pempel 1999a, 226; Cummings 1999, 36).

More broadly, there is another political interest that helps explain the Korean case: U.S. geopolitical interests. Here the focus is on the United States advancing its perceived broad strategic, rather than narrow economic, interest.[21] Once again, the evidence is consistent with an interpretation derived from this perspective—that the United States is using the financial crisis and its aftermath to advance its interests and reestablish its dominance in the region. Lawrence Summers, then deputy secretary of the treasury stated plainly, "Financial liberalization, both domestically and internationally, is a critical part of the U.S. agenda" (quoted in Kapur 1998). Changes in the global balance of power have also afforded the United States greater leeway in the pursuit of its interests. During the Cold War, the United States was forced to tolerate different national styles of capitalism, practices that in many ways limited U.S. influence in the region. With the passing of the Cold War it was now free to challenge these systems, despite the objection of states like Japan, Malaysia, Thailand, and Indonesia. With the financial crisis, it was in a position to impose a new set of economic and financial norms (Pempel 1999a, 236; Cummings 1999, 18, 41).

The IMF, in this interpretation, was an integral instrument of U.S. power. It was the United States that encouraged the IMF to focus increasingly on microeconomic reform and trade liberalization. Ultimately, Summers could boast that "the IMF has done more to promote America's trade and investment agenda in East Asia than 30 years of bilateral trade negotiations" (Hale 1998, 24). U.S. Trade Representative Mickey Kantor shared this assessment, referring to the IMF as a "battering ram" used to open Asian markets to U.S. products (*International Herald Tribune* 1/14/98). This also explains strong U.S. opposition to an "Asian Monetary Fund" (AMF).

---

21. U.S. pressure for the deregulation of capital more generally can also be explained as a conflict over the burdens of adjustment. As Blyth argues in his chapter, since the United States has deep and sound capital markets, it is likely to suffer less than others in an international financial crisis. In fact, it may attract capital during a crisis as investors "flee to quality." Thus, the United States might bear a disproportionately small share of the costs from a system prone to financial crisis, and, being home to some of the world's most powerful financial firms, might have the most to gain from a world free of barriers to capital and financial services.

The idea behind the AMF, championed by Japan's vice minister of finance, Eisuke Sakakibara, was to mobilize a large fund that would be available to Asian states facing financial crisis, but without the types of conditions imposed by the IMF. An AMF would address two concerns raised by Sakakibara: the "inherent instability of liberalized international capital markets" and doubts about whether all of the reforms demanded by the IMF were "absolutely necessary to resolve the crisis."[22] But the AMF proposal was killed "outright" by the United States and for "clearly geopolitical" reasons. The United States feared that the AMF would undercut the IMF and its ability to advance U.S. interests, and also feared that it would lose political influence in the region vis-à-vis Japan, which would be the main force behind the new AMF (quotes from Bhagwati 2000, 28; see also Altbach 1997, 2, 10, 11; Cohen 2000, 197; Wade 1998c, 702).[23] This was not the first time that the United States undercut an alternative arrangement to the IMF for "strategic considerations." In the mid-1970s the United States presided over the demise of the Financial Support Fund, a "safety net" for mutual balance-of-payments support that was designed to deal with the problems that emerged in the wake of the energy crisis (Cohen 1998b, 170; Spiro 1999).

In sum, there is no compelling or unambiguous case in favor of pressing for universal capital account deregulation. In fact, the balance of the available evidence would suggest coming down on the side of caution, or at the very minimum toleration for experimentation with some controls. But this has not been the position of the United States or the IMF, whose behavior, especially in the wake of the Asian financial crisis, can only be explained by taking into account ideology, narrow economic interests, and broad geopolitical calculations. The problem is that these three variables are not easily disentangled. The dense networks between the interested parties of Wall Street and the ideologues in Washington, for example, are such that, in the words of Jagdish Bhagwati (2000, 46), "anyone who has another point of view is unlikely to be heard, because everybody shares the same assumptions."

And even though the congruence between IMF conditions and U.S. material and strategic interests is undeniable, the people who work at the IMF don't look like willing tools of U.S. imperialism. Trained as economists, they are more likely to pride themselves on the way that they are "above" politics. Confident in their faith, and with a sincere hope to improve the world, they are more Billy Graham than Bismarck.

22. Eisuke Sakakibara, "Reform of the International Financial System", speech delivered at the Manila Framework Meeting, Melbourne, 3/26/99, www.mof.go.jp/english/if/ele070.htm. For more on the AMF, see Altbach 1997; Bergsten 1998. Grimes in his chapter also observed how Japan interpreted the crisis differently than the United States.

23. Grimes also noted China's opposition to the AMF, also for geopolitical reasons.

THE INESCAPABLE POLITICS OF MONEY

The chapters in this volume have looked at a broad set of choices about money, addressed theoretical and empirical puzzles, and applied them to a markedly diverse range of countries. But they share a common conclusion: where there is money, there is money politics. But money politics are too easily underappreciated. One reason for this is that money is special and features unique interconnections between the ideas, material interests, and institutions associated with its management. Ideas about money—shaping beliefs, hardening into ideologies, and constituting norms that circumscribe behavior—are especially important because of the crucial role of "market sentiment." Money, after all, has value because people believe it has value. But because of the unique role of credibility in the macroeconomic sphere, one policy can—for reasons unrelated to the underlying economic coherence of other choices—develop a sole, consequential, and self-reinforcing claim to economic legitimacy. This legitimization matters because it serves to mask the fact that every choice about money serves some material interests over others, and that despite the power and influence of markets, those choices take place in the context of state purpose and the shadow of international power. Greater attention needs to be paid to the political foundations—the political determinants—of choices about money in a global economy where monetary phenomena lead and the real economy follows.

References

Abdelal, Rawi. 1998. "The Politics of Monetary Leadership and Followership: Stability in the European Monetary System since the Currency Crisis of 1992." *Political Studies* 46: 236–259.

——. 2001a. "Contested Currency: Russia's Ruble in Domestic and International Politics." Harvard Business School, Cambridge. Draft manuscript.

——. 2001b. *National Purpose in the World Economy: Post-Soviet States in Comparative Perspective.* Ithaca, N.Y.: Cornell University Press.

——. Forthcoming. "Memories of Nations and States: Institutional History and National Identity in Post-Soviet Eurasia." *Nationalities Papers* 30 (3).

Ackley, Gardner. 1978. "The Costs of Inflation." *American Economic Review* 68 (2): 149–154.

Aftalon, Albert. 1931. "The Causes and Effects of the Movement of Gold into France." In *Selected Documents Submitted to the Gold Delegation of the Financial Committee.* Geneva: League of Nations.

Ageron, Charles-Robert. 1978. *La France coloniale ou parti colonial?* Paris: Presses Universitaires de France.

Aghevli, Bijan, Moshin Khan, and Peter Montiel. 1991. "Exchange Rate Policy in Developing Countries: Some Analytical Issues." IMF Occasional Paper 78, International Monetary Fund, Washington, D.C.

Agnenor, Pierre-Richard, and Mark Taylor. 1992. "Testing for Credibility Effects." *IMF Staff Papers* 39 (3): 545–571.

Aiaganov, B.G. 1994. *Politicheskie partii i obshchestvennye dvizheniia sovremennogo Kazakhstana* (Political parties and social movements in contemporary Kazakhstan). Almaty: Ministry of Publishing and Public Information of the Republic of Kazakhstan.

Akerlof, George, William Dickens, and George Perry. 1996. "The Macroeconomics of Low Inflation." Brookings Papers on Economic Activity 1, Brookings Institution, Washington, D.C.

Alesina, Alberto. 1988. "Macroeconomics and Politics." In *NBER Macroeconomics Annual 1988,* edited by Stanley Fischer. Cambridge: MIT Press.

Alesina, Alberto, and Lawrence H. Summers. 1993. "Central Bank Independence and Macroeconomic Performance: Some Comparative Evidence." *Journal of Money, Credit, and Banking* 25 (2): 151–162.

Alexandrov, Mikhail. 1999. *Uneasy Alliance: Relations between Russia and Kazakhstan in the Post-Soviet Era, 1992–1997.* Westport, Conn.: Greenwood.

Aliber, Robert. 1964. "The Costs and Benefits of the U.S. Role as a Reserve Currency Country." *Quarterly Journal of Economics* 78 (3): 442–456.

Almanac of China's Foreign Economic Relations and Trade. Various years. Beijing: Zhongguo Duiwai Jingji Maoyi Chubanshe.

Altbach, Eric. 1997. "The Asian Monetary Fund Proposal: A Case Study of Japanese Regional Leadership." *JEI Report* 47 (December 19): 1–14.

Anderson, Jeffrey. 1997. "Hard Interests, Soft Power, and Germany's Changing Role in Europe." In *Tamed Power: Germany in Europe,* edited by Peter J. Katzenstein. Ithaca, N.Y.: Cornell University Press.

Arestis, Philip, and Keith Bain. 1995. "The Independence of Central Banks: A Non-conventional Perspective." *Journal of Economic Issues* 29 (1): 161–174.

Åslund, Anders. 1995. *How Russia Became a Market Economy.* Washington, D.C.: Brookings Institution.

Balassa, Béla. 1984. "Adjustment Policies in Developing Countries: A Reassessment." *World Development* 12 (9): 955–972.

Balassa, Béla, and associates. 1971. *The Structure of Protection in Developing Countries.* Baltimore, Md.: Johns Hopkins University Press.

Ball, Laurence. 1997. "Disinflation and the NAIRU." In Romer and Romer, eds., *Reducing Inflation.*

Balogh, T. 1966. "The Mechanism of Neo-Imperialism." In *The Economics of Poverty.* London: Weidenfeld and Nicolson.

Banain, King, and Eugene Zhukov. 1995. "The Collapse of the Ruble Zone, 1991–93." In *Establishing Monetary Stability in Emerging Market Economies,* edited by Thomas D. Willett, Richard C.K. Burdekin, Richard J. Sweeney, and Clas Wihlborg. Boulder, Colo.: Westview.

Bangura, Yusuf. 1983. *Britain and Commonwealth Africa: The Politics of Economic Relations, 1951–1975.* Manchester, U.K.: Manchester University Press.

Bank of Sierra Leone. n.d. *Review of the General Manager's Department.* Freetown: Bank of Sierra Leone.

Barro, Robert J. 1995. "Inflation and Economic Growth." *Bank of England Quarterly Bulletin* 35 (2): 166–176.

———. 1996. "Inflation and Growth." *Federal Reserve Bank of St. Louis Review* 78 (3): 153–169.

Barro, Robert J., and David B. Gordon. 1983. "Rules, Discretion, and Reputation in a Model of Monetary Policy." *Journal of Monetary Economics* 12 (1): 101–120.

Basu, S. K. 1967. *Central Banking in the Emerging Countries.* Bombay: Asia Publishing House.

Bates, Robert. 1981. *Markets and States in Tropical Africa.* Berkeley: University of California Press.

Bayart, Jean-François. 1984. *La politique Africaine de François Mitterrand.* Paris: Karthala.

Bayoumi, Tamim, and Barry Eichengreen. 1992. *Shocking Aspects of European Monetary Unification.* Cambridge, Mass.: National Bureau of Economic Research.

Bayoumi, Tamim, and Jonathan Ostry. 1997. "Macroecoomic Shocks and Trade Flows within Sub-Saharan Africa: Implications for Optimum Currency Arrangements." *Journal of African Economies* 6: 412–444.

Becker, Gary. 1997. "Latin America Owes a Lot to Its Chicago Boys." *Business Week,* June 9, 22.

Beissinger, Mark R. 1996. "How Nationalisms Spread: Eastern Europe Adrift the Tides and Cycles of Nationalist Contention." *Social Research* 63 (1): 97–146.

Berg, Elliot. 1964. "The Economic Basis of Political Choice in West Africa." *American Political Science Review* 54 (2): 391–405.

Berger, Helge, Jakob De Haan, and Sylvester Eijffinger. 2001. "Central Bank Independence: An Update of Theory and Evidence." *Journal of Economic Surveys* 15 (1): 3–40.

Bergsten, C. Fred. 1975. *Dilemmas of the Dollar: The Economics and Politics of U.S. International Monetary Policy.* New York: Council on Foreign Relations.

——. 1998. "Reviving the 'Asian Monetary Fund.' " International Economics Policy Briefs 98-8, Institute for International Economics, Washington, D.C.

——. 2000. *The New Asian Challenge.* IIE Working Papers 00-4, Institute for International Economics, Washington, D.C.

Berman, Sheri. 1998. *The Social Democratic Moment: Ideas and Politics in the Making of Interwar Europe.* Cambridge: Harvard University Press.

Berman, Sheri, and Kathleen R. McNamara. 1999. "Bank on Democracy: Why Central Banks Need Public Oversight." *Foreign Affairs* 78 (2): 2–8.

Bernstein, Richard, and Ross Munro. 1997. *The Coming Conflict with China.* New York: Knopf.

Bhagwati, Jagdish. 1998. "The Capital Myth." *Foreign Affairs* 77 (3): 7–12.

——. 2000. "Lessons from the East Asian Experience." In *Building an Infrastructure for Financial Stability,* edited by Eric S. Rosengren and John S. Jordan. Conference Series 44 (June), Federal Reserve Bank of Boston, Boston.

Bhatia, Rattan. 1986. "The West African Monetary Union: An Analytical Review." IMF Occasional Paper 35, International Monetary Fund, Washington, D.C.

Bhattacharya, Rina. 1997. "Pace, Sequencing, and Credibility of Structural Reforms." *World Development* 25 (7): 1045–1061.

BIS (Bank for International Settlements). 2001a. *BIS Quarterly Review: Statistical Annex.* September.

——. 2001b. "Central Bank Survey of Foreign Exchange and Derivatives Market Activity in 2001: Preliminary Global Data." Press release, October 9.

Blackburn, Keith, and Michael Christensen. 1989. "Monetary Policy and Policy Credibility: Theories and Evidence." *Journal of Economic Literature* 27: 1–45.

Blanchard, Olivier, and Stanley Fischer. 1989. *Lectures on Macroeconomics.* Cambridge: MIT Press.

Bleaney, Michael. 1985. *The Rise and Fall of Keynesian Macroeconomics.* London: Macmillan.

Blinder, Alan. 1997a. "Is Government Too Political?" *Foreign Affairs* 76 (6): 115–126.

——. 1997b. "The Speed Limit: Fact and Fancy in the Growth Debate." *American Prospect* 34: 57–62.

——. 1998. *Central Banking in Theory and Practice.* Cambridge: MIT Press.

Block, Fred L. 1977. *The Origins of International Economic Disorder: A Study of United States International Monetary Policy from World War II to the Present.* Berkeley: University of California Press.

Blyth, Mark. 2000. "Economic Ideologies, Conventions, and Stability." Department of Political Science, Johns Hopkins University, Baltimore, Md. Draft manuscript.

Boche, Jörg. 1993. Franco-German Economic Relations." In *France-Germany, 1983–1993,* edited by Patrick McCarthy. New York: St. Martin's.

Bordo, Michael. 1975. "John E. Cairnes on the Effects of the Australian Gold Discoveries, 1851–73." *History of Political Economy* 7 (3): 337–359.

———. 1983. "Some Aspects of the Monetary Economics of Richard Cantillon." *Journal of Monetary Economics* 12 (2): 235–258.

Bowles, Paul, and Gordon White. 1994. "Central Bank Independence: A Political Economy Approach." *Journal of Development Studies* 31 (2): 235–264.

Braun, Oscar, and Leonard Joy. 1968. "A Model of Economic Stagnation: A Case Study of the Argentine Economy." *Economic Journal* 78 (312): 14868–14887.

Bremmer, Ian, and Ray Taras, eds. 1997. *New States, New Politics: Building the Post-Soviet Nations.* Cambridge: Cambridge University Press.

Bruno, Michael. 1995. "Does Inflation Really Lower Growth?" *Finance and Development* 32 (3).

Bruno, Michael, and William Easterly. 1996. "Inflation and Growth: In Search of a Stable Relationship." *Federal Reserve Bank of St. Louis Review* 78 (3).

Bulmer, Simon J. 1997. "Shaping the Rules? The Constitutive Politics of the European Union and German Power." In *Tamed Power: Germany in Europe,* edited by Peter J. Katzenstein. Ithaca, N.Y.: Cornell University Press.

Bulmer, Simon J., and William E. Paterson. 1996. "Germany in the European Union: Gentle Giant or Emergent Leader?" *International Affairs* 72 (1): 9–32.

Burdekin, Richard, Jilleen R. Westbrook, and Thomas Willett. 1993. "Exchange Rate Pegging as a Disinflation Strategy: Evidence from the European Monetary System." In *Varieties of Monetary Reform: Lessons and Experiences on the Road to Monetary Union,* edited by Pierre L. Siklos. Boston: Kluwer Academic.

Buria, Ariel. 1999. *An Alternative Approach to Financial Crises.* Essays in International Economics 212, International Economics Section, Princeton University, Princeton, N.J.

Burkett, Paul, and Richard Lotspeich. 1993. "Review Essay: The Order of Economic Liberalization: Financial Control in the Transition to a Market Economy." *Comparative Economic Studies* 35 (1): 59–84.

Burstein, Daniel. 1988. *Yen! Japan's New Financial Empire and Its Threat to America.* New York: Simon and Schuster.

Cairnes, John E. [1873] 1965. *Essays in Political Economy: Theoretical and Applied.* New York: Augustus Kelley.

Calvo, Guillermo. 1987. "Balance of Payments Crises in a Cash-Advance Economy." *Journal of Money, Credit, and Banking* 9 (1): 9–32.

Calvo, Guillermo, and Carlos Végh. 1991. "Exchange-Rate-Based Stabilization under Imperfect Credibility." International Monetary Fund Working Paper 91/77, International Monetary Fund, Washington, D.C.

Calvo, Guillermo, Leonardo Leiderman, and Carmen Reinhart. 1996. "Inflows of Capital to Developing Countries in the 1990s." *Journal of Economic Perspectives* 10 (2): 123–139.

Camara, Sariba Sylvain. 1976. *La Guinée sans la France.* Paris: Presses de la Fondation Nationale des Sciences Politiques.

Canitrot, Adolfo. 1980. "La disciplina como objetivo de la política económica: Un ensayo sobre el programa económico del gobierno Argentino desde 1976." Estudios CEDES 6, CEDES, Buenos Aires.

Cantillon, Richard. [1931] 1964. *Essai sur la nature du commerce en général.* Edited and translated by Henry Higgs. New York: Augustus Kelley.

Card, David, and Dean Hyslop. 1997. "Does Inflation 'Grease the Wheels of the Labor Market'?" In Romer and Romer, eds., *Reducing Inflation*.

Cardim de Carbalho, Fernando. 1995–96. "The Independence of Central Banks: A Critical Assessment of the Arguments." *Journal of Post-Keynesian Economics* 18 (2): 159–175.

Cargill, T. F., and M. M. Hutchison. 1990. "The Federal Reserve and the Bank of Japan." In *The Political Economy of American Monetary Policy*, edited by Thomas Mayer. Cambridge: Cambridge University Press.

Chang, Michelle. 2001. "Power and Interest in European Monetary Integration." Colgate University, Hamilton, N.Y. Draft manuscript.

Chen, Qi. 1999. "Dongya Jinrong Weiji: Diyuan zhengzhi jingji de xin xianshi" (East Asian financial crisis: New reality of geo-political economy). *Dongbeiya Luntan* 1: 12–16.

Chen, Xianqui. 1997. *Deng Xiaoping zhiguolun* (Deng Xiaoping's statecraft). Beijing: Huaxia Chubanshe.

Chen, Zhaohui, and Alberto Giovannini. 1994. "The Credibility of Adjustable Parities: The Experience of the European Monetary System." In *The International Monetary System*, edited by Peter B. Kenen, Francesco Papdia, and Fabrizio Saccomanni. Cambridge: Cambridge University Press.

China Financial Outlook. 1999. Beijing: China Financial Publishing House.

Chipman, John. 1989. *French Power in Africa.* Oxford: Basil Blackwell.

Cohen, Benjamin. 1971. *The Future of Sterling as an International Currency.* London: Macmillan.

———. 1993. "Beyond EMU: The Problem of Sustainability." *Economics and Politics* 5 (2): 187–202.

———. 1998a. *The Geography of Money.* Ithaca, N.Y.: Cornell University Press.

———. 1998b. "When Giants Clash: The OECD Financial Support Fund and the IMF." In *Institutional Designs for a Complex World*, edited by Vinod K. Aggarwal. Ithaca, N.Y.: Cornell University Press.

———. 2000. "Taming the Phoenix? Monetary Governance after the Crisis." In Noble and Ravenhill, eds., *The Asian Financial Crisis*.

Cohen, Samy. 1980. *Les conseillers du président: de Charles de Gaulle à Valéry Giscard d'Estaing.* Paris: Presses Universitaires de France.

Collins, Susan, and Francesco Giavazzi. "Attitudes toward Inflation and the Viability of Fixed Exhange Rate Regimes: Evidence from the EMS." In *A Retrospective on the Bretton Woods System*, edited by Michael Bordo and Barry Eichengreen. Chicago: University of Chicago Press.

Conley, John, and William Maloney. 1995. "Optimal Sequencing of Credible Reforms with Uncertain Outcomes." *Journal of Development Economics* 48: 151–166.

Connolly, Bernard. 1995. *The Rotten Heart of Europe.* London: Faber and Faber.

Conway, Patrick. 1995. *Currency Proliferation: The Monetary Legacy of the Soviet Union.* Essays in International Economics 197, International Economics Section, Princeton University, Princeton, N.J.

Cooper, Richard N. 1998. "Should Capital Account Convertibility Be a World Objective?" In *Should the IMF Pursue Capital Account Convertibility?* edited by Peter B. Kenen. Essays in International Economics 207, International Economics Section, Princeton University, Princeton, N.J.

——. 1999. "Should Capital Controls Be Banished?" Brookings Papers on Economic Activity 1, Brookings Institution, Washington, D.C.

Corden, W. Max. 2000. "The Financial Crisis: Are the IMF Prescriptions Right?" In Horowitz and Heo, eds., *The Political Economy of International Financial Crises.*

Corrigan, E. Gerald. 1996. "Building a Progressive and Profitable National Banking System in Argentina." Goldman, Sachs, press release, April 30.

Cottarelli, Carlo, and Curzio Giannini. 1997. *Credibility without Rules?* IMF Occasional Paper 154, International Monetary Fund, Washington, D.C.

Council on Foreign Relations Task Force. 1999. *Safeguarding Prosperity in a Global Financial System: The Future International Financial Architecture.* New York: Council on Foreign Relations.

Crow, John W. 1989. "Overview: Central Bank Perspectives." In *Monetary Policy Issues in the 1990s.* Federal Reserve Bank of Kansas City, Kansas City, Kans.

Cukierman, Alex. 1992. *Central Bank Strategy, Credibility and Independence.* Cambridge: MIT Press.

——. 1994. "Central Bank Independence and Monetary Control." *Economic Journal* 104: 1437–1448.

Cukierman, Alex, Steven Webb, and Bilin Neyapti. 1992. "Measuring Independence of Central Banks and Its Effect on Policy Outcomes." *World Bank Economic Review* 6 (3): 353–398.

Cullather, Nick. 1994. *Illusions of Influence: The Political Economy of United States–Philippines Relations, 1942–1960.* Stanford, Calif.: Stanford University Press.

Cummings, Bruce. 1999. "The Asian Crisis, Democracy, and the End of 'Late' Development." In Pempel, ed., *The Politics of the Asian Economic Crisis.*

Dabrowski, Marek. 1995. "From the Soviet Ruble to National Rubles and Independent Currencies: The Evolution of the Ruble Area in 1991–1993." In *Integration and Disintegration in European Economies,* edited by Bruno Dallago and Giovanni Pegoretti. Aldershot, U.K.: Dartmouth.

D'Anieri, Paul. 1997. "Dilemmas of Interdependence: Autonomy, Prosperity, and Sovereignty in Ukraine's Russia Policy." *Problems of Post-Communism* 44 (1): 16–26.

Davidson, Paul. 1999. "The Case for Capital Regulation." In *Capital Regulation: For and Against,* edited by Robert Sidelsky et al. London: Center for Post-Collectivist Studies.

Debelle, Guy, and Stanley Fischer. 1995. "How Independent Should a Central Bank Be." In *Goals, Guidelines and Constraints Facing Monetary Policymakers,* edited by Jeffrey C. Fuhrer. Boston: Federal Reserve Bank of Boston.

Degefe, Befekadu. 1995. "The Development of Money, Monetary Institutions and Monetary Policy, 1941–75." In *An Economic History of Modern Ethiopia.* Vol. 1, *The Imperial Era, 1941–74,* edited by Shiferaw Bekele. Dakar, Senegal: Codesria.

de Grauwe, Paul. 1993. "The Political Economy of Monetary Union in Europe." *World Economy* 16 (6): 653–661.

De Haan, Jakob, and Gurt Jan van Hag. 1995. "Variation in Central Bank Independence across Countries: Some Provisional Empirical Evidence." *Public Choice* 85: 335–351.

DeMartino, George. 2000. *Global Economy, Global Justice: Theoretical Objections and Policy Alternatives to Neoliberalism.* London: Routledge.

Deng, Xiaoping. 1994. *Deng Xiaoping wenxuan* (Selected works of Deng Xiaoping). Vol. 3. Beijing: Renmin Chubanshe.

Destler, I. M., and C. Randall Henning. 1989. *Dollar Politics: Exchange Rate Policymaking in the United States.* Washington, D.C.: Institute for International Economics.

Dhonte, Pierre. 1997. *Conditionality as an Instrument of Borrower Credibility.* IMF Working Paper on Policy Analysis and Assessment 2 (February), International Monetary Fund, Washington, D.C.

Diaz-Alejandro, Carlos. 1963. "A Note on the Impact of Devaluation and the Redistributive Effect." *Journal of Political Economy* 71: 577–580.

Díaz-Bonilla, Eugenio. 1996. "The Washington Consensus and the Myth of the Tequila Effect." Working Papers (September), Fundación Andina, Buenos Aires.

Dibooglu, Selahattin, and Julius Horvath. 1997. "Optimum Currency Areas and European Monetary Unification." *Contemporary Economic Policy* 15: 37–49.

Ding, X. L. 1994. *The Decline of Communism in China: Legitimacy Crisis, 1977–1989.* Cambridge: Cambridge University Press.

Di Tella, Guido. 1987. "Argentina's Most Recent Inflationary Cycle, 1975–85." In *Latin American Debt and the Adjustment Crisis,* edited by Rosemary Thorp and Laurence Whitehead. Pittsburgh: University of Pittsburgh Press.

Dominguez, Kathryn M., and Peter B. Kenen. 1992. "Intramarginal Intervention in the EMS and the Target-Zone Model of Exchange Rate Behavior." *European Economic Review* 36: 1523–1532.

Dornbusch, Rudiger. 1997. "Mexico Should Ditch the Peso for the Dollar." *Business Week,* May 19, 22.

———. 1998. "Capital Controls: An Idea Whose Time Is Past." In *Should the IMF Pursue Capital Account Convertibility?* edited by Peter B. Kenen. Essays in International Economics 207, International Economics Section, Princeton University, Princeton, N.J.

———. 1999. "Comment on Chapters 2, 3, and 4." In Feldstein, ed., *The Costs and Benefits of Price Stability.*

Dotsey, Michel, and Peter Richmond. 1996. "The Welfare Cost of Inflation in General Equilibrium." *Journal of Monetary Economics* 37 (1): 29–47.

Drake, Paul. 1989. *The Money Doctor in the Andes: The Kemmerer Missions, 1923–1933.* Durham, N.C.: Duke University Press.

Drazen, Allan, and Vittorio Grilli. 1993. "The Benefits of Crises for Economic Reforms." *American Economic Review* 83 (3): 598–607.

Drazen, Allan, and Elhanan Helpman. 1987. "Stabilization with Exchange Rate Management." *Quarterly Journal of Economics* 102 (4): 835–855.

Drezner, Daniel. 1999. *The Sanctions Paradox.* Cambridge: Cambridge University Press.

Dudwick, Nora. 1997. "Armenia: Paradise Lost?" In *New States, New Politics,* edited by Ian Bremmer and Ray Taras. Cambridge: Cambridge University Press.

Duesenberry, James. 1977. "Inflation and Income Distribution." In *Inflation Theory and Anti-inflation Policy,* edited by Eric Lundberg. Boulder, Colo.: Westview.

Dumont, René. 1966. *L'Afrique noire est mal partie.* Paris: Seuil.

Dunbar, Nicholas. 2000. *Inventing Money: The Story of Long Term Capital Management and the Legends behind It.* New York: Wiley.

Dyson, Kenneth, and Kevin Featherstone. 1999. *The Road to Maastricht.* New York: Oxford University Press.

EACB (East African Currency Board). 1965, 1966, 1967. *Report.* Nairobi: East African Currency Board.

———. 1972. *Final Report of the East African Currency Board.* Nairobi: East African Currency Board.

Eatwell, John. 1996. *International Financial Liberalization: The Impact on World Development.* UNDP Discussion Paper Series 64, United Nations Development Program, New York.

Eatwell, John, and Lance Taylor. 1998. "The Performance of Liberalized Capital Markets." Working Paper 8, Center for Economic Policy Analysis Working Paper Series 3, New School for Social Research, New York.

Edison, Hali J., and Michael Melvin. 1990. "The Determinants and Implications of the Choice of an Exchange Rate System." In *Monetary Policy for a Volatile Global Economy,* edited by William Haraf and Thomas Willett. Washington, D.C.: American Enterprise Institute.

Edwards, Sebastian. 1989. *Real Exchange Rates, Devaluation, and Adjustment.* Cambridge: MIT Press.

———. 1999. "How Effective Are Capital Controls?" *Journal of Economic Perspectives* 13 (4).

———. 2001. "Capital Mobility and Economic Performance: Are the Emerging Economies Different?" NBER Working Paper 8706 (January), National Bureau for Economic Research, Cambridge, Mass.

Eichengreen, Barry. 1987. "Conducting the International Orchestra: Bank of England Leadership under the Classical Gold Standard, 1880–1913." *Journal of International Money and Finance* 6.

———. 1989. "Hegemonic Stability Theories of the International Monetary System." In *Can Nations Agree?* edited by Richard N. Cooper, Barry Eichengreen, Gerald Holtham, Robert D. Putnam, and C. Randall Henning. Washington, D.C.: Brookings Institution.

———. 1992a. *Golden Fetters: The Gold Standard and the Great Depression.* Oxford: Oxford University Press.

———. 1992b. "Is Europe an Optimum Currency Area?" In *The European Community after 1992: Perspectives from the Outside,* edited by Silvio Borner and Herbert Grubel. London: Macmillan.

———. 1992c. *Should the Maastricht Treaty Be Saved?* Princeton, N.J.: Princeton University Press.

———. 1994. *International Monetary Arrangements for the 21st Century.* Washington, D.C.: Brookings Institution.

———. 1998. "Dental Hygiene and Nuclear War: How International Relations Looks from Economics." *International Organization* 52 (4): 993–1012.

———. 1999. *Toward a New International Financial Architecture.* Washington, D.C.: Institute for International Economics.

———. 2000. "The International Monetary Fund in the Wake of the Asian Crisis." In Noble and Ravenhill, eds., *The Asian Financial Crisis.*

Eichengreen, Barry, and Jeffry Frieden. 1993. "The Political Economy of European Monetary Unification." *Economics and Politics* 5 (2).

Eichengreen, Barry, and Donald Mathieson. 1998. "Hedge Funds and Financial

Market Dynamics." IMF Occasional Paper 166, International Monetary Fund, Washington, D.C.

———. 1999. "Hedge Funds: What Do We Really Know?" Economic Issues 19, International Monetary Fund, Washington, D.C.

Eichengreen, Barry, and Charles Wyplosz. 1998. "Stability Pact: More than a Minor Nuisance?" *Economic Policy* 26: 67–113.

Eijffinger, Sylvester, and Jakob De Haan. 1996. *The Political Economy of Central-Bank Independence.* Special Papers in International Economics 19, International Economics Section, Princeton University, Princeton, N.J.

EIU (Economist Intelligence Unit). 1999. *EIU Country Report: China and Mongolia: First Quarter.* London: Economist Intelligence Unit.

Enoch, Charles, and Anne-Marie Gulde. 1997. *Making a Currency Board Operational.* IMF Working Paper on Policy Analysis and Assessment 10 (November), International Monetary Fund, Washington, D.C.

Epstein, Gerald. 1992. "Political Economy and Comparative Central Banking." *Review of Radical Political Economics* 24 (1): 1–30.

Epstein, Gerald, and Juliet Schor. 1990. "Corporate Profitability as a Determinant of Restrictive Monetary Policy: Estimates for the Postwar United States." In *The Political Economy of American Monetary Policy,* edited by Thomas Mayer. Cambridge: Cambridge University Press.

Ernst, Dieter. 1994. "Mobilizing the Region's Capacities? The East Asian Production Networks of Japanese Electronics Firms." In *Japanese Investment in Asia: International Production Strategies in a Rapidly Changing World,* edited by Eileen Doherty. Berkeley, Calif.: Berkeley Roundtable on the International Economy.

Evangelista, Matthew. 1996a. "From Each according to Its Abilities: Competing Theoretical Approaches to the Post-Soviet Energy Sector." In *The Sources of Russian Foreign Policy after the Cold War,* edited by Celeste Wallander. Boulder, Colo.: Westview.

———. 1996b. "Stalin's Revenge: Institutional Barriers to Internationalization in the Soviet Union." In *Internationalization and Domestic Politics,* edited by Robert O. Keohane and Helen V. Milner. Cambridge: Cambridge University Press.

Ezenwe, Uka. 1983. *ECOWAS and the Economic Integration of West Africa.* London: C. Hurst.

Fallows, James. 1989. "Containing Japan." *Atlantic Monthly,* May, 40–54.

Fama, Eugene F. 1970. "Efficient Capital Markets: A Review of Theory and Empirical Work." *Journal of Finance* 25 (2): 383–417.

Faust, Jon. 1996. "Whom Can We Trust to Run the Fed? Theoretical Support for the Founder's Views." *Journal of Monetary Economics* 37: 267–283.

FEC (Foreign Exchange Commission). 1999. *Internationalization of the Yen for the 21st Century: Japan's Response to Changes in Global Economic and Financial Environments.* April 20. Tokyo: Ministry of Finance.

Feinberg, Richard. 1992. "Latin America: Back on the Screen." *International Economic Insights* 3 (4): 2–6.

Feldstein, Martin. 1979. "The Welfare Cost of Permanent Inflation and Optimal Short Run Economic Policy." *Journal of Political Economy* 87 (4): 749–768.

———. 1997. "The Costs and Benefits of Going from Low Inflation to Price Stability." In Romer and Romer, eds., *Reducing Inflation.*

———. 1999a. "Capital Income Taxes and the Benefit of Price Stability." In Feldstein, ed., *The Costs and Benefits of Price Stability.*

——, ed. 1999b. *The Costs and Benefits of Price Stability.* Chicago: University of Chicago Press.

——. 1999c. "Introduction." In Feldstein, ed., *The Costs and Benefits of Price Stability.*

Feldstein, Martin, and Charles Horioka. 1980. "Domestic Saving and International Capital Flows." *Economic Journal* 90: 314–329.

Felix, David. 1995. "Financial Globalization versus Free-Trade: The Case for the Tobin Tax." UNCTAD Discussion Papers 108, United Nations Conference on Trade and Development, New York.

Ferreira Rubio, Delia, and Mateo Goretti. 1996. "Cuando el presidente gobierna solo: Menem y los decretos de necesidad y urgencia hasta la reforma constitucional." *Desarrollo económico* 36 (141): 443–474.

Finance Yearbook of China. Various years. Beijing: Zhongguo Caizheng Zazhishe.

Finnemore, Martha. 1993. "International Organizations as Teachers of Norms: The United Nations Educational, Scientific, and Cultural Organization and Science Policy." *International Organization* 47 (4): 565–597.

——. 1996. *National Interests in International Society.* Ithaca, N.Y.: Cornell University Press.

Finnemore, Martha, and Kathryn Sikkink. 1998. "International Norm Dynamics and Political Change." *International Organization* 52 (4): 887–917.

Fischer, Stanley. 1982. "Seigniorage and the Case for a National Money." *Journal of Political Economy* 90 (2): 295–313.

——. 1993. "The Role of Macroeconomic Factors in Growth." *Journal of Monetary Economics* 32 (3): 485–512.

——. 1996. "Maintaining Price Stability." *Finance and Development* 33 (4): 34–37.

——. 1998a. "Capital Account Liberalization and the Role of the IMF." In *Should the IMF Pursue Capital Account Convertibility?* edited by Peter B. Kenen. Essays in International Economics 207, International Economics Section, Princeton University, Princeton, N.J.

——. 1998b. "In Defense of the IMF: Specialized Tools for a Specialized Task." *Foreign Affairs* 77 (4): 103–106.

——. 1998c. Presentation by first deputy managing director of the International Monetary Fund, to Midwinter Conference of the Bankers Association for Foreign Trade, Washington D.C. January 22. Transcript.

——. 1999a. "Comment on Feldstein." In Feldstein, ed., *The Costs and Benefits of Price Stability.*

——. 1999b. "On the Need for an International Lender of Last Resort." *Journal of Economic Perspectives* 13 (4): 85–104.

——. 2000. "Proposals and IMF Actions to Reduce the Frequency of Crises." In *Building an Infrastructure for Financial Stability,* edited by Eric S. Rosengren and John S. Jordan. Conference Series 44 (June), Federal Reserve Bank of Boston, Boston.

Fischer, Stanley, and Franco Modigliani. 1986. "Toward an Understanding of the Real Effects and Costs of Inflation." In *Indexing, Inflation, and Economic Policy,* edited by Stanley Fischer. Cambridge: MIT Press.

Fisher, Irving. 1920. *The Purchasing Power of Money.* Rev. ed. New York: Macmillan.

Fleming, J. M. 1962. "Domestic Financial Policies under Fixed and under Floating Exchange Rates." *IMF Staff Papers* 9: 369–379.

Foster, Edward. 1972. "Costs and Benefits of Inflation." In *Studies in Monetary Economics.* Minneapolis: Federal Reserve Bank of Minneapolis.

Frankel, Jeffrey. 1984. *The Yen/Dollar Agreement: Liberalizing Japanese Capital Markets.* Washington, D.C.: Institute for International Economics.

Frankel, Jeffrey, and Andrew Rose. 1998. "The Endogeneity of the Optimum Currency Area Criteria." *Economic Journal* 108 (449): 1009–1025.

Franzese, Robert J., Jr. 1999. "Partially Independent Central Banks, Politically Responsive Governments, and Inflation." *American Journal of Political Science* 43: 681–706.

Fratianni, Michele, and Jurgen von Hagen. 1990. "Asymmetries and Realignments in the EMS." In *The European Monetary System in the 1990s,* edited by Paul de Grauwe and Lucas Papademos. London: Longman.

Frieden, Jeffry. 1991. "Invested Interests: The Politics of National Economic Policies in a World of Global Finance." *International Organization* 45 (4): 425–451.

——. 1997. "Monetary Populism in Nineteenth Century America: An Open Economy Interpretation." *Journal of Economic History* 57 (2): 367–395.

——. 1998. "The Euro: Who Wins? Who Loses?" *Foreign Policy* 112: 24–32.

Frieden, Jeffry, and Ronald Rogowski. 1996. "The Impact of the International Economy on National Policies: An Analytical Overview." In *Internationalization and Domestic Politics,* edited by Robert O. Keohane and Helen V. Milner. Cambridge: Cambridge University Press.

Friedman, Milton. [1953] 1988. "The Case for Flexible Exchange Rates." Reprinted in *The Merits of Flexible Exchange Rates,* edited by Leo Melamed. Fairfax, Va.: George Mason University Press.

——. 1968. "The Price of the Dollar." In *Dollars and Deficits: Inflation, Monetary Policy, and the Balance of Payments.* Englewood Cliffs, N.J.: Prentice-Hall.

Friedman, Milton, and Anna J. Schwartz. 1963. *A Monetary History of the United States, 1857–1960.* Princeton, N.J.: Princeton University Press.

Frydman, Roman, and Edmund Phelps, eds. 1983. *Individual Forecasting and Aggregate Outcomes: Rational Expectations.* New York: CUNY Press.

Funabashi, Yoichi. 1995. *Asia Pacific Fusion: Japan's Role in APEC.* Washington, D.C.: Institute for International Economics.

Gaillard, Philippe. 1995. *Foccart parle.* Paris: Jeune Afrique.

Gale, Douglas. 1982. *Money: In Equilibrium.* Cambridge: Cambridge University Press.

Garrett, Geoffrey. 1998. "The Transition to Economic and Monetary Union." In *Forging an Integrated Europe,* edited by Barry Eichengreen and Jeffry Frieden. Ann Arbor: University of Michigan Press.

Gavin, Francis J. 2001. "The Myth of Flexible Response: American Strategy in Europe during the 1960's." *International History Review* 23 (4): 847–875.

——. 2002. "The Gold Battles within the Cold War: American Monetary Policy and the Defense of Europe, 1960–1963." *Diplomatic History* 26 (1): 61–94.

Gavin, Francis J., and Erin Mahan. 2000. "Hegemony or Vulnerability? Giscard, Ball, and the Gold Standstill." *Journal of European Integration History* 6 (2): 61–84.

Gervasoni, Carlos. 1997. "La sustentabilidad electoral de los programas de estabilización y reforma estructural: Los casos de Argentina y Peru." Paper presented at the XX International Congress of the Latin American Studies Association, Guadalajara, Mexico, April 17–19.

Geuss, Raymond. 1981. *The Idea of a Critical Theory: Habermas and the Frankfurt School.* Cambridge: Cambridge University Press.

Ghosh, Atish, Anne-Marie Gulde, and Holger Wolf. 1998. *Currency Boards: The Ultimate Fix?* IMF Working Paper of the Policy Development and Review Department 8 (January), International Monetary Fund, Washington, D.C.

Giavazzi, Francesco, and Alberto Giovannini. 1989. *Limiting Exchange Rate Flexibility: The European Monetary System.* Cambridge: MIT Press.

Gibson, Edward, and Ernesto Calvo. 2000. "Federalism and Low Maintenance Constituencies: Territorial Dimensions of Economic Reform in Argentina." *Studies in Comparative International Development* 35 (3): 32–55.

Gilpin, Robert. 1975. *U.S. Power and the Multinational Corporation.* New York: Basic Books.

———. 1987. *Political Economy of International Relations.* Princeton, N.J.: Princeton University Press.

———. 2000. *The Challenge of Global Capitalism: The World Economy in the 21st Century.* Princeton, N.J.: Princeton University Press.

Ginkō Tsūshinsha. 1976. *En no kokusaika* (Internationalization of the yen). Tokyo: Ginkō Tsūshinsha.

Giorgio, Luis, and Silvia Sagari. 1996. "Argentina's Financial Crisis and Restructuring in the 1980s." In *Bank Restructuring: Lessons from the 1980s,* edited by Andrew Sheng. Washington, D.C.: World Bank.

Girnius, Saulius. 1993. "Establishing Currencies in the Baltic States." *RFE/RL Research Report* 2 (22): 35–39.

Glaser, Antoine, and Stephen Smith. 1992. *Ces messieurs Afrique: Le Paris-village du continent noir.* Paris: Calmann-Lévy.

Goh, Keng Swee. 1991. "Why a Currency Board?" In *Wealth of East Asian Nations: Speeches and Writings of Goh Keng Swee,* edited by Linda Low. Singapore: Federal Publications, 1995.

Golay, Frank. 1961. *The Philippines: Public Policy and National Economic Development.* Ithaca, N.Y.: Cornell University Press.

Goldberg, Linda S., Barry W. Ickes, and Randi Ryterman. 1994. "Departures from the Ruble Zone: Implications of Adopting Independent Currencies." *World Economy* 17 (3): 293–322.

Gold Coast. 1956–57. *Legislative Assembly Debates, 1956–57.* First series, vol. 3. Accra: Government of the Gold Coast.

Goldstein, Judith. 1993. *Ideas, Interests, and American Trade Policy.* Ithaca, N.Y.: Cornell University Press.

Goldstein, Judith, and Robert O. Keohane, eds. 1993. *Ideas and Foreign Policy: Beliefs, Institutions, and Political Change.* Ithaca, N.Y.: Cornell University Press.

Goldstein, Morris. 1998. *The Asian Financial Crisis: Causes, Cures, and Systemic Implications.* Washington, D.C.: Institute for International Economics.

Gombeaud, Jean-Louis, Stephen Smith, and Corinne Moutot. 1992. *La guerre du cacao.* Paris: Calmann-Lévy.

Goodhart, Charles A. E. 1995. "The Political Economy of Monetary Union." In *Understanding Interdependence,* edited by Peter B. Kenen. Princeton, N.J.: Princeton University Press.

Goodman, David, and Gerald Segal, eds. 1994. *China Deconstructs.* London: Routledge.

Grabel, Ilene. 1996. "Financial Markets, the State, and Economic Development: Controversies within Theory and Policy." *International Papers in Political Economy* 3 (1): 1–42.

——. 1997. "Creating 'Credible' Economic Policy in Developing and Transitional Economies." *Review of Radical Political Economics* 29 (3): 70–78.

——. 1999. "Rejecting Exceptionalism: Reinterpreting the Asian Financial Crises." In *Global Instability and World Economic Governance,* edited by J. Michie and J. Grieve Smith. London: Routledge.

——. 2000. "The Political Economy of 'Policy Credibility': The New-Classical Economics and the Remaking of Emerging Economies." *Cambridge Journal of Economics* 24 (1): 1–19.

Granville, Brigitte. 1995. "Farewell, Ruble Zone." In *Russian Economic Reform at Risk,* edited by Anders Åslund. New York: Pinter.

Greenspan, Alan. 1998a. "The Current Asia Crisis and the Dynamics of International Finance." Testimony before the House Committee on Banking and Financial Services, U.S. House of Representatives, January 30. Transcript.

——. 1998b. "The Current Asian Crisis and the Dynamics of International Finance." Testimony before the Committee on Foreign Relations, U.S. Senate, February 12. Transcript.

——. 1998c. "The Current Asian Crisis. Testimony before the Subcommittee on Foreign Operations of the Committee on Appropriations, U.S. Senate, March 3. Transcript.

——. 1998d. "The Current Asian Crisis and the Financial Resources of the IMF." Testimony before the Committee on Agriculture, U.S. House of Representatives, May 21. Transcript.

——. 1998e. "International Economic and Financial Systems." Testimony before the Committee on Banking and Financial Services, U.S. House of Representatives, September 16. Transcript.

Gregory, T.E. 1931. "The Causes of Gold Movements into and out of Great Britain, 1925–29." In *Selected Documents Submitted to the Gold Delegation of the Financial Committee.* Geneva: League of Nations.

Grieco, Joseph M. 1990. *Cooperation among Nations.* Ithaca, N.Y.: Cornell University Press.

Grilli, Vittorio, Donato Masciandaro, and Guido Tabellini. 1991. "Political and Monetary Institutions and Public Financial Policies in the Industrial Countries." *Economic Policy* 13: 342–391.

Grimes, William W. 2000. "Japan and Globalization: From Opportunity to Constraint." In *East Asia and Globalization,* edited by Samuel Kim. Oxford: Rowman and Littlefield.

——. 2001. "Internationalization of the Yen." Boston University, Boston, Mass. Draft manuscript.

——. 2002. "Internationalization as Insulation: Dilemmas of the Yen." In *Japan's Managed Globalization: Adapting to the 21st Century,* edited by Ulrike Schaede and William W. Grimes. Armonk, N.Y.: M.E. Sharpe.

Gros, Daniel. 1993. "Costs and Benefits of Economic and Monetary Union: An Application to the Former Soviet Union." In Masson and Taylor, eds., *Policy Issues in the Operation of Currency Unions.*

Gros, Daniel, and Alfred Steinherr. 1991. *Economic Reform in the Soviet Union.*

Princeton Studies in International Economics 71, International Economics Section, Princeton University, Princeton, N.J.

Gros, Daniel, and Nils Thygesen. 1992. *European Monetary Integration.* New York, St. Martin's.

Groshen, Erica L., and Mark E. Schweitzer. 1999. "Identifying Inflation's Grease and Sand Effects in the Labor Market." In Feldstein, ed., *The Costs and Benefits of Price Stability.*

Grossman, Stephen, and Joseph Stiglitz. 1980. "On the Impossibility of Informationally Efficient Markets." *American Economic Review* 70 (3): 393–408.

Guidotti, Pablo, and Carlos Végh. 1992. "Losing Credibility: The Stabilization Blues." IMF Working Paper (September), International Monetary Fund, Washington, D.C.

Guyer, Jane. 1995. "Introduction." In *Money Matters: Instability, Values and Social Payments in the Modern History of West African Communities,* edited by Jane Guyer. London: James Currey.

Haas, Peter M. 1992a. "Introduction: Epistemic Communities and International Policy Coordination." In Haas, ed., *Knowledge, Power, and International Policy Coordination.*

——, ed. 1992b. *Knowledge, Power, and International Policy Coordination.* Special issue of *International Organization* 46 (1).

Hafer, Rik W., and Ali M. Kutan. 1994. "A Long-Run View of German Dominance and the Degree of Policy Convergence in the EMS." *Economic Inquiry* 32: 684–695.

Hahn, Frank. 1983. *Money and Inflation.* Cambridge: MIT Press.

Hale, David. 1998. "Dodging the Bullet—This Time." *Brookings Review* 16 (3): 22–36.

Hall, Peter C. 1986. *Governing the Economy.* Oxford: Oxford University Press.

Hall, Peter C., and Robert J. Franzese. 1998. "Mixed Signals: Central Bank Independence, Coordinated Wage-Bargaining, and European Monetary Union." *International Organization* 52 (3): 505–535.

Halpern, Nina. 1993. "Creating Socialist Economies: Stalinist Political Economy and the Impact of Ideas." In Goldstein and Keohane, eds., *Ideas and Foreign Policy.*

Hamilton, Gary. 1999. "Asian Business Networks in Transition: or, What Alan Greenspan Does Not Know about the Asian Business Crisis." In Pempel, ed., *The Politics of the Asian Economic Crisis.*

Hanke, Steve. 1997. "New Currency Boards Come to the Balkans." *Transition* 8 (1): 8–9.

Hanke, Steve, Lars Jonung, and Kurt Schuler. 1993. *Russian Currency and Finance.* London: Routledge.

Hansson, Ardo, and Jeffrey Sachs. 1992. "Crowning the Estonian Kroon." *Transition* 9: 1–2.

Hartendorp, A.V.H. 1958. *History of Industry and Trade of the Philippines.* Manila: American Chamber of Commerce of the Philippines.

Hatch, Walter, and Kozo Yamamura. 1996. *Asia in Japan's Embrace: Building a Regional Production Alliance.* Cambridge: Cambridge University Press.

Hayami, Masaru. 1995. *En ga sonkei sareru hi* (The day when the yen will be respected). Tokyo: Tōyō Keizai.

Hayek, F.A. 1990. *Denationalization of Money—The Argument Refined.* 3d ed. London: Institute of Economic Affairs.

Hayter, Teresa. 1966. *French Aid.* London: Overseas Development Institute.

Hazlewood, Arthur. 1979. *The Economy of Kenya: The Kenyatta Era.* Oxford: Oxford University Press.

Hefeker, Carsten. 1997. *Interest Groups and Monetary Integration.* Boulder, Colo.: Westview.

Heisenberg, Dorothee. 1998. *The Mark of the Bundesbank.* Boulder, Colo.: Lynne Rienner.

Helleiner, Eric. 1994. *States and the Reemergence of Global Finance.* Ithaca, N.Y.: Cornell University Press.

——. 1998. "National Currencies and National Identities." *American Behavioral Scientist* 41.

——. 1999. "Denationalizing Money? Economic Liberalism and the 'National Question' in Currency Affairs." In *Nation-States and Money,* edited by Emily Gilbert and Eric Helleiner. London: Routledge.

——. 2000. "Still an Extraordinary Power, but for How Much Longer? The United States in World Finance." In *Strange Power: Shaping the Parameters of International Relations and International Political Economy,* edited by Thomas Lawton, James Rosenau, and Amy Verdun. Aldershot, U.K.: Ashgate.

——. 2001. "Departing from Orthodoxy: Southern Monetary Reforms in the 'Embedded Liberal' Era." Trent University, Peterborough, Ontario. Draft manuscript.

Henning, C. Randall, and Pier Carlo Padoan. 2000. *Transatlantic Perspectives on the Euro.* Washington, D.C.: Brookings Institution.

Heo, Uk. "South Korea: Democratization, Financial Crisis, and the Decline of the Developmental State." In Horowitz and Heo, eds., *The Political Economy of International Financial Crises.*

Hinshaw, Randall. 1958. *Toward European Convertibility.* Essays in International Economics 31, International Economics Section, Princeton University, Princeton, N.J.

Hirsch, Fred, Michael Doyle, and Edward L. Morse. 1977. *Alternatives to Monetary Disorder.* New York: Council on Foreign Relations.

Hirschman, Albert. [1945] 1969. *National Power and the Structure of Foreign Trade.* Berkeley: University of California Press.

——. 1985. "Reflections on the Latin American Experience." In *The Politics of Inflation and Economic Stagnation,* edited by Leon Lindbergh and Charles Maier. Washington, D.C.: Brookings Institution.

Hiwatari, Nobuhiro. 1996. "The Domestic Sources of U.S.-Japan Economic Relations." Paper presented at the 1996 Annual Meeting of the American Political Science Association, San Francisco, August 29.

Hoffmaister, Alexander, and Carlos A. Végh. 1996. "Disinflation and the Recession-Now-Versus-Recession-Later Hypothesis: Evidence from Uruguay." *IMF Staff Papers* 43: 355–394.

Hong, Kiseok, and Jong-Wha Lee. 2000. "Korea: Returning to Sustainable Growth?" In Woo, Sachs, and Schwab, eds., *The Asian Financial Crisis.*

Honohan, Patrick. 1990. "Monetary Cooperation in the CFA Zone." In *Economic Reform in Sub-Saharan Africa,* edited by Ajay Chhibber and Stanley Fischer. Washington, D.C.: World Bank.

Horowitz, Shale, and Uk Heo, eds. 2001. *The Political Economy of International Financial Crises: Interest Groups, Ideologies, and Institutions.* London: Rowman and Littlefield.

Hoskins, W. Lee. 1991. "Defending Zero Inflation: All for Naught." *Federal Reserve Bank of Minneapolis Quarterly Review* 15 (2): 16–20.

Houphouët-Boigny, Félix. 1957. "Black Africa and the French Union." *Foreign Affairs* 35 (4).

Hua, Chang, and Pei Huang. 1998. *Hanwei Renminbi* (Defending RMB). Chengdu: Sichuan Chubanshe.

IIMA (Institute for International Monetary Affairs). 1999a. "Internationalization of the Yen: Implications for Stabilization of Financial Systems and Currencies in Asia." Conference Report, March, Institute for International Monetary Affairs, Tokyo.

——. 1999b. "Prescriptions for Recovery of the World Economy." IIMA Occasional Paper 7, Institute for International Monetary Affairs, Tokyo.

Ikenberry, G. John. 1992. "A World Restored: Expert Consensus and the Anglo-American Postwar Settlement." In Haas, ed., *Knowledge, Power, and International Policy Coordination.*

——. 1993. "Creating Yesterday's New World Order: Keynesian 'New Thinking' and the Anglo-American Postwar Settlement." In Goldstein and Keohane, eds., *Ideas and Foreign Policy.*

——. 2000. *After Victory.* Princeton, N.J.: Princeton University Press.

IMF (International Monetary Fund). Various years. *Direction of Trade Statistics.* Washington, D.C.: International Monetary Fund.

——. 1995. *Argentina: Recent Economic Developments, 1995.* Washington D.C.: International Monetary Fund.

——. 1998a. *Argentina: Recent Economic Developments, 1998.* Washington, D.C.: International Monetary Fund.

——. 1998b. *International Capital Markets: Developments, Prospects, and Key Policy Issues.* Washington, D.C.: International Monetary Fund.

——. 1998c. *World Economic Outlook: Financial Turbulence and the World Economy.* Washington, D.C.: International Monetary Fund.

——. 1999. "A Guide to Progress in Strengthening the Architecture of the International Financial System." Statement by the managing director on Progress in Strengthening the Architecture of the International Financial System, IMF Executive Board Meeting, April 16, 1999.

Inoki, Takenori. 2000. "Ōshū no shiren, Ajia no kibō" (Lessons from Europe, hopes for Asia). *Chūō kōron* 1339 (December): 34–37.

Ishihara, Shintarō. 1998. "Writer Ishihara Blames US for Asian Crisis." *Bungei Shunjū* (August): 110–124 [FBIS translation].

Jackson, Patricia, David J. Maude, and William Perraudin. 1998. "Bank Capital and Value at Risk." Bank of England Working Paper Series 79, Bank of England, London.

Jackson, Robert. 1993. "The Weight of Ideas in Decolonization: Normative Change in International Relations." In Goldstein and Keohane, eds., *Ideas and Foreign Policy.*

Jevons, W. Stanley. 1881. "Richard Cantillon and the Nationality of Political Economy." *Contemporary Review* 39 (January): 61–80.

Jin, Yanshi. 1998. "Renminbi bianzhi yufou de zhengce xuanze jiqi zhengzhi houguo" (Policy choice regarding whether to devalue the RMB and its political consequences). *Zhanlue yu guanli* 2: 49–54.

Johnson, Harry G. 1973. "The Panamanian Monetary System." In *Further Essays in Monetary Economics,* edited by Harry G. Johnson. Cambridge: Harvard University Press.

Johnson, Juliet. 2000. *A Fistful of Rubles: The Rise and Fall of the Russian Banking System.* Ithaca, N.Y.: Cornell University Press.

Johnson, Peter A. 1998. *The Government of Money: Monetarism in Germany and the United States.* Ithaca, N.Y.: Cornell University Press.

Jones, William. 1976. *Planning and Economic Policy in Mali.* Ph.D. thesis, Université de Genève.

Jorion, Philippe. 1997. *Value at Risk.* New York: McGraw Hill.

Joseph, Richard. 1976. "The Gaullist Legacy: Patterns of French Neo-colonialism." *Review of African Political Economy* 6 (May–August): 4–14.

Julienne, Robert. 1987. *Vingt ans d'institutions monétaires Ouest-Africaines, 1955–75.* Paris: Harmattan.

Kallas, Siim. 1993. "Pros and Cons of the Reintroduction of the Estonian Kroon." In *Conference on the Reintroduction of the Estonian Kroon.* Tallinn: Bank of Estonia.

Kallas, Siim, and Mart Sorg. 1995. "Currency Reform." In *Transforming the Estonian Economy.* Tallinn: Institute of Economics, Estonian Academy of Sciences.

Kaltenthaler, Karl. 1997. "The Sources of Policy Dynamics: Variations in German and French Policy Towards European Monetary Cooperation." *West European Politics* 20 (3): 91–110.

——. 1998. *Germany and the Politics of Europe's Money.* Durham, N.C.: Duke University Press.

Kaneko, Tarō. 1999. "En wa kijiku tsūka ni narenai" (The yen cannot become a key currency). *Kokusai Kin'yū* 1030 (November 8): 4–10.

Kaplan, Ethan, and Dani Rodrik. 2001. "Did the Malaysian Capital Controls Work?" NBER Working Paper 8142 (February), National Bureau for Economic Research, Cambridge, Mass.

Kapur, Devesh. 1998. "The IMF: A Cure or a Curse?" *Foreign Policy* 111 (Summer): 114–129.

Karlik, John. 1968. "The Costs and Benefits of Being a Reserve Currency." In *The Open Economy: Essays on International Trade and Finance,* edited by Peter B. Kenen and Roger Lawrence. New York: Columbia University Press.

Karunatilake, Halwalage N.S. 1973. *Central Banking and Monetary Policy in Sri Lanka.* Colombo, Sri Lanka: Lake House Investment.

Katzenstein, Peter J. 1997. "United Germany in an Integrating Europe." In *Tamed Power: Germany in Europe,* edited by Peter J. Katzenstein. Ithaca, N.Y.: Cornell University Press.

Katzenstein, Peter J., and Takashi Shiraishi, eds. 1997. *Network Power: Japan and Asia.* Ithaca, N.Y.: Cornell University Press.

Kawai, Masahiro. 1998. "The East Asian Currency Crisis: Causes and Lessons." *Contemporary Economic Policy* 16 (April): 157–172.

Keeler, John. 1993. "Opening the Window for Reform: Mandates, Crises, and Extraordinary Policy-Making." *Comparative Politics Studies* 25 (4): 433–486.

Keizai Dōyūkai. 2000. *A Private-Sector Perspective on the Internationalization of the Yen: A Study on Japanese and Asian Stability and Growth.* Tokyo: Keizai Dōyūkai.

Kenen, Peter B. 1969. "The Theory of Optimum Currency Areas." In *Monetary Problems of the International Economy,* edited by Robert A. Mundell and Alexander K. Swoboda. Chicago: University of Chicago Press.

———. 1985. "Macroeconomic Theory and Policy: How the Closed Economy Was Opened." In *Handbook of International Economics,* vol. 2, edited by Ronald W. Jones and Peter B. Kenen. Amsterdam: North-Holland.

Kennedy, E. 1991. *The Bundesbank: Germany's Central Bank in the International Monetary System.* New York: Council on Foreign Relations Press.

Keohane, Robert O. 1984. *After Hegemony.* Princeton, N.J.: Princeton University Press.

Keynes, John Maynard. [1930] 1971. *A Treatise on Money I: The Pure Theory of Money.* Reprinted in *The Collected Writings of John Maynard Keynes,* edited by Donald Moggridge and Elizabeth Johnson. Vol. 5. London: Macmillan.

———. 1936. *The General Theory of Employment, Interest and Money.* New York: Harcourt, Brace, and World.

———. 1937. "The General Theory of Employment." *Quarterly Journal of Economics* 51 (2): 213–214.

———. [1942] 1980. "Letter to Roy Harrod, April 19." Reprinted in *The Collected Writings of John Maynard Keynes,* edited by Donald Moggridge and Elizabeth Johnson. Vol. 25. London: Macmillan.

Kiguel, Miguel. 1994. "Exchange Rate Policy, the Real Exchange Rate, and Inflation: Lessons from Latin America." *Cuadernos de economía* 31 (93): 229–249.

Kiguel, Miguel, and Nissan Liviatan. 1992. "The Business Cycle Associated with Exchange Rate-Based Stabilization." *World Bank Economic Review* 6 (May): 279–305.

Kihon Seisaku Kenkyūkai. 1999. "'Yūro' shutsugen to kongo no kokusai tsūka chitsujo no henka" (The introduction of the euro and future changes in the international monetary order). JSI/FIF Report 4 (March 12), Japan Strategy Institute and Fujita Institute of Future Management Research, Tokyo.

Kikkawa, Mototada. 1998. *Manē haisen* (Defeat in the money wars). Tokyo: Bunshun Shinsho.

Kim, Byong Kuk. 1965. *Central Banking Experiment in a Developing Economy: Case Study of Korea.* Seoul: Korea Research Center.

Kim, Samuel. 1997. "China as a Great Power." *Current History* 96 (September): 246–251.

Kindleberger, Charles P. 1967. *The Politics of Money and World Language.* Princeton Essays in International Economics 61. International Economics Section, Princeton University, Princeton, N.J.

———. 1970. *Power and Money: The Economics of International Politics and the Politics of International Economics.* New York: Basic Books.

———. 1985. "The International Monetary Politics of a Near-Great Power: Two French Episodes, 1926–1936 and 1960–1970." In *Keynesianism vs. Monetarism, and Other Essays in Financial History.* London: George Allen and Unwin.

———. 1989. *Manias, Panics, and Crashes: A History of Financial Crises.* New York: Basic Books.

———. 2000. *Manias, Panics, and Crashes: A History of Financial Crises.* 4th ed. New York: Wiley.

Kingdon, John. 1984. *Agendas, Alternatives, and Public Policies*. New York: Harper-Collins.

Kirman, Alan P. 1992. "Whom or What Does the Representative Individual Represent?" *Journal of Economic Perspectives* 6: 117–136.

Kirshner, Jonathan. 1995. *Currency and Coercion: The Political Economy of International Monetary Power*. Princeton, N.J.: Princeton University Press.

———. 1998. "Disinflation, Structural Change, and Distribution." *Review of Radical Political Economics* 30 (1): 53–89.

———. 1999a. "Inflation: Paper Dragon or Trojan Horse?" *Review of International Political Economy* 6 (4): 609–618.

———. 1999b. "Keynes, Capital Mobility, and the Crisis of Embedded Liberalism." *Review of International Political Economy* 6 (3): 313–337.

———. 1999c. "The Political Economy of Realism." In *Unipolar Politics*, edited by Michael Mastanduno. New York: Columbia University Press.

———. 2000. "The Study of Money." *World Politics* 52 (3): 407–436.

———. 2001. "The Political Economy of Low Inflation." *Journal of Economic Surveys* 15 (1): 41–70.

Kishimoto, Shūhei. 1999. "Shin Miyazawa kōsō no shimei to Ajia tsūka kikin" (The mission of the New Miyazawa Plan and the Asian Monetary Fund). *Fainansu* (May): 31–48.

Kobayashi, Hideo. 1997. "Ajia to kyōchō shite koso han'ei wa aru, keizaikai/keizaishi no tachiba kara" (Prosperity can be had through cooperation with Asia, from the perspective of the economic community and economic history). *Sekai* 635: 200–205.

Kondō, Takehiko. 1979. *"Kokusai tsūka" toshite no en* (The yen as an "international currency"). Tokyo: Kyōikusha.

Kramer, John M. 1993. "'Energy Shock' from Russia Jolts Baltic States." *RFE/RL Research Report* 2 (17): 41–49.

Krasner, Stephen D. 1978. *Defending the National Interest*. Princeton, N.J.: Princeton University Press.

Krugman, Paul. 1979. "A Model of Balance of Payments Crises." *Journal of Money, Credit, and Banking* 11 (3): 311–325.

———. 1984. "The International Role of the Dollar: Theory and Prospect." In *Exchange Rate Theory and Practice*, edited by John Bilson and Richard Marston. Chicago: University of Chicago Press.

———. 1999. *The Return of Depression Economics*. New York: Norton.

Kukk, Kalev. 1997. "Five Years in the Monetary Development of the Baltic States: Differences and Similarities." *Bank of Estonia Bulletin* 5, Bank of Estonia, Tallinn.

Kutan, Ali M. 1990. "German Dominance in the European Monetary System: Evidence from Money Supply Growth Rates." *Open Economies Review* 2 (3): 269–293.

Kwan, C. H. 1997. "Ajia no tsūka kiki, sono taishitsu to kyōkun" (The Asian financial crisis, its characteristics and lessons). *Sekai* 640 (October): 35–38.

———. 2001. *Yen Bloc: Toward Economic Integration in Asia*. Washington, D.C.: Brookings Institution.

Kydland, Finn, and Edward Prescott. 1977. "Rules Rather than Discretion: The Inconsistency of Optimal Plans." *Journal of Political Economy* 85 (3): 473–491.

Laban, Raul, and Federico Sturzenegger. 1994a. "Distributional Conflict, Financial Adaptation and Delayed Stabilizations." *Economics and Politics* 6 (3): 257–276.

——. 1994b. "Fiscal Conservatism as a Response to the Debt Crisis." *Journal of Development Economics* 45 (2): 305–324.

Laidler, David. 1979. "The Welfare Costs of Inflation in Neoclassical Theory: Some Unsettled Problems." In *Inflation Theory and Anti-inflation Policy,* edited by Erik Lundberg. Boulder, Colo.: Westview.

——. 1991. *The Golden Age of the Quantity Theory of Money.* Princeton, N.J.: Princeton University Press.

Lainela, Seija, and Pekka Sutela. 1995. "Escaping from the Ruble: Estonia and Latvia Compared." In *Integration and Disintegration in European Economies,* edited by Bruno Dallago and Giovanni Pegoretti. Aldershot, U.K.: Dartmouth.

Laitin, David D. 1998. *Identity in Formation: The Russian-Speaking Populations in the Near Abroad.* Ithaca, N.Y.: Cornell University Press.

Lakatos, Imre. 1970. "Falsification and the Methodology of Scientific Research Programmes." In *Criticism and the Growth of Knowledge,* edited by Imre Lakatos and Alan Musgrave. Cambridge: Cambridge University Press.

Lake, David A. 1993. "Leadership, Hegemony, and the International Economy." *International Studies Quarterly* 37: 459–489.

Lam, Willy Wo-Lap. 1998. "Fiscal Crisis Pulls Hong Kong Closer to Motherland." *South China Morning Post,* July 1, 6.

Lardy, Nicholas. 1994. *China in the World Economy.* Washington, D.C.: Institute of International Economics.

——. 1998a. "China and the Asian Contagion." *Foreign Affairs* 77 (4): 78–88.

——. 1998b. *China's Unfinished Economic Revolution.* Washington, D.C.: Brookings Institution.

Laso, Eduardo. 1957–58. "Financial Policies and Credit Control Techniques in Central America." *IMF Staff Papers* 6: 427–460.

Lauristin, Marju, and Peeter Vihalemm. 1997. "Recent Historical Developments in Estonia: Three Stages of Transition (1987–1998)." In *Return to the Western World.* Tartu, Estonia: Tartu University Press.

LDPSIY (Liberal Democratic Party Subcommittee on the Internationalization of the Yen). 1998. *"En no kokusaika" ni muketa gutai sochi ni tsuite.* www.jimin.or.jp /jimin/saishin/seisaku-18.html.

Lee, Sheng-Yi. 1986. *The Monetary and Banking Development of Singapore and Malaysia.* 2d ed. Singapore: Singapore University Press.

Leymarie, Pierre. 1974. "Interview with Didier Ratsiraka." *Revue française d'études politiques africaines* (January): 29–40.

Li, Fuxiang. 1998. "Renminbi huilu de zhengce mubiao yu qushi fenxi" (An analysis of the policy goals and trends of RMB exchange rate). *Zhongguo jinrong,* April.

Li, Shuyi, and Jianxiong Yong. 1997. *Ershiyi Shiji Zhongguo Jueqi* (The rise of China in the 21st century). Beijing: Zhonggong Zhongyang Dangxiao Chubanshe.

Lieven, Anatol. 1993. *The Baltic Revolution: Estonia, Latvia, and Lithuania and the Path to Independence.* New Haven, Conn.: Yale University Press.

Little, Ian, Tibor Scitovsky, and Maurice Scott. 1970. *Industry and Trade in Some Developing Countries.* Oxford: Oxford University Press.

Loedel, Peter H. 1999. *Deutsche Mark Politics: Germany in the European Monetary System.* Boulder, Colo.: Lynne Rienner.

Louge, Dennis E., and Richard James Sweeney. 1981. "Inflation and Real Growth: Some Empirical Results." *Journal of Money, Credit, and Banking* 13: 497–501.

Loungani, Prakash, and Nathan Sheets. 1995. "Central Bank Independence, Inflation and Growth in Transition Economies." Federal Reserve System International Finance Discussion Papers 519, United States Federal Reserve System, New York.

Lowenstein, Roger. 2000. *When Genius Failed*. New York: Random House.

Lucas, Robert, Jr. 1973. "Some International Evidence on Output-Inflation Trade-offs." *American Economic Review* 63: 326–334.

Ludlow, Peter. 1982. *The Making of the European Monetary System*. London: Butterworths Scientific.

Malthus, T.R. [1811] 1963. "Depreciation of Paper Money." Reprinted in *Occasional Papers of T.R. Malthus,* edited by Bernard Semmel. New York: Burt Franklin.

Marsh, David. 1992. *The Bundesbank: The Bank That Rules Europe*. London: Mandarin.

Mas, Ignacio. 1995. "Central Bank Independence: A Critical View from a Developing Country Perspective." *World Development* 23 (10): 1639–1652.

Masson, Paul, and Mark Taylor. 1993. *Policy Issues in the Operation of Currency Unions*. Cambridge: Cambridge University Press.

Mastel, Greg. 1997. *The Rise of the Chinese Economy: The Middle Kingdom Emerges*. Armonk, N.Y.: M.E. Sharpe.

Maxfield, Sylvia. 1994. "Financial Incentives and Central Bank Authority in Industrializing Nations." *World Politics* 46: 556–588.

——. 1997. *Gatekeepers of Growth: The International Political Economy of Central Banking in Developing Countries*. Princeton, N.J.: Princeton University Press.

Mazzucelli, Collette. 1995. "Germany at Maastricht: Diplomacy and Domestic Politics." In *Dimensions of German Unification,* edited by A. Bradley Shingleton, Marion J. Gibbon, and Kathryn S. Mack. Boulder, Colo.: Westview.

McCallum, Bennett, and Marvin Goodfriend. 1989. "Demand for Money: Theoretical Studies." In *The New Palgrave: Money,* edited by John Eatwell, Murry Milgate, and Peter Newman. New York: Macmillan.

McDonough, William J. 1994. "An Independent Central Bank in a Democratic Country: The Federal Reserve Experience." *Federal Reserve Bank of New York Quarterly Review* (Spring): 1–6.

McKinnon, Ronald. 1962. "Optimum Currency Areas." *American Economic Review* 53: 717–725.

McKinnon, Ronald, and Kenichi Ohno. 1997. *Dollar and Yen: Resolving Economic Conflict between the United States and Japan*. Cambridge: MIT Press.

McNamara, Kathleen R. 1998. *The Currency of Ideas*. Ithaca, N.Y.: Cornell University Press.

McNamara, Kathleen R., and Erik Jones. 1996. "The Clash of Institutions: Germany in European Monetary Affairs." *German Politics and Society* 14 (3): 5–30.

Medhora, Rohinton. 1992. "The West African Monetary Union." *Canadian Journal of Development Studies* 13 (2): 151–179.

Melitz, Jacques. 1988. "Monetary Discipline and Cooperation in the European Monetary System: A Synthesis." In *The European Monetary System,* edited by F. Giavazzi, S. Micossi, and M. Miller. Cambridge: Cambridge University Press.

Meri, Lennart. 1993. "Estonia Has More Gold Than Europe." In *Conference on the Reintroduction of the Estonian Kroon*. Tallinn: Bank of Estonia.

Merton, Robert C. 1975. "The Theory of Finance from the Perspective of Continuous Time." *Journal of Financial and Quantitative Analysis* 10 (4): 659–674.

Meunier, Sophie. 2000. "The French Exception." *Foreign Affairs* 79 (4): 104–116.

Meyer, John, John Boli, George Thomas, and Francisco Ramirez. 1997. "World Society and the Nation-State." *American Journal of Sociology* 103 (1): 144–182.

Michailof, Serge, ed. 1993. *La France et l'Afrique: Vade mecum pour un nouveau voyage*. Paris: Karthala.

Michalopoulos, Constantine, and David G. Tarr. 1992. *Trade and Payments Arrangements for States of the Former USSR*. Washington, D.C.: World Bank.

Millman, Gregory J. 1995. *The Vandals Crown*. New York: Free Press.

Miura, Kiyoshi. 2000. "Workshop on Framework for Regional Monetary Stabilization in East Asia." IIMA Newsletter 6 (September 29), Institute for International Monetary Affairs, Tokyo.

Miyoshi, Hiroko. 1999. "'21 seiki ni muketa en no kokusaika' konfarensu kaisai" (Conference on internationalization of the yen toward the 21st century). *Fainansu* (August): 2–11.

Moravcsik, Andrew. 1998. *The Choice for Europe*. Ithaca, N.Y.: Cornell University Press.

Morgenthau, Hans J. 1967. *Politics among Nations: The Struggle for Power and Peace*. 4th ed. New York: Knopf.

Mundell, Robert A. 1960. "The Monetary Dynamics of International Adjustment under Fixed Capital." *Quarterly Journal of Economics* 74: 227–257.

———. 1961. "The Theory of Optimum Currency Areas." *American Economic Review* 51 (3): 657–665.

Murillo, Maria Victoria. 2001. *Labor Unions, Partisan Coalitions, and Market Reforms in Latin America*. Cambridge: Cambridge University Press.

Murphy, Antoin E. 1986. *Richard Cantillon: Entrepreneur and Economist*. Oxford: Clarendon Press.

Nauseda, Gitanas. 1997. "Development of the Lithuanian Monetary System and the European Union." In *Lithuania's Integration into the European Union*, edited by Klaudijus Maniokas and Gediminas Vitkus. Vilnius, Lithuania: European Integration Studies Center.

Nihon Keizai Chōsakai. 1998. *Ajia no keizai-tsūka kiki to Nihon no yakuwari* (Asia's economic and financial crisis, and Japan's role). Tokyo: Nihon Keizai Chōsakai Gikai.

Nkrumah, Kwame. 1965. *Neo-colonialism: The Last Stage of Imperialism*. London: Nelson.

Noble, Gregory W., and John Ravenhill, eds. 2000a. *The Asian Financial Crisis and the Architecture of Global Finance*. Cambridge: Cambridge University Press.

———. 2000b. "Causes and Consequences of the Asian Financial Crisis." In Noble and Ravenhill, eds., *The Asian Financial Crisis*.

Noland, Marcus, Li-Gang Liu, Sherman Robinson, and Zhi Wang. 1998. *Global Economic Effects of the Asian Currency Devaluations*. Washington, D.C.: Institute for International Economics.

Nordhaus, William. 1975. "The Political Business Cycle." *Review of Economic Studies* 42 (April): 169–190.

Nouaille-Degorce, Brigitte. 1982. "La politique française de coopération avec les états africains et malgaches au sud du Sahara, 1958–1978." Ph.D. dissertation, University of Bordeaux.

Oatley, Thomas H. 1997. *Monetary Politics: Exchange Rate Cooperation in the European Union.* Ann Arbor: University of Michigan Press.

Odell, John S. 1982. *U.S. International Monetary Policy.* Princeton, N.J.: Princeton University Press.

Ohno, Kenichi. 1999a. "Exchange Rate Management in Developing Asia." ADB Institute Working Paper 1, Asian Development Bank Institute, Tokyo.

——. 1999b. "Tojōkoku sekai to gurōbaru shijō keizai" (The world of developing nations and the global market economy). *Sekai* 657 (January): 78–88.

Oka, Masao. 1996. *En ga kijiku tsūka ni naru hi* (When the yen will become a key currency). Tokyo: Kadokawa Shoten.

Olcott, Martha Brill. 1995. *The Kazakhs.* 2d ed. Stanford, Calif.: Hoover Institute Press.

——. 1996. *Central Asia's New States.* Washington, D.C.: United States Institute of Peace Press.

——. 1997a. "Democratization and the Growth of Political Participation in Kazakhstan." In *Conflict, Cleavage, and Change in Central Asia and the Caucasus,* edited by Karen Dawisha and Bruce Parrott. Cambridge: Cambridge University Press.

——. 1997b. "Kazakhstan: Pushing for Eurasia." In *New States, New Politics,* edited by Ian Bremmer and Ray Taras. Cambridge: Cambridge University Press.

Olcott, Martha Brill, Anders Åslund, and Sherman Garnett. 1999. *Getting It Wrong: Regional Cooperation and the Commonwealth of Independent States.* Washington, D.C.: Carnegie Endowment for International Peace.

Onishi, Junya, 1999. "Should the Current Arguments on the Internationalization of the Yen Be Reconsidered?" Occasional Paper 99-11, Harvard University Program on U.S.-Japan Relations, Harvard University, Cambridge.

Onoh, J.K. 1982. *Money and Banking in Africa.* London: Longman.

Orlowski, Lucjan. 1994. "The Disintegration of the Ruble Zone: Driving Forces and Proposals for Policy Change." *Aussenwirtschaft* 49 (1): 101–129.

Ostrup, Finn. 2000. *Money and the Natural Rate of Unemployment.* Cambridge: Cambridge University Press.

Oye, Kenneth. 1992. *Economic Discrimination and Political Exchange.* Princeton, N.J.: Princeton University Press.

Parks, Richard W. 1978. "Inflation and Relative Price Variability." *Journal of Political Economy* 86 (1): 79–95.

Parsons, David Wayne. 1981. "Was Keynes Khunian? Keynes and the Idea of Theoretical Revolutions." *British Journal of Political Science* 15 (2): 451–471.

Patinkin, Don. 1989. *Money, Interest, and Prices.* 2d ed., abridged. Cambridge: MIT Press.

Péan, Pierre. 1990. *L'homme de l'ombre.* Paris: Fayard.

Pempel, T.J. 1997. "Transpacific Torii: Japan and the Emerging Asian Regionalism." In Katzenstein and Shiraishi, eds., *Network Power.*

——. 1999a. "Conclusion." In Pempel, ed., *The Politics of the Asian Economic Crisis.*

——, ed. 1999b. *The Politics of the Asian Economic Crisis.* Ithaca, N.Y.: Cornell University Press.

———. 1999c. "Regional Ups, Regional Downs." In Pempel, ed., *The Politics of the Asian Economic Crisis.*

Perkins, Dwight Heald, and Wing Thye Woo. 2000. "Malaysia: Adjusting to Deep Integration with the World Economy." In Woo, Sachs, and Schwab, eds., *The Asian Financial Crisis.*

Petrei, A. Humberto, and James Tybout. 1985. "Microeconomic Adjustments in Argentina during 1976–1981: The Importance of Changing Levels of Financial Subsidies." *World Development* 13 (August): 946–967.

Piga, Gustavo. 2000. "Dependent and Accountable: Evidence from the Modern Theory of Central Banking." *Journal of Economic Surveys* 14 (5): 563–595.

Plumptre, A. 1940. *Central Banking in the British Dominions.* Toronto: University of Toronto Press.

Polanyi, Karl. 1944. *The Great Transformation.* New York: Farrar and Rhinehart.

Posen, Adam. 1993. "Why Central Bank Independence Does Not Cause Low Inflation: There Is No Institutional Fix for Politics." In *Finance and the International Economy 7: The AMEX Bank Review Prize Essays,* edited by Richard O'Brien. Oxford: Oxford University Press.

———. 1995a. "Central Bank Independence and Disinflationary Credibility: A Missing Link?" Federal Reserve Bank of New York Staff Reports 1 (May), Federal Reserve Bank of New York, New York.

———. 1995b. "Declarations Are Not Enough: Financial Sector Sources of Central Bank Independence." NBER Macroeconomics Annual 10, National Bureau of Economic Research, Cambridge, Mass.

Putnam, Hilary. 1981. *Reason, Truth, and History.* Cambridge: Cambridge University Press.

Raun, Toivo A. 1997. "Estonia: Independence Redefined." In Bremmer and Taras, eds., *New States, New Politics.*

Reeves, Richard. 1993. *President Kennedy: Profile of Power.* New York: Touchstone.

Rist, Charles. [1940] 1966. *History of Monetary and Credit Theory: From John Law to the Present Day.* Translated by Jane Degras. New York: Augustus M. Kelley.

Rivlin, Alice. 1998. Remarks at the Hyman P. Minsky Conference on Financial Structure, the Levy Institute, Annandale on Hudson, N.Y., April 23. Transcript.

Robson, Peter. 1968. *Economic Integration in Africa.* London: Allen and Unwin.

Rockoff, Hugh. 1990. "The 'Wizard of Oz' as a Monetary Allegory." *Journal of Political Economy* 98 (4).

———. 2000. "How Long Did It Take the United States to Become an Optimal Currency Area?" NBER Working Paper Series on Historical Factors in Long Run Growth 124, National Bureau of Economic Research, Cambridge, Mass.

Rodriguez, Carlos. 1982. "The Argentine Stabilization Plan of December 20th." *World Development* 10 (September): 801–811.

Rodrik, Dani. 1998. "Who Needs Capital Account Convertibility?" In *Should the IMF Pursue Capital Account Convertibility?* edited by Peter B. Kenen. Essays in International Economics 207, International Economics Section, Princeton University, Princeton, N.J.

Romer, Christina D., and David H. Romer. 1997a. "Introduction." In Romer and Romer, eds., *Reducing Inflation.*

———, eds. 1997b. *Reducing Inflation: Motivation and Strategy.* Chicago: University of Chicago Press.

Rosenberg, Emily. 1985. "Foundations of US International Financial Power: Gold Standard Diplomacy, 1900–1905." *Business History Review* 59 (2): 169–202.

Rosenbluth, Frances McCall. 1989. *Financial Politics in Contemporary Japan.* Ithaca, N.Y.: Cornell University Press.

Rothchild, Donald, ed. 1968. *Politics of Integration: An East African Documentary.* Nairobi: East African Publishing House.

Rowland, Benjamin M., ed. 1976. *Balance of Power or Hegemony: The Inter-war Monetary System.* New York: Lehrman Institute.

Ruggie, John Gerard. 1982. "International Regimes, Transactions, and Change: Embedded Liberalism in the Postwar Economic Order." *International Organization* 36 (2): 379–415.

——. 1993. "Unravelling Trade: Global Institutional Change and the Pacific Economy." In *Pacific Economic Relations in the 1990s: Cooperation or Conflict?* edited by Richard Higgott, Richard Leaver, and John Ravenhill. Boulder, Colo.: Lynne Rienner.

Rutland, Peter, and Timur R. Isataev. 1995. "Kazakhstan." In *First Steps toward Economic Independence: New States of the Postcommunist World,* edited by Michael L. Wyzan. Westport, Conn.: Praeger.

Sachs, Jeffrey D., and David Lipton. 1993. "Remaining Steps to a Market-Based Monetary System in Russia." In *Changing the Economic System in Russia,* edited by Anders Åslund and Richard Layard. London: Pinter.

Sachs, Jeffrey D., and Wing Thye Woo. 2000. "Understanding the Asian Financial Crisis." In Woo, Sachs, and Schwab, eds., *The Asian Financial Crisis.*

Sakakibara, Eisuke. 1998. *Kokusai kin'yū no genba: Shihonshugi no kiki o koete* (The arena of international finance: Moving beyond the crisis of capitalism). Tokyo: PHP Shinsho.

Salant, William A. 1964. "The Reserve Currency Role of the Dollar: Blessing or Burden to the United States?" *Review of Economics and Statistics* 46 (2): 165–172.

Sandholtz, Wayne. 1993. "Choosing Union: Monetary Politics and Maastricht." *International Organization* 47 (1): 1–39.

Santoni, G.J. 1986. "The Effects of Inflation on Commercial Banks." *Federal Reserve Bank of St. Louis Review* (March): 15–26.

Sargent, Thomas J. 1982. "The Ends of Four Big Inflations." In *Inflation: Causes and Effects,* edited by Robert E. Hall. Chicago: University of Chicago Press.

——. 1999. *The Conquest of American Inflation.* Princeton, N.J.: Princeton University Press.

Schadler, Susan, Maria Carkovic, Adam Bennett, and Robert Kahn. 1993. "Recent Experiences with Surges in Capital Inflows." IMF Occasional Paper 108, International Monetary Fund, Washington, D.C.

Schamis, Hector. 1999. "Distributional Coalitions and the Politics of Economic Reform in Latin America." *World Politics* 51 (January): 236–268.

——. 2002. *Re-Forming the State: The Politics of Privatization in Latin America and Europe.* Ann Arbor: University of Michigan Press.

Schamis, Hector, and Christopher Way. 2000. "The Politics of Exchange Rate-Based Stabilization." Cornell University, Ithaca, N.Y. Unpublished manuscript.

Schenk, Catherine. 1993. "The Origins of a Central Bank in Malaysa and the Transition to Independence, 1954–59." *Journal of Imperial and Commonwealth History* 21 (2): 409–431.

Schmieding, Holger. 1992. *Lending Stability to Europe's Emerging Market Economies.* Tübingen, Germany: J. C. B. Mohr.

Segal, Gerald. 1999. "Does China Matter?" *Foreign Affairs* 78 (5): 24–36.

SGPIY (Study Group for the Promotion of the Internationalization of the Yen). 2000. Interim Summarization, June 30, Study Group for the Promotion of the Internationalization of the Yen, Tokyo.

———. 2001. *Report.* June 27, Study Group for the Promotion of the Internationalization of the Yen, Tokyo.

Sheng, Yumin. 2000. "Synergistic Globalization: The Political Economy of China's GATT/WTO Accession." Department of Political Science, Yale University, New Haven, Conn. Draft manuscript.

Shi, Yinhong. 1999. "Guanyu Zhongguo de daguo diwei jiqi xingxiang sikao" (Thoughts on China's great power status and its image). *Guoji Jingji Pinglun* (September–October): 43–44.

Shiller, Robert J. 1986. "Do Stock Prices Move Too Much to Be Justified by Subsequent Movements in Dividends?" *American Economic Review* 76 (3): 421–436.

———. 2000. *Irrational Exuberance.* Princeton, N.J.: Princeton University Press.

Simmons, Beth. 1994. *Who Adjusts?* Princeton, N.J.: Princeton University Press.

Sinn, Stefan. 1992. "Savings-Investment Correlations and International Capital Mobility: On the Evidence from Annual Data." *Economic Journal* 102: 1162–1170.

Smyth, Russell. 1998. "Recent Developments in Rural Enterprise Reform in China: Achievements, Problems and Prospects." *Asian Survey* 38 (8): 784–800.

Solomon, Robert. 1999. *Money on the Move: The Revolution in International Finance since 1980.* Princeton, N.J.: Princeton University Press.

Song, Qiang, Zangzang Zhang, and Bian Qiao. 1996. *Zhongguo keyi shuobu* (China can say no). Beijing: Zhonghua Gongshang Lianhui Chubanshe.

Song, Wenbin. 1999. "Zhongguo de ziben waitao wenti yanjiu" (A study of China's capital flight). *Jingji Yanjiu* 5: 39–48.

Sorg, Mart. 1994. "Estonian Strategies in the Reconstruction of Its Monetary System." In *The Competitiveness of Financial Institutions and Centers in Europe,* edited by Donald E. Fair and Robert Raymond. Dordrecht: Kluwer.

Spencer, Grant, and Adrienne Cheasty. 1993. "The Ruble Area: A Breaking of Old Ties?" *Finance and Development* 30 (2): 2–10.

Spiro, David E. 1999. *The Hidden Hand of American Hegemony: Petrodollar Recycling and International Markets.* Ithaca, N.Y.: Cornell University Press.

Stasavage, David. 1995. "The Political Economy of Monetary Union: Evolution of the African Franc Zone, 1945–1994." Ph.D. dissertation, Harvard University.

———. 1997. "The CFA Franc Zone and Fiscal Discipline." *Journal of African Economies* 6 (3): 132–167.

Stasavage, David, and Dominique Guillaume. 2002. "When Are Monetary Commitments Credible? Parallel Agreements and the Sustainability of Currency Unions." *British Journal of Political Science* 32 (1): 119–146.

Stein, Ernesto, and Jorge Streb. 1995. "Political Stabilization Cycles in High Inflation Economies." IADB Working Paper Series 309 (August), Inter-American Development Bank, Washington, D.C.

Steinfeld, Edward. 1998. *Forging Reform in China.* Cambridge: Cambridge University Press.

Stiglitz, Joseph. 2000. "What I Learned at the World Economic Crisis." *New Republic*, April 17.

Strange, Susan. 1987. "The Persistent Myth of Lost Hegemony." *International Organization* 44 (4): 551–574.

———. 1998a. "Finance in Politics: Epilogue to *Mad Money*." Paper prepared for "Power and Order: Change in World Politics—A Festschrift in Honor of Robert G. Gilpin," Princeton University, Princeton, N.J., October 2–3. Draft manuscript.

———. 1998b. *Mad Money: When Markets Outgrow Governments*. Ann Arbor: University of Michigan Press.

Suny, Ronald Grigor. 1993. *Revenge of the Past: Nationalism, Revolution, and the Collapse of the Soviet Union*. Stanford: Stanford University Press.

———. 1998. *The Soviet Experiment: Russia, the USSR, and the Successor States*. New York: Oxford University Press.

———. 1999/2000. "Provisional Stabilities: The Politics of Identities in Post-Soviet Eurasia." *International Security* 24 (3): 139–178.

Swietochowski, Tadeusz. 1995. *Russia and Azerbaijan: A Borderland in Transition*. New York: Columbia University Press.

Szporluk, Roman, ed. 1994. *National Identity and Ethnicity in Russia and the New States of Eurasia*. Armonk, N.Y.: M. E. Sharpe.

Taagepera, Rein. 1993. *Estonia: Return to Independence*. Boulder, Colo.: Westview.

Tarr, David G. 1994. "The Terms-of-Trade Effects of Moving to World Prices on the Countries of the Former Soviet Union." *Journal of Comparative Economics* 18 (1): 1–24.

Tavlas, George S. 1994. "The Theory of Monetary Integration." *Open Economies Review* 5: 211–230.

Temple, Jonathan. 1998. "Central Bank Independence and Inflation: Good News and Bad News." *Economics Letters* 61: 215–219.

———. 2000. "Inflation and Growth: Stories Short and Tall." *Journal of Economic Surveys* 14 (4): 395–426.

Thucydides. 1972. *History of the Peloponnesian War*. Harmondsworth, U.K.: Penguin Books.

Tobin, James. 1983. "Inflation: Monetary and Structural Causes and Cures." In *Inflation through the Ages: Economic, Social, Psychological and Historical Aspects*, edited by Nathan Schumukler and Edward Marcus. New York: Columbia University Press.

Tornell, Aron, and Andres Velasco. 1995. "Money-Based versus Exchange Rate–Based Stabilization with Endogenous Fiscal Policy." NBER Working Paper 5300, National Bureau of Economic Research, Cambridge, Mass.

Touré, Ahmed Sékou. 1979. *Africa on the Move*. London: Panaf.

Toye, John. 1991. "Is There a New Political Economy of Development?" In *States or Markets? Neo-Liberalism and the Development Policy Debate*, edited by Christopher Colclough and James Manor. Oxford: Oxford University Press.

Toyoda, Maria. 2001. "Malaysia: Ethnic Cleavages and Controlled Liberalization." In Horowitz and Heo, eds., *The Political Economy of International Financial Crises*.

Triffin, Robert. 1944. "Central Banking and Monetary Management in Latin America." In *Economic Problems of Latin America*, edited by Seymour Harris. New York: McGraw-Hill.

——. 1946. *Monetary and Banking Reform in Paraguay.* Washington, D.C.: Board of Governors of the Federal Reserve System.

——. [1947a] 1966. "International Versus Domestic Money." In *The World Money Maze: National Currencies in International Payments.* New Haven, Conn.: Yale University Press.

——. [1947b] 1966. "National Central Banking and the International Economy." In *The World Money Maze: National Currencies in International Payments.* New Haven, Conn.: Yale University Press.

——. 1960. *Gold and the Dollar Crisis.* New Haven, Conn.: Yale University Press.

Uche, Chibuike Ugochukwu. 1996. "From Currency Board to Central Banking: The Politics of Change in Sierra Leone." *African Economic History* 24: 147–158.

——. 1997. "Bank of England vs. the IBRD: Did the Nigerian Colony Deserve a Central Bank?" *Explorations in Economic History* 34: 220–241.

Ungerer, Horst, Owen Evans, and Peter Nyberg. 1983. *The European Monetary System: The Experience, 1979–1982.* Washington, D.C.: International Monetary Fund.

Urquidi, Victor. 1991. "Monetary Management in Latin America." In *Evolution of the International and Regional Monetary Systems,* edited by Alfred Steinherr and Daniel Weiserbs. London: Macmillan.

USFR (United States Federal Reserve). 1944. "New Monetary and Banking Measures in Paraguay." *Federal Reserve Bulletin* 30 (1): 42–51.

——. 1945. "Monetary Developments in Latin America" *Federal Reserve Bulletin* 31 (6): 519–530.

Utsumi, Makoto. 1999. "Yūro ga Nihon keizai to en ni ataeru eikyō" (The effect of the euro on the Japanese economy and the yen). In *Yūro to Nihon keizai* (The euro and the Japanese economy), edited by Utsumi Makoto. Tokyo: Tōyō Keizai.

Vallée, Olivier. 1991. *Le prix de l'argent CFA: Heurs et malheurs de la zone franc.* Paris: Karthala.

van de Walle, Nicolas. 1991. "The Decline of the Franc Zone: Monetary Politics in Francophone Africa." *African Affairs* 90: 383–405.

Velasco, Andres. 1994. "Are Balance of Payments Crises Rational?" C.V. Starr Center for Research Economics Working Paper 94-08 (March), New York University, New York.

Verdun, Amy. 1999. "The Institutional Design of EMU: A Democratic Deficit." *Journal of Public Policy* 18 (2): 107–132.

Verkhovsky, Alexander. 1993. *Central Asia and Kazakhstan: A Political Spectrum.* 2d ed. Moscow: Information and Expert Analysis Agency "Panorama."

Vinelli, Paul. 1950–51. "The Currency and Exchange System of Honduras." *IMF Staff Papers* 1: 420–431.

Wade, Robert. 1992. "East Asia's Economic Success." *World Politics* 44: 270–320.

——. 1998a. "The Asian Crisis and the Global Economy: Causes, Consequences, and Cure." *Current History* 97 (November): 361–373.

——. 1998b. "The Asian Debt-and-Development Crisis of 1997–?" *World Development* 26 (8): 1535–1553.

——. 1998c. "From 'Miracle' to 'Cronyism': Explaining the Great Asian Slump." *Cambridge Journal of Economics* 22.

Wallich, Henry, and Robert Triffin. 1953. *Monetary and Banking Legislation of the Dominican Republic.* New York: Federal Reserve Bank of New York.

Walsh, Carl E. 1995. "Central Bank Independence and the Short-Run Output–Inflation Trade-off in the European Community." In *Monetary and Fiscal Policy in an Integrated Europe,* edited by Barry Eichengreen, Jeffry Frieden, and Jakob van Hagen. Berlin: Springer.

Walter, Andrew. 1991. *World Power and World Money: The Role of Hegemony and International Monetary Order.* New York: St. Martin's.

Watson, Matthew. 2000. "Sand in the Wheels, or Oiling the Wheels of International Finance? New Labour's Appeal to a New Bretton Woods." Paper presented to the 50th Annual Conference of the Political Studies Association, London School of Economics, London.

Weber, Axel. 1991. "Reputation and Credibility in the European Monetary System." *Economic Policy* 12: 58–102.

Weber, Robert J. 2000. "Games with Incomplete Information." In *The New Palgrave Dictionary of Economics,* edited by John Eatwell, Murry Milgate, and Peter Newman. London: Palgrave.

Weyland, Kurt. 1998. "Swallowing the Bitter Pill: Sources of Popular Support for Neoliberal Reform in Latin America." *Comparative Political Studies* 31 (5): 539–568.

Whiting, Allen. 1997. "ASEAN Eyes China: The Security Dimension." *Asian Survey* 37 (4): 299–322.

Willett, Thomas D. 2000. *International Financial Markets as Sources of Crisis or Discipline: The Too Much Too Late Hypothesis.* Princeton Essays in International Economics 218, International Economics Section, Princeton University, Princeton, N.J.

Williamson, John, ed. 1994. *The Political Economy of Policy Reform.* Washington, D.C.: Institute for International Economics.

Williamson, John, and Molly Mahar. 1998. *A Survey of Financial Liberalization.* Princeton Essays in International Economics 211, International Economics Section, Princeton University, Princeton, N.J.

Winkler, Bernhard. 2000. "Which Kind of Transparency? On the Need for Clarity in Monetary Policy-Making." European Central Bank Working Paper Series 26, European Central Bank, Frankfurt.

Woo, Wing Thye, Jeffrey D. Sachs, and Klaus Schwab, eds. 2000. *The Asian Financial Crisis: Lessons for a Resilient Asia.* Cambridge: MIT Press.

Woodruff, David. 1999. *Money Unmade: Barter and the Fate of Russian Capitalism.* Ithaca, N.Y.: Cornell University Press.

Woodward, Bob. 2000. *Maestro: Greenspan's Fed and the American Boom.* New York: Simon and Schuster.

Woolley, John T. 1994. "Linking Political and Monetary Union: The Maastricht Agenda and Domestic Politics." In *The Political Economy of European Monetary Unification,* edited by Barry Eichengreen and Jeffry Frieden. Boulder, Colo.: Westview.

World Bank. 1962. *The Economic Development of Uganda.* Baltimore, Md.: Johns Hopkins Press.

———. 1988. "Argentina, Industrial Sector Study." Industrial Development Division, World Bank, Washington, D.C.

———. 1993a. "Argentina, Public Finance Review: From Insolvency to Growth." Country Department IV, World Bank, Washington, D.C.

——. 1993b. *The East Asian Miracle.* London: Oxford University Press.

——. 1998. *East Asia: The Road to Recovery.* Washington, D.C.: World Bank.

——. 1999. *Global Economic Prospects and the Developing Countries, 1998/99: Beyond Financial Crisis.* Washington, D.C.: World Bank.

Wu, L. 1997. "Retraining Economics Lecturers in Russia." *Transitions* 8 (2): 17.

Wyplosz, Charles. 1989. "Asymmetry in the EMS: Intentional or Systemic?" *European Economic Review* 33: 310–320.

Xi, Laiwang. 1996. *Waijiao molue* (Strategies of diplomacy). Beijing: Hongqi Chubanshe.

Yahuda, Michael. 1999. "China's Search for a Global Role." *Current History* 98 (September): 266–270.

Yan, Xuetong. 1996. *Zhongguo guojia liyi fenxi* (Analyzing China's national interest). Tianjin: Tianjin Renmin Chubanshe.

Yang, Fan. 1999. *Zuji fengbao: Renminbi zoushi yu fan weiji* (Halt the storm: RMB trend and resistance of the crisis). Beijing: Zhongguo Jingji Chubanshe.

Yansane, Aguibou. 1979. "Monetary Independence and Transition to Socialism in Guinea." *Journal of African Studies* 6 (3): 132–143.

——. 1984. *Decolonization in West African States with French Colonial Legacy.* Cambridge: Scheckman.

Yoshitomi, Masaru, and Kenichi Ohno. 1999. "Capital-Account Crisis and Credit Contraction." ADB Institute Working Paper 2, Asian Development Bank Institute, Tokyo.

Yu, Zhengliang. 1998. *Daguo zhanlue yanjiu: Weilai shijie de Mei, E, Ri, Ou he Zhongguo* (A study of great power strategy: US, Russia, Japan, Europe and China in the future). Beijing: Zhongyang Bianyi Chubanshe.

Zainal-Abidin, Mahani. 2000. "Implications of the Malaysian Experience on Future International Financial Arrangements." *ASEAN Economic Bulletin* 17 (2).

Zhang, Xiaopu. 1998. "Woguo guoji shouzhi pinghengbiao wucha yu yilou fenxi" (An analysis of the errors and omissions of our country's balance of payment account). *Guoji Jinrong Yanjiu* 7: 29–31.

Zhang, Xuebin. 1999. "Lun Zhongmei Liangguo Zhengfu zai Yazhou Jinrong Weiji zhong de Biaoxian" (On the performance of the Chinese and the American governments during the Asian financial crisis). *Guoji Zhengzhi Yanjiu* 2: 40–48.

Zhongguo Jinrong (*ZGJR*). 1998. "Renminbi buxuyao ye buhui bianzhi" (RMB need not and will not devalue) [Editorial]. September.

Zhu, Chenghu, Ning Pu, and Yongsheng Tang. 1999. *Zouxiang ershiyi shiji de daguo guanxi* (Great power relations toward the 21st century). Nanjing: Jiangsu Renmin Chubanshe.

Zhu, Tianye. 1999. "Juebuke yinxiao shida" (Don't lose the big to gain the small). *Guoji Maoyi* 3: 53–55.

Zolberg, Aristide. 1967. "The Political Use of Economic Planning in Mali." In *Economic Nationalism in Old and New States,* edited by Harry Johnson. Chicago: University of Chicago.

Index

CORNELL STUDIES IN POLITICAL ECONOMY
A series edited by
Peter J. Katzenstein